WHAT A DIFFERENCE A DAY MAKES

WHAT A DIFFERENCE A DAY MAKES

African American Women Who Conquered 1950s Music

STEVE BERGSMAN

Foreword by LILLIAN WALKER-MOSS

University Press of Mississippi / Jackson

What a Difference a Day Makes: Women Who Conquered 1950s Music is part of a two-book set about the great female singers of the 1950s. The companion volume, *All I Want Is Loving You: Popular Female Singers of the 1950s*, describes the white woman performers of the decade. This volume is about the Black female singers of the same era. Due to the types of music they sang and, of course, race issues, the two groups of singers had completely different career arcs. In addition, the advent of rock 'n' roll decimated the careers of the white soloists, but enhanced the glory of the Black singers.

The University Press of Mississippi is the scholarly publishing agency of the Mississippi Institutions of Higher Learning: Alcorn State University, Delta State University, Jackson State University, Mississippi State University, Mississippi University for Women, Mississippi Valley State University, University of Mississippi, and University of Southern Mississippi.

www.upress.state.ms.us

The University Press of Mississippi is a member of the Association of University Presses.

∞

Library of Congress Cataloging-in-Publication Data

Names: Bergsman, Steve, author. | Walker-Moss, Lillian, writer of foreword.
Title: What a difference a day makes : women who conquered 1950s music / Steve Bergsman, Lillian Walker-Moss.
Other titles: American made music series.
Description: Jackson : University Press of Mississippi, 2023. | Series: American made music series | Includes bibliographical references and index.
Identifiers: LCCN 2023027631 (print) | LCCN 2023027632 (ebook) | ISBN 9781496844965 (hardback) | ISBN 9781496848956 (trade paperback) | ISBN 9781496848963 (epub) | ISBN 9781496848970 (epub) | ISBN 9781496848987 (pdf) | ISBN 9781496848994 (pdf)
Subjects: LCSH: Popular music—United States—1951–1960—History and criticism. | African Americans—Music—20th century—History and criticism. | Girl groups (Musical groups)—United States—History—20th century. | African American women singers. | Women singers—United States. | African American singers.
Classification: LCC ML82 .B4305 2023 (print) | LCC ML82 (ebook) | DDC 782.42164092/52—dc23/eng/20230705
LC record available at https://lccn.loc.gov/2023027631
LC ebook record available at https://lccn.loc.gov/2023027632

British Library Cataloging-in-Publication Data available

CONTENTS

FOREWORD

LILLIAN WALKER-MOSS

Our managers took us to see Jerry Leiber and Mike Stoller because they were the be-all of hit makers. They had hits with Elvis Presley and the Drifters in the 1950s and in the girl group era with the Dixie Cups and Shangri-Las. When we went to perform for them, we blew their minds; they went bonkers for us. Physically, we were so tiny, but after they heard us sing, they called us the little girls with big voices. We sang aggressively.

We called ourselves the Masterettes. We were four girls, but on the day of our audition with Leiber and Stoller, one couldn't make it. Penny Carter, who took Sylvia Wilbur's place, was still in high school, and her father made her quit. Herb Rooney was our musical director, and he took her place. If I remember correctly, we sang our own compositions. Herb fit in so well, Leiber and Stoller decided to keep that lineup. It was unique, three girls and a guy. Leiber and Stoller had this song for us called "Tell Him," which had been recorded by a singer named Johnny Thunder (as "Tell Her"). It had made a little noise but didn't do much nationally. They thought the song was a good fit and told us to take it home and make it our own. Herb gave us the doop-do-doops and showed us a different way of singing the melody, and that's what we got. When we sang it for Leiber and Stoller they were thrilled. What they said was, "Your sound is so exciting we are going to change the name of your group to the Exciters."

"Tell Him" by the Exciters went to #4 on the pop charts in early 1963.

Music has been a part of my life since as far back as I can remember. I grew up in Harlem, but when I was about twelve years old, my family moved to the borough of Queens. In 1950, I was six and I remember that the radio was on all the time. My parents were young. When I was born in 1944, my mother was twenty-one and my father was twenty-three. I had an older brother and two younger siblings.

Not only did my parents listen to the radio but they also bought records. They loved the standards, big bands, and jazz. We had records by Dinah Washington, Ella Fitzgerald, Sarah Vaughan, Carmen McRae, and Peggy Lee. Two of my parents' favorites were Sarah Vaughan and Ella Fitzgerald, but there was someone who topped even them in esteem: Billie Holiday. My folks used to say she was the best singer who ever lived. My parents would go to the Apollo all the time, and when I was old enough, in elementary school, they took me and my older brother with them. I remember seeing LaVern Baker, Ruth McFadden, and Ruth Brown. Years later, the Exciters sang backup on one of Ruth Brown's tunes. She had contacted our manager because she really wanted us to do it. Of course, we said, "Sure, we would love to be on her record."

My favorite songs by women singers in the 1950s included "I Sold My Heart to the Junkman" by Dinah Washington, "Bewitched, Bothered, and Bewildered" by Ella Fitzgerald, and "Fever" by Peggy Lee. Oh, my goodness, did Peggy Lee put that song away! One time the family was watching television, and Carmen McRae was on the screen. She could be singing a melody, then break it down to a whisper. I would think, "Oh my God, this lady could sing so great." My father said, "You never paid attention to her before." I said, "I love her, love her." He got such a kick out of me liking her music.

I don't want to forget Eartha Kitt. I just loved "C'est Si Bon." My sister and I used to make believe we had a long cigarette holder and feather boa and walk around the house singing that song.

I always wanted to be singer, probably since I was three years old. My parents encouraged my interest by putting me in amateur talent shows. It wasn't until I was about twelve that I decided to put my musical interests (and talent) into action. I was good friends with Sylvia Wilbur, who was a cousin of Lois Harris Powell of the Chantels. We all used to go to Sylvia's and Lois's grandmother's house. One day, Sylvia and I went there, and Lois and her friends (who became the Chantels) were rehearsing. I had no idea they had a singing group and was amazed. They sounded like birds; their music was heavenly. I had always wanted to sing by myself, but when I saw the group, I said to Sylvia, "Let's make a singing group. I want to be like Lois and her friends."

Sylvia and I started singing together when we were twelve in 1956. We used to get other girls to sing with us, usually just for a couple of weeks. The longest one lasted was two months. They would get tired of. On the first day of high school, I met Brenda Reid and she joined Sylvia and me in our group. She had a best friend named Carolyn Johnson, who would hang around with us at rehearsals. One day, we were listening to records and singing along when Carolyn joined in. She had a good voice, and I said, "I didn't know you knew how to sing." She answered, "I can sing a little bit." That was enough. I asked her if she wanted to be in the group. Of course, she said yes—we were very cool girls.

We met Herb Rooney and Clayton Williams, who we called Dickie. They were in a group called the Masters. (That's how we became the Masterettes.) They heard us singing and said, "You girls can really sing, but you're not harmonizing right." They would drop by and teach us how to harmonize and put on a show. Every weekend, they would take us to their show so we could see how it was done. We eventually wanted a chance. Our first show was in Oyster Bay, Long Island. We sang "Please Say You Want Me" by the Schoolboys and some Shirelles songs.

When we signed with Leiber and Stoller, we hit right away with "Tell Him," but everything was a struggle after that even though we had good songs like "He's Got the Power." The biggest disappointment was "Doo Wah Diddy Diddy." It hit the charts with a bullet and then started slowing down. It picked back up, and everyone said it was a sleeper. Then the Manfred Mann version was released, and we were off the charts.

I don't want to say anything negative about the British Invasion because the Exciters opened for the Beatles on the group's first North American tour. They were great guys. One of the stops was the Gator Bowl in Jacksonville, which wasn't an integrated venue. The Gator Bowl informed us that we couldn't perform there. The Beatles were not happy and told the Gator Bowl officials if the Exciters can't perform, they wouldn't either. The Beatles stood their ground. We were so honored and proud they stuck up for us. The Gator Bowl finally conceded.

For the past decade, I've been singing with other ladies from the girl group era in our group called the Super Girls. The ladies include me, Louise Harris Murray of the Hearts and the Jaynetts, Margaret Williams of the Cookies, Nanette Licari of Reparata and the Delrons, and Beverly Warren of the Raindrops.

My father wasn't into the blues as much as he was into jazz. Growing up, I knew about more jazz singers than blues singers. However, regarding the blues or R&B, the Exciters worked with a number of performers from the 1950s. We did a lot of shows with Big Maybelle, whose music I've liked since I was a kid. We also sang with her daughter, who was a singer as well. We worked a couple of shows with Faye Adams. One of the songs I really loved when I was young was her version of "Shake a Hand." As the Super Girls, we did that song at Foxwoods. Louise Harris Murray sang the lead. We put a new spin on it, and the result was awesome. Good songs live forever.

—LILLIAN WALKER-MOSS was an original member of the 1960s girl group the Exciters, which recorded such popular songs as "Tell Him," "You Got the Power," and "Do Wah Diddy Diddy." She currently sings with the Super Girls.

WHAT A DIFFERENCE A DAY MAKES

TEARDROPS FROM MY EYES

MABEL SCOTT—OTIS AND LEON RENÉ—
SISTER ROSETTA THARPE—RUTH BROWN—RUDY TOOMBS

As the tumultuous decade of the 1940s concluded, Americans opened their brand-new calendars for 1950, and optimism ran rampant. All they had to do was fill in the empty spaces with appointments and chores, greeting a new decade with an America at the peak of postwar prestige and ready for all things shiny and new.

However, not all things, especially the prosaic, change so quickly with a new year or new decade. Radio noise filled the quiet, and in the world of popular music, the juvenile holiday song from December 1949, "Rudolph, the Red-Nosed Reindeer" by cowboy singer Gene Autry was still the #1 pop song at the start of the year. It would quickly be replaced by "I Can Dream, Can't I," a tune by the most successful singing group of the 1940s, the Andrews Sisters.

Few people remember "I Can Dream, Can't I," but everyone knows "Rudolph, the Red-Nosed Reindeer," which is why as 1950 tumbled toward its end, a bunch of performers, as early as October, rushed into the studio to record a holiday song of their own. One of those singers was Patti Page, who strolled into a New York sound studio to record a tune called "Boogie Woogie Santa Claus," because, as she said at the time, nothing would sell at the end of the year except a Christmas song. The B-side to "Boogie Woogie Santa Claus" was a remake of the moderately successful country tune "Tennessee Waltz," which turned out to be a monster record, in fact an eternal classic, and the Christmas ditty on the platter's reverse side was quickly ignored. Page noted in her autobiography that some deejays may have heard her "Boogie Woogie Santa Claus" song, but "I don't know who ever played it."

That was a bit disingenuous. "Boogie Woogie Santa Claus" in 1950 was on the cusp of being a holiday classic, just not by Patti Page.

3

The song goes back to just a few years before when Mabel Scott, a popular Black nightclub singer, signed a recording contract with Exclusive Records, a Hollywood company founded and run by African American entrepreneurs and songwriters Otis and Leon René. It was on the Exclusive label in 1948 that Scott boasted a hit record with "Boogie Woogie Santa Claus."

Exclusive excelled in R&B, and as one writer noted, Leon René was an important figure in early R&B and rock 'n' roll with the Exclusive, Excelsior (directly run by Otis René), and then later Class labels. Before that, he was best known for writing "When the Swallows Come Back to Capistrano." He also wrote "I Sold My Heart to the Junkman" by Patti LaBelle and the Bluebelles and "Rockin' Robin" by Bobby Day.[1]

Mabel Scott (Mabel Bernice Scott) was a corker. Born in Richmond, Virginia, in 1915, her family moved around before finally ending up in New York in the early 1920s, first in the Bronx and then in Harlem. As a child, she took piano lessons and sang in the local church, and by age fifteen began appearing in musicals performed at Harlem's Alhambra Theater. Two years later, she appeared at the famous Smalls Paradise in Harlem and then at the Cotton Club with Cab Calloway. She was a determined and popular trouper, eventually moving to England, where she recorded on Parlophone Records. When World War II broke out, she returned to the United States. In 1946, she first stepped into an American studio for Hub Records, for whom she recorded "Do You Know the Game?" and "Just Give Me a Man," the latter cowritten by Otis René.[2] The September 2, 1946, issue of *Cash Box* magazine took notice, especially because the latter song was somewhat risqué for the time. The reviewer wrote: "Mabel Scott's version of 'Just Give Me a Man' comes out on the purple side. She sings with gusto, and the orchestra is pretty much in the background all the time, but it's a good buy for the Harlem and Central Avenue [Los Angeles] locations."[3]

The song has such captivating lyrics as: "I've prayed for a honey, or Mister Five by Five. He can be conscious or unconscious, dead or alive! Bring him in, bring him in, I'll help him do the jive! Ooh, just gimme a man." The subject was definitely not unknown to Scott; she boasted at least seven marriages.

Singer/songwriter Billy Vera, who knew Scott in her later years, once asked her about her trip to the altar with smooth-singing Charles Brown, the avatar of laid-back blues. His best-known recording is "Merry Christmas Baby," which he recorded with Johnny Moore's Three Blazers. Charles Brown was gay, so Billy Vera asked Scott, "How did you not know that?" Scott answered, "He was on the road a lot, and I was on the road a lot. We didn't really see much of each other."[4] A perfect marriage for both!

In 1946, Scott thrust a knife into the side of Willie Ward, her husband at the time, but apparently not too deep. Music historian Marv Goldberg tracked down an article in the July 11, 1946, *California Eagle*, which reported: "Mabel

Scott, who gained a terrible following here [Los Angeles] with her risqué songs, last week was freed of assault charges in New York. . . . Miss Scott explained satisfactorily to the court that a recent argument between the two climaxed in years of disagreements, finally ending in physical violence on Ward's part, and that he was stabbed as she tried to protect herself."

Scott had her first recording session with Exclusive Records in January 1948, notching more than a dozen different cuts. In February, she married husband number four, Will Jones. In May, she was back in the studio, where she recorded her most popular song, "Elevator Boogie," which climbed to #6 on the R&B charts. Some of the more interesting lyrics included "Step in, Mr. Brown, right now we're going down, with the elevator boogie." According to Marv Goldberg, the piano player on the tune was Charles Brown.[5]

In July, Scott and Jones divorced. She went into the studio again in August and for the last time in November, recording a song written for her by Leon René, "Boogie Woogie Santa Claus." Although *Cash Box* didn't get around to reviewing the record until January 1, 1949, declaring Mabel Scott, "hotter than a 10-dollar pistol," the song did quite well, reaching #12 on the R&B charts in 1948. It was Scott's second and last hit record.[6]

Vera, who met Scott through his work at the Rhythm & Blues Foundation, said she was very "chatty" and would call him often. "I went to her funeral. It was held in a tiny church in Los Angeles, and it was very hot that day," he recalled. "I spoke at the funeral, but there were few people there. No one famous, just older neighbors and friends."[7]

For the winter season, "Boogie Woogie Santa Claus" was brimming with good tidings. The song was hotter than a hot toddy and tastier than eggnog. It boasted a pre–rock 'n' roll rhythm that gives a nod to Wynonie Harris's "Good Rockin' Tonight" or anything by Joe Turner. When she blasts "well it's rock rock rock Mr. Santa" she was many years ahead of Bill Haley.

The success of "Boogie Woogie Santa Claus" wasn't enough to save Exclusive, which went bust, selling its masters to Swing Time Records, which in November 1950 reissued Mabel Scott's "Boogie Woogie Santa Claus" paired with "That Ain't the Way to Love" just about the time Patti Page was letting go with her version of the song coupled with that little tune called "Tennessee Waltz." Also in the mix that year was another version of the song by Lionel Hampton's band with Sonny Parker on the lead.

A lot of yuletide sparks were caused by "Boogie Woogie Santa Claus," but in the R&B world of 1949–50, the real flames were fanned by another female singer, Sister Rosetta Tharpe, who bragged the biggest selling Christmas tune "Silent Night," which was recorded with the Rosetta Gospel Singers. It's not as if there wasn't a lot of competition in the winter of 1949–50. Besides three versions of "Boogie Woogie Santa Claus," Lowell Fulson offered up "Lonesome Christmas

(Parts 1 and 2)," Amos Milburn scored a hit with "Let's Make Christmas Merry, Baby," Little Willie Littlefield chortled "Merry Christmas," and "The Christmas Song" by Nat King Cole returned once again to the R&B charts, as did "Merry Christmas Baby" by Johnny Moore's Three Blazers (the song is credited to Lou Baxter and Johnny Moore but was actually written by Charles Brown).

Music writer Larry Birnbaum offhandedly noted, "Sister Rosetta Tharpe, for one, had injected gospel music into rhythm & blues," an important precursor of rock 'n' roll. Indeed, the gospel-singing, electric guitar–playing Tharpe, who pioneered fretboard distortion, eventually became known as "the Godmother of rock 'n' roll."[8] In 2017, she was inducted into the Rock & Roll Hall of Fame.

Perhaps the first great gospel singer to become a nationally known performer, Tharpe had been recording since the 1930s, but her music was esoteric. She never became a recording star, only notching four songs on the R&B charts over her long career. Her first blossom in the R&B world, "Strange Things Happening Every Day," climbed all the way to #2 on the R&B charts in 1945. It would be her biggest crossover into popular markets. In 1948, she charted twice with "Precious Memories" at #13 and "Up above My Head, I Hear Music in the Air," which flew all the way to #6.

Her last charted record, "Silent Night (Christmas Hymn)," reached #6 on the R&B charts at the end of 1949, but the bulk of sales were apparently accounted for in 1950, so that's how the record ended up as one of the top songs that year. Even with Christmas just a memory, *Cash Box*'s review of individual markets for the January 7, 1950, issue charted "Silent Night" as the sixth best-selling record in San Francisco. The week before, it was the seventh best-selling record in New Orleans.[9]

There's probably not one year in the past one hundred that someone didn't record the traditional Christmas hymn "Silent Night," but what made this a hit for Tharpe were her bluesy intonations, clarity, and stretched wording and spacing. The arrangement didn't stray far from the musical core of the song; nevertheless, if you hear Tharpe's version of this traditional piece you know you're listening to a unique interpretation—and the predominantly Black audience of 1949–50, including radio listeners, jukebox feeders, and record buyers, thought so as well.

Sister Rosetta Nubin Tharpe was born in Cotton Plant, Arkansas, in 1915. Her mother was a singer, stringed instrument player, and preacher who quickly pulled her daughter into the circuit. Tharpe was playing guitar and singing by the age of four and a regular evangelical trouper by six.[10] In her early twenties she was lucky enough to sign with Decca Records, and in 1938 she recorded for the first time, backed by Lucky Millinder's jazz orchestra. This is what made Tharpe revolutionary: her ability and skill in mixing secular and gospel. She would sing gospel before secular audiences, appear with blues and jazz singers, or warble straight-up secular songs that bordered on risqué. She married three times although she was gay.[11]

By 1943, Tharpe, tired of recording with Lucky Millinder, wanted to return to her gospel roots. The next year, she stepped into the studio to record the extraordinary "Strange Things Happening Every Day," a gospel song that easily passed for something secular.[12] The song boasted a galloping boogie beat, tinkling piano, and a rockin' vocal by Tharpe. Some musicologists skip Roy Brown's "Good Rockin' Tonight" or Jackie Brenston's "Rocket 88" when looking for the first rock 'n' roll record and go straight to "Strange Things Happening Every Day."

By 1949–50, Tharpe was still recording with Decca, which was happy to have her. In the March 26, 1949, issue of *Cash Box*, Decca took out a full-page ad to tout its top singers, including Bing Crosby, Guy Lombardo, the Mills Brothers, the Andrews Sisters, the Ink Spots, Red Foley, and Sister Rosetta Tharpe.[13] In July, the magazine reviewed a new Tharpe record, "Down by the River Side" backed by "My Lord's Gonna Move this Wicked Race." The reviewer gushed: "We've always been one of Sister Rosetta Tharpe's fans, and with this new platter, we just simply bow to the 'Queen of Spirituals' as she sings and plays two numbers that are going to zip coins into many a jukebox. . . . Sister Tharpe is in gorgeous voice, in her famed lively tempo and laughing, happy rhythm, and sells the tune right over the top."[14]

With the start of the new decade, Decca reaffirmed its commitment to Tharpe. In April 1950, the record company announced it had renewed her contract for another four years. She had already been with the company for the prior decade. Although she was no longer a singles' recording star, she was a well-known and beloved gospel performer. Later in 1950, she was the first gospel singer to perform at the Philharmonic in Hollywood.[15]

For some moderately successful, Black, female, recording acts such as Mabel Scott and Sister Rosetta Tharpe, 1950 was the end of the line for hit singles, although they would continue as successful performing acts, or in Tharpe's case as a gospel singer.

The start of a new decade also meant the end of Leon René's Exclusive label, which, on the surface, suffered from an infusion of new technologies that were expensive to acquire and maintain. The whole music world was changing in ways that would adversely affect some of the older independent labels. Three factors hurt Exclusive, said Billy Vera, who wrote a book about the competition, Specialty Records: the mob was bootlegging his records on the East Coast, and when he was riding high with records such as "The Honeydripper," he invested in expensive Los Angeles real estate. Most of all, the introduction of the 45-rpm record format was the last straw; René didn't have the capital to make the changeover from 78s.[16]

Leon and Otis René were brothers from Covington, Louisiana, who went to Los Angeles in 1930, when they were twenty-eight and thirty-two, respectively. They hit quickly, writing "When the Swallows Come Back to Capistrano" and "When It's Sleepytime Down South," which became a theme song for Louis Armstrong.[17]

The René brothers got into the record business during the Depression because the major record companies had cut back. As Leon René noted, "the majors cut off most of their Negro talent" and, regarding the brothers specifically, they found it difficult to get their material recorded. Their Exclusive Records hit paydirt in 1945 when Joe Liggins and his Honeydrippers' song "The Honeydripper" topped the R&B charts for eighteen weeks. Also roaring through for Exclusive that year was Herb Jeffries's huge hit "Left a Good Deal in Mobile." In an interview with author Arnold Shaw, Leon René reminisced: "We had things going our way until [RCA] Victor introduced the seven-inch vinyl, 45-rpm record, which revolutionized the record business and made the 78-rpm record obsolete overnight."[18]

Two financial aspects of the 45 rpm's introduction were destructive to independent labels such as Exclusive. First, switching production was expensive, and second, to get the public to switch formats, as René recalled, the majors "reduced the price of R&B records from a dollar-five to 75 cents, retail. This forced many independent labels out of business."

There also was an important socioeconomic issue as well. The 45 was introduced in 1949 at a time when poverty and underemployment were rampant in geographic markets where country & western and R&B were strongest. Many consumers could not afford to purchase the advanced record players that spun the new formats, so they continued to buy 78s for a few more years. In 1950, the 78 outsold the combined sales of both new record formats, the 45 rpm and 33⅓ rpm.

Columbia Records officially introduced the 33⅓ format, called the LP, in June 1948. In March 1949, RCA Victor unveiled the 45 rpm. Capitol was the first label besides RCA to issue 45s, followed by MGM and Mercury, with Decca, Coral, and Brunswick following suit. In England, it took EMI two years to move away from 78s. Due to confusion about the formats, record sales actually declined in 1948 and 1949.

Once the product known as the record was introduced into the American market at the start of the twentieth century, it quickly became a very successful technological advancement in home entertainment. By 1921, 100 million records were sold annually. Then the radio industry introduced electrical microphones and better speakers, so consumers turned their attention to the music coming out of the radio. Sales declined for five years until Victor Records introduced "electrical process" records and electric record players. By 1929, global sales leaped to 200 million records. Then came the Depression and World War II, which almost shut down the young record industry; first people lost jobs and income, and then raw materials were sidetracked for the war effort. Sales didn't surpass 1920s levels until 1946, when 350 million units were sold in 1946 and 375 million in 1947.[19]

The overarching change in the music business at the start of the 1950s was due to the rising importance of records, particularly in the form of the 45, which was smaller and more flexible than the 78, which was larger, more brittle, and breakable. The 33⅓ (LP) was introduced the year before the 45 but its prominence in pop music would not increase until the 1960s.

Due to the importance of the single (increasingly the 45), when looking at the Black female singers who strived for success in the 1950s, we can track their performance on the record charts. Generally, the pop charts published by *Billboard* were the most important indicators. For much of the early 1950s, *Billboard* segregated its charts into Popular Music, where mostly white singers and groups appeared; Country & Western, a different market from pop, although its performers were primarily white as well; and R&B, which largely tracked Black musicians.

Billboard published its first music chart, Best-Selling Retail Records, in 1940, and much to its credit, two years later, recognized the burgeoning country & western and R&B sectors. The former was initially labeled American Folk Records and the latter the Harlem Hit Parade, which was based on record sales from a handful of record stores in Harlem, New York. Of the initial Top Ten on the Harlem Hit Parade of October 24, 1942, familiar names such as Louis Jordan, Earl Hines, Lucky Millinder, and Four Ink Spots dominated. There was just one female on the chart: Billie Holiday singing with Paul Whiteman. Their song "Travelin' Light" came in at #2.

Trying to keep abreast with the pace and origin of record sales, *Billboard* in 1945 renamed the Harlem Hit Parade as Race Records, which demonstrated an awareness that there was a wider market for blues and R&B records beyond the streets of Harlem. Nevertheless, this alteration was extremely naïve in terms of labeling and didn't sit well with African American musicians. In 1949, the chart was renamed Rhythm & Blues Records.

The problem for *Billboard* was that the dominant pop record market was being assaulted by swarms of gnats. For many reasons, outliers in the music business were luring away traditional record buyers. Starting in the 1940s, a host of financial, structural, and production issues affected the record industry. The raw materials for shellac, for example, came from Asia, and with the advent of World War II, sources dried up. In response, the major labels decided to concentrate recording activity on their biggest stars. That left the R&B and country & western performers to fend for themselves, usually moving to independent labels.[20]

Big bands recorded for large, nationally distributed companies such as RCA Victor, while new artists signed on to independent labels that began appearing during the war and would proliferate over the next seven years. While the majors had problems identifying the new music—MGM called it "ebony," while Decca and Capitol preferred "sepia"—the new labels were R&B from the start, although bebop, country, electric blues, and gospel were all recorded by the new labels, noted author Nelson George: "In 1949, when *Billboard* changed the name of its Black pop music chart from Race to Rhythm & Blues, it wasn't setting a trend but responding to a phrase and a feeling the independent labels had already made part of the vocabulary."[21]

Record sales were also boosted by several other factors, including radio, retail sales, and jukeboxes. According to a report in *Billboard*:

> Corresponding to the growth of the independent label was the emergence of the independent radio station. In 1940, when the FCC ceased licensing new stations, the number of AM radio stations in the U.S. totaled 813. After World War II, from 1945 to 1949, the number of AM stations more than doubled from 943 to 2,127, mostly due to the rise of the small independent, "which was the type empowered and encouraged to program current phonograph records" and became the fastest-growing entity in radio. By 1948, independents were the most numerous kind of station broadcasting to American audiences.
>
> Most homes did not have phonographs, but popular gathering spots from bars to bowling alleys did have an appliance to play records; it was the jukebox. By the mid-1940s, 75% of the records produced in America went into jukeboxes. In 1950, the Seeburg Corporation introduced an all 45-rpm jukebox, which became the dominant jukebox technology in the last half of the twentieth century.
>
> According to *Billboard* magazine, in 1950, there were at least 12,000 record retailers in the U.S.[22]

Recognizing the importance of the "single," on March 24, 1945, *Billboard* unveiled the Honor of Hits, which was a chart recognizing the top records in the country. This was more than just a list of best-selling records. Using a complicated formula, the magazine blended five sources to create its chart: best-selling records via retail, best-selling sheet music, songs most played on jukeboxes, songs most played on the radio, and a stream called "songs with the most radio plugs." The mix would change over time.[23]

Like most African American male singers, an underlying goal of female performers was to transcend the R&B musical ghetto and make it to the pop charts, which meant their songs sold to a vastly wider and less segregated

audience. Many Black songwriters sold their song rights or were swindled out
of their due, but for the smart and persistent ones, the payoff was extreme.
Harvey Fuqua, who wrote "Sincerely," a #1 R&B hit for his group the Moonglows, saw the McGuire Sisters cover the record and take it to #1 on the
pop charts. Vera, who knew Fuqua, once asked him what he thought of the
McGuire Sisters. Fuqua answered, "I love the McGuire Sisters." In those days,
a #1 R&B record might sell 100,000 copies. The McGuire Sisters version of
the song sold 3.5 million. "Do I love the McGuire Sisters? You bet your ass
I do!" he exclaimed. Vera called Fuqua a "good businessman" but noted that
even he had to share writing credits with Alan Freed, who was the Moonglows'
manager at the time.[24]

In addition, in some large cities such as New York and Los Angeles that
didn't ban integrated audiences at nightclubs, a hit record meant bigger and
better-paying gigs. From the 1940s onward, non-jazz male acts as such as Cecil
Gant, Louis Jordan, the Ink Spots, the Mills Brothers, and by 1950 Nat King
Cole and Billy Eckstine, were veterans of the pop charts. It was a more difficult
journey for the popular Black female singers of the day, who were generally less
pop and more rhythm and bluesy, at least at the start of the 1950s. As noted,
Black songstresses appeared on the first *Billboard* listing of top records in 1942.
For the remainder of the decade, no Black female singer had a Top Thirty "pop"
hit record except in 1948, when Ella Fitzgerald's version of "My Happiness"
made it to #24 on *Billboard*'s year-end charts.

In 1949, not one African American was listed as the performing artist on
Billboard's Top Thirty singles of the year. In 1950, Nat King Cole and Billy
Eckstine made the leap. One person who didn't was Ruth Brown, who had the
top R&B song in 1950 with "Teardrops from My Eyes," nosing out such big hits
as "Mona Lisa" by Nat King Cole and "Pink Champagne" by Joe Liggins and
his Honeydrippers.

"Teardrops from My Eyes" is a beautiful mid-tempo song with a proto–rock
'n' roll beat. Thematically, it's about a woman missing her man. It was composed
especially for Ruth Brown by Rudolph "Rudy" Toombs, who rolled some nice
lyrics: "Well, if you see clouds in my eyes / it's just because you said goodbye /
Although the sun is shining, there's no summer skies / Still it's raining teardrops
from my eyes." Brown sang it with warm affection, but as the years went on it,
she associated it with incidents of violence.

On tour to promote her new hit song, Brown was doing a show in Newport
News, Virginia, all decked out in a beautiful new red dress. She didn't get far into
her set when a woman from the audience lurched toward the stage, holding a
paper cup tipped almost to the brim with beer. "Sing 'Teardrops,'" the woman
spit. Brown, already a veteran performer, mouthed the word "later" to the inebriant and continued singing her big hit from 1949, "So Long." The woman was

besotted and determined. "Sing 'Teardrops' right now," she continued. Brown ignored her, finished the song, waited until the applause began to settle, and cued the band for the next song, which wasn't 'Teardrops,' as it was saved for the big finale. The lady from the audience took umbrage and yelled "Hey don't get cute with me, bitch! I know you're from over there in Portsmouth," and to accent the point, she hurled the cup at Brown, which splashed all down her new red dress. In a flash, Brown lifted that dress over her head, tossed it to one side and went after the drunken woman. After rolling all over the floor, her brother Leonard jumped in to separate the warriors, pulling his sister away and holding her hands to keep her from swinging. Trying to control Ruth, Leonard didn't see that the woman suddenly flashed a knife. Thankfully, someone else saw the blade, grabbed the lady before she could swing it at Brown, and dragged her away. Incensed, Brown turned on her brother, yelling, "I could have been cut open!" He let her rage on screaming and swinging her fists at him until she tired. The concert ended right there.[25]

That wasn't Brown's saddest story about "Teardrops."

Songwriter Rudy Toombs was born in Monroe, Louisiana, in 1914. He came into his own in the 1950s with a varied array of hits such as the novelty tune "One Mint Julep" for the Clovers, the bluesy "5–10–15 Hours" for Ruth Brown, the drinking tune "One Bourbon, One Scotch, One Beer" for Amos Milburn, and then in 1960 the rock 'n' roller "I'm Shakin'" for Little Willie John. Brown called him a dear friend, writing "a man full of life, effervescent and happy. He showed that in his songs—all bouncy and jolly."

Brown considered herself a ballad-y torch singer at the time, but Toombs, an in-house Atlantic Records songwriter, came to her with melodies that were different rhythmically from what she had been doing.

In the early 1950s, R&B songs were introduced, worked on for a few hours, and then recorded the next day, but Brown recalled toiling over "Teardrops" for about a week.

Afterward, Toombs and Brown worked closely as a team, writing several hits. "He could sit down at the piano and produce a new song in a matter of hours," Brown said of Toombs.

Sorrow came later. In 1962, Toombs was walking down a street when he was slammed in the head by someone who was trying to rob him. When he was found, he wasn't dead yet, but as Brown recalled, he was "too far gone to live. Very sad."[26]

The April 8, 1950, issue of *Cash Box* reviewed a new Ruth Brown song that caused the reviewer to go ga-ga over the singer. And no, it wasn't "Teardrops from My Eyes." Before the big hit, Atlantic Records decided to issue a single with Brown singing two golden nuggets: "Sentimental Journey" on the A side and "I Can Dream, Can't I" on the B side (covers of hit records by Doris Day/

Les Brown and the Andrews Sisters, respectively). Although the single never caught on, *Cash Box*'s reviewer thought Brown was stupendous, writing: "The bewitching pipes of chirp [female singer] Ruth Brown take up with a pair of well-known tunes and come through for music ops [jukebox operators]. Both ends of this platter show that gal's pipes in top-notch style, with the music resounding excellently from start to finish . . . this rendition, with Ruth purring the golden lyrics in captivating tones that score from the word go, is tailor made for the jukebox trade. The gal's tonsils trill the enticing lyrics in smooth pitch all the way, with great music seeping thru the background."[27]

Atlantic Records was equally high on its performer, re-signing her in August 1950 with substantial advances in a royalty agreement over what Brown had initially gotten with the firm. *Cash Box*, in discussing the "pact," noted, "Ruth Brown is top-flight blues singer with many of her records among the most popular issued. The chirp is slated shortly for a personal appearance at the local [New York] Café Society Downtown."[28]

According to Brown, "Teardrops from My Eyes" was Atlantic's first record available on 45-rpm vinyl as well as the standard 78-rpm shellac.

One of the first *Billboard* reviews of "Teardrops from My Eyes" was published in the November 11, 1950, issue, except it wasn't the one by Ruth Brown. It was the Lucky Millinder version.[29] The magazine was a little behind the eightball because just the next week, rival *Cash Box* listed Ruth Brown's version as the #1 record in the most important African American market in the country, Harlem. At that moment, Brown's competition among the other Black female singers included Helen Humes with "Million Dollar Secret" and Dinah Washington with two songs moving in opposite directions, "Harbor Lights" going up and "I'll Never Be Free" going down.[30]

These were all good songs, but "Teardrops from My Eyes" was like a steam locomotive running down a steep hill, and the music world knew it. This led to a free-for-all to get the publishing rights. The trade press covered the rumble closely, with *Cash Box* reporting "Several publishers have been bidding for Atlantic Records' torrid tune, 'Teardrops from My Eyes.' Not only does Atlantic have a smash record with it by Ruth Brown, which by the way has been hitting the #1 spot in *Cash Box*'s hot columns [regional lists], but Progressive Music, Atlantic's subsidiary, also published the song."[31] The winner was Simon House, which quickly boasted about the acquisition with a quarter-page ad in *Cash Box*, noting all the different recordings of the song: Jo Stafford and Gene Autry, Fran Warren, Louis Prima, Hawkshaw Hawkins, Joy and Wes Holly, Ruth Brown, June Hutton, Red Kirk, Wynonie Harris and Lucky Millinder, Bill Haley, Helen O'Connell, and Frank DeVol.[32]

All were good singers, but Ruth Brown was tops. On December 9, 1950, *Billboard* listed Brown's version of the song as the #1 best-selling R&B record in the country. The Top Ten that week included two other females, Helen Humes with "Million Dollar Secret" and Little Esther (Phillips) and Johnny Otis with "Oh Babe." This was a great moment for the women because the Little Esther/ Johnny Otis hit outperformed two other versions of the same song on the chart that week.[33] Although Brown was battling Little Esther, who was cruising along with novelty song "Wedding Boogie," this time with the Johnny Otis Congregation (Mel Walker and Lee Graves), as the only female representative on the best-selling R&B charts, she was the one singled out for a major career and lifestyle break when it was announced that Brown would be headlining at the Apollo Theater in New York, coming off a grueling southern tour of one-nighters.[34]

As if things weren't already going Ruth Brown's way, on December 23, 1950, she made the cover of *Cash Box*. A svelte-looking Brown wearing an embroidered jacket over a white blouse and a straight-line skirt is standing between two Atlantic executives. In her right hand she's holding a large white handkerchief that she had brought to the corner of her right eye. The cutline reads: "Songstress Ruth Brown dries her tears as Atlantic Records *prexy* Herb Abramson and VP Ahmet Ertegun assure her that there's no reason at all to cry with her terrific recording of 'Teardrops from My Eyes' hitting the #1 spot in most blues & rhythm locations throughout the country."[35]

Brown, Abramson, and Ertegun were crying all the way to the bank.

I WANNA BE LOVED (1950)

HELEN HUMES—NELLIE LUTCHER—JEWEL KING— DAVID BARTHOLOMEW—LEW CHUDD—TOMMY RIDGLEY— FATS DOMINO—DINAH WASHINGTON—LIONEL HAMPTON

Toward the end of autumn 1950, Aladdin Records in Los Angeles announced it would break into the LP (33⅓) field with a flurry of albums. Aladdin, which specialized in R&B music, had been strictly a 78-rpm company, and to promote its adoption of the new record technology it brought into the recording studio a host of blues, jazz, and R&B performers including Illinois Jacquet, Amos Milburn, Lester Young, and Wynonie Harris. All of the initial artists recording on the LPs were men except for one woman: Helen Humes, a jazz/blues singer who had worked with the Count Basie Orchestra.[1]

She once recorded a great double-entendre song called "You Played on My Piano," which boasted the following fun opening lyrics: "You played on my piano, and now you want to beat my drum / You think I'm gonna let you but, baby, I ain't so dumb / Now, I let you try my fiddle, now you don't wanna stop / If you don't stop fiddlin', then I'm gonna blow my top."

She also recorded another guess-the-true-meaning song called "They Raided the Joint," which had the chorus line: "They raided the joint, took everyone down but me / I was over in the corner just as high as I can be."

Many of the female jazz and swing orchestra veterans found the start of the new decade amenable to their song styling, although that window would only be open for a short period of time as the audience for Black songstresses was shifting toward blues and R&B.

Humes was fortunate to have a long career as a jazz singer, playing festivals, receiving awards, and still recording albums even into the 1980s. She was never a real singles artist, bragging only two popular hits, "Million Dollar Secret" and "Be-Baba-Leba." The latter was a 1945 hit, but with a bit of controversy, so Humes rerecorded it for Discovery Records in 1950 as "E-Baba-Le-Ba." Even with that familiar sound, Humes's surprising big hit for 1950 was "Million Dollar Secret."

Discovery Records, which was founded by jazz promoter Albert Marx, signed Humes around the start of the new decade and tried to make her a singles artist, dropping several of her platters into the market early in 1950. In June, *Cash Box*'s competitive "Jazz 'n' Blues Reviews" column showcased three female singers among the men, with top honors (Award of the Week) going to Little Esther for "Cupid Boogie" backed by "Just Can't Get Free." Also in the mix was Julia Lee crooning the golden nugget "Nobody Knows You When You're Down and Out" with "There Goes My Heart" on the B-side. The third female singer reviewed was Helen Humes with "Rock Me to Sleep" with "Sad Feeling" on the B-side. The reviewer, who knew of Humes, noted, "Great pipes of chirp [female singer] long missing from the vocal spotlight."[2]

Humes was back again the next month in the "Jazz 'n' Blues Reviews." This time, five females made the column: Florence Wright with "Pie in the Basket" / "The Real Gone Tune"; Sister Wynona Carr joining Prof. Donald E. Thomas on "Don't Miss that Train" / "I Heard Mother Pray One Day"; with "I've Got the Boogie Blues" / "Is Love a Game," and the "Award o' the Week" winner Thelma Carpenter with "Pie in the Basket" / "Melody." Humes joined the crowded slate with "This Love of Mine" / "He May Be Yours." The reviewer tossed a quick thumbs-up to Humes: "Plaudits on this version go to both the top-notch singing of Helen Humes and the excellent baton waving of Marshall Royal (orchestra leader)."[3] None of these singles became a hit.

Despite the ineluctable surmise that Humes's recent offerings were not scoring in the slightest with radio listeners and record buyers, the aggressive Bihari brothers picked off the singer from Discovery for their Modern Records label.

Helen Humes was born June 23, 1913, in Louisville, Kentucky. She was an only child in a middle-class family. Her mother was a teacher and her father was one of the first Black attorneys in the city.[4] As a child she took piano and vocal lessons. When she was thirteen years old, she appeared at an amateur singing contest where she caught the attention of local blues singer Sylvester Weaver. By the next year, she was making her first record on the OKeh label with such adult-sounding titles as "If Papa Has Outside Lovin'" and "Do What You Did Last Night." She recorded one other single for OKeh, "Everybody Does It Now" backed by "Alligator Blues."[5] Her next break came when she began singing with saxophonist Big Al Sears, who at the time was fronting his own band.

Humes moved on to the Count Basie Orchestra, where she replaced Billie Holiday in the touring band.[6] In 1938, she recorded with Harry James, and in

1939, she recorded with Count Basie (and James Rushing) on "Blame It on My Last Affair" backed by "The Blues Like I Want to Hear."

Humes snagged her first big R&B hit in 1945 with the novelty song "Be-Baba-Leba," which was recorded on the Philo label. Its surprising success led to a squabble among the upstart West Coast independent labels for the song rights. Charlie Barnet, who owned an independent music publishing company, worked out a deal for the exclusive publishing rights to "Be-Baba-Leba" with Harold Oxley, an agent who controlled the tune's original copyright when it was first sung (but not recorded) by Tina Dixon, whom Oxley managed. This is where it all got messy. Dixon recorded the song for the Excelsior label, which was run by Otis René. However, Dixon's cut came after the Humes's recording on Philo. Barnet first tried to negotiate with Humes before learning that Dixon featured the song in her nightclub act before the Humes's recording, which meant Dixon version of the song had a prior copyright.

The tale of the tune was covered by *Billboard* magazine on January 16, 1946, which highlighted the back story, that is, the emergence of the independent West Coast record industry. The magazine noted: "'Be-Baba-Leba' is sweeping the country in the same manner as 'The Honeydripper.' Both tunes started off to nationwide popularity through recordings by West Coast independent diskers. Exclusive Records started the ball rolling with Joe Liggins's recording of 'The Honeydripper.' Another localite, Philo Records, hit the jackpot with their cutting of 'Be-Baba-Leba' by songstress Helen Humes, and now a Barnet-Decca version is skedded [scheduled] for release in a few weeks."[7]

Humes didn't have her next and only other big hit until 1950, when Modern Records released a live version of her singing "Million Dollar Secret."

Gene Norman, who was a popular Los Angeles disk jockey and jazz aficionado, promoted jazz concerts in the city. His Blues Jubilee programs at the Shrine Auditorium were some of the first integrated jazz and blues concerts in the United States. Some of the shows were recorded and the songs released on major labels such as Decca and Capitol but also on local labels like Modern.[8] "Million Dollar Secret" was recorded at one of Norman's Blues Jubilee shows. It was matched with "I'm Gonna Let Him Ride" on the B-side. It was a pairing of the fun and bluesy "Million Dollar Secret" with the raucous and rocking R&B tune "Let Him Ride." "Secret" met the post-swing, semi-R&B sensibilities of the time, but "Ride" was the future. After a rollicking piano lead, the high-pitched Humes launched: "Well, he may be her man, but he comes to see me sometimes / He comes so often, I'm beginning to think he's mine."

Early notice of the song arrived via *Cash Box*'s "Jazz 'n' Blues Reviews" on October 7, 1950, with this review: "There's no stopping this one, chirp [female singer] Helen Humes comes up with a sensational side in the upper lid [A-side], tagged 'Million-Dollar Secret.' The disk is from a Gene Norman jazz concert and has Helen wailing a sock R&B side. Lyrics, background music, and the noise of the crowd all go toward making this end a must in your machine [jukebox]. Flip side shows just as well, but we give the edge to the top deck [A-side]."[9]

In early December, the song was holding its own in a slew of local markets, where the competition from other female singers for R&B chart position was intense with Margie Day's "Street Walkin' Daddy," Little Esther's "Wedding Boogie," Ruth Brown's "Teardrops from My Eyes," and two by Dinah Washington, "I'll Never Be Free" and "It Isn't Fair."

What probably was unfair but certainly legitimate was Humes's former record label trying to cash in on her sudden popularity. On December 2, 1950, with "Million Dollar Secret" still hot in such cities as Detroit and Los Angeles, Discovery ran a quarter-page ad in *Cash Box* touting a recording by Humes it hadn't released before, a remake of "Be-Baba-Leba." The sly-as-a-fox ad read: "Million $$$ Secret: Helen Humes, 'If I Could Be with You One Hour Tonight,' backed by 'E-Baba-Le-Ba.'"[10] A similar ad ran in *Billboard*.

Cash Box reviewed the song first among the trades, giving a full, if somewhat tepid, accounting in its "Jazz 'n' Blues Reviews" column: "Helen Humes shows up here with an unusual rendition of an old standard. With a party going on in the background, Helen really rides along with this one. Flip is a gibberish sort of thing again with the sound of a huge crowd making itself felt in the background. Ops [jukebox operators] who cleaned up with 'Million Dollar Secret' will want to get on this bandwagon."[11]

Humes continued recording for Modern, Decca, Dootone, and Contemporary, but never made her way back to the singles charts. She caught some slings and arrows along the way. In May 1952, *Jet* magazine, in what could only be called a gossipy, fat-shaming column, commented on the weight growth of popular female singers. The unknown columnists dissed: "Generally good natured about their avoirdupois, many of today's successful fat women show contemptuous disregard for waistline routines. Typical is Ella Fitzgerald, often called the 'First Lady of Song,' whose appetite for fattening foods is commonly known in show business. Such is also the case of personable Dinah Washington and Helen Humes, both of whom are good box office in personal appearances."[12]

What the column did get right was that Helen Humes put on a very good show and was, indeed, good box office. The next year, *Jet* atoned for its sins and proudly headlined, "Benny Carter, Helen Humes to tour Europe." The brief notation read: "Former bandleader Benny Carter, now featured saxophonist-trumpeter with Norman Granz's Jazz at the Philharmonic All-Stars, will team with blues singer Helen Humes, ex-Count Basie vocalist as headliners in a scheduled jazz concert tour of Europe next year. The concert tour, booked

October thru December 1954, was arranged by Southern California's impresario Irwin Parnes. It will be billed under the title, 'The Evolution of American Jazz: More than 50 Torrid Years of Afro-American Music.'"[13]

In 1964, after two tours of Australia, Humes briefly moved there. She returned three years later to take care of her ailing mother. At one point, she sold all her music wares, including her piano and albums, vowing never to sing again, but she did. She passed away in 1981.

Humes's contemporary, singer Nellie Lutcher, also had a sporadic recording career with numerous highs and lows. Her final singles also came in 1950, when she teamed up with Nat King Cole for a couple of duets.

Lutcher was born a year before Humes in 1912. A native of Lake Charles, Louisiana, she had a family experience the complete opposite of that of Humes, at least until she was a preteen. She was one of fifteen children, and both her parents were musically inclined. Her father was a bass player, and her mother was a church organist. Like Humes, she took piano lessons. Her brother Joe Lutcher became a well-known bass player.[14] On February 1, 1950, the *Ohio Daily Express* picked up a syndicated gossip column, which ran a story on the Lutcher siblings, first mentioning Joe, who was trying to decide whom to sue for wages after getting stiffed on a recent tour. The column said the musicians' union promised action, but it seemed a little slow to Joe and his eight musicians. Unfortunately, that type of incident with unscrupulous promoters was fairly common at the time. That story was immediately followed by one about Nellie having to scurry around the West Coast chasing gigs while she "would have liked to just stretch out in the silken super king-sized bed in her house of mirrors boudoir."[15]

Joe and Nellie's father played with Clarence Hart's Imperial Orchestra, and when Nellie turned twelve she was brought into the band, which mostly played regionally in Louisiana and Texas. One story about her prowess on the piano was that when celebrated blues singer Ma Rainey came to Lake Charles and was short a pianist, little Nellie stepped up. By the early 1930s, she was playing with the Southern Rhythm Boys.[16] In 1935, Lutcher moved to Los Angeles, where she found a regular gig playing at the Dunbar Hotel earning two dollars a night. Her sister Vida, who helped manage Lutcher's career, remembered her playing a lot of honky-tonks in Los Angeles.[17]

"Nellie came to Los Angeles because she was being offered a lot of deals and, of course, Hollywood was the place to be," said Darryl "Munyungo" Jackson, percussionist, four-time Grammy winner, and nephew of Nellie Lutcher. "She was from Lake Charles, and many musicians at that time would leave the South for opportunity, go east, north to Chicago or Detroit, or out west. She sang jazz, often playing in a trio: drummer, bass, and piano. They were swinging in a mix of jazz and pop. It wasn't R&B. The music was rhythmic."[18]

In 1947, Lutcher caught her big break. She volunteered to sing at a March of Dimes Cancer Drive at Hollywood High School. The show was broadcast live. One of the people listening was Dave Dexter, who worked for Capitol Records. He rushed out to sign her. He quickly got her into the studio, where he produced her first recordings, including a song called "Hurry on Down," which went to #2 on the R&B charts. That wasn't even her best effort. Her next release, "He's a Real Gone Guy," was a Top Ten R&B song for 1947, while "Hurry on Down" settled at #13 on the annual charts.[19]

The year 1948 was even more productive for Lutcher, with four big hits: "Fine Brown Frame," "The Song Is Ended (But the Melody Lingers On)," "Come and Get It," and "Honey and Cool Water." Singer Louise Harris Murray, of the group the Hearts in the mid-1950s and the Jaynetts in the early 1960s, was not yet a teenager in 1948, but as a bored young girl she spent hours listening to the radio, which was always on in her or her grandmother's apartments. One of her favorite songs in those early years was Lutcher's "Fine Brown Frame." "That was a hot song to me back then," Murray recalled. The lyrics were simple: "Oh, he got a fine brown frame / I wonder what could be his name? / He looks good to me and all I can see / is his fine brown frame."[20]

The songwriters were listed as Guadalupe Cartiero and J. Mayo Williams. Cartiero was a relative unknown, but Williams was a veteran producer and recording executive who worked for a number of record companies, including Decca. His specialty was "race records," and unfortunately, he had a reputation for taking advantage of blues musicians and songwriters, getting them to sign away the rights to their own records. He probably had little to do with the creation of "Fine Brown Frame" (other than producing), which was written from the female perspective.

Capitol Records kept the pump on, pushing out five more Nellie Lutcher singles in 1949, but it was the year of the stumble, and not one of her records caught on with the public.

It looked like 1950 was going to end the same way. The first single Capitol released was "Little Sally Walker" with "Only You" on the B-side. Not even *Billboard* could get behind this one. Its review of "Little Sally Walker" was grim: "Rhythmic, spirited rendition of some flimsy jive material." The B-side wasn't liked any better: "Up-tempo affair has a strong, taut beat, but little more."[21]

Nevertheless, Lutcher had stage appeal. She had been performing live for more than thirty-five years and had created a popular floor show and loyal following. When the television show *This Is Your Life* spotlighted Lutcher in 1952, host Ralph Edwards called her "one of the world's greatest nightclub entertainers."[22]

Lutcher was in good form as 1950 unwound, appearing at the Palomar in Seattle in January. Reviewer Wil Stevens noted: "This house's new expanded policy registered with Nellie Lutcher as this week's feature. At the late show, caught Nellie in her first Seattle appearance; she was wonderful. While the gal may frame better in a room, she showed fine techniques in playing to a vaude [vaudeville] crowd. Using 'Hurry on Down' as a torpid, well-paced starter . . . the gal hit straight for the mitts [applause], with 'Real Gone Guy,' furnishing a socko recall with 'Fine Brown Frame.'"[23]

The Palomar was so excited to have Lutcher, it brought her back to Seattle in August, where she also appeared in a big holiday parade. The local independent paper extolled: "the inimitable Nellie Lutcher on stage at the Palomar will ride in the process . . . on a theater float."[24]

As Capitol was unleashing "Little Sally Walker" on America, Lutcher was back in Los Angeles appearing at the Oasis and volunteering for another March of Dimes benefit. In March, Lutcher was in Chicago glad-handing at the Music Operators of America (MOA) conference at the Palmer House along with other popular stars at the time: Red Foley, Hank Williams, Spike Jones, the Ames Brothers, and Johnny Desmond.[25] She also performed at the Oriental for a local disk jockey's ABC Club, which, according one reviewer, was a real mess. He reticently scorched Lutcher with this comment, "Nellie Lutcher starts poorly. Does two numbers strictly for a Negro audience before launching into her standard click hits, 'Real Gone' and 'Brown Frame.' The Capitol chirp won solid hand [applause] at the close."[26]

In January 1950, Nat King Cole was in Los Angeles to record a bunch of new songs. He brought in his regular group of musicians to back him in the studio. The band consisted of veterans, including saxman Charlie Barnet. Although they had never worked together before, Cole invited Lutcher to the studio to record a couple of songs, including "Can I Come In for a Second" and "For You, My Love."[27] Lutcher was still in the studio when *Cash Box* executives came by to give the Nat King Cole Trio the magazine's award for Best Small Combo for the second year in a row. As a reporter who was there recalled, when Cole was given the statue, he said, "Gee, this is one of the really great moments in my life," and then turned to the reporter. Together they burst out laughing because they both knew Cole had said the exact same words when he got the award the year before. A photo of Lutcher standing next to Cole and *Cash Box*'s Leo Simon appeared in the magazine's February 18, 1950, issue. The cutline read: "'You dood it again,' says Nellie Lutcher, congratulating Nat King Cole on his win."[28]

At first it appeared that the top song on the duet's single would be "Can I Come In for a Second," a repartee between the two singers. It was a fun, breezy nightclub kind of song; thematically the lead (Cole) tries to convince a woman (Lutcher) to let him come into her apartment/home. *Cash Box*'s reviewer, who got to sit in on the session, exclaimed, "Another unusual flip to this session was the doubling on vocal by Nat and Nellie Lutcher, their first time on wax together, and if what we heard 'em run through is any indication, they're going to be a sockeroo team . . . The number was 'Can I Come In for a Second' and whatever 'Baby, It's Cold Outside' [thematically and structurally similar] left undone, this one does—or gets mighty close."²⁹ And that was a problem. What seems innocent today was considered very "blue" or risqué for the times.

As was the practice at the start of the 1950s, when a record had the potential to be a hit, almost every other label would rush in with its own singers to take on the song. That was the case with "Can I Come In for a Second," with versions by the famous Patty Andrews and Dick Haymes and the not-so-famous Betty Garrett and Larry Parks. The latter duo recorded on the MGM label, which had contested a decision by the American Broadcasting Company (ABC) to not play the song. MGM circulated petitions among various show business figures protesting what it called "an unfair, narrow-minded decision for censorship." It also submitted the record to the Catholic Legion of Decency seeking its approval of the tune.

Probably because it featured two Black singers and would play on more independent radio stations instead of big network pop stations, there was no controversy for Capitol's release. Despite such big names as Frank Sinatra, Pearl Bailey, Dick Haymes, and Artie Shaw coming out with new songs, on February 25, 1950, *Cash Box*'s "Record Review" chose to highlight the Nat and Nellie single with its "Sleeper of the Week" full review. Focusing on "Can I Come In for a Second," the magazine turned up the volume: "Nellie and Nat share the vocal limelight on 'Can I Come In for a Second' and come up with a side that'll last for lots more time than that. Ditty is a bright, pert novelty with a set of wonderful lyrics. Split vocal on the side, with Nellie and Nat taking several spots in their own inimitable styling, makes the disk shine and glow brightly. Tempo is merry throughout, with the ork [orchestra] backing provided rounding out the side in great manner."

As for "For You, My Love," the reviewer called it another excellent side and highlighted the fact that it was a mellow up-tempo blues ditty, with great orchestra backing and a fine solo sax break.

Taken together, the assessment was: "Blue ribbon winner in the offing for music ops [jukebox operators] is this biscuit [single] by Nellie Lutcher and King Cole. Both sides of this platter are loaded with dynamite and are sure to go like wildfire and wear white in the phonos [phonographs] once they get around. It's the type of platter that makes you want to step up and play a jukebox."³⁰

Billboard magazine hated "Can I Come In for a Second" in what turned out to be the B-side, curtly commenting "Nat and Nellie fill out the platter with a windy and unimpressive side." On the other hand, *Billboard* just adored the A-side, remarking, "Powerhouse teaming for the fast-stepping blues item turns out successfully. Should do business in R&B sectors as well as with the pop hipsters."³¹

As it turned out, *Billboard* got it right. The big hit on the Nat and Nellie single was "For You, My Love" and not "Can I Come In for a Second." It would be her last charting single.

On December 2, 1950, *Billboard* ran a Discovery Records block advertisement. Discovery was still trying to gain some heat from a red-hot Helen Humes, with its release of an older previously unreleased single, "If I Could Be with You One Hour Tonight" / "E-Baba-Le-Ba." Right next to the ad in the nightclub column, one could read that Ella Fitzgerald and Dinah Washington would be headlining at Birdland in New York, where Sarah Vaughan was already ensconced. Meanwhile, Nellie Lutcher would be playing the Club Harlem in Philadelphia.[32]

Lutcher continued to record with Capitol, at least through 1951, but with nothing going on, the label dropped her the next year. She was still such a popular and well-known performer that she appeared on the *This Is Your Life* television show in 1952. The next year, *Jet* caught up with her in its gossip column with the header: "Nellie Lutcher's Sister Weds." The news item: "Shortly after Lydah Lutcher and Staff Sergeant Sam J. Dixon exchanged vows in Los Angeles, the bride's famous sister Nellie Lutcher played the piano and sang at the couple's reception."[33]

The final irony of Lutcher's career came in 1958. Jack Webb wanted her for his new television pilot, *Pete Kelly's Blues*. At first, Lutcher accepted the gig, only to withdraw from the show for "personal reasons." Taking her place was Helen Humes.[34]

Remembering his youth, Munyungo Jackson said, "When we were kids, we used to go to her [Nellie Lutcher's] house for the holidays and Christmas time. She would have a lot of people come by, hang, and play music. She played the piano. I was too young to know who everyone was. I was a kid and didn't know that she was famous, but you could tell the way she handled herself that she was not a regular person."[35]

In 1957, she retired from recording and only sporadically performed live. She served as director of the Musicians' Union. On June 8, 2007, Lutcher died at age ninety-five.

The year 1950 was a good one for Black female singers. Of the Top 100 R&B songs for the year, fourteen were by women including two in the Top Five. Joining Ruth Brown in that select group was Esther Phillips, whose "Mistrusting Blues" came in at #5 for the year. In addition, there was a lot of diversity, with eight different ladies pushing onto a list that included some of the top jazz and R&B singers of the time: Nat King Cole, Louis Jordan, Johnny Otis, Ivory Joe Hunter, Fats Domino, Amos Milburn, Billy Eckstine, and Larry Darnell. Add these names to the 1950s list: Ruth Brown, Esther Phillips, Dinah Washington, Jewel King, Helen Humes, Sister Rosetta Tharpe, Margie Day, and Nellie Lutcher.

One might say of that list of female performers, the one who sang the most important record regarding the eventual rise of rock 'n' roll in the mid-1950s was the lady with the briefest career, Jewel King. She was a distaff addition to the New Orleans hothouse that was one of the key talent nodes of the proto–rock 'n' roll era. In 1950, as R&B was twisting into rock 'n' roll, outside of Los Angeles or New York, New Orleans was the place to be. That was due to a number of odd musical tentacles all coming together. First, of course, was the wealth of talent not just in New Orleans but across the whole bayou area stretching from Houston through Crescent City to Mississippi. Second, New Orleans already boasted a long history of being the most welcoming southern city for different strains of Black music and offering venues where that music could be played. Third, up until the World War II years, there wasn't a major recording studio in the South. Nashville came first, then New Orleans in 1947. Memphis didn't get its first professional studio until 1950, when Sam Phillips opened his Memphis Recording Service to record R&B musicians.

As a result of all those strands coming together, when the independent companies that were recording R&B began looking for talent outside of New York or Los Angeles, one of the first places they scouted was the Texas-Louisiana gulf region.

After World War II, Cosimo Matassa was selling records at his J&M Music Shop in New Orleans when he realized that there was no professional recording studio in the city. So, in 1947, he opened J&M Recording Service. It was good timing because De Luxe Records out of New Jersey had come to town scouting for talent and recorded at J&M locals such as Dave Bartholomew, Paul Gayten, and Annie Laurie.

While that was being organized, New Orleans singer Roy Brown was talking with Cecil Gant, who was playing at Foster's Rainbow Room, about a song he had written called "Good Rockin' Tonight." Gant knew Jules Braun of De Luxe Records was in town and got the two of them together. Squeezing in Brown before the Paul Gayten/Annie Laurie session at the J&M Studio, Braun recorded four Roy Brown songs, including "Good Rockin' Tonight," which became a big hit nationally and is one of the tunes considered to be among the earliest rock 'n' roll records.

Two years later, Lew Chudd, who owned Imperial Records in Los Angeles, arrived. He, too, was in search of talent, but he was on a particular mission. A local disk jockey told him about a "fat kid" who could be heard playing piano in Good Town, a rough Black section of New Orleans. There was still a law prohibiting Caucasians and Blacks from mixing in such venues as nightclubs, so he and Dave Bartholomew took a cab to the Dew Drop Inn, lying on the floor until it dropped them off at the club.[36]

"The clubs were segregated through the 1950s, and you could get arrested if you were a white person in a Black club," explained New Orleans music producer Wade Wright, locally known as "Wacko," who started out in the music business as a drummer. "When I began playing with Huey 'Piano' Smith in the 1950s, I was always worried I would be arrested. The police never came and got me."[37]

Chudd later told an interviewer what happened at the Dew Drop Inn: "Lloyd Price was on the bill, and he was accompanied by the stout youngster we came to hear. I was offered Price, but I wanted the fat man who played the piano . . . I had Dave Bartholomew with me. He was a former Duke Ellington trumpet player who had his own band and was very popular in New Orleans . . . with Bartholomew's, help I finally got to talk with Fats Domino—that was his name—and signed him to a contract."[38]

Before Bartholomew and Chudd would whisk Fats Domino into the J&M Studio to record a song called "Fat Man" built around on old tune known as "The Junker's Blues." Bartholomew brought his own band into record. On Tuesday, November 29, 1949, Bartholomew conducted his first session for Imperial Records, recording his band with lead singer Tommy Ridgley. Jewel King, a "reedy-voiced New Orleans blues songstress" who occasionally sang with Bartholomew's band, accompanied Ridgley to the recording session.[39]

Writer Rick Coleman called Mary Jewel King "a lithe Creole beauty." She was born June 1910 in Bexar County, Texas, and as far as anyone could recall, didn't make it to New Orleans until sometime in the 1940s. By the end of the decade, she was working steadily, making a name for herself in places like Club Rocker, Club Desire, and the Dew Drop Inn. Her first recordings, "Go Now" and "Passion Blues," were for Jules Braun and his De Luxe Records.

The next time she was in a recording studio was November 29, 1949, with Dave Bartholomew's band, which included some great session musicians such Red Tyler on the sax, Frank Fields on bass, and Earl Palmer on drums. Also at the session were Lew Chudd and up-and-coming music executive Al Young, who at the time owned a record store in New Orleans. Wearing the producer hat, bandleader Bartholomew split the session, giving the initial round to Tommy Ridgley, who was in the studio for the first time. He recorded both sides of a single, "Early Dawn Boogie" and "Shrewsbury Blues." This platter was marketed by Imperial Records in 1949. Ridgley was born in Shrewsbury, Louisiana, and the good feelings about this record turned it into a local hit.[40]

Although Ridgley was Bartholomew's main interest, he was a shrewd judge of talent, and when Jewel King got lined up for her stint in the recording studio, he had her record not two but four cuts: a new version of "Passion Blues," "Low-Down Feeling," "Don't Marry Too Soon," and "3 × 7 = 21." The latter song featured the kind of horn riffs and beat that became Bartholomew's trademark, wrote Fats Domino biographer Coleman, who also noted that Al Young, who was trying to impress Lew Chudd, kept acting like he was running the session, which led to bad blood between Young and Bartholomew.

How it all went down in that recording session remains debatable. New Orleans music historian Jeff Hannusch interviewed Earl Palmer, who explained that Bartholomew's band hadn't quite jelled when it made its first recordings. R&B hadn't yet taken hold in New Orleans; nevertheless, the band had a funkier beat to it, with a lot of quintet-type arrangements and ballads. Sometimes Palmer, Bartholomew, or Theard Johnson would sing, then came old "pregnant eyes" Tommy Ridgley. Tommy had a high-pitched, thin voice and was more of a blues singer, said Palmer.

According to Hannusch, "these earlier sessions lacked the drive and distinctiveness that Bartholomew's later productions would flaunt. In contrast, these sides had a jazzy uptown blues approach," reflecting, perhaps, Lew Chudd's more sophisticated Los Angeles approximation of the burgeoning R&B sound. Chudd, more used to the professional recording studios of Los Angeles, didn't cotton to the primitive J&M studio, where he felt the sound was always muddy.[41]

Despite all of the consternation about the studio and the looseness of Bartholomew's early recordings, that first session hit the big time immediately, with Jewel King's "$3 \times 7 = 21$" quickly climbing the national charts. Red Tyler's sax dominates the opening of the song before King launches—explaining that the "21" refers to her age. She sings, "Yes, I'm 3×7, just made 21 / I'm going out baby and have myself some fun." This was rock 'n' roll before there was rock 'n' roll.

Lew Chudd, who had a very productive stay in New Orleans, saw the future for his Imperial Records and told a reporter in February 1950 that his firm was in the "hot and rhythm business" for keeps following the great reception throughout the country of his label's "Fat Man" and "$3 \times 7 = 21$." He also hinted that he was signing more singers out of the South. Imperial grabbed Lloyd Price, who Chudd first passed over when signing Fats Domino.[42] The first single by Price, who was from Kenner, Louisiana, was cut with Bartholomew's band backing him and was called "Lawdy, Miss Clawdy." It went to #1 on the R&B charts in 1952.

Chudd had a right to boast in February 1950. In New Orleans that month, the Top Ten tunes included Imperial Records' "$3 \times 7 = 21$" at #3, "Fat Man" by Fats Domino at #4, and "Carnival" by David Bartholomew at #5. (At #6 was Nellie Lutcher's brother Joe Lutcher with "Mardi Gras" on the Modern label.) Nellie was also hot in Kansas City and Oakland. In March, the song burned in San Francisco and Richmond. In May, the rocker was still in the Top Ten in Newark and Seattle.[43]

Imperial quickly got King and Fats Domino back into the studio again. In March, Imperial took out a half-page ad in *Cash Box* promoting "Sensational

New Releases," which were Jewel King's "Broke My Mother's Rule" / "I'll Get It," Cecil Gant's "When You Left Me Baby" / "You'll Be Sorry," and Fats Domino's "Little Bee" / "Boogie Woogie Baby." None of these songs became hits, although "Little Bee" generated controversy because it was about a girl with a bumble-bee posterior and included the noun "bust," referring to breasts, and the verb "ball," implying sexual activity ("She's 42 in the hip, 31 in the bust. . . . Man, she likes to ball and she likes to play"). Some stations refused to play it.

Imperial tried again in July 1950 with another quarter-page ad with different wording: "Better than 'Fat Man' on Imperial, 'Hey! La Bas Boogie/Brand New Baby,' and Hotter than '3 × 7 =21' on Imperial, 'I Love a Fellow/Low-Down Feeling.'" These songs didn't make a dent in the charts, either.[44]

Fats Domino went on to become a huge recording star throughout the 1950s and 1960s with such songs as "Ain't It a Shame," "Blueberry Hill," and "I'm Walkin'." He's in the Rock & Roll Hall of Fame. But what happened to Jewel King?

With "Fat Man" and "3 × 7= 21" rocketing up the R&B charts, Lew Chudd rapidly had Bartholomew set up a western tour for the two acts, with King as the headliner. What happened next has become a bit muddy over the decades. King either demanded that her boyfriend (or husband?) Jack Scott, a guitarist (or bandleader?), join the entourage, and when Bartholomew said no, she replied, in that case she wasn't going to go, either. Or King bailed because Scott refused to let her tour without his band. In either case, King didn't travel, and Ridgley ended up performing her songs.

According to legend, Bartholomew warned King she was making a big mistake by not going on the tour. King (or Scott?) was obstinate, and in the end, Bartholomew was right. King recorded a dozen tracks for Imperial only to end up as a one-hit wonder. In the mid-1950s, she was still singing with her husband's band in New Orleans clubs and then disappeared from the music scene.[45]

When all the great and famous New Orleans contributors—Fats Domino, Lloyd Price, David Bartholomew, Smiley Lewis, and Huey "Piano" Smith—are discussed regarding the rise of rock 'n' roll, there are a couple of females to add to that list, one of whom is Jewel King.

As noted, 1950 was a very good year for Black female songstresses, particularly Ruth Brown, who had the #1 R&B song of the year, and Esther Phillips, who had eight Top Ten songs that year, including three #1 hits, "Double-Crossing Blues," "Mistrusting Blues," and "Cupid's Boogie." Even with all that success, Dinah Washington, then known as "Queen of the Jukeboxes" before becoming "Queen of the Blues," accomplished something no other female singer did that year: one of her songs crossed over to the pop charts. The song was called "I Wanna Be Loved," and it only reached #5 on the R&B charts, but also became a mid-tier hit on the pop charts, rising as high #21. It wasn't

Washington's first time crossing over. Back in 1946, a song called "Blow-Top Blues," which she recorded with the Lionel Hampton Band, tracked the same way. It reached #5 on the R&B chart (then called Race Records) and #21 pop.

Dinah Washington first entered a recording studio at the tail end of 1943 when she was touring with the Lionel Hampton Band. The story as told by Leonard Feather, a songwriter and agent, was that he heard Washington singing in New York and approached a friend, Eric Bernay, who had an independent jazz label called Keynote, with the idea of recording Washington with a group of Lionel Hampton band members, including Joe Morris on trumpet, Arnett Cobb on tenor sax, and Milt Buckner on piano. Bernay agreed, and on a late December evening after a show at the Apollo, the group walked into RKO studios at Radio City, where they recorded four cuts, including "Salty Papa Blues" and "Evil Gal Blues." According to Feather, Lionel Hampton sat in on the session. As Feather averred: "She [Washington] had a very biting tone quality to her voice, a unique timbre. Nobody else had quite that sound. She had a style that reflected her church and gospel background and the whole tradition of the blues. She didn't sound like Bessie Smith, but it was in the same tradition, just a generation later—a more sophisticated sound, with a more sophisticated background accompanying music." "Salty Papa Blues" and "Evil Gal Blues" were Top Ten R&B hits in 1944.

Two years later, what looked like a repeat recording session ended up being a big break—in all interpretations of the word "break"—for Washington. In May 1945, Washington, now recording with a major, Decca Records, entered a recording studio with another small band consisting of the Lionel Hampton All-Stars to record the Leonard Feather song "Blow-Top Blues." By this time, Hampton was at the top of his game, performing at Carnegie Hall, and was squabbling with Washington, who was feeling squelched by the bandleader. On the label of the record "Blow-Top Blues," the listed performers are Lionel Hampton and his Septet with "blues chorus by Dinah Washington." While he got the credits, what he couldn't do was get the publishing rights to the song, which didn't make Hampton happy with the whole setup. He feuded with Washington, who wanted to quit the band, and as punishment Hampton held up releasing the record. Legend has it that Washington pointed a gun at Hampton's head, thus persuading him to release her from her contract and release the record.[46] She was twenty-two at the time, a veteran of the music business about to go out on her own. Whether she actually pointed a gun at Hampton is unknown, but she was right about one thing, "Blow-Top Blues" needed to be released, which happened in 1946. It became Washington's first record to jump to the pop charts, and it's easy to see why. Despite the low-down name of the song, this was a slow, sophisticated tune with a top-of-the-line orchestra. It was the kind of tune that would become her signature form—jazzy, bluesy, sophisticated, and precisely performed, something like Nat King Cole would do. Washington sang: "I used to be a sharpie, always dressed in the latest styles / Now I'm walking down Broadway, wearing nothing but a smile / . . . I try to push the A train, and poured whiskey in my hair / I'm a girl you can't excuse, I've got those blow-top blues."

Four years later, she would cross over again with "I Wanna Be Loved."

If one looked at the R&B charts for 1950, "I Wanna Be Loved" wasn't even her best record. She was recording for Mercury at the time, who released five Dinah Washington singles that year—and all were Top Ten R&B hits. Two of the songs, "I Only Know" and "I'll Never Be Free," reached #3 on the R&B charts. Her other hits that year were "It Isn't Fair" (#5) and "Time Out for Tears" (#6). Washington scored her first R&B #1 in 1948 with "Am I Asking Too Much" and did it again the following year with "Baby Get Lost." The latter success story was somewhat unusual. The song was teamed on a single with "Long John Blues," a typical double-entendre blues song, this time about a dentist called Long John. The lyrics were crazy blue: "He took out his trusted drill, and told me to open wide / He said he wouldn't hurt me, but he'd fill my hole inside."

Feather, who produced the record, speculated that most buyers actually wanted to hear "Long John Blues" but were too embarrassed to ask for it, so they requested "Baby Get Lost," which became a #1 record, while "Long John Blues" did almost as well, settling in as a #3 song.

The good tidings from 1949 flowed into 1950. In January, *Billboard* ranked the top R&B artists by retail sales and jukebox plays. The only female on both lists was Dinah Washington, who notched the #12 slot on both charts.[47] In March, the magazine conducted its Fourth Annual Music-Record Poll as to the top R&B artists playing on jukeboxes, and once again, Dinah Washington was the sole female, coming in at #12. Among the names ahead of her on all of the charts were Amos Milburn, Charles Brown, Louis Jordan, Roy Brown, and one group, the Orioles.[48]

In March of that year, Washington played with the Joe Thomas Band at the 421 Club in Philadelphia. She was also in the suburbs. A wire service story out of Chester, Pennsylvania, covered the Blue Heaven Supper Club, which had just unveiled a new policy of bringing in major artists as headliners. The first female to top the bill was Dinah Washington.[49]

She could be found that month in Washington, DC, where a club called Louis and Alex premiered Sunday shows. Coverage by *Billboard* read: "Louis and Alex's, one of the better clubs in the capital's Negro district, pursues a non-segregation policy, and the audience was about 60% white. Music was provided by the five-piece ork [orchestra], the Capital City Jazz Band, whose Dixieland style was lapped up by the crowd. Dinah Washington, an added attraction, also went over big."[50] This story was bigger news to Black Americans who followed their favorite performers. Another wire service story picked up by the *Detroit Tribune* was headlined: "Dinah Washington Breaks Sabbath Rule." The story began colorfully: "Dinah Washington, dynamic delineator of songs and unchallenged 'Queen of the Jukeboxes,' broke with her oldest personal tradition: she agreed to open a one-week engagement" beginning on a Sunday. Apparently, Washington never opened on Sundays because of her years touring with a gospel group, and it became an "obsession almost amounting to a superstition."[51] That all ended at the Louis and Alex nightclub.

The Queen of the Jukeboxes was such a formidable presence in that very important jukebox market that she ended up being a singular integrationist pioneer. Under a headline that read "Café Chain Honors D'nh [Dinah]" it was reported that the nationally famous Howard Johnson Restaurant chain decided for the first time in 1950 to include "female Negro artists" among those recordings selected for the jukeboxes in their establishments. The first female "race artist" to be accorded a place on the music boxes was Dinah Washington via her hit recording of "I Wanna Be Loved." The chain didn't have an official ban against "Negro artists" who were women, it just happened that none had ever appeared, although the Ink Spots and Billy Eckstine both integrated the company's jukeboxes in the late 1940s.[52]

After a successful two-week run at the Strand Theater in Detroit, Washington, along with the singing group the Ravens, moved over to the Paradise Theater in January 1950. The *Detroit Tribune* noted: "Sharing the spotlight (with the Ravens) of entertainment will be that blues-singing gal, Dinah Washington. Dinah has earned the distinction of being the 'Queen of the Jukeboxes' throughout America. Her styling of the blues has made her one of the outstanding singers of 1949."

The next month in *Billboard*'s "Record Reviews" column, it was the Ravens versus Dinah Washington among the highlighted songs soon to hit the market. The magazine gave a thumbs up to the Ravens and a thumbs down to Washington's release of "I Only Know" / "I've Been a Fool," saying, "Dinah W. delivers the blues bottled with plenty of punch, but the material is pretty routine stuff."[53] What do reviewers know anyway? The song climbed all the way to #3 on *Billboard*'s own R&B chart and was the twenty-sixth best-selling R&B tune of the year.[54] The #25 best-selling R&B cut that year was "I Wanna Be Loved," and it was very loved by *Cash Box*. The only woman to be reviewed in the magazine's "Jazz 'n' Blues Reviews" for June 17, 1950, the reviewer of "I Wanna Be Loved" / "Love With Misery" was all amour: "There's no doubt about the upper lid [A-side] here. Dinah Washington really turns in a great performance with this blues rendition of the currently popular 'I Wanna Be Loved.' Side-A natural for the boxes [jukeboxes]. Flip [B-side] is a slow torchy melody, which Dinah handles in the same brilliant style. The top deck [A-side] can't miss."[55]

The song, written by Johnny Green with lyrics by Edward Heyman and Billy Rose, was intended for the 1933 remake of the theatrical production *Billy Rose's Crazy Quilt*. The song was revived in 1950 by the Andrews Sisters, who had a #1 smash on the pop charts with it, ending up as the seventeenth best-selling song of the year, and it was the last #1 tune for the famous singing group. As was common practice at the time, when a song looked like a potential hit, all of the record companies would pile in with their own versions by their own singers. Considering the competition, it was a tremendous feat that Washington's cover of the song crossed over the pop charts and did as well as it did.

Scrambles were commonplace in the early 1950s. It happened, for example, with Washington's recording of "Time Out for Tears," a Top Ten R&B tune in 1948 by Savannah Churchill that crossed over to the pop charts, where it climbed to #24. In fact, the *Billboard* review of the Washington version referred to Churchill, a Louisiana native. It read: "Tune was an R&B click a couple of seasons back via Savannah Churchill's waxing [recording]. Miss Washington sells it soulfully, with big and pretty orking [orchestration]."[56]

The week before that review, *Billboard* spotlighted a bunch of new songs for the pop market. One of those was "Time Out for Tears" by a singer called Bill Lawrence. The review was similar: "The rhythm & blues click of two years ago gets a fine boost revival as a pop. Lawrence gets plenty of feeling into it."[57] Not much would be heard about Bill Lawrence, who sang with the Tommy Dorsey Band for about a year. However, in one of those odd twists of fate, backing Lawrence on the tune was a group of young ladies called the Chordettes. A lot more would be heard about them starting in 1955, when their song "Mr. Sandman" was everywhere across the airwaves on the way to becoming a monster hit.

CHAPTER TWO

SMOOTH SAILING (1951)

SAVANNAH CHURCHILL—JOE DAVIS—ELLA FITZGERALD— BOSWELL SISTERS—NORMAN GRANZ—MARGIE DAY— GRIFFIN BROTHERS—RUTH BROWN—WILLIS JACKSON— DINAH WASHINGTON

Savannah Churchill had lotsa luck, but it couldn't be counted on. Sometimes it was really, really good. Sometimes it was so bad, it was catastrophic. Take that time in 1956, when Churchill was playing the Midwood Club in Brooklyn, New York. There she was dressed to the nines, crooning her wonderfully seductive, torchy songs when a besotted fan, hooked up with a full tank, leaned unsteadily over the ledge of the balcony. As she sang, the inebriant lost his balance, pitched over the rail, and landed full force on Churchill, breaking her pelvis and causing painful injuries that would keep her out of action for longer than a career could survive.[1] Five years later, *Jet* caught up with Churchill, calling her the comeback story of the year. "Crippled by an accident several years ago, [Churchill] had considered retirement," the magazine columnist scribed. "Now with a hit record (a remake of her old hit 'I Want to Be Loved'), she's back in demand on the nightclub circuit."[2]

Except it didn't all go down that way. Churchill did record an album with the Jamie label in 1961, but it was obvious her best days as a singer were far in the past. Some Churchill aficionados maintain she never fully recovered from the Midwood Club disaster.

When one talks of R&B singers from the 1950s finally gaining acceptance with the pop audience, it should be remembered there were a handful of jazz and torch singers from swing-time America in the 1930s and 1940s who often found a regular audience in white America, even more so than in Black

America. Ella Fitzgerald was of those singers, and Savannah Churchill was another. Both would have crossover hits in 1951.

It would be reasonable to conclude that Churchill's big record that year, "(It's No) Sin," often listed just as "Sin," was not a crossover record because it rose to #5 on the pop charts and was not at all a hit on the R&B charts. This was her pattern. She recorded between thirty to forty singles in her lifetime, and only six charted. Four adorned the R&B charts, four the pop charts; two songs charted on R&B, but not pop, two on pop but not on R&B, and two on both. Here's another way to look at it: she charted six songs, and four of those made it to the pop charts.

Savannah Churchill (Savannah Valentine Roberts) is often referred to as a Creole singer because she was very light-skinned, and it was assumed that she came from New Orleans. The reality was that she was born in 1915 in the tiny burg of Colfax, Louisiana, over 200 miles from the Crescent City. She wasn't even there for very long as her family migrated to Brooklyn before she started elementary school. By the time she was in her early twenties, she had married her high school sweetheart, Arthur Churchill, briefly attended New York University, and worked as waitress in a couple of Harlem restaurants.[3] In 1937, she auditioned for Ed Smalls, the owner of the popular nightspot Smalls Paradise. He listened, looked her over, and finally responded, "Baby, you can't sing much, but you ain't bad to look at. With experience, you might improve, so I'll give you a job." It paid $18 a week. As Churchill told a *Jet* reporter, "That $18 a week Smalls offered me wasn't as much as I made in tips at the Anchor Inn, but it was my beginning in show business."[4] For two years, she trod the stage at Smalls as a second-string singer, refining her act and arguing with Smalls to give her a chance. It took a bit of luck to finally get there. The featured vocalist for a weekend gig couldn't make it, so Smalls gave Churchill her moment.

Joe Davis, who worked with Fats Waller, had already spent a lifetime in the music industry when he founded Manhattan-based Beacon Records in 1942. He was the kind of music man who didn't have a clean reputation, and although he moved around a lot, he always landed on his feet. He was able to create Beacon because he bought the rights to the wartime shellac ration of another record company, which needed the money to refurbish a record-pressing plant in Richmond, Virginia. One of the first decisions he made as a record label boss was to record Savannah Churchill backed by Jimmy Lytell and his All-Star Seven.[5] The single was a jump blues extraordinaire, with the somewhat blue "Fat Meat Is Good Meat" on the A-side and "Two-Faced Man" on the B-side. It was Churchill's first time in a recording studio, and she conquered.

Two years later, big band veteran Benny Carter, whose orchestras in the 1930s included guys like Cozy Cole and Teddy Wilson, was then residing in Los

Angeles. He put together another band with Max Roach and Miles Davis and began recording for Capitol Records. In 1944, when he needed a female singer for a couple of songs, "Hurry, Hurry" and "Just a Baby's Prayer at Twilight," he invited Churchill to take the lead.

Then came her big break—actually two big breaks! First, Manor Records decided to sign Churchill in her own right, not as part of someone else's group, and she did the company proud with "Daddy, Daddy," which was a #3 hit on the R&B charts. Savannah took on the cowriting chore, and the singing credits read: Savannah Churchill and Her All-Star Orchestra. She sings: "I keep a knockin', you tell me I can't come in / But if a party comes [?] out, I swear you'll make me sin."

Her second lucky break came in May 1945, when Ella Fitzgerald failed to turn up for a show at the Howard Theater in Washington, DC. Churchill, who was appearing at a local club, was called on to replace her.[6]

Toward the end of 1946, Churchill returned to the studio to record what became her signature song, "I Want to Be Loved (But Only by You)" with "Foolishly Yours" on the B-side. The song went to #1 on the R&B charts and became her first crossover hit, rising to #21 on the pop charts. This time, Churchill took full songwriting credits, and the performers are listed as Savannah Churchill and the Four Tunes. The surprising kick in the sultry song was the hint of a country & western melody instead of the basic blues beat. "I Want to be Loved" foreshadowed so many of the powerhouse ballads that white female crooners sang in the early to mid-1950s.

Her luck continued through the next year with more hits, including "I Want to Cry," which climbed to #14 on the R&B charts, and most importantly, "Time Out for Tears," #10 on the R&B charts and #20 pop. Then in 1949 through 1950, nothing seemed to work for her. She suffered a two-year cold streak with no charted records despite moving from Manor to the Arco label. Oddly, her songs worked for others. In 1948, a fledging songwriter named Deborah Chessler penned a song called "Tell Me So," which Churchill recorded. It didn't do much for her, but the Orioles took it to #1 on the R&B charts and it became the fifth best-selling R&B tune of 1949.

Tennessee Ernie Ford and Kay Starr did well in 1950 with "I'll Never Be Free," which Churchill recorded in 1949. Other ladies taking it on included fellow Louisianan Annie Laurie with Paul Gayten, Dinah Washington, and Ella Fitzgerald with Louis Jordan.

Although Churchill wasn't scoring any hits, the late 1940s and 1950 were not fallow years for her. She was so well-known that she appeared in a couple of movies, and in 1951, she even appeared in an ad program for Sparkling Champale Malt Liquor. It featured a head and shoulder photo of Churchill with a quote from her saying: "Celebrate with Champale, it's so powerful, powerful good."7 She also toured when she could. In November 1950, she found herself on an Erroll Garner tour in Detroit. The local paper noted, "Erroll Garner returns to the Paradise . . . a fast revue featuring Gene Ammons and his orchestra . . . Other stars include Savannah Churchill, torrid blues singer . . ."8

Churchill recorded some fine uncharted tunes from 1949–50, including "Let's Call a Spade a Spade" and "Once There Lived a Fool." She recorded the latter song for the Regal label. In January 1951, *Cash Box*'s review noted: "Savannah Churchill's first record on the Regal label is one to shout about. Taking a currently sensational number, Savannah joins with the Striders to turn out a first-rate rendition of it."9

Again, no action for a Churchill recording, so in March 1951, Regal released another chestnut redone, "Wedding Bells Are Breaking Up That Old Gang of Mine" with "And So I Cry" on the B-side. *Cash Box* couldn't get enough of Churchill, commenting: "Savannah Churchill takes a wonderful oldie and gives it dynamic rendition on the top deck [A-side]. With a good chorus to back her up, Savannah sends it out of this world."10 One thing for sure was that *Cash Box*'s reviewers and the rest of the America weren't in the same groove. That record also struck out.

With Regal's strategy of Churchill remaking oldies a failure, she caught another break, moving to a major label, RCA Victor, in September 1951. A story in *Cash Box* crowed: "Two outstanding stylists of blues and ballads, Savannah Churchill, popular headliner, and Terry Timmons . . . have signed exclusive RCA Victor contracts." The story filled out with a Churchill backgrounder: "Savannah Churchill's hit record 'I Want to be Loved' skyrocketed her into the front ranks of the top recording artists after she had sung her way from church choirs to featured vocalist . . . she had won initial recognition with 'Daddy, Daddy' and then was featured in top nightclubs and vaudeville houses from coast to coast."11

RCA Victor wasted no time getting Churchill into the recording studio almost immediately, where she recorded what might be considered her biggest hit, "(It's No) Sin." This song was a truly amazing accomplishment for several reasons. First, while this tune never scored on the R&B charts, it was a #5 best-selling record in the pop world. And to get there, Churchill's recording had to fend off more competitors than a gladiator in a coliseum. This was a time when a potential hit record would attract all labels, and "Sin" was like catnip to felines.

The first recording of "Sin" was not by Churchill, but a group called the Four Aces. The song, on the small label called Victoria, broke in Philadelphia and then careened all over the country, stressing pressing plants from the onslaught of orders. Then came the scramble, with not only Churchill recording the song but also Billy Williams, Eddy Howard, Sammy Kaye, Arthur Prysock, Arthur "Guitar Boogie" Smith, the Four Buddies, the Four Knights, and the Larks.12 This is how crazy it got. On November 24, 1951, *Cash Box* surveyed sixteen deejays across the country to gather their Top Ten hits: "Sin" was listed in fourteen cities. Billy Williams's version scored in New Hampshire and New York City; Eddy Howard's in Massachusetts, Chicago, Texas, and Rochester, New York; the Four Aces' in Philadelphia, Cleveland, and Boston; Sammy Kaye's in Louisville and Atlanta; and Churchill's across the South in Alabama, Mississippi, and Washington, DC.[13]

The reason the song didn't resonate with R&B listeners is the tune as vocalized by Churchill was given a standard pop format made popular by former big band vocalists like Dinah Shore. The background singers were so lamentable it could have been the barbershop quartet–sounding Ames Brothers, who were popular at the time. Still, against a jungle of male voices, Churchill's version sounded much more fetching.

It was almost Churchill's last hurrah as a hitmaker. In 1953, she would have one more charted record, which was kind of a repeat performance of 1951. Her version of "Shake a Hand" did not score in the R&B world but was a moderate hit at #22 in the pop realm. About that time, Churchill decided to leave mainstream music to concentrate on spiritual songs, explaining that she was tired of one-nighters, and sales of songs with a spiritual or gospel tinge such as "Shake a Hand" were catching on.[14]

She tried to come back to the pop music world without a great deal of success. It didn't help that a drunk patron fell from a balcony and landed directly on top of her, ruining her health. She died in 1974 at the age of fifty-eight.

"Sin" had made Savannah Churchill the rare crossover success story outside of a select group of jazzy singers such as Ella Fitzgerald, who was the reigning queen of crossover appeal. She became a recording star before the creation of *Billboard*'s Harlem Hit Parade in 1942. From her first hit record "All My Life" with bandleader Teddy Wilson in 1936 to "My Heart and I Decided" in 1943, Fitzgerald bragged thirty-five Top Twenty hits before ever appearing on anything resembling a segregated music chart. Over that time period, she snagged two #1 songs. In 1944, she boasted two more #1 songs on the pop charts. It was not unusual for Fitzgerald to have songs chart higher on the pop charts than on the R&B listings, sometimes having a Top Ten pop hit without even making a dent in the R&B world. That wasn't the case in 1951, when "Smooth Sailing" hit #3 on the R&B charts and crossed over to the pop charts. It was also the top song by a Black female singer that year on the R&B charts. However, it wasn't the top song by a female voice on the R&B charts.

The pop world in 1951 heralded the next singing sensation, a weird white R&B singer named Johnnie Ray. His lachrymose songs such as "Cry" and "The Little White Cloud That Cried" attracted to concerts hordes of screaming teenage girls not seen since Frank Sinatra's heyday and not to be repeated until Elvis Presley's arrival. Johnnie Ray crossed over to the R&B charts as did a smattering of other white acts, most notably guitarist Les Paul, who with his wife vocalist Mary Ford, also crossed over to the R&B world with "How High the Moon." It was a Top Twenty R&B song in 1951, making Mary Ford the most successful female on the list. Fitzgerald almost got there. Her "Smooth Sailing" was #22 on the R&B best-seller list for 1951.

Both "How High the Moon" and "Smooth Sailing" were not novelty songs but were two of the most unusual cuts that year: "How High the Moon" for its layered, almost experimental guitar approach (Ella Fitzgerald also recorded this song and sang it at Carnegie Hall in 1947), and "Smooth Sailing" because there is not an actual "word" in the whole song. Ella Fitzgerald jazz-scatted the whole tune. Crazy, man, crazy!

This doesn't mean that Fitzgerald wasn't hip to what was happening in the pop world. Toward the end of January 1951, Ella rolled into the Paramount, a "nitery" in New York. She was headlining a multifaceted show including a couple of new acts. Not feeling well, she let young guys like Russ Emery and comic Harvey Stone do some of the heavy lifting. She opened tentatively with such golden nuggets as "My Heart Cries for You," not really capturing the audience's attention until she launched into "How High the Moon."[15]

In 1951, Ella Fitzgerald was one of the most famous singers in the world, already earning her eventual nicknames "First Lady of Song" or "Queen of Jazz." Through the 1940s, about the only female act that competed with her in Top Twenty singles was the Andrews Sisters. From 1937 through 1949, the Andrews Sisters snagged six #1 songs, and Fitzgerald four. Which is the better jazz swing tune, "A Tisket, a Tasket" by Fitzgerald or "Boogie Woogie Bugle Boy" by the Andrews Sisters? Your choice.

Both acts were heavily influenced by the almost forgotten Boswell Sisters, who rose to stardom in the 1930s on the first growth wave of the new technological innovation of the time, the radio. Their first recordings were more blues-oriented than jazz.

The three Boswells, Martha, Connee, and Helvetia, were born (1905 through 1911) and raised in New Orleans during the first decade of the twentieth century at a time when the Crescent City was a laboratory of a new sound in America, jazz. Their mother was an enthusiast of this new music, and although the girls received classical music training, they were taken at a young age to hear the vibrant jazz sound emanating from the streets of New Orleans.

By the 1930s, they were the first female musical stars famous for being on the radio, although they did make movies as well. From 1931 to 1938, the Boswell Sisters charted twenty Top Twenty records, including their biggest hit, the 1934 #1 "The Object of My Affection."

As music writer Larry Birnbaum noted, "the Boswell Sisters were one of the most innovative American vocal groups ever . . . adopting jazz rhythms and

African American inflections with an authenticity that few other white artists could match."[16]

The Andrews Sisters (LaVerne, Maxene, and Patty) began their career by imitating the Boswell Sisters. And so did Ella Fitzgerald.

In 1934, at the age of seventeen, Fitzgerald was slated to perform at the famed Amateur Night at the Apollo Theater in Harlem. She intended to do a dance routine, but on the bill that night was the Edwards Sisters (Ruth and Louise), one of the few female tap acts that became dance stars. Fitzgerald was smacked with a sudden bout of insecurity and at the last moment decided she would sing instead. She opted for the song "The Object of My Affection," trying to imitate the voice of Connee Boswell.

As Birnbaum wrote, so genuine was the Boswell Sisters' approach to jazz that Ella Fitzgerald modeled her style after Connee Boswell. He quoted Fitzgerald: "I tried so hard to sound just like her."

Ella Fitzgerald won Amateur Night, which attracted the attention of bandleader Chick Webb.

Ella Fitzgerald was born April 1917 in Newport News, Virginia. After her father died, Ella and her mother moved to Yonkers, New York, in 1920. At an early age, she sang in the church choir, danced, and listened to jazz on the radio and the myriad records her mother brought home. At fifteen, her mother died, and Ella moved in with her aunt in Harlem. That was the beginning of a dark period in Fitzgerald's life, which soon included street crime, orphan asylum, reform school, and then back on the street, essentially as a homeless person.[17]

Winning Amateur Night at the Apollo saved her because she soon joined the Chick Webb Orchestra, which often played the Savoy Ballroom in Harlem. In fact, Fitzgerald was paroled to Chick Webb's band. Good things happened quickly. First, she was on a salary of $12.50 a week, and eventually Moe Gales, cofounder of the Savoy, became her first manager. In 1936, she started recording with Chick Webb and bandleader Teddy Wilson. Four of those cuts became Top Twenty pop songs. The next year, she recorded songs under her own name with the Mills Brothers and a tune called "Goodnight My Love" with the Benny Goodman Orchestra. It was her first #1 record. Chick Webb must have been wondering what the heck was going on with his star vocalist because he pulled her into the recording studio with his own band. In 1938, seven Ella Fitzgerald tunes backed by Chick Webb's orchestra went Top Twenty, including the song the made her a household name, her second #1 "A Tisket, a Tasket," a jazzy rendition of the old nursery rhyme that Fitzgerald reworked and embellished with Al Feldman. In 1937, there was no *Billboard* chart of the top songs in the country, but the magazine did tabulate sheet music and record sales. "A Tisket, a Tasket" was #1 on both lists as well as on radio's *Your Hit Parade*. In 1938 and

1939, the song appeared in three movies, and in 1942, Ella famously swings the tune in an Abbot and Costello comedy *Ride 'em Cowboy.*[18]

Fitzgerald would get her second and third #1 songs in 1944 with "I'm Making Believe" and "Into Each Life Some Rain Must Fall," both with the Ink Spots.

Since the 1930s, Fitzgerald had been recording with Decca Records, and her last contract with the record company would come to a conclusion in 1951. Starting in 1950, Decca made sure Fitzgerald was back in the studio recording singles, which the company pushed into the market as quickly as possible. The trouble was that Fitzgerald's jazzy sound was becoming outdated. In 1950, only two of her songs charted: "I'll Never Be Free" was a #3 hit on the R&B charts while "Can Anyone Explain (No, No, No)" with Louis Armstrong reached #30 on the pop charts. In 1951, Decca was relentless, recording about ten more singles, most of which were pushed into record stores and radio stations as the next great Ella Fitzgerald tune. She was still highly respected and often received excellent reviews. *Cash Box* just loved Fitzgerald and always reviewed her tunes with affection. Here are samples from 1951:

> "The Hot Canary" / "Two Little Men on a Flying Saucer." Ella Fitzgerald takes a novelty that is causing a lot of excitement as an instrumental and sings some lyrics to it on the upper half. With Sy Oliver's orchestra doing the backing, Ella makes this sound very cute. The second side is another item with clever lyrics, which Ella delivers in her well-known style.[19]

> "Because of Rain" / "The Chesapeake and Ohio." Ella shows up with her most commercial side in years with a tune titled 'Because of Rain.' Ella really sends this one flying and her interpretation of it is sure to zoom it into the hit class. It's simply great . . . Ella brings her unique phrasing to this ballad and highlights everything that's in it.[20]

Despite *Cash Box*'s boosterism, none of these songs became a hit. Decca was struggling with its star female singer in the new decade, and to make matters worse, it was common knowledge that Irv Green at Mercury Records wanted to steal her away. In the end, Decca took control.[21] In the autumn of 1951, *Jet* announced that the record company had signed Ella Fitzgerald to a new five-year contract, reminiscing that she had been singing for Decca since 1936, a year after she won first prize at Amateur Night at the Apollo Theater.[22]

The trade papers treated the story with a bit more news. *Cash Box* reported that Leonard W. Schneider, executive vice president of Decca Records, was on the record as announcing Fitzgerald's signing a new five-year contract. The magazine closed its story with this note: "Currently, she is heading the top of the lists with her terrific version of 'Smooth Sailing.'"[23]

This was one of the oddest stories of 1951. Ella's jazzy approach to songs had quickly become outdated on the pop charts, but her most swing-oriented song, a tune that was ultra-jazz, became her only hit record of the year and her biggest hit in two years. Called "Smooth Sailing," it was nontraditional song, from start to finish all scat, which had become Ella's hallmark.

Scat, or to put it bluntly the singing of nonsense syllables, was employed in old blues and jazz songs. Then it was accidentally raised to a jazz art form by Louis Armstrong, who, in 1926, while recording a rendition of "Heebie Jeebies," dropped his lyric sheet and ad-libbed sounds. The session continued, and anyone listening to the record could not tell it was not done on purpose.[24] Eventually, the dominant style of scat became associated with Fitzgerald, particularly after she did a version of "Flying Home" all in phonetic improvisation or scat.[25]

The thing about "Smooth Sailing" was that it had pedigree written all over it. The tune was written by Houston native Arnett Cobb, who played tenor sax with Lionel Hampton for six years in the 1940s. On the piano was Hank Jones from Vicksburg, Mississippi, who played with many of the famous bop jazzmen, including Charlie Parker. On the organ was the great Bill Doggett from Philadelphia, who played with Helen Humes on her first hit "Be-Baba-Leba" in 1945 and later scored a tape-measure home run with "Honky-Tonk" (#1 R&B, #2 pop in 1956). As an added bonus, the background harmony was by the Ray Charles Singers.

Even with all those great musicians, "Smooth Sailing" still caught everyone by surprise. *Cash Box* first reviewed the song in August 1951 as the B-side, barely taking notice. The A-side was initially intended to be "Love You Madly." On the B-side, the quick review read: "Bottom half [B-side] is one of the things Ella is famous for, singing without words. It makes for good listening."[26]

By the following month, when *Billboard* was predicting the next big hits, it chose "Smooth Sailing," recognizing that it had already begun picking up steam. A surprised reviewer wrote about the song: "A recent issue, this unusual side, intended as a jazz item, has taken a pop foothold in several sectors and is making a concerted bid for general favor."[27]

As for the song itself, the reviewer added, "Ella does a scat from start to finish on a simple Arnett Cobb riff off an exciting assist from a driving organist, rhythm section, and the Ray Charles singers."

Decca, which was riding high, took a whole page in the November 3, 1951, *Billboard* to tout all its great songs. At that point, "Smooth Sailing" was the second biggest best-selling song for the label in the popular market, behind Louis Armstrong and ahead of the Mills Brothers.[28]

A small article deep within *Billboard* magazine on April 14, 1951, concerned the popularity of what it called "rhythm & blues niteries" in the Los Angeles area. These were generally blues clubs and nightclubs that catered to African

American audiences but were increasingly attracting a white audience as they shifted to R&B (about 30–60 percent of the audiences were white). The article mentioned clubs that operated "with all-Negro shows," noting: "Besides R&B clubs, there are from 6 to 10 intimate niteries that feature a combination of blues and jazz." One club that was mentioned was the Oasis, which had featured Ella Fitzgerald, Louis Armstrong, and Cab Calloway but was now getting "strong box office" from all sorts of musicians, featuring such talents as Little Esther, Johnny Otis, and Charles Brown.[29]

Through 1950, one could still catch Ella Fitzgerald at New York's Bop City or Birdland. A reviewer who attended Fitzgerald's Birdland set wrote, "That great gal of songs, Ella Fitzgerald, is really wooing the customers at Broadway's Birdland. There is constantly a line wrapped around the corner from Broadway waiting to get into Birdland to see and hear America's First Lady of Swing. She's great."[30]

A year earlier, Norman Granz, the impresario of the Jazz at the Philharmonic series, invited her to go on the road with what was essentially a "touring jam session" that brought jazz to the hinterlands as well as premier venues such as Carnegie Hall. The 1950–51 season of Jazz at the Philharmonic, for example, meant eleven weeks on the road in fifty-one US cities and a six-week tour of Europe. Among the players were Coleman Hawkins and Lester Young in the reed section, Hank Jones on piano, and "taking over the vocal department . . . is our Lady of Swing, Queen Ella Fitzgerald."[31]

After her Decca contract expired, Norman Granz, by then her manager, signed her to Verve, where she undertook the series of landmark *Songbook* albums. Although she continued to release singles through the 1950s and '60s, by the time of the *Songbook* sets, she was essentially an album recording star. She died in 1996 at the age of seventy-nine, having recorded close to 600 single tracks and selling over 40 million albums. The "Lady of Swing" had become the "First Lady of Song."[32]

On October 7, 1950, *Cash Box* ran its "Jazz 'n' Blues Review" spotlighting, among other artists, Helen Humes and her song "Million Dollar Secret," which went on to become a big hit. However, for its "Award o' the Week," the magazine's reviewers instead chose the unknown Margie Day recording with the Griffin Brothers. The song was "Street Walkin' Daddy" with "Riffin' with Griffin'" on the B-side. Day coos deep in the blues: "Ooooh, street walkin' daddy, tell me what's on your mind / Say, street daddy why treat me so unkind? / When I first met you, you said you loved just me / Since then, things have changed, now you have two or three."

For that particular column, the magazine included eight regular reviews and the "Award o' the Week." None of the other songs were successful releases, only the platters by Helen Humes and Margie Day.

"Street Walkin' Daddy" was another song that caught the market by surprise, and the reviewer noted the tune was "causing quite a stir in rhythm & blues spots." The song "whirls in slow blues tempo and has chirp [female singer] Margie Day wailing a tender low-down melody. It's a wax [record] that will surely earn repeat plays on the boxes [jukeboxes] and wear white in no time at all. Tempo is slow and mellow, with ork [orchestra] backing fitting the mood and patter of the music like a glove. Ivory [piano] tickling in the background, added to a tempting wall of a tenor sax all go toward making the wax the grade A-side it is."[33]

The reviewer predicted that Margie Day had what it took to become a top jukebox attraction, which was a heady and commercially appealing compliment in its day. Although a talented singer, her career would peak in 1951 with the hit record "Little Red Rooster," not to be confused with the Howlin' Wolf song of the same name. Well, maybe a little confused, since both tunes evolved from early blues songs that used "the little red rooster" or "red rooster" themes, such as ditties by Memphis Minnie and Charley Patton.

Margie Day (born Margaret Hoffler, later Margie Day Walker) was born April 1926 in Norfolk, Virginia. She began her professional career playing with local bands and took a chance and moved to New York. It was a break, but not a big break. She sang in lounges and even produced her first recording on the Savoy label, but in the end returned to Norfolk. That turned out to be the real break for her career. Local boys Jimmy and Buddy Griffin had formed their own band playing clubs throughout the Mid-Atlantic region, including Washington, DC. When Day returned to town, they asked her to join them.[34] Their first recording together was "Street Walkin' Daddy," a #7 hit on the R&B charts. The song did well in some urban locales but was not expansively a hit. In December 1950, for example, the song was #1 in Detroit, outperforming "Million Dollar Secret" and "Teardrops from My Eyes" but wasn't charting at all in cities such as Los Angeles, Oakland, or Dallas.[35]

"Street Walkin' Daddy" was recorded on the brand-new Dot label, which was an aggressive promoter. As early as November, the label was buying space for promotions in trade publications. In the November 4, 1950, issue of *Billboard*, it took the top position on the far-right column of the page to tout its Margie Day record. Four ads below it was the Modern label promoting "Million Dollar Secret" by Helen Humes.[36]

In February 1951, the Margie Day follow-up tune "Little Red Rooster" was already charting, ironically in places where "Street Walkin' Daddy" stumbled, like Los Angeles and Dallas. The song was written by the Griffin Brothers and attributed to Margie Day with the Griffin Brothers Orchestra. It was a solid blues number, much livelier than Day's big hit from the prior year. The song reached #5 on the R&B charts and was in the Top Fifty R&B songs for the year. In March 1951, it was a Top Ten best-selling R&B song,[37] which might account for the Griffin Brothers getting new management. *Billboard* reported, "The Griffin Brothers ork, Dot Records artist, has inked a management pact with Shaw Artists Corporation. The band's vocalist is Margie Day. The group currently has a hit waxing, 'Little Red Rooster.'"[38]

In support of their hit, Day and the Griffin Brothers hit the road. A major ad in the *Miami Times* showcased a "Battle of the Bands" with Ivory Joe Hunter plus the Griffin Brothers featuring Margie "Little Red Rooster" Day. A news story in the same paper reported that ". . . the famous Griffin Brothers and their sensational orchestra, plus the one and only Margie 'Little Red Rooster' Day, will all be presented on one giant attraction . . . as well as other parts of southeast Florida."[39]

And Ohio as well: in April 1951, Dayton's *Ohio Daily Express* boasted a promotion for the Palace Theater of "a bombshell of entertainment" of the Griffin Brothers Orchestra and Margie Day.[40]

Most musical partnerships don't last very long, and this happened with Day and the Griffin Brothers. One could see it coming. Day got first billing on the records, while the Griffin Brothers took the top name plate at live performances—although it should be added that Day got to use the sobriquet "Little Red Rooster" as part of her promo. As late as October 1951, they still toured together, although the Griffin men were already preparing for the future. Reportage in the *Miami Times* about the Griffin Brothers Orchestra noted, "Led by Jimmy Griffin and his brother . . . the band dishes out tunes in the manner that the people like to hear. Featured with the band was none other than the incomparable Margie 'Little Red Rooster' Day, who needed no introduction to popular music lovers and who was all that the patrons expected and then some."

The same article then took a turn, focusing on another singer with the band, Tommy Brown, "who kept the crowd calling for more."[41]

By the next month, *Cash Box*'s gossip column broke the news that Margie Day was now singing with Floyd Dixon while also recording on her own. The Griffin men did not suffer. With Tommy Brown on lead vocal, 1952 was their year. They scored with "Tra-La-La," which rose to #7 on the R&B charts, and their biggest hit ever "Weepin' and Cryin'," which was a #1 R&B tune.[42]

Margie Day performed with other bands, such as those led by Paul Williams, but her bluesy recordings were no longer catching the ears of radio listeners and buyers—although she was a favorite of the critics. Her 1952 release "Midnight" / "My Story" got this nod: "Margie Day sings the Chet Atkins tune that everyone is covering and with the aid of some chorus chanting and good orking [orchestration] waxes a new disk."[43] In 1953, Day signed with Decca. Its initial Margie Day platter that year, "Snatchin' It Back" / "Do I," was greeted as "a belted, up-tempo item with a low-down vocal that comes through in strong fashion. A go-go time

with a wild sax that lends sock to the disk."[44] And 1954's "I'm Too Busy Crying" /
"Take Out Your False Teeth, Daddy" seduced the reviewer as well: "Margie Day
etches a melodic lilt that is very pop flavored. Pretty tune puts soul into the
reading that seems aimed at the pop market."[45] None of these songs did well.

In 1956, *Jet* noted a life change, writing in its gossip column, "Margie Day,
ex-singer with Buddy Griffin's ork, is waiting for the stork to visit her Norfolk
home. Her hubby, Robert Walker, is her manager."[46]

She returned to recording after the birth of her child, although her time
had come and gone. She retired in the early 1960s and then went back into
the business. Her life had come full circle; she died in the town where she was
born, Norfolk, Virginia, in 2014, at eighty-eight years of age.

For most of early 1951, Ruth Brown was on the road. In the pop world, live
performances were lucrative endeavors that helped boost interest in the singles.
For Black female singers, live shows were the main means of making a living. A
successful single for R&B artists generally didn't bring in much money, unless
songwriting royalties were involved, but it did boost interest in the singer.
With a big R&B hit, a singer could play the best segregated venues—although
nothing like the pay from famous nightclubs in the big cities or an up-and-
coming Las Vegas.

For Black performers, an extensive string of smaller venues had long been
established throughout the country. These clubs and honky-tonks, as a group,
were often referred to as the Chitlin' Circuit.

"It was a different America," remembered Carlo Ditta, a New Orleans record
producer. "Every little region had its own little place where local people supplied
the music. It was all segregated. The Black communities were much more about
having their own things going on. They had their own prosperity to spend at
their own clubs and music circuit. To tour, you had to go into their clubs. Very
rarely did Black singers cross over into the white world. The patrons were Black,
and most of the singers were Black men. It wasn't an easy circuit, especially
for woman singers."[47]

In the South, different geographic loops on the Chitlin' Circuit were controlled by various promoters. Ruth Brown held a booking contract with a
company called Universal Attractions, which then subcontracted with local
agents, basically little Mafioso types. As Brown explained, "You worked through
them [locals]; even in those days, these guys had a stranglehold on the business."
A father-and-son team that Brown referred to as the Weinbergs controlled
Virginia, North Carolina, and some areas in Louisiana. Two Black promoters,
Henry Winn and B. B. Beamon, worked in Georgia, while in Texas, "the Black
kingpins" of the business were Don Robey and Howard Lewis.

After "Teardrops from My Eyes" became an R&B smash, Brown hit the road
big time, starting in the northeast and drifting through Virginia deep into the

Chitlin' Circuit. Brown wrote that she felt like the Queen of the One-Nighters: "one-night dance dates followed into the Carolinas and all the way down to Georgia, Alabama, and Tennessee, bringing me face to face with all those racial problems, rubbing my nose in them. We did close on 70 one-nighters on the trot, spending most days riding the tour bus."

Outside of the South, urban centers boasted better venues, some of which were famously pedigreed on the Black circuit. The crème de la crème of the Black venues included a handful of large theaters such as the Apollo in New York, the Regal in Baltimore, the Howard in Washington, DC, and the Regal in Chicago.

While she was playing the Regal in Chicago, a tenor sax musician began flirting with Ruth Brown. His name was Willis "Gator" Jackson, and they soon fell into close contact, which was not difficult as this was a week's engagement and all of the entertainers stayed at the same accommodations. She introduced him to Atlantic Records, which quickly employed his considerable talents. As Brown noted, "you could hear Jackson's bootin' dirty sax behind me" on "I Know," one of her two big hits of 1951. The other was "I'll Wait for You."[48]

Brown and Jackson became a couple, although at first not married, and his band backed her throughout 1951. Brown was generous to Jackson, first giving him a career because he always got separate billings. For example, a quarter-page ad promoting a show at Detroit's Paradise Theater had Ruth Brown at the top of the bill, Charlie Parker in the middle, and Willis Jackson and his orchestra listed third.[49]

A syndicated story about Brown's April shows at the Café Society in New York was used as part of a promotional story in the *Arizona Sun*, which included these lines: "As you will find her very first entrance the personification of all things that go to make beauty, loveliness, charm, and a fresh tone, plus admirably competent technique, when the Atlantic recording star comes to Phoenix to appear with Willis Jackson and his orchestra at Riverside Park . . . the orchestra has . . . the talented composer, arranger, and musician Willis Jackson himself, in person on the tenor sax."[50]

After New York, Brown, Jackson, and his orchestra were on the West Coast for a month. As for the other women of song, Dinah Washington was playing one-nighters across Texas, while Little Esther joined Johnny Otis for an East Coast swing.[51]

Sometimes Jackson even squeezed Brown out of the media glare. Ignoring the singer, a *Miami Times* headline reported "Willis Jackson's Scores at B'way Club," and the copy was all about the bandleader, exclaiming, "The mad man of the sax played B'way's Birdland Café to capacity last week. The Florida lad with Ruth Brown spotlighting the vocals did himself 'saximoniously' scored a terrific hit with his Atlantic recordings . . . The band moves into Harlem's Apollo in November, and brother, that should be sumpin.'"⁵² The article could not have made Brown happy, as it was completely misleading. Brown wasn't part of Willis Jackson's gig; he and his band were the background players to her spotlight.

The road was how Black entertainers made money. In 1951, the average income for a wage-earning American was $2,200. For men alone, it was $3,000. Not only did women earn less, but there was almost no change in the average women's salary from 1945 to 1951. According to Brown, she and her band could make $1,000 a night, obviously a lot of money back then. The problem was everyone got a piece. At first, Universal Attractions took care of transport, including a driver, but that cost $350.

"We practically lived in that darn thing when we were on the road, and I had to pay for everything—wages, accommodation, and meals, and still hope to clear something at the end of it for the kitty," she wrote. And none of that included unscrupulous promoters who wouldn't pay or ran off with the ticket money. Still, if you worked hard enough and long enough on the road, the money was better than excellent compared to other jobs available for Black women. How good was it to be an entertainer? Brown bought a Cadillac for herself—and one for Willis Jackson. Not only did she feel she earned the right to own a Cadillac, but it eliminated the need to use the expensive Universal Attractions transport and driver. At $2,900 for a Cadillac coupe in 1951, it was a good investment.⁵³

This doesn't mean there weren't hiccups. A cutline underneath a picture of Ruth Brown in the *Detroit Tribune* on June 23, 1951, noted that she signed to do a European tour, adding that twice she had contracts to appear at the local Flame Show Bar and both times she didn't show up.⁵⁴

Brown ranted to the press that if wannabe singers "knew that the road to success is paved with hundreds of sleepless nights on buses and trains and in dingy hotel rooms," they might think twice about trying to be a star. To which she continued, "If they only knew about the long and humiliating hours spent waiting in bookers and agents' offices, the meals in coffee joints (and sometimes no meals at all), and the years of backbreaking work," maybe they wouldn't be so anxious to be a star.⁵⁵

However, she added, if you do succeed, it's worth it.

As a point of comparison to the white world of entertainment, in early 1951, the old swing bandleader Guy Lombardo got together with the red-hot Ames Brothers (both had Top Thirty best-selling records in 1950) for an aggressive two-month tour that began in New Orleans and headed west into Texas and Oklahoma and then swung north through the Midwest and wound up in Syracuse, New York. After a month on the road, the tour grossed around $200,000, and when it was all over was expected to bring in somewhere between $400,000 to $500,000.⁵⁶ Even if Ruth Brown played every night on the road for two months, she would only have grossed about $60,000.

Considering she had such a big hit in 1950, Brown didn't do a lot of recording either that year or in 1951. In the latter year, Atlantic released just three Ruth Brown singles, of which only two charted: "I Know" climbed to #7 on the R&B charts and "I'll Wait for You" went to #3. The latter was pop-blues number, the kind of song that was right in Brown's wheelhouse: "Along about the evening, I feel so blue / And though my heart is grieving, I'll wait for you."

It was released early in 1951, and *Cash Box* gave it the "Award o' the Week" in its "Jazz 'n' Blues Reviews." Oddly, the magazine preferred what eventually became the B-side, "Standing on the Corner." The reviewer spent little time with "I'll Wait for You," simply noting that it was a "subdued item with a good beat." Nevertheless, deejays preferred this tune, and in the end, so did record buyers.[57]

By summer, Atlantic released "I Know" with "I Don't Want Anybody," a livelier blues number with great Ruth Brown inflections. This time *Billboard* got there first with its "Rhythm & Blues Record Reviews," where it was Roy Brown versus Ruth Brown. The reviewer's comments for Ruth Brown were that she "belts stylishly on this fine, medium-jump blues, framed in a 'Teardrop' ork [orchestra] setting, with combo swinging."[58]

When *Cash Box* finally released its review, it observed that Ruth Brown "apparently doesn't know how to turn out anything but smash hits." Regarding the record, the reviewer wrote, "Letting go with her terrific style of delivery, she goes every which way on this disc as the backing of Budd Johnson's orchestra plays right along."[59]

By November 1951, the only Brown on the charts was Charles Brown with his hit "Seven Long Days." Nevertheless, Ruth Brown got to headline the magazine's candid-camera inquiries, where she touted her next record, "Shine On (Big Bright Moon)," which she said was a different type of song for her in that it had a new beat with shades of calypso, Latin, and blues.[60] *Billboard* labeled the song "tango blues."[61] Meanwhile, *Cash Box*'s reviewers, who were enamored with her, once again gave Ruth Brown the "Award o' the Week": "Ruth belts the lyrics home in a dynamic and feelingful [*sic*] manner, while the orchestra joins in with a musical backing that's tailor made."[62]

The song didn't make it. Still, in the magazine's year in review, Ruth Brown was the highest-rated female and the Best Jazz 'n' Blues Artist of 1951, one position ahead of Ella Fitzgerald and many notches in front of Little Esther and Margie Day. In the category Best Jazz 'n' Blues Record of 1951, Brown's holdover from the prior year, "Teardrops from My Eyes," narrowly beat Margie Day's "Little Red Rooster."

In the most interesting of the magazine's year-end polling, the category of Best Female Vocalist of 1951 was fully integrated, so readers could vote for singers in any ethnic group. Traditional jazz singers Sarah Vaughan and Ella Fitzgerald squeezed in amid Rosemary Clooney, Jo Stafford, and Doris Day.

Also on the list, just managing to push into the Top Twenty from voters, was Dinah Washington, right behind Peggy Lee and Teresa Brewer.[63]

While it was nice to be recognized, it wasn't nearly at the level of esteem Dinah Washington deserved, because just like the prior year, as a female singer there was no one close to her in R&B chart activity. In 1950, Washington boasted five Top Ten R&B hits; in 1951 she had another four: "Harbor Lights" (#10 in 1951 but recorded in 1950), "My Heart Cries for You" (#7), "I Won't Cry for You" (#6), and "Cold, Cold Heart" (#3).

Washington was recording for the Mercury label, which at the time and for better or worse, would drag Washington back into the studio to recast in her inimical style whatever song came into prominence. So, the Hank Williams's standard "Cold, Cold Heart" was transformed into a wonderful jazzed-up revision barely recognizable as the country song it was at its genesis. At the end of the year, *Cash Box* listed the Top Fifteen Rhythm & Blues Tunes for 1951, and only two females made the list. The first was the white songstress Patti Page with her pop-but-soulful version of the country song "Tennessee Waltz" (#7) and then Dinah Washington's "Cold, Cold Heart" (#12).[64] Through the voices of these women, country crossed over to both the pop and R&B charts.

Also in 1951, Mercury pushed Washington to record such popular fare as "My Heart Cries for You" and the seemingly indestructible "Harbor (or Harbour) Lights," which was probably a bigger hit in the 1950s than when it was written in 1937. It seemed as if everyone from Bing Crosby to Guy Lombardo to Ray Anthony took a whack at it 1950 and 1951. Indeed, in 1951 alone there were a dozen recordings of the song. Sammy Kaye's version was the ninth best-selling single in 1950. Washington gave the song some deep-seated soul, although for baby boomers, the supreme recording came in 1960, when the Platters did a smooth doo-wop rendition.

With "My Heart Cries for You," which was adapted from an old French melody dating back to Marie Antoinette, singer Guy Mitchell with Mitch Miller had a big hit with it after releasing the song at the end of 1950. About ten other versions flooded the market from the likes of Vic Damone to Dinah Shore, although by 1951, Washington was the only Black entertainer to tackle the tune.

Dinah Washington (Ruth Lee Jones) was born in Tuscaloosa, Alabama, in August 1924. Her mother worked as a domestic and her father was a gambler who was often gone for months at a time. She had one older brother. Sometime in the late 1920s (no later than 1928), the family moved to Chicago. The family was poor, and her mother, Alice Jones, was able to make extra money playing piano at Saint Luke's Baptist Church. Alice taught her daughter the piano, and by the time Washington was in elementary school, she was a regular performer at church, both playing piano and singing.

In the early 1930s, gospel singer Sallie Martin joined Thomas A. Dorsey to perform and train gospel choruses in Chicago. By 1937, Dorsey's University Gospel Singers snagged a regular radio show on WLFL. The good times didn't last, and Martin split from Dorsey to perform as a solo act. She hired Washington to help her—and sing. From Washington's perspective, the problem with gospel was that there no money in it, so she switched from spirituals to the secular and began appearing at small Chicagoland clubs. To make sure her break from Martin was permanent, she married an older guy named John Young, the first of seven marriages. At first, he acted as her manager, getting her gigs at Chicago's South Side bars, but the relationship fell apart and after three months Young went into the service. Meanwhile, Dinah was able secure a gig with a group called the Cats and the Fiddle at a better venue, the upstairs club at the Garrick Stage Bar (Garrick Lounge). The singer downstairs was Billie Holiday. Dinah was making $50 a week at the upstairs bar.

Her big break came in 1942, when bandleader Lionel Hampton heard her sing and invited her to join his band for his opening at Chicago's Regal Theater. Hampton is given credit for changing her name to Dinah Washington. She stayed with the band for four years and then signed with Mercury Records as a solo act. It was one of the best moves Mercury ever made. For ten years, from 1948 to 1958, almost every Dinah Washington tune released by Mercury was a Top Ten R&B record. Before her most famous song, "What a Diff'rence a Day Makes," she had three crossover hits on the pop charts and two #1 hits on the R&B charts.[65]

The difference between the big female stars on the pop charts and those on R&B charts was the investment in the singers. Ladies such as Patti Page or Rosemary Clooney would spend endless hours in the studios recording up to twenty different songs in one year, so their label could flood the market. Even Mercury, which was a bigger player, was judicious with their major R&B talent. In 1951, Dinah Washington recorded fewer than ten songs, and Mercury released only a handful; plus, it had a strong holdover from the year before, "Harbor Lights," which was probably why it performed the worst of the charted songs, only making it as high as #10 on the R&B charts. Otherwise, the best-performing Dinah Washington song in 1951 was "Cold, Cold Heart," which peaked at #3.

Washington began 1951 with a tour of major theaters in the East before swinging into the Midwest, where she toured with Amos Milburn, who was hot with "Bad Bad Whiskey," and comic relief Jackie "Moms" Mabley. In February, she was at the Paradise Theater in Detroit, where she was billed as the "Queen of the Jukeboxes," which was akin to calling her "Queen of Streaming" today, so it was high praise.[66]

In May, she was in Arizona, where the local newspaper hailed her as "a great performer" and one of the most unique entertainers of the radio, stage, TV, and nightclub fields. It added that Dinah Washington was "an artist who could well hold her own on the legitimate stage as well. She is the unchallenged 'Queen of the Jukeboxes' and darling of the record industry and nation's disk jockeys."[67]

After three months on the road, Washington finished her tour in New York, where she played the Renaissance Ballroom. According to the press, upward of three thousand music and dance lovers jam-packed the venue. A downpour began one hour before the hall opened and continued most of the night, but the overflow crowd did not slip away. The Dominoes (#1 R&B hit "Sixty-Minute Man") opened the show, and she was backed by the Arnett Cobb Orchestra.[68]

Except for another divorce, this one from Walter Buchanan, a former bass player with Arnett Cobb's band, it was some kind of year for Washington. In August, she was on the cover of *Cash Box*, standing in front of a piano with Ike Carpenter and Ben Bart of Universal Attractions. According to the cutline, the picture was taken on the West Coast as she was appearing at the Club Oasis in Los Angeles after she had "scored a tremendous success at Birdland in New York."[69] The next month, the music industry folks in Philadelphia threw a birthday party for her at a reported price tag of $2,500 (about $28,000 in 2021 dollars). According to press reports, stars from stage, screen, and radio were in attendance. To entertain the multitudes, Dinah sang "I Wanna Be Loved."[70]

Later that month, it was announced that she would again be joining Earl Bostic for another tour of major African American theaters, beginning with the Apollo, the Howard in Washington, DC, and the Earle in Philadelphia, then heading south to play seventeen one-nighters before ending the tour in Miami. According to the trade press, Washington and Bostic toured together in 1950, and it was "one of the hottest box office entries in the R&B personal appearance field." This time around, the "package" was being sold for $750 and $1,000 per date against 50 percent of the gross. Universal Attractions was booking the duo.[71]

How happy was Mercury to have Dinah Washington in its stable of performers? On November 24, 1951, the label took out a full-page ad in *Billboard* to tout its top performers. In a tour de force of white faces, including Patti Page, Eddy Howard, Georgia Gibbs, and Vic Damone, there was one African American, Dinah Washington. And she was the only Mercury artist to be listed twice, for her songs "Cold, Cold Heart" and "Hey Good Lookin'."[72]

Earlier that month, Mercury went one better. On November 3, 1951, the label promoted just one of its performers with a full-page ad. The header read: "Disc Jockeys All over America Acclaim Dinah Washington's 'Baby (Did You Hear Me).'" The promo featured quotes from disc jockeys all over the country, from Chicago to Charlotte to Chicopee, Massachusetts, from Cleveland to Cedar Rapids to Camden, New Jersey.[73]

As Marv Henry of WLOL in Minneapolis/St. Paul declared in the promotion, "Dinah's our gal for hits."

CHAPTER THREE

5-10-15 HOURS (1952)

RALPH BASS—LITTLE ESTHER (ESTHER PHILLIPS)— JOHNNY OTIS—JERRY "SWAMP DOGG" WILLIAMS— WINI BROWN—MARIE ADAMS—EDNA MCGRIFF— DINAH WASHINGTON—RUTH BROWN— LUCKY MILLINDER—RUDY TOOMBS

Back in the 1970s, writer Arnold Shaw sat down with Ralph Bass, who was a highly regarded, if not legendary, R&B record producer. At the time, he was toiling in Chicago for Chess Records, where he had worked with Etta James. Bass had been in the business since the 1940s, beginning with Black & White Records and in the recording studio with Lena Horne. His killer run as a promoter and discover of R&B talent came in the late 1940s and early 1950s, when he was on contract to the independent label Savoy, which was owned by Herman Lubinsky, and Federal, a subsidiary of King Records, owned by Syd Nathan.

Shaw was interested in Bass's years at Savoy and King. Although the independent R&B record companies performed a tremendous service to America by discovering and recording African American talent that the major record labels ignored, thus bringing to listeners' attention some of best musicians and songwriting talent the country had to offer, the men who ran these companies were not necessarily the finest of citizens. They might have, deep in their heart of hearts, believed in the music, but on a personal level, many of them were cheats, creeps, and charlatans.

Bass began his Shaw interview with these comments: "Syd Nathan [King Records], Herman Lubinsky [Savoy Records], they're all the same except for a few personal traits. Like Lubinsky was the cheapest motherfucker in the world. Both Nathan and Lubinsky thought the same way . . . I could tell you some real weird things about Syd . . . and Lubinsky was a tyrant. Everybody was afraid to cross him."

It was through Bass's rant that a reader could learn one outlier story of how a young teenager named Esther Mae Jones became the R&B world's hottest female recording star at the beginning of the 1950s under the name Little Esther (later Esther Phillips).

The time was the late 1940s, and Bass was in Los Angeles working with an R&B group called the Robins (two of whom, Bobby Nunn and Carl Gardner, would later form the Coasters). While there, he watched a talent contest at a movie theater in Watts on 103rd Street. The girl who won the contest was about thirteen or fourteen years old and named Esther Jones. Bass was at that time recording the Robins, who were being backed by the Johnny Otis band at Radio Recorder. Just as an afterthought, he brought in the soon-to-be Little Esther to sing the Johnny Otis tune "Double-Crossing Blues." The very adult-sounding Little Esther was backed by the Robins, and the male solo on the song was by Bobby Nunn.

Bass sent the record to Lubinsky in New Jersey and asked for five dollars for Little Esther's expenses. Lubinsky said nah, he ain't gonna to fork over five dollars for the girl. However, when a local disc jockey came into Lubinsky's office looking for something new, he came upon the Little Esther recording and flipped, excitedly exclaiming the song was going to be a hit record. At the time, the song didn't even have a name, so the deejay ran a contest on his station to name the song, and that's how it came to be "Double-Crossing Blues." Lubinsky suddenly realized he had a hot record and called Bass in the middle of night. On the West Coast, Bass picked up the phone to a screaming voice, "Get me that girl!" The ironic Bass answered, "What girl? The one you wouldn't give me the five bucks for?" Lubinsky whispered that Bass would get whatever money he needed but to sign that girl immediately—the record was prematurely blowing up in New Jersey.

Johnny Otis had his own take on how Little Esther was discovered. She was just shy of her fourteenth birthday when she won a talent contest, and sitting in the audience that night was Otis, because he knew who she was. At the time, Otis had a nightclub called the Barrel House across the street from Watts Towers. Down the same street, he also owned a poultry ranch where people could buy live chickens. And one of the neighborhood kids who was a real good chicken-catcher was Esther.

In Otis's recollection, her recording with the Robins was not planned. That session ran too smoothly, and when all of the Robins' songs were recorded, there was still twenty minutes of recording time left. Studio minutes didn't come cheap, so one used what one contracted for. Otis quickly wrote out a song. He remembered, "We only had time to make one take. It sold a million."

The 78 platter on the gold-and-red Savoy label reads "Double-Crossing Blues," with Johnny Otis as the songwriter. Otis also made sure he got credit for the song's delivery, so underneath the title, an upper line reads "Johnny Otis Quintette" in all-capital letters and then sub-lines in smaller lettering: "Vocals by the Robins and Little Esther." (Despite the wording, Little Esther is always given credit as the song's artist.)

Otis's song-credit-stealing from a novice performer was a slick move, but in the end, the record companies were smarter. As Bass recalled, "Everybody who was involved with that record got double-crossed . . . Johnny and I, the Robins, everybody connected with it."[1]

Nevertheless, Otis knew talent. He brought the teenager into his band, billing her as Little Esther, and they toured together heavily into 1952, when things changed for the singer.

Little Esther (Esther Mae Jones) was born in December 1935 in Galveston, Texas. Her parents divorced when she was an adolescent, and her mother moved to the Watts area of Los Angeles. For awhile, Esther bounced back and forth between her parents. Her first entrée into the song world was through the church. At that singing contest when she was thirteen, her sister talked a hesitant Esther into taking part. The year was 1949, but that song "Double-Crossing Blues" was released in 1950 and became a #1 hit. At the time, Little Esther was the youngest person ever to have a #1 record.[2]

Little Esther was back in the studios big time that year, recording fourteen more songs, or seven double-sided records. Savoy got those records to radio stations and record stores as fast as heavy cartons could be ferried around the country. The result was astonishing. Before the year was out, Little Esther could boast seven Top Ten hits, including three #1 songs: "Double-Crossing Blues," "Mistrusting Blues," and "Cupid's Blues." 1950 was anything but a blue year for Little Esther.

Then she switched recording labels to Federal, and she and Johnny Otis hit the road together. A large ad in the *Miami Times* on February 17, 1951, reads: "Rockland Palace Proudly Presents Little Esther with Johnny Otis, his Orchestra, and Barrel House Revue Plus Mel Walker, Redd Lyte, and the Four Blue Notes."[3] By the next week, the same paper was reporting a Saturday night dance at the VFW and American Legion Hall with Johnny Otis and "that one and only Little Esther, Federal Recording Artist."[4]

By September, as syndicated columnist Ted Yates reported, Johnny Otis, after a vacation on the West Coast, opened to a standing-room-only crowd in Tulsa but was headed, along with Little Esther and Mel Walker, to the eastern seaboard, where they were to run a series of concerts along the "southern route."[5]

In May 1951, the *Detroit Tribune* ran a newswire photo from New York with a cutline that read: "Frank Schiffman of Harlem's Apollo Theater introduces two

distinguished artists, Johnny Otis, bandleader, and juvenile blues singing star
Little Esther, on the stage of the Apollo Theater, before a capacity crowd. The
outstanding stars both received awards for being the Best Jazz 'n' Blues Artist
winners in the Fifth Annual *Cash Box* Poll for making the most money in that
field for jukebox operators. Because the stars had been on a tour triumphant
for the past five months, the ceremonies did not take place until last week."[6]

A couple of months before, Federal Records took a full-page ad in *Cash Box*
promoting Little Esther, who was voted Best Jazz 'n' Blues Artist of 1950. The ad
copy read: "Now on her way to surpassing all past records in '51."[7]

That didn't happen, probably because she was too long on the road; Little
Esther's recording output in 1951 was small, with a handful of songs released
and little to no chart action.

At the very end of the year, Federal released one more record, "The Crying Blues," with "Ring-A-Ding-Doo" on the B-side. *Billboard* gave it a quick
review: "Mark this up as Esther's most potent entry in some time, certainly
her strongest for Federal. It's a sock blues with meaning gimmick provided
by a lad billed as 'Mel' and a strong orking [orchestration] by the J&O Band."
The review gave short shrift to "Ring-A-Ding-Doo," which it called "a try to
come up with a 'Hucklebuck' [a popular 1949 dance tune]. The riff pattern is
agreeable and the performance and beat infectious, but the lyrical idea lacks a
matching spark. Should catch some coin from the dancers."[8]

It caught a lot of coin, because "Ring-A-Ding-Doo" was Little Esther's
comeback record. On February 23, 1952, it reached the Best-Selling Retail R&B
Record chart, coming in at #8 its first week in the Top Ten.

The erratic first years of Little Esther's career can partly be blamed on the
instability of recording contracts. To some extent, she was tethered to Johnny
Otis, who was no more trustworthy than guys like Lubinsky and Nathan, which
would always mean someone was not getting paid what they should have been
paid, and it was time to walk away or file a lawsuit. When Ralph Bass was told
by Lubinsky to sign Esther Jones, he grabbed Otis, and the two of them found
Esther's mother, who worked as a domestic in Pasadena. She and Esther signed,
but the guardianship bit, because she was going to be on the road with Otis, got
lost in the shuffle. Due to that legal glitch, when Bass moved on from Savoy to
King (Federal) Records, he was able to take Little Esther with him.[9]

In February 1951, the trade papers were reporting "Little Esther's first
[recording] date for Syd Nathan's King diskery was done with Nathan's recently
inked vocal group the Dominoes."[10] Those happy times didn't last long, because
on December 1, 1951, a headline in *Cash Box* read, "Little Esther, Otis Switch,"
with an article reporting that Little Esther and Johnny Otis had signed recording contracts with Mercury Records, with Little Esther coming from Federal

and Otis from Savoy. Syd Nathan cranked up his lawyers to prevent that from happening.[11] In January 1952, the gossip column "Round the Wax Circle" in *Cash Box* noted, "Ralph Bass of Syd Nathan's Federal label buzzed us with the news that they still have Little Esther under contract, as just approved here [Los Angeles] in Superior Court. . . . This, according to Ralph, supersedes any other label's previous announcement regarding Little Esther's services."[12]

If you might be scratching your head and wondering what all of these changes were about, some of it was revealed a little later in 1952, when it was announced that Little Esther and Savoy settled "contractual differences" through arbitration. Those differences were, of course, about money. Little Esther felt she was owed more, and Savoy didn't want to pay up. According to the press, the decision called for Little Esther to get a lump sum payment of $6,000 (about $60,000 in 2021 dollars). This figure was based on a disputed 650,000 records on which the artist received one and a half cents per record, providing both sides were done by her, and three quarters of a cent if only one side was done by her.[13]

African American recording artists in the 1950s through the 1960s often felt that they were cheated out of royalties, forced to sign bad contracts, or had to share songwriting rights—and they were usually correct. Little Esther's time with Johnny Otis soon ended because he refused her request for a salary increase. Money was always an issue early in Little Esther's career. In 1954, *Jet* reported that Little Esther was being sued for $2,398 in Los Angeles Superior Court by a Mrs. Love Jordan, who was hired to be the singer's teacher during a nationwide tour in 1953. The lawsuit was for back wages.

Little Esther had much more serious issues in the 1950s: an alcohol and heroin addiction.

Even before that, the unanswered question was what happened to Little Esther after her tremendous success at Savoy? As European music writer Dik De Heer blogged, "It is hard to understand why Esther was not as successful on Federal as she was on Savoy. She worked with the same producer (Ralph Bass) and the same musicians (the Johnny Otis Band) that she had on Savoy, and the material . . . was generally superior to the songs she had cut earlier."[14] Little Esther recorded thirty-two sides for Federal, but only "Ring-A-Ding-Doo" was a national hit.

Jerry "Swamp Dogg" Williams Jr. cut his first record as Little Jerry in 1954. He was twelve years old. He then spent the next six decades as singer, song-writer, musician, and record producer. For a while, he was working as an A&R man at Atlantic Records, which was where he first met Esther Phillips. They crossed paths again in 1972, when she was working on an album called *Alone Again, Naturally*. She recorded one of his songs, "You and Me Together" for the album. They finally sang together as a duet in 1981, singing one of Williams's more lightweight tunes, "The Love We Got Ain't Worth Two Dead Flies"—not exactly the high point of her career.[15]

Competition is not an excuse for Little Esther, but 1952 was a very good year for female R&B voices, with eight different women charting big time. Twelve songs by R&B songstresses made the Top 100 R&B songs in 1952, a year that included such classics as Johnny Ace's "My Song," Lloyd Price's "Lawdy, Miss Clawdy," B.B. King's "3 O'Clock Blues," and the Clovers' wonderful novelty doo-wopper "One Mint Julep." Of the Top Twenty R&B songs in 1952, only Ruth Brown cracked that group with "5–10–15 Hours." In the first three years of the 1950s, Brown, Dinah Washington, and Little Esther were the dominant names, but in 1952, several female first-timers hit the charts.

In 1945, Ben Bart had founded Universal Attractions Agency, which through the 1960s was the dominant talent and booking agency for Black performers. In 1952, it paid for a promotion in African American newspapers extolling its growth and listing all of the performers it had booked during the year, including Roy Brown, Jackie Brenston, the Ravens, and Percy Mayfield, and for the women, Little Esther, Ruth Brown, Dinah Washington, and a few relatively unknowns such as Wini Brown.[16]

This a good time to mention Wini Brown, because 1952 was her moment in the sun as she scored her one and only Top Ten hit (#10 for one week) "Be Anything—Be Mine."

Most of what music historians know about Wini Brown comes from writer Marv Goldberg, who retraced her history, because a lot of the existing information about her was mostly incorrect. That was partly due to Duke Ellington, who in his memoirs talked about Wini Brown when he was actually referring to Wini (Winifred) Johnson.

Wini Brown didn't help herself much because she recorded as Wini Brown and Her Boyfriends, which was clearly a rip-off of singer Julia Lee, who since the 1940s had been recording as Julia Lee and Her Boy Friends and in 1952 released one record, "Going to Chicago Blues" / "Last Call."

Wini (Winifred) Brown was born in June 1927 in Chicago. When she was still a teenager, Brown caught her first music business break when Lionel Hampton hired her for his vocal group called the Hamptones with Madeline Green and Sammy Jennings. In 1947, she recorded "Gone Again," which was written by Lionel Hampton's wife Gladys, and got enough play that Hampton gave her a solo spot to sing it at concerts. The following year, she did some recordings with Earl "Fatha" Hines. The next year, she married saxman Charlie Fowlkes, who got her a contract at National Records. The label quickly got Wini Brown into the studio, where she recorded four cuts. She would have a few more sessions with National going into 1949, but no hits resulted. Wini Brown failed upward by getting picked up in 1950 by a major label, Columbia. That hookup didn't last long, because by the end of 1951, she was with Mercury Records, for which she recorded "Be Anything—Be Mine."

Brown toured and continued to record with different labels into the early 1960s but never became a star, although she was for a long time associated with the Cootie Williams Orchestra. She died in 1978 at the age 50.[17]

In April 1952, Federal Records released Little Esther's "Better Beware" / "I'll Be There," which was chosen by *Cash Box* for its "Award o' the Week" in its reviews of new songs. The reviewer noted, "Little Esther belts out a fast-moving bounce with zest and the force of a tornado as she gives a dynamic reading to a number that has what the doctor ordered to put life into the jukes." Also up for review that week was a song by Marie Adams called "I'm Gonna Play the Honky-Tonks" with "My Search Is Over" on the B-side. The reviewer liked this cut as well, saying, "Strong-voiced Marie Adams belts out slow blues with much feeling as she sells the fitting lyrics. Bill Harvey's Band backs Marie solidly as they give the expressive arrangement a sock coverage."[18]

The Adams song looked good. Not so much Little Esther's. So Federal released Little Esther's "Aged and Mellow," which appeared to have legs. The syndicated column "Spinning with Sy" made it the "Record of the Week," saying "Sixteen-year-old Esther will really knock you out with her latest recording—just like she likes her whiskey, she likes her men aged and mellow. This is a catchy tune, and the lyrics are very clever."[19] One assumes no one thought it weird that a sixteen-year-old girl would be singing about aged men and booze. (Considering her later addictions, maybe it wasn't the right tune for her.) Nevertheless, in July, "Aged and Mellow" made the Top Ten in Los Angeles—and only that city. Other women singers were making the R&B charts interesting and competitive at that moment in 1952, in particular Marie Adams, as her song "I'm Gonna Play the Honky-Tonks" was taking off around the nation. Adams sang: "I'll play the high-class joints, I'll play the low-class joints, and baby, I'm gonna even play the honky-tonks."

She would play them all as "I'm Gonna Play the Honky-Tonks" rose to #3 on the R&B charts and made her a star. It was the third best-selling female R&B song in 1952. When *Jet* caught up with the rising singer the next year, it reported ". . . a corpulent songbird out of Houston, Texas, named Marie Adams. She gained overnight fame late last summer with a Dinah Washington–like recording of a rousing tune entitled 'I'm Gonna Play the Honky-Tonks,' which within six months sold over 250,000 discs."[20]

Marie Adams (Ollie Marie Givens) was born on October 19, 1925, in Linden, Texas, a hamlet spitting distance from both Louisiana and Arkansas. After singing in gospel groups, she made her way down to Houston, where Black entrepreneur Don Robey was creating a music empire. One story has it that in 1951, Marie's husband talked her into auditioning for Robey at his record shop. He also owned the premier entertainment venue for African Americans in Houston and a growing record label. Robey, who was as caustic as he was charming, put a copy of Dinah Washington's "Harbor Lights" on a turntable and asked Adams if she could sing it. She nailed the song.[21] Robey didn't have the suave Dinah Washington under contract as a recording artist, but he liked her music, which might also be why some fans of the "Honky-Tonks" song believe it has that Dinah Washington ring to it.

Marie Adams recorded sparingly for Robey's Peacock, the first platter being "I'm Gonna Play the Honky-Tonks" in 1951 but not released until 1952. She recorded only seven singles for Peacock between 1951 and 1955, partly because Robey liked to have his recording artists on the road as he also owned a booking agency and controlled a wide swath of the Chitlin' Circuit in the Mississippi Delta and Gulf Region from Texas to Memphis. It was almost as if Peacock's hit records supported Robey's road shows instead of Robey's road shows supporting Peacock's records.

At the end of 1952, Adams was back in the studio to record one new record, "Sweet Talking Daddy" with "My Song" on the B-side. The latter song was an absolute monster hit for newcomer Johnny Ace, recorded for Duke Records out of Memphis. In 1952, Robey bought Duke Records. *Cash Box* columnist Sam Evans led off in his November 8, 1952, "Kickin' the Blues Around" feature with this tidbit: "Marie 'The Honky-Tonk Gal' Adams going into a string of club dates up and down the West Coast. Her popularity was sparked by Peacock's release of 'Sweet Talking Daddy.'"[22]

The song wouldn't have helped Marie Adams's tour much; it couldn't muster nearly the popularity of "Honky-Tonks." By 1953, she was touring with Johnny Otis. A curious "Holiday Dance" promotion in the May 8, 1953, (Roanoke, Virginia) *Tribune* featured Johnny Otis and his orchestra "featuring" Marie Adams, with a picture of Otis but not of Adams. Also on the bill were the "5" Royals, with a picture, who were listed as the singers of "Baby, Don't Do It" and "I'm Gonna Play the Honky-Tonks."[23] Ooh, that hurt.

In the summer of 1952, when Little Esther's "Aged and Mellow" and Marie Adams's "I'm Gonna Play the Honky-Tonks" were trying to make headway on the R&B record charts, other women were crashing the party. Dinah Washington's "Mad about the Boy" was doing well in some cities, as was "Easy, Easy Baby" by newcomer Varetta Dillard, who would hit her prime over the next couple of years. Also making it to the charts for the first time was teenager Edna McGriff with "Heavenly Father."

Edna McGriff was born in December 1935 in Tampa. At an early age, her family moved to New York. She was still attending Washington Irving High School when her world, like an oyster, opened wide.[24]

At sixteen, McGriff's family was living in Harlem. She was already an accomplished pianist and attempting to be a songwriter as well. According to *Jet*, she took one of her compositions to Atlantic Records, where she met Jack Walk. He was so impressed with the teenager that he coached her for a year and then got her a Jubilee Records session. Jubilee was cofounded by Herb Abramson in 1946. A year later, Abramson sold his half of the partnership to Jerry Blaine and went on to cofound Atlantic Records with Ahmet Ertegun.[25]

That sounds like a straightforward story except for a June 23, 1951, article in *Billboard* that read, "Apollo Records signed fifteen-year-old Little Edna McGriff to a long-term contract. The teenage blues singer . . . writes much of her own material. Her first waxing [recording] session includes three of her originals, 'Come Back,' 'Note Droppin' Papa,' and 'Rain.' Orchestral backing for the gal's first disks will be by Budd Johnson, a tenor man who is organizing a road band."[26]

Considering McGriff's later spiritual-sounding songs, signing with Apollo Records made sense because the label concentrated on gospel from 1948 to 1952, which is what you do when the best singer on the label is Mahalia Jackson, the "Queen of Gospel." However, it is possible that *Billboard* just confused Apollo and Jubilee, because the latter was the company that issued McGriff's first record. In the December 22, 1951, issue of *Billboard*, Jubilee took out a half-page vertical ad to promote its talent, including Edna McGriff, a new blues star, singing "Come Back" with "Note Droppin' Papa" on the B-side.[27]

It was the B-side that attracted attention—just not enough to break out. That problem was quickly solved when early in 1952 Jubilee unleashed "Heavenly Father" with "I Love You" on the B-side. *Cash Box* reviewers were the first to sniff out the song's potential, giving it the "Award o' the Week" in its "Jazz 'n' Blues Reviews" on March 8, 1952: "The slow ballad is waxed impressively by Edna McGriff as she doles out her own tune, 'Heavenly Father.' The title might lead one to believe the song is a religious number, but while it is in a way, it certainly gives a new twist in its treatment. Lyrics are timely, and Buddy Lucas and his Band of Tomorrow provide a soothing backdrop as they offer their dramatic arrangement of this slow piece. The artists plus the material bring a waxing that will get a big share of the jukebox play."[28]

In the May 10, 1952, issue of *Billboard*, with "Heavenly Father" in its sixth week ensconced as one of the country's best-selling retail R&B records, Jubilee posted a congratulatory advertisement reading: "No. 1 in the nation in rhythm & blues and now, WOW!! You jocks and ops are making it Tops in Pops: Edna McGriff with the Buddy Lucas Ork original Jubilee recording of 'Heavenly Father.'"[29]

McGriff was hailed by New York disk jockeys as the "greatest find since Ella Fitzgerald," and bookings rolled in.[30] One year after the song's debut, it reportedly sold 500,000 records.[31] All of the buyers got their seraphic money's worth. "Heavenly Father" was a tune that slipped away from the traditional blues structure with the kind of easy rock 'n' roll beat that someone such as Connie Francis would sing at the end of the 1950s. It was a tune ahead of its time, delivered by a teenager who sounded like love-weary adult.

In September, a *Billboard* poll titled "Juke Operators Name 1952's Most Profitable R&B Records to Date" had "Heavenly Father" sitting at #9.[32]

A syndicated column about the record business in May 1952 observed MGM was releasing a version of the song by Fran Warren. The notation ended with this comment: "Edna should make lots of money on the song."[33]

That was naïve. Young performers, especially African American singers and songwriters, were notoriously exploited by sharp-elbowed managers and record companies, who knew endless ways to enhance earnings at the expense of talent.

The syndicated "Theatrically Yours" column broke the news about the song this way: "Edna McGriff, who sings on Jubilee Records, her own song 'Heavenly Father' won't get any of the profits from her song. She sold the song to her manager for $25 [$250 in 2021 dollars]."[34]

Managers, promoters, and record label owners knew that many African American songwriters were coming from impoverished backgrounds and needed every cent that their songwriting could bring in, so they offered pennies on the dollar for tunes that would go on to earn millions. In the 1950s, the business was no different in New York, Los Angeles, New Orleans, or Houston.

Someone took umbrage at the "Theatrically Yours" column about Edna McGriff because two weeks later, the column reported: "Edna McGriff's manager says he didn't buy her song 'Heavenly Father' from her for $25 as reported." The manager said, "I didn't cheat her out of the number." However, he didn't say whether or not he bought the song from her at all or how much interest (if any) she now had in her own song.[35]

According to musicologist Marv Goldberg, in 1955, McGriff stopped singing for a while because she was having contract problems. In 1957, a *Cleveland Call and Post* article summed up the issues this way: "Two years ago, misfortune set-in in the form of troubles with her manager, who wanted a bigger share of the money than he was entitled to. So she decided to temporarily quit show business until her contract expired."[36]

Since McGriff was young, pretty, and single, the Black media had a weird preoccupation with her love life. The *Detroit Tribune* picked up a syndicated column out of New York, which declared "Edna McGriff Hits Marriage Rumors" that went on to deny the "persistent" show business rumor that she'd marry blues singer Floyd Dixon. The story reported "Edna, who is taking a week off prior to a 45-day Theater tour of the Midwest, stated that although the popular blues stylist was making a terrific itch for her hand in matrimony with an average of three long distance phone calls per day and in letter, she has personally never met Floyd Dixon." The article added that the seventeen-year-old singer's name had been linked with several other top names in marriage rumors, but she stated that the idea of marriage was "a little far-fetched."[37]

Two years later, *Jet* picked up the marriage stream with a story about singer Lee Richardson and McGriff being "the hottest new *woomance* in show business. He calls her every time he is near a telephone."[38]

The 1957 *Cleveland Call and Post* article reported that she married Leon Dixon, a childhood sweetheart. If that was accurate, it didn't last long, because in 1959, she married Leroy Minors.

As Goldberg summed up, "We know she didn't marry Floyd Dixon; we know she didn't marry Johnny Wallace; we know she didn't marry the tall, handsome carpenter from Bermuda; and we know she didn't marry Lee Richardson. But she did marry . . ."[39]

McGriff struck gold once with "Heavenly Father," but after recording with numerous record labels and heavy touring, she never had another hit. She died in 1980 at age forty-four.

Edna McGriff, Marie Adams, and Wini Brown could boast just moderate success (if any!) as hitmakers after 1952. The same could not be said of two other female rookies, Harlem native Varetta Dillard and New Orleans born Shirley Goodman, who would have better songs and better years ahead, Dillard as a song stylist, and Shirley as part of the successful duo Shirley and Lee. This is not to be dismissive of their 1952 hits, Dillard's "Easy, Easy Baby" and Shirley and Lee's "I'm Gone"—both were very cool songs.

Dinah Washington would also have better songs in the years ahead, yet that didn't stop the dynamo from dominating the R&B record charts from a female perspective, with one-third of the dozen releases by females making the Top 100 R&B hits of the year.

Remember that competitive month in July 1952 when Little Esther, Marie Adams, Varetta Dillard, and Edna McGriff were all driving up the regional charts. Dinah Washington was also in the mix with a revival of an oldie, "Mad about the Boy." The tune was written by famed British playwright and songster Noel Coward for a Broadway revue in 1932. Dinah gave it an assertive interpretation over a lush, horn-driven orchestration. It did well in selected cities but didn't travel widely and wasn't a hit record.

Washington was still recording for Mercury and successful at what she was doing. The question was not necessarily could she be more successful, but could she gain a wider pop audience the way that Ella Fitzgerald had done? That meant a change of attitude. Going as far back as 1951, Redd Foxx, who knew her on the Chitin' Circuit, said, "She wouldn't sing white, and because of that, she couldn't get the big downtown jobs."⁴⁰ It's hard to say what Foxx actually meant; did Washington not sing white or pop songs or not sing in front of white audiences? In either case, that all was about to change.

Before 1952, Washington had been touring with Earl Bostic. She had been married to Walter Buchanan, but that union was not long in duration and about to be over because Washington had gotten friendly with one of Bostic's musicians, a cat named Jimmy Cobb. *Cash Box*'s gossipy "Rhythm 'n' Blues Ramblings" column picked up on the news just about the time Washington decided against a European tour. The story began this way: "Dinah Washington's wedding date with Jimmy Cobb will wind up in the profit-and-loss sheet for the incomparable chanteuse. She'll gain a hubby and new personal manager and lose a previously slated European booking. Apparently, the tax equation on the other side of the pond worried her. 'I like it here, and the possibility of my having to leave more than half of my earnings abroad is out,' she told the press."⁴¹

It's not that Dinah Washington didn't play fast a loose with her schedule. Later in 1952, she would face a lawsuit after she didn't appear at a July 4 dance concert in Trenton, New Jersey. The promoter, a local disk jockey, sued. The legal dustup was settled when Washington agreed to headline his first prom of the season at Trenton's arena.⁴²

After leaving Earl Bostic, Jimmy Cobb headed Dinah Washington's band, and they took off in two cars for a string of one-nighters in the South. It was grueling and humiliating in equal measure. Cobb remembered, "In the South, there were a lot of towns where the musicians couldn't stop, with 'whites only' signs everywhere." They generally stayed in private homes and the occasional hotel that accepted African Americans. The theaters were small, and in the course of a three-month tour, that could mean almost ninety one-nighters because there were no nights off. Afterward, Washington's schedule improved because she played bigger venues on the Chitlin' Circuit such as the Apollo, the Royal in Baltimore, or the Earle in Philadelphia. Being with Washington was a big break for Cobb, because Dinah put his name up front as the house orchestra leader. It also led to his first recordings, backing up Washington at a Los Angeles session date, where they recorded four sides: "Trouble in Mind," "Wheel of Fortune," "Tell Me Why," and "When the Sun Goes Down."⁴³

Later in the year, they were in Chicago to record again, and Washington did a new version of her 1946 hit with Lionel Hampton, "Blow-Top Blues." The 1952 re-recording was called "New Blowtop Blues," with credits going to Dinah Washington and the Jimmy Cobb Quintet. The song was another hit, shooting to #7 on the R&B charts, and was a Top 100 R&B song that year.

Washington did well with another blues number, "Trouble in Mind," which shot to #4 on the R&B charts. The song's antecedents date back to spirituals from the 1800s, although the first recording of the song wasn't until 1924.

Washington didn't shy away from the tune's inherent blues, while the orchestration was crisp and modern with tinkling piano keys and a horn introduction. "Trouble in Mind" was Washington's second biggest hit of the year.

For Dinah Washington's R&B fans, who came into her orbit back in the 1940s or the first years of the 1950s, it was a musical salve to hear her sing the blues considering her deviations that year into the pop world.

An ongoing debate in the African American cultural world during 1952 was how pop-oriented Dinah was going to be. Syndicated writer Ria Darley, who shared bylines under the "Theatrically Yours" column that ran in most African American newspapers in the early 1950s, carried the load on this issue. The breezier version of a Dinah-goes-pop column began this way: "Dinah Washington, the enchanting songstress whose style is *copped* by many singers, is being *ought* by her recording boss, Bob Shad of Mercury Records, to leave its Blues and Rhythm department and invade its 'pop' department."[44] The rationale was that Washington could reach all races, especially as it appeared to Mercury that many white singers were copying and capitalizing on the Dinah Washington style.

The problem was that, although the big booking agencies such as Universal Attractions had Washington busy on the Chitlin' Circuit, if she went pop they could book her in better venues. Ria Darley sat in with Washington and previewed a "pop" recording session, where the background orchestration included instruments such as violins. Darley thought the session was terrific and noted, "She [Washington] can record in the 'popular' field, where she belongs."

As late as October 1952, Ria's co writer of the column Larry Douglas noted, "Dinah Washington is still going great, and it seems from her latest recording of 'Stormy Weather' that she will hit the 'pop' field."[45]

The perennially popular song "Stormy Weather" wasn't a hit for Washington, nor was another oldie-but-goodie, "I Cried for You," which was released toward the end of the year. Many fine ladies had tackled "I Cried for You" going as far back as Connee Boswell and Mildred Bailey in the 1930s and on through Kate Smith and Judy Garland to Sarah Vaughan and Billie Holiday. *Cash Box* liked Washington's rendition, noting: "The thrush [singer] belts out a fast tempo oldie with a personality treatment that sends this side soaring. Her lush vocal of the spirited arrangement."[46] It didn't sell, unlike Washington's forays into the pop field at the beginning of the year.

In the mid-1950s, white singer Georgia Gibbs would salvage what had been a strong career in the early 1950s by covering songs that were big hits on the R&B charts as sung by Black female artists. She was excoriated for her appropriations, although in the 1950s, any song that had hit potential was like a hot potato. It was more usual than unusual to see ten recordings of a potential hit, no matter the genre—R&B, pop, or country. In 1952, Kay Starr boasted a monster hit "Wheel of Fortune," which ended up as the #2 best-selling song of the year. Somehow, the forgotten "Blue Tango" was the #1 song of the year, but Starr's "Wheel of Fortune" should have taken the prize. Dinah Washington covered it with a much more bluesy interpretation. On the B-side was another popular tune, "Tell Me Why," which was a #2 pop hit for the Four Aces in 1951. Eddie Fisher also tackled the song that year.

Billboard's quick review of the songs was a mixed bag. It liked "Wheel of Fortune," saying, "Dinah really . . . reads down this current pop hit. Figures to be one of her strongest recent entries. Reading [recording] could grab a small corner of the pop field." The reviewer wasn't so kind about the B-side, "Tell Me Why," writing: "The thrush isn't up to her best in covering the current smash item. The original . . . will be hard to compete with in the R&B field."[47]

Both songs were hit singles. "Tell Me Why" jumped to #7 on the R&B charts, and "Wheel of Fortune" flew all the way to #3.

Neither song crossed over to the pop charts, but in real time and space, Washington crossed over into the pop world, which meant better bookings.

When jazzman Stan Kenton played Carnegie Hall early in 1952, his gross from the sold-out show was a record $8,500 ($83,500 in 2021 dollars). Afterward, he would go on the road for sixty days, with most of the shows expected to sell out. It was estimated that Kenton's tour would gross about $250,000 ($2.5 million in 2021 dollars). It was not quite Carnegie Hall, but Dinah Washington playing with the Cootie Williams Band would be residing for the week at the Town Hall, also a well-regarded New York venue.[48]

In April, she played the esteemed jazz venue Birdland in Manhattan, where she set attendance records. *Cash Box*'s "Rhythm & Blues Rambling" column also reported she would be going on an integrated tour, noting "Dinah Washington will add her distinctive vocal stylings to a package that will include the Mills Brothers, Woody Herman's Ork [orchestra], and two other acts. Miss Washington will choose her latest Mercury recordings for this concert tour."[49] This was such a successful tour that *Billboard* reported in May that the lineup of Woody Herman, Dinah Washington, Tommy Edwards, the Mills Brothers, and comic Herkie Styles would be booked into Carnegie Hall. A news report on July 2 noted: "Woody Herman and Tommy Edwards, MGM platter mates, joined the Mills Brothers and Dinah Washington in a show at the Pittsburgh Mosque, packing the 3,800-seat auditorium to capacity."[50]

By July, Washington was back at Birdland, and the press was all over the venue. First, because the stars came out to see her perform, a wire-service photo of her with actor Robert Mitchum was printed in African American papers.[51] If the papers did not use that photo, the Black press ran another of Washington just singing on the Birdland stage. The *Echo* of Meridian, Mississippi, ran that picture with the headline "Songsational Singing Star Solid, Superb, and Sparkling!"[52]

The Birdland appearance was big news because Washington received several awards during her extended gig. Bob Austin of *Cash Box* presented her with a scroll designating Washington as "Queen of the Jukeboxes." The award was the result of a national survey conducted by a poll of 168 leading Negro newspapers' weekly ratings coast to coast. Also, jazz pianist, composer, and journalist Leonard Feather presented her with a trophy for "outstanding performances in the field of entertainment." The ceremonies were aired by WJZ, which inaugurated its midnight-to-six a.m. disk jockey show at the Birdland.

In 1952, Dinah Washington was "songsational."

Even with all that, Washington wasn't the top female R&B star of 1952. That honor belonged to Ruth Brown, who had two monster hits that year, "Daddy, Daddy," which went to #3 on the R&B charts, and the stupendous "5–10–15 Hours," a #1 song, the thirteenth best-selling R&B tune of the year, and the only song by a female in the R&B Top Twenty.

On October 25, 1952, Ruth Brown got a measure of revenge on bandleader Lucky Millinder. When *Cash Box* ran a full page of new record reviews, it chose Brown's "Three Letters" / "Good for Nothin' Joe" for its coveted "Award o' the Week" with an extended review. Among the fifteen also-rans was Lucky Millinder with "Backslider's Ball" / "Please Be Careful."[53]

Unfortunately, both Brown and Millinder's records ended up in the same place—nowhere. This was a strange occurrence despite this lavish note from a reviewer: "That magical something that was born into the voice of Ruth Brown and has enabled her to turn out one hit after another again comes to the fore as the thrush etches another, labeled 'Three Letters,' that will undoubtedly follow in the footsteps of her most recent clicks, e.g., '5–10–15 Hours' and 'Daddy, Daddy.'"

The revenge factor had to do with a window of opportunity early in Ruth Brown's career. In 1948, she was still an unknown playing at the Frolic Show Bar in Detroit when the famous Lucky Millinder accompanied by guitarist Chico Alvarez of the Stan Kenton Orchestra strolled in. They were playing at the Paradise Theater, the prestige Black venue in Detroit. Millinder liked what he saw and offered Brown an audition the next morning. He said, "You're hired," and suddenly Brown figured she was hitting the big time. After about a month on tour with the Lucky Milliner Band, they went to Washington, DC, where she sang, among other songs, Dinah Washington's "Evil Gal Blues." After her set, she was walking backstage when one of the musicians asked if she wouldn't mind getting sodas for the band at the refreshment stand. She did just that and dispersed the drinks to the band. The talented but short-tempered Millinder called her over and snapped, "I hired you to sing, not be a waitress. You're fired."

Brown was stranded in DC but managed to get a job singing at the Crystal Caverns. One night, local deejay Willis Conover came in with singer Sonny Til of the Orioles. While Brown was singing, Conover left the room and called

Atlantic Records in New York. Atlantic was a fledgling label on the lookout for fresh talent. Before long, Ahmet Ertegun and Herb Abramson, the founders of Atlantic, were in the Crystal Caverns audience to check her out. They wanted to sign her. As an added bonus, she would be getting a gig at the Apollo. Driving to New York, she was in a car with four other people when it slammed into a tree at full speed. One passenger died immediately. Brown ended up with two broken legs.

She was still on crutches in May 1949 when she recorded a song called "So Long," which Little Miss Cornshucks had sung. Within a few weeks of its release, the song sold well enough to climb to #6 on the R&B charts. It was the company's second hit record after Stick McGhee's "Drinkin' Wine, Spo-dee-o-dee." Ruth Brown had made it.

Ruth Brown (Ruth Alston Weston) was born in January 1928 in Portsmouth, Virginia. Her father was active in the church choir of the Emanuel A.M.E. (American Methodist Episcopal) Church, which is where the young girl made her debut, playing the piano and singing. Eventually, she was singing with church groups and at affairs such as weddings. Portsmouth was a Navy town, and as a teenager, Brown would sneak out of her house to sing at the numerous clubs where sailors went for drinks. She even snuck away to New York for the famous Amateur Night at the Apollo, which she won. After an incident in which her boyfriend was killed, Brown left home for good to play clubs near military bases scattered up and down the East Coast. Brown was appearing at a club in Petersburg, Virginia, when she was offered a gig in Detroit.[54]

Ruth Brown's career was always good news, bad news, good news, bad news, and good news, and 1952 started the same way. In January, *Jet* labeled Brown "the best voice since [Sarah] Vaughan." The article noted that Brown was a "buxom, brown girl with a sparkling personality . . . a visual and vocal delight. She seems to put all the oomph of her size 16 [for some reason, *Jet* was always concerned about the size of Black female singers] figure into the mournful ballads that she sings in a lazy, half-sobbing manner, and into the vigorous blues which she delivers in a brash, naughty style . . . although seriously injured in 1949 and invalided for six months, Ruth made a courageous comeback and has been keeping people feet tapping ever since."[55]

The same article reported Brown's fee for a one-night show was $1,000 and $2,500 for weekly theater engagements.

She must have been making good money because in February 1952, *Cash Box* reported that Brown had been robbed of jewels, furs, gowns, and musical arrangements valued at $10,000. The robbery occurred in Pittsburgh while Ruth parked her car in front of the Bailey Hotel to eat dinner.[56]

The year would immediately turn around, and much of it was due to Atlantic's songwriter and arranger Rudy (Rudolph) Toombs. The native Louisianan began his music career as a vaudeville-style song-and-dance man. He eventually got off the road to write songs for R&B singers—and he was a master.

He was working at Atlantic Records when they signed Ruth Brown, and the two were immediately thrown together. Brown recalled, "The things he was doing were different rhythmically from what I was into. I was more of a pop torch singer. I preferred ballads. But since Ahmet Ertegun and Herb Abramson seemed a step ahead of what was going to be the accepted sound, I went along with them and picked up on the tunes that Rudy wrote for me."

One of the first tunes they worked on was the #1 R&B hit "Teardrops from My Eyes." Again, according to Brown, "We worked on 'Teardrops' for at least a week. At that time, working on one tune for a week was quite a long time . . . I don't know whether 'Teardrops' was one of my best ventures, because actually I wasn't a rhythm singer . . . I had a sense of timing that was very natural because of my church singing. When 'Teardrops' was played back after I recorded it, it just scared everybody . . . it seemed to start a whole trend of things because a number of singers covered it afterwards."

After that big hit, Toombs was more or less assigned to Brown. Their next big hit was "5–10–15 Hours."

In her memoir, Brown remembered a funny anecdote about the song: "Rudy Toombs was responsible for my next smash I enjoyed. His original title was '5–10–15 Minutes (Of Your Love)' until Herb [Abramson] coolly informed him that 'minutes' was no longer enough now that we were in the era of Billy Ward and the Dominoes' 'Sixty-Minute Man.' Presto, it became '5–10–15 Hours (Of Your Love).'"[57]

Brown's rendition of the new Rudy Toombs song was released in March 1952, and *Cash Box*'s "Jazz 'n' Blues Reviews" made the tune its "Award o' the Week," overcoming other entries from Wini Brown, Margie Day with the Griffin Brothers, and a group called the Lightning Trio with a song called "Annie Laurie."

The reviewer gushed: "A real low-down blues tune is belted out by Ruth Brown as she gives a solid set of lyrics a zestful send-off. The upper lid ([A-side], titled '5–10–15 Hours,' is a pretty thing that is treated to a dramatic arrangement. Ruth Brown's dynamic chanting receives solid support from the ork [orchestra], which features a muted trumpet in the backing. The result is an exciting etching [record] that should make merry in the jukes."[58] Brown sang: "Just give me five, ten, fifteen hours of your love / Give me fifteen hours while that shiny moon's above."

The Toombs arrangement of the song would not be unfamiliar to anyone listening to the radio in the mid-1950s—the same blues beat would become universal whether speeded up for a Bill Haley cut or slowed down for a dance like the stroll.

The unknown author of the "Rhythm 'n' Blues Ramblings" column in *Cash Box* took notice of the songwriter, leading off the April 12, 1952, column with these remarks: "Tin Pan Alley tunesmith Rudy Toombs, who's phenomenal 'Teardrops' sold over one and one-half million disks last year, is hitting again with two Atlantic disks, '5–10–15 Hours' (Ruth Brown) and 'One Mint Julep' (the Clovers). Rudy's been penning tunes for about 10 years now, since he gave up his vaudeville song-and-dance bit to become a songwriter. His dancing and singing experience served him in good stead, aiding his sense of rhythm and teaching him what music should be."[59]

About a month later, "5–10–15 Hours" debuted on *Billboard*'s Best-Selling Retail Rhythm & Blues Records chart at #2. It would quickly go to #1 and still be there ten weeks later. Its only decline was on the chart for Most Played Jukebox Rhythm & Blues Records, where it had fell to #2 behind the Dominoes' "Have Mercy Baby."[60]

The record performed so strongly that Atlantic Records issued a flyer about Ruth Brown, who *Cash Box* referred to as Atlantic's "hot money-maker." Using pictures and blurbs from Black magazines and the trades, the flyer told "the spectacular and dramatic" story of a young miss who rose from a choir singer in Emanuel A.M.E. Church to the star who was earning $200,000 at the age of 22."[61]

With a hit record came star power. The syndicated "Spinning with Sy" column, in a week where "Sy" chose as the Top Three records Wini Brown's "Be Anything—Be Mine," Edna McGriff's "Heavenly Father," and Ruth Brown's "5–10–15-Hours" (the Clovers' "One Mint Julep" at #5), also focused on the comings and goings of Ruth Brown, writing: "Ruth Brown, the very fabulous 'Teardrops' girl whose current big number is '5–10–15 Hours,' opened last week at Harlem's Apollo Theater. Her triumphant return to New York after a record-smashing road tour saw a huge turnout of her fans. Friends informed me that they called her back for seven encores opening day."[62]

In August, Atlantic released Brown's follow-up record, "Daddy, Daddy" with "Have a Good Time" on the B-side. Again, she was bestowed by *Cash Box*'s "Jazz 'n' Blues Reviews" its "Award o' the Week" over singers such as Little Esther and Sister Rosetta Tharpe. The reviewer noted: "Ruth Brown, whose past successes have been such tremendous jukebox hits and have brought her into such prominence in the rhythm & blues field, throws two new ones onto the market . . . to raise the star to new heights."[63]

That was just the prelude. The reviewer was elated by Brown singing torridly over a calypso-like beat that "gripped listeners with excitement." In addition, the reviewer exclaimed that the moderate tempo was "pulsatingly arranged."

"Daddy, Daddy" did well, climbing all the way to #3 on the R&B charts in a strong market. On October 11, when it began its decline, "Daddy, Daddy" was the only record by a female on the *Billboard* chart.[64]

By the end of the year, rumors swirled where Brown would tour next, with columnists whispering she would appear with singer Billy Eckstine in a "huge" run of one-nighters.[65]

The real present came the month before Christmas. She inked a new five-year $100,000 record contract with Atlantic Records. Brown explained that the new contract guaranteed her a minimum income from record royalties of 100,000 skins [dollars] over the contract's period. No fool, she was also seeking ways and means to convert this reward (called "neat loot" by columnists) into a capital gains deal, hoping to pay lower taxes.[66]

CHAPTER FOUR

HOUND DOG (1953)

ELVIS PRESLEY—BIG MAMA THORNTON—JERRY LEE LEWIS—BIG MAYBELLE—DENVER FERGUSON—LINDA HAYES—MITZI MARS—ANNISTEEN ALLEN—EARTHA KITT—VARETTA DILLARD—DINAH WASHINGTON—CHRISTINE KITTRELL—SARAH LAWLER—RUTH BROWN—BLIND LEMON JEFFERSON—FAYE ADAMS—JOE MORRIS

Elvis Presley's first recording session for RCA Records was in Nashville on January 11, 1956. The first two tunes recorded for his new label were "I Got a Woman," a Ray Charles hit, and "Heartbreak Hotel," which made history as the singer's first #1 record. Over the next few months, he did a couple of television shows and toured the South before heading to New York. He had been slammed by a critic after he performed on the Milton Berle show and was angry when a reporter caught up with him in Charlotte. "Them critics don't like to see nobody win doing any kind of music they don't know nuthin' about," Presley lamented. "The colored folk been singing it, and it's just the way I'm doin' it now . . ."

Rock 'n' roll was something new, and the older generation assumed it was a passing teenage fad, which was the inference from the reporter, who thought Presley would be boxed in by a music trend that would quickly fade away. Presley replied, "I like to sing ballads the way Eddie Fisher does and the way Perry Como does, but the way I'm singing now is what makes the money. Would you change if you were me?"

When he was back in New York, Presley made an appearance on *The Steve Allen Show*, a variety program on NBC. He had a new song he was working on called "Hound Dog," and the show devised a goofy premise where Presley, dressed in tie and tails, would sing the song to a real basset hound. While it all sounded banal at best, there was a serious purpose in devising such a scene. Elvis Presley would not be seen gyrating on television.

No one was happy with Presley's performance, but work was work. The next day, he promptly arrived at RCA studios in Manhattan for another recording session. Again, an underlying conservatism abounded, and this compromised RCA's plans. At the session, Elvis recorded "Don't Be Cruel" and "Hound Dog." The smarter play would have been to issue two records backed by minor songs on the B-sides, but RCA wasn't sure what it had with Elvis: was he a rising star or just a flash in the pan? The corporate decision was to issue one record with "Hound Dog" on the A-side and "Don't Be Cruel" on the B-side.[1]

"Hound Dog" bit first, rising to the top of the charts. Deejays then flipped the record over, and "Don't Be Cruel" followed the same path. For eleven weeks straight, the two-sided hit was #1 on the record charts. As musicologist Joel Whitburn noted, "Because of the enormous strength of each side, and with *Billboard* alternating the sides shown first, its 11 weeks at Number One are a combined total of the two sides as each song flip-flopped at Number One on both the best-seller and jukebox charts."[2]

Presley was not happy that RCA had issued both songs on one record because with two records, he would have made twice the amount of money. Presley biographer Albert Goldman observed: "The simple fact was that RCA was just pumping out the product as it came to hand . . . Nobody at Victor [RCA] knew anything about the new world of rock. The idea was to exploit him [Elvis Presley] to the limit now that he was hot."[3]

At that moment in 1956, what young listeners to local radio stations and teenage record buyers didn't realize, in the adulation of Elvis Presley and the coming of rock 'n' roll, how much of the music was based on blues or R&B. The best example of that was the song "Hound Dog," which like an old family pet was accustomed to certain rewards just for being as good as good can be—such as being a #1 song. In 1953, singer Willie Mae "Big Mama" Thornton's initial recording of the tune was a monster hit on the R&B charts, where it resided for fourteen weeks, including seven at #1.

Presley was trying to capture Big Mama's mojo. "It was obvious from 'Heartbreak Hotel,' 'Hound Dog,' and 'That's Alright Mama' that Elvis did more than listen to the records of 'Big Boy' Crudup and Big Mama Thornton," wrote Nelson George. "He attempted, with amazing success on his early records, to inhale their passion in his soul. The sound emanating from a white Southerner of all people scared white parents and the guardians of separation [segregation] just as if Presley were Black."[4]

"Hound Dog" was written by two young white men, Jerry Leiber and Mike Stoller. Their families were from the East Coast, but by the mid-1940s, when they were preteens and early teenagers, both the Leiber and Stoller families had moved to Los Angeles. The two hung out in one of the most bustling blues scenes in the country, South Central Los Angeles. Blues singer Jimmy

Witherspoon was the first to record a Leiber-Stoller song, "Real Ugly Woman," around 1950. The songsters continued writing with moderate success for local blues singers, including Little Esther, throughout the first years of the 1950s. Their big break came in August 1952, when Big Mama Thornton recorded "Hound Dog," a song it had taken them less than fifteen minutes to write.[5]

Willie Mae Thornton was born December 1926 in Ariton, Alabama, in the southeast corner of the state. The tiny hamlet boasted a population of about 600 people in the 1920s. Thornton claimed Montgomery was where she was born, which is a possibility if she wasn't born at home; it is doubtful that Ariton had even a doctor's office. Her father was a minister, her mother sang in the church, and Willie Mae followed her parents into the Lord's work. When she turned fourteen, Thornton found cleaning work at a local saloon, which was fortuitous because, whenever possible, the bar's owners allowed her to sing on stage. Somehow, an Atlanta music promoter stumbled upon her and asked her to join his Atlanta-based Hot Harlem Revue, which toured throughout the South. She was billed as the "New Bessie Smith" and stayed with the tour for seven years before finally settling down in Houston.[6]

She did her first recording in Houston even before joining Don Robey's growing stable of artists at Peacock Records. For a while, Robey employed Johnny Otis as a bandleader, and around 1952 Thornton went west with Otis's touring show. When they got to Los Angeles, Otis's old stomping grounds, he brought Thornton into the studio for Peacock Records. He also wanted Leiber and Stoller to provide material for Thornton. As Stoller recalled for *Rolling Stone* magazine, Johnny Otis told Leiber and Stoller to come down to his garage, where he used to rehearse. "We saw Big Mama, and she knocked us out cold. She looked like the biggest, badass you would ever see. And she was mean. She must have been 350 pounds, and she had these scars all over her face."[7]

Considering Big Mama's look and demeanor, thematically, Leiber and Stoller had to write a song that said "go fuck yourself," but in a nicer way. It took them fifteen minutes to write "Hound Dog." Stoller recalled, "We wanted her to growl it." But Thornton was not going to take direction from two white boys. Instead she growled at Leiber and Stoller, "Don't tell me how to sing no song."

Otis, who never let a writing credit get past him, always claimed he helped the boys put the song together and that warranted him putting his name on the record as part of the songwriting team, so underneath the song title, it reads "J. Leiber, M. Stoller, J. Otis." After a lawsuit concerning creative ownership of the song that was won by Leiber and Stoller, Otis's name was omitted from all subsequent "Hound Dog" records.

As writer Ken Emerson noted, "Set to a relaxed rumba beat, the original 'Hound Dog' was about sass and sex. Thornton . . . notorious for her foul language, scars on her cheeks . . . and mannish garb of khaki trousers and plaid shirts, sang with a deep growl and a broad wink. She inveighed against her shiftless lover, but she didn't get too hot and bothered."[8]

"Hound Dog" was a big R&B hit immediately. In April, *Jet* declared that "Hound Dog" by Willie Mae (Big Mama) Thornton, a Peacock recording artist, ranked first in sales in New York, Chicago, New Orleans, San Francisco, Newark, Memphis, Dallas, Cincinnati, Los Angeles, and St. Louis. The magazine also commented that "Miss Thornton" was an unknown until discovered by Don Robey, president of Peacock Records, "a Negro firm in Houston."[9]

As late as August the same year, the "Theatrically Yours" syndicated column remarked, "It's a toss-up in our book between Willa Mae Thornton's 'Hound Dog' and Willie Mabon's 'I Don't Know' as the hottest R&B record of this or any other season."[10]

Like most Peacock/Duke recording stars, Thornton didn't do much recording. Owner Don Robey much preferred his talent to be on the road, which was more lucrative for him. There was never another "Hound Dog"–level hit for Thornton, although she was popular in live performances. In 1952, she and the Johnny Otis Show played the Apollo Theater, initially as an opening act to Little Esther and Mel Walker, but she eventually took over as the premier guest performer. In 1954, she was teamed with Johnny Ace, the James Dean of Black America, on a successful tour until he accidentally killed himself. It was the darkest of times for her, but she would have her moment in the sun again with the dawning of the Age of Aquarius.

Elvis Presley covering Big Mama Thornton's hit record of 1953 was not a unique phenomenon. Big Maybelle, one of the major R&B hitmakers of 1953, boasted an eerily similar experience a few years down the road. This time it was about a non-hit record. The song was "Whole Lotta Shakin' Goin' On," which she recorded in 1955.

In 1956, an unknown Jerry Lee Lewis was in Sam Phillips's recording studio in Memphis trying to come up with a song that he could take to deejays. They tried the Big Maybelle song "Whole Lotta Shakin' Goin' On," adhering closer to prior versions. It wasn't working, so with a new band and new direction, they went back into the studio to recut the song. It only took one take to get it right. And just like with the relatively unknown Elvis one year before, Jerry Lee Lewis secured a gig on *The Steve Allen Show*. It was April 15, 1957, and Lewis was the last performer on the show, given the final five minutes. This is the way writer Ed Ward described the performance: "Swinging into 'Whole Lotta Shakin',' he [Jerry Lee Lewis] slowly stood, riding the piano like a madman, kicking the piano stool out of his way so he could get a better purchase on the keyboard. Caught up in the spirit of the moment, Steve Allen threw the stool back at him and then a hail of other objects after it. Undaunted, Jerry Lee started playing with his foot. It was scandalous, and it gave Jerry Lee his big break. Recognizing the debt, he later named his son Steve Allen Lewis."[11]

Big Maybelle's opening lyrics:

> Twenty-one drums and an old bass drum
> An' somebody beatin' on a ding-dong

Jerry Lee Lewis's opening:

> Come on over baby, whole lot of shakin' goin' on
> Yes, I said come on over baby, baby you can't go wrong

So how did Jerry Lee Lewis end up with Big Maybelle's obscure record from 1955?

The original tune was written by African American songwriter Dave (Curly or Curlee) Williams and in 1955 recorded on the Decca label by Roy Hall, a white boogie-pianist. Either Jerry Lee Lewis heard the song when he worked at a Nashville club owned by Roy Hall or later when he was working with Johnny Littlejohn's band in Natchez, Mississippi, a bend in the river away from Lewis's hometown of Ferriday, Louisiana. That was 1956 and later that year, Lewis would travel upriver to Memphis to try his luck with Sun Records.[12]

That wasn't the only oddity about Big Maybelle's "Whole Lotta Shakin'" song. On some recordings, the B-side was "One Monkey Don't Stop No Show," which was an old Southern adage and title of an unrelated Stick McGhee song from 1950. The same title would be used twice more in the 1960s on completely unrelated songs by Joe Tex (#20 on the R&B chart and #65 pop) and Honey Cone (#5 R&B and #15 pop).

Big Maybelle (Mabel Louise Smith) was born in May 1924 in Jackson, Tennessee. Like most R&B performers, she began singing in church but was lured away by the devilish sounds of the blues. Memphis promoter Dave Clark discovered her as a preteen, and her big break came when she began touring with the all-female International Sweethearts of Rhythm.[13]

Operating out of the Midwest in the early to mid-1940s, Denver Ferguson built up a fine roster of musicians as a promoter, booking agent, artist representative, and all-around Black entrepreneur. At first he didn't have any big stars, but his roster grew as "Boogie-Woogie Piano and Accordion Queen" Christine Chatman left a prior band to go on her own, as did singer Big Maybelle, sometimes known as "Hey Lawdy Mama" from her best-known song. Ferguson had her touring the Chitlin' Circuit with Sax Kari and his band (for a while, one of his guitar players was jazz great Wes Montgomery). Big Maybelle began to get noticed. In 1943, the *Indianapolis Recorder* published a column noting, "Maybelle, new Ferguson Bros. singing find, knocked the house out . . . This buxom bit of rhythm is sure to go places as she is in the class with America's leading feminine vocalists." Also in 1943 from the *Chicago Defender*: "Maybelle, the 'Hey Lawdy Mama,' really came on in this city last night when she set the Memorial Auditorium on fire with the blues . . . when she fell in the groove on her favorite number, 'Hey Lawdy Mama,' the house started jumping until the wee hours of the morning."[14]

According to writer Larry Birnbaum, Big Maybelle first entered a recording studio in 1944 while singing with Christine Chatman's band, cutting "Hurry, Hurry," which had been a big hit for Savannah Churchill and Benny Carter.[15]

Ferguson had also represented Tiny Bradshaw and his band, so when Big Maybelle, recording as Mabel Smith, stepped into the recording studio for King Records in 1947, they backed her up. On her next session with King, she was backed by "Hot Lips" Page's band. Nothing happened with these recordings, and it wasn't until she was picked up by Fred Mendelsohn at OKeh that things turned around for her.[16] Perhaps it was all because Mendelsohn locked in the sobriquet under which she would become famous: Big Maybelle. Her first OKeh sessions were in late 1952, with those recordings hitting the market in 1953. Three of those songs would be big hits: "Grabbin' Blues" rose all the way to #3 on the R&B charts; "My Country Man" did almost as well, coming in at #5 on the R&B charts; and "Way Back Home" hit at #10.

The latter song was the most interesting in that it was the B-side to the A-side cut "Just Want Your Love." Deejays flipped the record and began playing "Way Back Home." It was so new to the turntables not everyone got the title right. The Lincoln, Nebraska *Voice* on April 9, 1953, ran a column by a local writer who noted, "If you're looking for real gone [the ultimate compliment!] music, you must hear . . . Big Maybelle's disking [recording] of 'On My Way Back Home.'"[17]

Big Maybelle also found herself compared to Big Mama Thornton. Of her 1953 release "Jinny Mule," *Cash Box*'s "Rhythm 'n' Blues Reviews" called the song "A middle beat novelty very reminiscent in approach and tune to 'Hound Dog' zestfully read by Big Maybelle. Gal berates her man as being a stubborn fool."[18]

Big Maybelle's career slumped after 1953. She would record sporadically over the 1950s, charting just one more song, "Candy," in 1956. Jerry "Swamp Dogg" Williams was from Portsmouth, Virginia, which was where he met Big Maybelle. He was a young teenager, and she was appearing at the Capitol Theater. He recalls just three things from that concert. First, she sang "Candy" and, second, she appeared on stage barefoot. He went backstage to meet her, and the third thing he remembered was how big she was. "You could have gotten two and a half women out of her," he said, laughing at the memory.[19]

Big Maybelle obviously was not a petite young lady. In 1954, during a farcical boxing match with comedienne Jackie "Moms" Mabley at the Apollo Theater, Big Maybelle put a little too much oomph in a roundhouse kick and, according to the press, Moms Mabley went down for the count. The audience thought it was part of the act.[20]

In the 1960s, Big Maybelle's career was put on hold as she suffered through poor health. She died in 1972 of a diabetic coma.

In the R&B world, 1953 was a big tent year for female singers. No matter the format—blues, rock 'n' roll, or jazz-pop—audience excitement expanded for many different voices, from veterans like Dinah Washington and Ruth Brown to a host of new talent. It was not as if the men's world of R&B was suddenly accommodating. It was more that it wasn't a particularly strong year for the guys. The one classic tune from the guys that year was the Orioles' version of "Crying in the Chapel," which was the #1 R&B song of 1953. That was it, although there were strong contenders from such handsome young men as Johnny Ace ("The Clock") and Clyde McPhatter and the Drifters ("Money Honey"). If someone had to choose a second classic R&B tune for the year, they would have had to turn to the women, where the nod would go to either (or both!) Big Mama Thornton's "Hound Dog" or the fabulous gospel-pop sound of "Shake a Hand" by Faye Adams.

Of the Top Ten R&B songs in 1953, the women took three positions: Faye Adams with "Shake a Hand" at #2, Ruth Brown with "(Mama) He Treats Your Daughter Mean" at #4, and Big Mama Thornton with "Hound Dog" at #7. If one looks at the R&B Top Twenty, the expanded list included Faye Adams's "I'll Be True" at #11; Shirley Goodman (as part of Shirley and Lee) at #14 for "I'm Gone," which was introduced at the end of 1952 but held strongly through early 1953; and newcomer to the charts, Linda Hayes, at #19 for "Yes! I Know (What You're Putting Down)."

Also new to the R&B charts that year were Annisteen Allen for "Baby I'm Doin' It" and Mitzi Mars for "I'm Glad."

As noted, Big Maybelle boasted three top records of the year. So did Ruth Brown. Reliable Dinah Washington had two big songs for the year, and Varetta Dillard one.

One of the most unusual songs released by any R&B singer in 1953 was Linda Hayes's "Yes! I Know (What You're Putting Down)", which was an answer song to the very popular "I Don't Know" by Willie Mabon from the prior year.

Mabon was a debonair and devilishly handsome piano player from Memphis. By the early 1940s, he moved north to Chicago and eventually began recording for Chess Records. In 1952, Chess released "I Don't Know" by Willie Mabon and his combo. The songwriting credits on the record read W. Mabon, but it is now recognized that Mabon lifted much of it from a tune by Cripple

Clarence Lofton, a Tennessee blues pianist who also ended up in Chicago. In Mabon's cut, as the singer, he begins in talk-song mode about the possibility of poisoning his girl. Her answer is the chorus that ends with "I don't know what my baby's puttin' down."

Hayes's delightfully humorous answer record follows Mabon's bluesy format but with the female talking about her no-good man instead of the other way around. Hayes does a little hesitation trick with the line "talkin' about what should I say this time baaaaby" that's pure earworm.

The two songs collided. Mabon's "I Don't Know," which was released in 1952, was still the #1 R&B best-selling record on January 31, 1953, when *Billboard* columnist Bob Rolontz wrote: "The Recorded in Hollywood label has rushed out a disking by thrush Linda Hayes titled 'Yes! I Know (What You're Putting Down)' the long-awaited reply to the smash Willie Mabon slicing of 'I Don't Know' on Chess, which has swept the R&B field and invaded the pop market as well."[21]

The newsy tidbit preceded the magazine's review of the record, which came the next week: "The Willie Mabon hit, 'I Don't Know,' is answered with feeling on this powerful reply. Linda Hayes chants the ditty with great ability. Material and performance make this an effort that can't miss."[22]

Then things got weird. By the third week in February 1953, one could find the two songs intensely competitive in individual markets. So, for example, in Philadelphia, "Yes! I Know" was the #2 song with "I Don't Know" the #3 song. Conversely, in Charlotte, "I Don't Know" was the #3 song and "Yes! I Know" was the #4 song.[23]

That was just the beginning of answer record mania. Mabon recorded for Chess Records in Chicago, and that label decided it would cash in on itself by getting local R&B singer Edna McRaney into the studio to record a version of the answer song, not subtly titled "Yes I Know."

Chicago bluesman Bobby Rush knew McRaney because they used to play together at West Side clubs such as the Sidewinder and Castle Rock. Rush's good friend Cash McCall also played on gigs with her. Her style, he said, was singing what was big on jukeboxes at the time.[24]

Although McRaney's answer record didn't work out, when Mabon torched the record charts in 1953 with another #1 record "I'm Mad," Chess decided to try again, bringing in a different local singer named Mitzi Mars to warble the answer song "I'm Glad" with Sax Mallard and his orchestra. Recorded for Checkers, a subsidiary label of Chess, this time the strategy worked, and the company had a secondary hit record.[25]

Not much is known about Mitzi Mars. Prior to "I'm Glad," she had only one recording, a 1951 debut called "Scrunch" with "Jump Boy" on the B-side. "Scrunch" appeared on an obscure Chicago label called J.O.B. Records, and the credits read "Henry Palmer and his Boys/Mitzi Mars, vocalist." Palmer, a pianist who was born in 1898, played the Chicago clubs. At the time, Mars was a semi-regular performer at the South Side's Club DeLisa while Palmer worked the Mill's Inn.[26]

"I knew the Club DeLisa and I knew Mitzi Mars," said Bobby Rush. "I was playing Robert's Show Lounge around 1956 or 1957 but I went to Club DeLisa to meet Ruth Brown, who was performing there. That night I also met Dinah Washington there. As for Mitzi, she was known locally mostly with the South Side clubs. I always associate her with another local singer Little Madeline because they were lovers of ladies. Mars sang jukebox hits while Little Madeline was more gutsy. Both just disappeared from the scene."

Two years after the J.O.B. recording, Mars got her big break. According to Chess Records' historical notes, on March 29, Mars cut two sides for Checker, "I'm Glad" and "Let It Roll." She was defined as a "brassy nightclub singer," who had been singing in South Side (Chicago) clubs for the past two years, often wearing a blond wig.[27] The song broke regionally in Atlanta, Pittsburgh, and Memphis. In 1953, Willie Mabon's "I'm Mad" was the tenth best-selling R&B cut; Mitzi Mars's "I'm Glad" made the R&B best-seller list at #79.

The #78 R&B best-seller was another answer song, "Baby I'm Doin' It," by a slightly better-known performer Annisteen Allen.

The year 1953 was a dandy one for a quintet out of North Carolina that called themselves the "5" Royales. That year, the group bagged three major hits: "Crazy, Crazy, Crazy," "Too Much Lovin' (Much Too Much)," and their biggest song, "Baby Don't Do It." The unofficial rule in answer songs was always answer the big hit, so "Baby I'm Doin' It" was a response to "Baby Don't Do It."

Annisteen Allen (Ernestine Letitia Allen) was born in 1920 in Champaign, Illinois. In her path toward stardom, she would tread some very familiar ground—in 1945 going to work for the Lucky Millinder band. Millinder seemed to find every up-and-coming female singer, renamed each girl for his band, and then quickly lost them. Millinder was from Anniston, Alabama, and billed his new singer as Annisteen Allen. She, perhaps, stayed with Millinder too long. In 1951, Annisteen singing with Big John Greer had two big hits, but no one really knew that because label credit only went to Lucky Millinder and his Orchestra. She finally caught a break recording that year under her own name one record, "Too Long" / "Hard to Get Along" on the Federal label, a subsidiary of King Records. Two years later, she moved to the parent label, where she had her only hit record under her own name, "Baby I'm Doin' It."[28] The "5" Royales pleaded: "If you leave me pretty baby / I'll have bread without no meat." Annisteen's response: "You gotta lot nerve to think we ain't through."

In February 1953, the "Theatrically Yours" syndicated column reported that Annisteen Allen's recording of "Yes, I Do" backed with "I'm Doing It" was breaking all the over the country. In the first five days of its release, it sold 75,000 copies. Larry Douglas, who wrote the column, got almost everything backwards in that small item. What was selling was the B-side, "Baby I'm Doin' It."[29]

"Baby Don't Do It" was the twelfth best-selling R&B song of 1953, and "Baby I'm Doin' It" rolled in at #78. In the annals of music history, the "5" Royales and Annisteen Allen would end up with another thing in common: their most famous songs were more famous for other performers.

In 1954, Allen recorded a tune called "Fujiyama Mama." Not much happened with the song until the next year, when rockabilly artist Wanda Jackson recorded it. American record buyers didn't cotton to the wild tune, but it became a #1 record in Japan—the first rock 'n' roll song to become a hit in that country.

In 1957, the "5" Royales recorded a song called "Don't Be Ashamed" paired with the B-side "Dedicated to the One I Love." What happened to that B-side cut? Beverly Lee of the Shirelles says her group first heard the song when they shared a billing with the "5" Royales at the Howard Theater in Washington, DC. "Dedicated to the One I Love" was part of the "5" Royales' act, and the Shirelles liked it so much, they sang it all the time. Their producer thought it was a song the Shirelles had created and suggested they record it. The four Shirelles confessed the song wasn't theirs, but they got to record it anyway.[30] It was a #3 best-seller in 1961 and a classic tune of the girl group era.

It wasn't just the women answering the men in song. In 1953, the flow worked in the reverse direction as well. Another answer record that garnered substantial airtime in 1953 was Rufus Thomas's "Bear Cat," on Sun Records, which was an answer song to Big Mama Thornton's "Hound Dog."

With money pouring into the coffers of record labels pushing answer songs, the original song publishers suddenly realized they weren't getting a cut of the melodies to which they held song rights. Lawsuits began to fly, or as a *Billboard* headline screamed, "Pubbers Train Legal Guns on Tail-Riding Indie Labels," which proclaimed that "publishers are putting up a fight to protect their originals from unauthorized or infringing answers."[31] The problem was that the "answers" stole melodies and themes from the originals. Don Robey at Peacock, the label for "Hound Dog," went after Sun Records and Republic Music, which bought the rights to Mabon's song, reporting to the press it was going to protect the firm against "infringements" on "I Don't Know."

Answer records were historically popular in the R&B field, where the trend flew under the radar of the mainstream music industry, but as a lawyer for Republic Music told *Billboard*, "If someone does not stop this practice, it will spread to fields other than rhythm & blues." And that's when the issue became important.

In 1953, the great divide between the pop world and the R&B scene had not closed, which led to another unusual phenomenon: a recording by a Black female singer that did not dent the R&B charts but was a major hit on the pop charts. That was a rare occurrence except for specific jazz singers such as Ella Fitzgerald in the 1940s.

It's fitting that the 1953 pop song anomaly was by none other than Eartha Kitt, a performer who was as well known for her activism, controversies, and liaisons as she was for her presence in movies, television shows, and the stage. While she was extremely popular as a singer in nightclubs and on albums, as a singles recording artist, she had climbed the pop charts for just a couple of years. In 1954, she could brag two Top Twenty pop hits, but that was a continuation and conclusion to the extraordinary year she had in 1953, charting four hits, two of which were Top Twenty. The lesser hits were "Uska Dara," which she sang in Turkish and rose to #23 on the charts, and the tantalizing "I Want to be Evil," which did a little better, climbing to #22 on the pop charts.

Her biggest hits of the 1953 were "C'est Si Bon" and "Santa Baby," and comparing the two involves a bit of craziness as well.

Eartha (Mae) Kitt was born in January 1927 in North, South Carolina. Her father was unknown to Eartha and her mother was a sharecropper of African American and Cherokee descent. As to her unusual name, the story Kitt told was that "after many years of small and sickly crops, my family's farm yielded a rich and abundant harvest the same year I was born. My mother said, 'we must call our daughter Eartha to thank the earth for our fine crop.'" Good times didn't last long, and soon mother and daughter went north to Harlem in search of a better life. Things got worse. At the age of nine, Eartha was given away by her mother. Although pretty much homeless as a teenager, she found jobs as a singer and dancer, getting a break at sixteen when she signed to the Katherine Dunham Dance Troupe just as it was leaving for a European tour.[32] According to the *Chicago Sun-Times*, after that experience, she was a featured singer at Carroll's, a Paris nightspot, until Orson Welles heard her sing. Impressed by both her voice and dramatic abilities, he offered her a role as his wife in a production of *Faust*. The newspaper noted that the language complications of that international production were of little matter, as Kitt spoke seven languages.[33]

RCA Victor signed Kitt, but she recorded just one song for the label in 1952. The next year, she recorded twelve songs for six records. As noted, her two biggest hits were "Santa Baby" and "C'est Si Bon." This is where things were different for Kitt. "Santa Baby" appeared to be the bigger hit, shooting all the way to #4 on *Billboard*, while "C'est Si Bon" made it only as far as #8. However, as a seasonal song, "Santa Baby" had a shorter time on the charts, and "C'est Si Bon" ended up as the twenty-ninth best-selling song of the year. Two things to note, however. First, none of Kitt's songs made it to the R&B charts, and Kitt, along with Nat King Cole ("Pretend"), were the only African American performers to crack the Top Thirty best-selling list of pop songs of 1953. Time is the determinant between a good song and one of eternal greatness. Decades and decades later, "C'est Si Bon" has become a forgotten tune while "Santa Baby" is considered a Christmas classic.

Of course, it didn't start out that way. Larry Douglas, the syndicated columnist of the "Theatrically Yours" column that ran in many independent African American newspapers, boldly predicted that "Santa Baby" would not be a hit. Douglas wrote, "It is too sexy. After all, Christmas is for children."[34]

Kitt was sultry, beautiful, and controversial. These were the same attributes ascribed to her when she first gained fame. In November of her breakout year 1953, she and other performers were invited to entertain the king and queen of Greece, who were visiting Los Angeles. Kitt sang "Santa Baby" and "I Want to Be Evil," and the next day, the mayor, city councilmen, and concerned citizens complained to the press that her performances for the royal guests were too risqué. Said the mayor of Los Angeles, "I personally found some of the lyrics offensive."[35]

As for "C'est Si Bon," the song was written in 1947 by French composer Henri Betti, with lyrics by André Hornez. The first versions of the song from 1948 were all by French singers, including the very popular Yves Montand. Although an English version of the song was first recorded in 1950, Kitt, backed by Henri Betti and his orchestra, sang the words in French. The B-side was "African Lullaby."

In June, *Billboard* teased the singer with the headline "She'll Sing in Sanskrit Yet," reporting: "Eartha Kitt, RCA Victor songstress who startled tradesters with her rendition of 'Uska Dara' in Turkish, is off on a linguistic binge of sorts. Her newest disking couples a French ditty 'C'est Si Bon,' sung in the original, of course, with a tune called 'African Lullaby.'"[36] The latter contains a chorus or two in apparently authentic Swahili. Eartha Kitt was an authentic in any language.

Time is not only a determinant in placing once-esteemed (sometimes obscure) songs on a pedestal, but also snags older, highly regarded tunes in modern constructs as to what is now acceptable. Reconsideration has wounded Varetta Dillard's 1953 hit song—and maybe the best of her oeuvre—"Mercy, Mr. Percy," which shot to #6 on the R&B charts and was one of best-selling songs by an R&B singer for the year.

Here are the lyrics that are no longer deemed appropriate: "Your arms are so inviting, your love is so exciting / I don't care if you hit me, As long as you don't quit me."

Abuse is not something that should be valued in a pop song, although in 1953, no one thought twice about it.

Cash Box's "Rhythm 'n' Blues Reviews" selected "Mercy, Mr. Percy" as its "Award o' the Week," saying: "Varetta Dillard comes up with a natural for her talented pipes. The thrush has a piece of material that is tailor made. Called

'Mercy, Mr. Percy,' Varetta employs her bag of tricks to sell it and sell it she does. She displays her histrionic talents as she pleads for mercy from Mr. Percy. She begs him to do anything, even hit her, but don't 'quit her.'"[37]

Time also hasn't played well for Dinah Washington's biggest hit of 1953, "TV Is the Thing (This Year)." This has to do with topicality, that is, what was new and exciting technology in 1953 became ubiquitous very quickly. At the start of 1953, television was already in twenty million households across America, an increase of 33 percent from the prior year.[38] However, if Washington's song has been culturally cancelled because it is out of date, well, that's because people haven't been listening close enough. The song is a humorous slice of bluesy sex-talk. *Billboard*'s quick review in October 1953 hit the nail on the head when it said: "Ribald effort, full of laughs, has many suggestive double entendres. Dinah Washington punches across a great performance. Juke [jukebox] coin should be heavy. Looks like a hit."[39] And it was. By the end of October, the "Stars Over Harlem" column in *Cash Box* checked in with Leonard Spivey and Duetta Maxwell of the Harlem River Record Shop, who reported that they were "ordering like mad" Dinah Washington's "TV Is the Thing (This Year)" and "Fat Daddy."[40] Washington sang: "Now he turned my dial to channel one, I knew that this was gonna be fun / He turned my dial to channel two, that station thrilled me through and through / He moved one notch to channel three, I said oh how I love what you're doin' to me."

The B-side was a song called "Fat Daddy," which also garnered major play, so the record became a two-sided hit. Both songs were Washington's only charted hits of the year.

It could be Washington was less often in the recording studio because she was experiencing the usual trouble in her personal life. Unofficially, she was married eight times—and those eight times came quickly. Toward the end of 1953, she and Jimmy Cobb were through. Washington once wrote about it this way: "He [Jimmy Cobb] had another interest besides me, one of my closest girlfriends. As it turned out, he got closer and closer to this girl and further and further away from me." Although Washington was hurt, she rebounded quickly. In mid-November, she announced her marriage to drummer Larry Wrice. That was one union that never really happened; she was just getting ahead of rumors and having a good time.[41]

Washington was beginning to have a reputation for having a short-temper and foul mouth. Sometimes these stories would appear obliquely in the Black press. For example, in September 1953, the "Theatrically Yours" column observed, "Songstress Dinah Washington should watch her step. Many of her fans have been heard to opine that her actions are not exactly ladylike."[42]

When Bobby Rush first saw Dinah Washington perform, he remembered her "cussing men out, cutting them, and talking shit." Rush was a well-known musician in Chicago but still a young bluesman on the make, and when he went backstage to meet Washington, she teased him. "C'mon over here, boy, you still got buttermilk on your chin. C'mon youngblood, you know what this is" and she had her hand below her stomach. "She was a rough talker and would scare the daylights out of you if you didn't know her," Rush said.[43]

While all that might have been true, Washington could be incredibly friendly and helpful. Once you got to know her, Rush added, you realized she was a kind person.

On April 4, 1954, *Cash Box*'s "Rhythm 'n' Blues Reviews" selected Dinah Washington's "You Let My Love Grow Cold" / "Ain't Nothin' Good" as its "Award o' the Week" record, noting in summary: "When this gal is mellow, you melt, when she is frigid, you freeze, when she is sexotic, you sizzle, and when she belts it, you bounce." One of her competitors that week was Little Esther, who was unleashing "Street Lights" / "You Took My Love Too Fast." There was still professionally a bit of rivalry between these top acts, who were sometimes lumped together in the Black press.[44] A 1953 interview with veteran bandleader Noble Sissle for the Global syndicate came up with this quote: "Little Esther is one of the most promising young blues singers I have heard in the last two years. She's going to develop into another Dinah Washington."[45]

When Esther Phillips was still a teenager, she appeared at the Apollo along with Dinah Washington. Phillips was singing with Johnny Otis's band, and he was managing her. Every night, Otis would have Phillips dressed up "like a little southern girl," much to the dismay of Washington. After the first couple of shows, Washington had had enough of that foolery and took Phillips out for makeover: new hairdo, high heels, nylon stockings, and a form-fitting dress. As Otis recalled, Washington said to him, "That's disgraceful, having her look like she's in the cotton fields."[46]

In March, some African American newspapers picked up a syndicated photo of Dinah Washington with Ben Bart of Universal Attractions. The two were at a recording session on the West Coast because Washington had "waxed a series of hit tunes."[47]

Mercury, Washington's record company, liked to have her in the studio, although—and despite the photo cutline—1953 wasn't a particularly busy year for her regarding recording sessions. She cut twelve tunes for six platters. A busy year for many singers, but not for Dinah Washington.

The year 1953 was so wide open for female R&B singers that a slew of relatively unknowns tried to crash the party. Despite poise, talent, beauty, and/or creativity, success on the singles chart, which meant better-paying gigs, passed them by. A few would go on to long careers in other genres such as jazz or gospel.

For the week of June 6, 1953, *Cash Box* picked Dillard's "Mercy, Mr. Percy" as its "Award o' the Week." Among the also-rans was "I'll Help You Baby" / "L&N

Special" by a singer named Christine Kittrell. On the B-side, the reviewer noted, "Christine sings a quick beat bounce with a New Orleans feel. Gal gives the etching drive."[48]

That Big Easy sound emerged because Kittrell bounced between New Orleans and Nashville for most her career—always on the verge of stardom, but never crossing over.

She was born in August 1929 in Nashville and was a member of the church choir as a youth. Kittrell made her recording debut in 1951 for Nashville-based Tennessee Records, when she cut one platter: "Old Man, You're Slipping" / "Sittin' Here Drinking." She was backed by a couple of guys from Fats Domino's band, and that led to a lengthy engagement at the Pelican Club in New Orleans. In 1952, still with Tennessee Records, she cut "Heartache Blues" / "You Ain't Nothing but Trouble," which attracted regional attention, especially in New Orleans, where it was a Top Ten song.[49]

Tennessee Records, along with the associated label Republic, were owned by Alan and Reynolds Bubis. Their A&R man was an African American, Theodore Roosevelt "Ted" Jarrett, who would become a well-known songwriter and producer. For some reason, the Tennessee Records brain trust moved Kittrell over to the Republic label and in 1953 got her into the studio to record a bunch of new songs. A handful got some notice, including the aforementioned "I'll Help You Baby" / "L&N Special" and "Gotta Stop Loving You" / "Slave to Love." The latter record was reviewed by *Cash Box*, which revealed that the A-side had Kittrell teaming up with Gay Cross in a slow, rhythmic, appealing, and interestingly arranged tune. The B-side was deemed a "feelingful" slow tempo blues tune, dramatically chanted and called "a swaying exotic thing with a fine rambling piano."[50] However, the only Kittrell cut to make any headway was a song called "Every Night in the Week," which late in 1953 was a #3 hit in Nashville, where Kittrell had made a name for herself.[51] Her career slowly faded with a few odd highlights: in 1954, she recorded "Sittin' Here Drinking Again" with Little Richard on the piano; in 1962, she recorded Leiber and Stoller's "I'm a Woman"; and in 1967, she was wounded in Vietnam while entertaining the troops. She passed away in 2001.[52]

Another talent who tried to dent the charts in 1953 was Sarah McLawler, who years later would become well known in the jazz world. She was highly regarded for her keyboard skills on the organ from the start of her professional career, when she was a whiz kid on the Hammond B3. One of the records she unleashed in 1953 was "Blues for Rex" on the Brunswick label. *Cash Box*'s reviewer immediately noted her keyboard skills, writing about the song: "An original by Sarah is treated to the great sounds the gal can produce from a Hammond. A dramatic and tense piece that would be great for production dramas."[53]

Sarah McLawler was born in 1928 in Louisville. She began to play the piano by ear at the age of seven. She rollicked in church, where her father was a minister, and later attended Fisk University. Like other female R&B and jazz musicians, she ended up on road with the Lucky Millinder orchestra (didn't everyone!) and later pioneered an all-woman band called the Syncoettes. She made her first recording in 1950 and the following year signed with King Records, where she recorded eight songs (four records). In 1953, she moved over to the Brunswick label, where she recorded just four songs, including "Blues for Rex."[54] To really hear the lady swing, find the second record that she put down for Brunswick, a double-sided instrumental with tenor saxman Georgie Auld. The first side, "The Blue Room," is a fine, groovy foot-tapper. No slight to the singer P!nk with her "Let's Get the Party Started," but fifty years earlier, the McLawler, organ, and sax jam "Let's Get the Party Rockin'" would get any club shakin'.[55]

In later years, McLawler was a denizen of New York jazz spots and international festivals.[56] She died in 2017.

Of all the female singers to have hit records in 1953, not one out-shown Ruth Brown, who had another spectacular year. She boasted three Top Ten hits, including "Mend Your Ways," which climbed to #7 on the R&B charts, and "Wild, Wild Young Men," a #3 R&B hit.

Her third starburst was the superlative #1 "(Mama) He Treats Your Daughter Mean," the fourth best-selling R&B song of 1953. *Down Beat* magazine voted it the top R&B record of 1953. This was Brown's third R&B #1 tune and the first to cross over to the pop charts, climbing as high as #23. It's a classic.

In an interview with *Rolling Stone* magazine, Little Richard explained the origins of his unique singing style: "When I first came along, I never heard of rock 'n' roll. I only heard of Elmore James, Sonny Boy Williamson, Ruth Brown . . . and this thing you hear me do—'Lucille-uh'—I got that from Ruth Brown. I used to like the way she'd sing 'Mama-uh, he treats your daughter mean.'"[57]

Little Richard knew his music. When Ruth Brown launches into "(Mama) He Treats Your Daughter Mean," as a listener you know you are in for a treat because the first exclamations are "Mama," or as she sang it "Mama-uh," with the second syllable wrapped in an idiosyncratic Ruth Brown squeal. That sound is not easy to pull off, but Brown maintains it throughout.

The origins of the tune are deep Texas blues. Blind Lemon Jefferson, born in 1893 in Coutchman, Texas, is sometimes known as the "Father of Texas Blues" and the man who created the thrashing guitar sound later adopted by guys like Clarence "Gatemouth" Brown and Guitar Slim (Eddie Jones), who influenced the next generation of guitar masters such as Jimi Hendrix. Blind Lemon also composed his own songs, one of which was "One Dime Blues," featuring these lyrics: "Mama, don't treat your daughter mean / That's the meanest woman a man 'most ever seen."[58]

This was a very esoteric song even in the early 1950s and accidentally made the transition to pop. The story Herb Abramson of Atlantic Records told was that singer Herb Lance wrote the song with his friend Johnny Wallace after they heard a busker on an Atlanta street sing what was probably the Blind Lemon Jefferson tune, which is a kinder way of saying the two songwriters just appropriated an existing ditty and called it their own. Lance, who had some fine moments in a long career, was a man burdened with a lot of psychological ticks. In 1953, when Ruth Brown was making Lance a lot of stash singing his "(Mama) He Treats Your Daughter Mean," he had to deal with a not very pretty public scandal. A "shake dancer" named Sandra Fields accused Lance of treating her very mean at a New York nightclub. Fields claimed Lance bit and kicked her while they were backstage at the Club Savannah in Greenwich Village. Fields said injuries caused by Lance's attack would disable her for six months. She intended to sue.[59] The next year, while drinking at a nightspot, he got into a scuffle with singer Titus Turner over who was the better crooner. In 1958, after the death of his two-year-old son, Lance attempted suicide with sleeping pills, slashing his wrists and, for good measure, turning on his stove's gas jets. He survived.[60]

When Atlantic Records brought the song to Brown, she wasn't comfortable with the tune thematically and couldn't, as she said, "relate to it." At the time, she was in the throes of another hot romance, this time with singer Chuck Willis, and was thinking the song would put a jinx on the relationship. Herb Abramson coaxed her into singing it partly by making the song more appealing to Brown. He upped the tempo from the slow ballad it originally was.

Brown recalled the recording session: "There was a lot of joking around the night we recorded it, for everyone present knew I was less than keen. And Willis was absent, off doing a session on his own. 'Does your man treat you mean, Ruthie?' drummer Connie Kay inquired, with mock anxiety written all over his teasin' face. 'Anybody here seen Gator?' trumpeter Taft Jordan chimed in."

After the first take, the studio musicians, with heightened concern, turned to Brown. She had to smile because everyone was so worried about how she would take to the song. That relaxed her, and the second take was spot-on.

Brown, in retrospect, mulled about the success of the song: "I can't put my finger on what was so special about that record, for the rhythm pattern was similar to a lot of stuff that was out there, but boy, did it take a trick. I was never so wrong about any piece of material in my life."[61]

Later in 1953, Brown was touring with Billy Eckstine and his band, and they put together a comedic repartee, which was really just the two of them doing Willie Mabon's talk-song "I Don't Know." It was a natural crowd pleaser and allowed Brown to hold back on what she called the "all-conquering" "(Mama) He Treats Your Daughter Mean" to the end of her set.

In April 1953, *Billboard* columnist Bob Rolontz observed the competition between "Mama" by Ruth Brown and "Hound Dog" by Willie Mae Thornton, as the two songs were "slugging it out" for top honors on the R&B charts. His observation: "This is the first time in quite a while that the women have led the field with the strongest R&B waxings [records]."[62]

As good as those songs were, in 1953, the platters were outdone by another classic female cut, Faye Adams's "Shake a Hand," the #2 R&B record of the year. Adams was so hot in 1953 she even had the #11 song, "I'll Be True," squeezed in between the answer song originals Willie Mabon's "I'm Mad" and the "5" Royales' "Baby Don't Do It."

"Shake a Hand" benefited from a religious revival of sorts on the R&B charts. It was what some trade magazines referred to as "religioso" or songs that tended in the direction of being religious but never got there.[63] In some cases, the names of the songs appeared sanctified, and that was as close as the tunes got to being blessed. For example, late in 1953, when Herald Records introduced "I'll Be True," the Faye Adams follow-up to her big hit of the year, the song had to compete with new holiday tunes such as Billy Ward and the Dominoes singing "Christmas in Heaven" or Dinah Washington getting into the act with "Silent Night" / "The Lord's Prayer."

The most obvious example is the tune that beat out "Shake a Hand" as song of the year, "Crying in the Chapel" by the Orioles. Johnny Ace sang "Cross My Heart," which sounded faintly committing—and it was, just not to God. Fats Domino lumbered on about "Going to the River," but it wasn't the Jordan River he was singing about. Finally, Billy Ward and the Dominoes unleashed "The Bells," a song that might have reeled in the naïve thinking of the Bells of St. Mary. Regarding the latter, any follower of Christianity would end up stuffing his or her ears with cotton so as not to listen to one of the most bizarre tunes of 1953.

"Shake a Hand" was written by performer and songwriter Joe Morris. The year before, Morris and his band had been touring with Little Laurie Tate as their female lead. In December, Tate was replaced by Faye Scruggs (her agent Phil Moore would change her name to Faye Adams).[64] In the spring, Morris and his Apple Jackers bagged a minor hit with the "The Applejack" on Atlantic. Soon afterward, Morris moved to the Herald label and in July it pushed into the market "Shake a Hand" with "I've Gotta Leave You" on the B side. The record read "Shake a Hand," with songwriting credit to Morris and the artist listed as Faye Adams with the Joe Morris Orchestra.

The always in-the-know *Billboard* columnist Bob Rolontz commented on August 1 about R&B artists switching labels, first mentioning Joe Morris, who was now "pacted" with Herald, and his first release would be "Shake a Hand." Then he mentioned a few more names before saying "Fay [sic] Adams, formerly Fay Scruggs with Atlantic, was now with Herald Records"—not realizing the tie-in between Morris and Adams.[65]

Three weeks later, the song noticeably began to catch on. *Cash Box*'s gossipy "Rhythm 'n' Blues Ramblings" led off its August 22, 1953, column with this note: "Excitement of the week. The 'Shake a Hand' disk put out by Herald and vocaled by Faye Adams is stirring up loads of action around New York, New Jersey, and Philadelphia. Points south are beginning to report the disk, and indications are that this will be a ree-eel BIG one."[66]

As was the practice at the time, if a song had potential, other labels would quickly issue their own versions with their own stars. One of the first to join the parade was Savannah Churchill. In one of those infrequent occurrences, *Cash Box*'s "Rhythm 'n' Blues Reviews" gave its "Award o' the Week" to both the Faye Adams and Savannah Churchill issues. The Adams review noted that, while the song wasn't a "religious item," the treatment had just enough touch of the spiritual kick. The reviewer added, "The tune is good, and the Adams vocal is top drawer." Regarding Churchill's version, the reviewer said it was "tender, warm, and well done," but differed from the Adams song in that it had more of a R&B kick with a "lapover" to the pop field.[67] And that's what happened. Churchill's "Shake" did not chart at all in the R&B field, only on the pop charts, where it did slightly better than Adams's version, climbing to #22. It would be Savannah Churchill's last charted record.

By September 19, 1953, "Shake a Hand" was the best-selling R&B song and the most played R&B tune on jukeboxes.[68] Atlantic Records realized it made a mistake letting Joe Morris and Faye Scruggs (the name change hadn't happened when she had previously signed with Atlantic) get away and wondered what could be done about it. The company still had a few Scruggs songs in the can, so it grabbed one called "Sweet Talk," added licentious jive-talk from a local disk jockey and pushed it into the market with a Joe Morris tune it also owned on the B-side. Atlantic made one mistake with the record's release. Instead of listing the singer as Faye Scruggs, it used Faye Adams, which was the name she signed contracts with at Herald Records. The company threatened to sue Atlantic. The best overview of the two record labels that refused to shake a hand was from *Jet*, which reported: "Herald Record executives threatened to file a legal action against Atlantic Records, claiming that Atlantic illegally published an 'over-sexed' record by Faye Adams. . . . Herald executives said Atlantic, which once had Miss Adams under contract, released a record she made for them called 'Sweet Talk' after dubbing in sizzling lover words . . ."[69]

Not even "Sweet Talk" could slow down "Shake a Hand," which by the first week in November had been the #1 record on the R&B charts for eight straight weeks.[70] When it became a category killer, the African American press took note. The *Detroit Tribune*, picking up a wire service story, reported the song had begun to "move onto the popularity charts usually reserved for so-called 'pop' tunes." As the story explained, it had been "generally assumed that R&B record styles were salable only in limited markets. Not long ago, they were even referred to as 'race' records and were beamed primarily to Negro audiences. With 'Shake a Hand,' the results have been different."[71]

When Faye Adams began touring with the Joe Morris Band in October, Morris tried to maintain the superior position. An ad for the District Theater in Roanoke, Virginia, reads: "On Stage: National Sensations of 'Shake a Hand' and Joe Morris 'Torrid Trumpet King' and his Famous Apple Jackers starring Faye Adams."[72] That didn't last long, as seen by this news item one month later: "Coming to Key West Wednesday, December 16, in person, Faye Adams's 'Shake a Hand' with the Joe Morris Band."[73]

It wasn't the official tally, but on December 19, 1953, *Billboard* listed 1953's top R&B records according to retail sales. The top three songs on that list were all by women in descending order from #1: "(Mama) He Treats Your Daughter Mean," "Shake a Hand," and "Hound Dog."

CHAPTER FIVE

TEACH ME TONIGHT (1954)

FRED MENDELSOHN AND AL SILVER—CHARLES SINGLETON— FAYE ADAMS—HENRY GLOVER—LULA REED—LINDA HAYES— RUTH BROWN—CHUCK WILLIS—DINAH WASHINGTON— PATTI AUSTIN—BOSWELL SISTERS—ANDREWS SISTERS— THE DREAMERS (THE BLOSSSOMS)— SHIRLEY GUNTER AND THE QUEENS

The rise of Faye Adams had a lot to do with the murky, double-dealing contentiousness of the independent labels on the East Coast, which were pushing to enter the R&B market.

The story begins with Fred Mendelsohn, a thirty-year-old former jukebox operator who decided to get into the rough-and-tumble record business by starting his own label, Regent Records, in New Jersey. He had limited capital and distribution capabilities, so he began discussions with another New Jersey operator, Herman Lubinsky of Savoy Records. They struck a deal whereby Savoy would take on distribution and Mendelsohn would remain president of Regent. One year later, Mendelsohn was bought out as Lubinsky took control of Regent. Mendelsohn landed on his feet, ending up with another New Jersey independent, Regal Records, owned by David and Jules Braun. Regent didn't press its own records. Instead, it turned to a small company owned by Al Silver and his brother-in-law that operated a record-pressing plant in lower Manhattan.

Mendelsohn itched to have his own label and in 1952 talked Silver and his brother-in-law into joining him to create Herald Records in Elizabeth, New Jersey. Silver recalled, "He [Mendelsohn] had no capital when he started Herald. We had little, but we had a pressing plant, so we formed a corporation. He brought us a bunch of Little Walter masters, which we put out. Nothing happened." The start-up wasn't paying anyone a salary, and Mendelsohn had a family to support, so he had to walk away. Silver and his brother-in-law decided to maintain Herald because the one thing they learned from Mendelsohn was that there was plenty of R&B talent in the New York metropolitan area, and that talent was very, very hungry.

One of those insatiable guys was a songwriter named Charles Singleton (he would be best known for his song "Strangers in the Night"), who had recently moved to New York from Florida. Singleton not only kept pushing songs to Silver, but would bring Herald up-and-coming singers that he knew, one of whom was trumpeter Joe Morris. The talented musician had previously been at Atlantic Records, where he had wanted to record a song called "Shake a Hand." It never happened, and Joe Morris's Atlantic contract expired. Morris was hungry for a new label, so his buddy Singleton did him a big favor, arranging a meeting with Silver at the ballroom in the Hotel America in Manhattan. It was like an audition. Morris and his band played a number of tunes, which Silver recalled as being low-down Southern blues. Morris also had brought along other performers with whom he was connected. Silver was impressed by Morris and ready to end the meeting when Morris pushed a singer named Al Savage forward. He sang a tune called "I Had a Notion," which Silver liked. Great, okay, two good performers to sign, business concluded, or so Silver thought. Then Morris called forward a slight young lady who had been sitting quietly in the back of the ballroom.

"Faye Scruggs—that was her name then," Silver remembered. "After he introduced her to me, she sang 'Shake a Hand' without a mike in front of that big, blasting band—and I got goose pimples."

Silver signed them all: Morris, Savage, a kid named Stringbean, and Faye Scruggs, although he claimed he didn't know that she was still signed to Atlantic at the time.

Silver, who had been a record manufacturer before starting Herald, now had to become a record producer. Singleton had to help him because Silver really didn't know what he was doing in the recording studio. Herald booked time at the Bell Sound Studio in Manhattan and brought in Joe Morris's band as backing musicians. They cut four singles (eight songs) with Faye Adams; one single, "I Had a Notion" / "I'll Be True," with Al Savage; and even a single with Stringbean.

(Silver claims he was the one who didn't like the name Faye Scruggs, so he changed it to Faye Adams, which sounded more professional. Her manager Phil Moore made the same claim.)

A short time later, Silver was vacationing with his wife at a Catskills resort when he was paged. There was a phone call for him. He picked up the receiver and it was his brother-in-law breathlessly screaming, "Al, I don't know what you want to do. That 'Shake a Hand' broke wide open! We're getting orders from Cincinnati for 10,000, from Chicago for 20,000 . . ." Herald hadn't yet fully pressed the record, and in the first three to four days, 300,000 to 400,000 orders had come in.

"That record went on to sell a million copies," Silver said. "When 'Shake a Hand' was tapering, we put out Al Savage's 'I Had a Notion." That hit and sold 400,000. To follow 'Shake a Hand,' we put out Faye Adams doing "I'll Be True," and that sold 800,000."[1]

Faye Adams (Fannie Tuell) was born in Newark (possibly Montclair), New Jersey, in 1923. Her father was a gospel singer, and at the age of five, she joined with her two sisters to form the Tuell Sisters, a gospel group. According to the *Afro-American* of September 5, 1953, the Tuell Sisters earned a regular Sunday morning gig at WHBI radio station in Newark.

At the age of sixteen, she won first prize at the Apollo's famous Amateur Night. Three years later, she married Tommy Scruggs, who, in a time-honored tradition, became her business manager. Her big break came when Ruth Brown saw her perform in an Atlanta nightclub and recommended Adams to talent manager Phil Moore. The amazing "Shake a Hand" came in 1953.[2]

At the close of that year, Adams recorded "I'll Be True" with "Happiness to My Soul" on the B-side. Despite the romantic lines "just treat me kind and tender and I'll be true to you," this was a blues rocker of a song. Her backing band was once again the Joe Morris Orchestra. The song rolled into 1954 building momentum, and early in the year dropped into the #1 slot on regional R&B charts. It was one of four songs by females to make the Top Twenty R&B in 1954. Adams and Ruth Brown split the successes: Ruth Brown's "Oh What a Dream" at #7, Faye Adams's "Hurts Me to My Heart" at #11, Faye Adams's "I'll Be True" at #13, and Ruth Brown's "Mambo Baby" at #15.

Adams hit the road to support the song, usually as part of a wide package of performers. These tours were real moneymakers. The *Arizona Sun* reported a Faye Adams/Orioles/Joe Morris Orchestra show grossed $4,000 (about $40,000 in 2021 dollars) in Charleston. Herald Records wisely strung together its own show for an early 1954 appearance at the Apollo. This one had Faye Adams teamed with the other Herald stalwarts Joe Morris, Al "I Had a Notion" Savage, and Mr. Stringbean. Then came the female blockbuster show in Detroit during the middle of the summer. LaVern Baker, Big Maybelle, and Faye Adams really turned up the July thermostat on that one.[3]

With the women packing venues, "I'll Be True" arrived at a strange moment in 1954. It was a desert out there for female voices on the radio. In March, when "I'll Be True" was riding high on *Billboard*'s Best-Sellers in Stores and Most Played on Jukeboxes charts, there were no other female singers in the Top Ten. It just shows how appealing that record was because at the time, Guitar Slim's "The Things That I Used to Do" was #1 just about everywhere on R&B charts across the country. Also not doing badly were "Money Honey" by

Clyde McPhatter and the Drifters, "You'll Never Walk Alone" by Roy Hamilton, "You're So Fine" by Little Walter, and "I'm Your Hoochie Coochie Man" by Muddy Waters.[4]

Meanwhile, Herald Records got Adams back in the recording studio, where she recorded "Hurts Me to My Heart" with "Ain't Gonna Tell" on the B-side. It was irrepressible. On August 21, 1954, *Billboard* rushed out its review of the song: "It looks as if Faye Adams has come up with another good one. The platter is getting attention throughout the country and is particularly strong in the South."[5] The trade publication was a little late. In the same issue, on the same page, *Billboard* ran its best-sellers, and in its first week on the market, "Hurts Me to My Heart" made the chart. Ahead of it, for its third week, was Ruth Brown's "Oh What a Dream." Columnist Rolontz, who had noticed the dearth of successful female recordings early that year, commented, "The thrushes have proved they can come back, took, this week, with both Ruth Brown and Faye Adams on the chart."[6]

One month later, Rolontz returned to the same theme, writing: "A few weeks ago, *Billboard*'s Best-Sellers and Most Played in Jukeboxes R&B charts were dominated by groups or male singers. At the time, the girls were having a tough time coming up with a hit." He then cited Ruth Brown's "Oh What a Dream" as "now in the top slot on the juke chart," and Faye Adams's "Hurts Me to My Heart," the "third best-selling record," as showing that "you can't keep a good woman down." He then mentioned Ruth Brown out on the road doing one-nighters and Faye Adams "scoring big in her first engagement as a single" with the giant R&B one-nighter package.[7] Stringing one-nighters on a long road trip was grueling, but it was where the money was made.

What was an interesting coincidence to the last Rolontz meanderings about the dearth of successful records by female singers was that on the same page as the "This Week's Best Buys" column, which reviewed new records that were already showing significant sales, was "I Don't Hurt Anymore" by Dinah Washington. A commentary explained that the song was moving slowly but steadily forward since its release the month before and had the potential to make the national charts.[8] It already was on the St. Louis and Los Angeles Top Ten charts and was a strong seller in Nashville and Cleveland, while still climbing in five other major cities.[9]

By the first week in October, it was "Oh What a Dream" versus "Hurts Me to My Heart" for the top position in metro record charts across the country. Meanwhile, coming into Top Ten lists were Dinah Washington's "I Don't Hurt Anymore" and "Oop Shoop," the first successful single by an all-female doo-wop group, Shirley Gunter and the Queens.

One month later, the ladies were back in force. "I Don't Hurt Anymore" was now #1 in a handful of cities, while still on the charts were "Oh What a Dream,"

"Hurts Me to My Heart," and "Oop Shoop." There was also one newcomer crashing the Top Ten, Ruth Brown's "Mambo Baby."[10]

In the first week of November 1954, *Cash Box* finally caught on to the year's female renaissance. Its gossip column "Rhythm 'n' Blues Ramblings" began this way: "The women are back! Whereas some months back, the only fem represented in the charts was Lula Reed, today the lists are headed by Ruth Brown, Atlantic; Faye Adams, Herald; and Dinah Washington, Mercury, with two songs. Also headed straight for the big numbers is Ruth Brown's latest, 'Mambo Baby.' Shirley Gunter on Flair was a recent occupant of the charts and still is in certain cities with her 'Oop Shoop.'"[11]

The big question in all that naming of names was: Who was Lula Reed? To answer that question, it's first necessary to recall an overlooked African American music pioneer named Henry Glover, who was not only a fine trumpet player, but over a long career touched every point in the creation of a hit song, including being an excellent songwriter. When Syd Nathan founded Cincinnati-based King Records in 1945, his shrewdest move was bringing in Glover, who became the company's arranger, producer, and just about everything else. As a songwriter, he wrote (among many, many other tunes) "Peppermint Twist" for Joey Dee and the Starliters, "Let the Little Girl Dance" for Billy Band, "Annie Had a Baby" for Hank Ballard, "Baby, I'm Doin' It" for Annisteen Allen, "I'll Be There" for Esther Phillips, and "It Ain't the Meat (It's the Motion)" for "Bull Moose" Jackson.[12] In 1951 and 1952, Glover wrote two tunes for singer and bandleader Sonny Thompson, "I'll Drown in My Tears" and "Let's Call It a Day," which went to #5 and #7 on the R&B charts, respectively. The lead singer for Sonny Thompson was a young lady named Lula Reed with a high Dinah Washington pitch.

Lula Reed was born Lula Marietta McClelland in 1926 in Mingo Junction, Ohio, which at the time was a bustling up-and-coming community with a population of 4,600.[13] In January 1953, she caught the attention of *Jet*, which lushly, if not dubiously, described Lula in January 1953 as: "A pretty 22-year-old vocalist, who was singing in a Port Clinton, Ohio, church choir a year ago, was acclaimed by recording officials and disc jockey as the singing find of the year. After racking up five successive songs as a vocalist for Sonny Thompson's band . . . Lulu was awarded a gold record of each of the five songs she made jukebox favorites for King Records and was named the Girl of the Year by the Southwest Association of Disc Jockeys."[14]

Reed was considered a very attractive songstress, which according to *Jet* made her a favorite among servicemen. She was voted "Favorite Pinup Girl" by GIs at Fort Smith in Arkansas.

Reed began singing in the local church choir. In 1952, she defeated fifty other contestants for a vocal spot with Sonny Thompson's band. Her first recordings were with Sonny Thompson for King Records in 1951.[15] Around 1953, King decided to record Reed as a singles act, and toward the end of that year she recorded "Your Key Don't Fit No More" with "Watch Dog." The very soulful "Your Key" was a powerfully deliberate groove that *Billboard* in January 1954 noted was "an attractive slow blues reading by the thrush." As for the B-side, "Watch Dog," the magazine mentioned, "More good stuff here via the gal's style and projections."[16] As good as "Your Key" sounded, it was the prefeminist anthem "Watch Dog" ("I don't want no man being a watchdog over me") that got the attention of disk jockeys and made some of the local Top Ten charts. Although it wasn't a national hit, the beautiful singer was voted fourth most popular R&B singer of the year by *Cash Box*. She never had another hit, occasionally switching back to her roots to sing gospel.

Her name was forgotten, but not some of her songs. "I'll Drown in My Tears" was transformed by Ray Charles into "Drown in My Own Tears," a #1 song for him in 1956. In 1955, Reed released a Henry Glover song called "Rock Love," which was exactly what it claimed to be, a chirpy pre-rock 'n' roll tune. The Fontane Sisters quickly covered it. Lula Reed's version was forgotten, while the Fontane Sisters had a hit song that rose to #13 on the pop charts.

Another female singer who occasionally recorded for King Records did a little better in terms of record-buyer recognition despite being born with a name to similar to Lula. She was born Bertha Lulu Williams in December 1923 in Linden, New Jersey, and was known professionally as Linda Hayes, which was the appellation underneath "Yes, I Know," her successful answer record to Willie Mabon's "I Don't Know."[17]

Hayes's first big break occurred when her family moved to Los Angeles. This was at a time when South Central Los Angeles was beginning to feed the local nightspots with musicians, and the independent labels were looking for local R&B talent to record. There was so much talent in South Central, the guys were always bumping up against each other, forming singing groups that would disband, form again with new players, and then re-form under a different name. For example, as a young teenager, Gaynel Hodge (co writer of the doo-wop classic "Earth Angel") played with the Hollywood Flames ("Buzz Buzz Buzz," a #11 best-selling song in 1957) and a couple of other groups in the early 1950s. He was doing very well for himself when his mother asked him, "Can you help your brother Alex get a group together?" Gaynel introduced Alex to Cornell Gunter, and with the addition of Herb Reed and Joe Jefferson, a new group called the Platters was formed. That was in 1952. A year later, Gunter left to become a member of the Flares ("Foot Stompin', Part 1," a Top Twenty-Five best-seller in 1961), a group that originally formed in 1952 as the Debonairs and included Richard Berry, who wrote "Louie Louie" (a #2 record for the Kingsmen in 1963). Gunter was replaced by Tony Williams, who was Linda Hayes's brother.[18]

Gaynel Hodge's "Earth Angel" was recorded by another local group, the Penguins, which quickly became unhappy with its label, Dootone. That caught the attention of talent manager Samuel "Buck" Ram, who had already taken on the Platters. He snagged the Penguins and pitched both groups to Mercury Records, which jumped to get the "Earth Angel" singers. Ram was smarter. He used the devolving Penguins to get the unknown Platters signed.

The Platters' first recording in January 1953 was "Hey Now" backed by "Give Thanks." Singing with the group for that recording session was Linda Hayes— the first female to sing with the Platters. Her slot would be taken by Zola Taylor, who became a regular in the classic Platters lineup.

While her brother was recording with Federal Records, Hayes signed with Recorded in Hollywood, a small LA label. Her first platter in her own name was "Yes! I Know (What You're Putting Down)," which was recorded with the Red Callender Sextette. The tune went to #3 on the R&B charts. She followed that up with a bomb of a record, "Atomic Baby."[19] Hayes melodically warned: "I've got a high potential and a low resistance point / Better handle me with care or baby I'll blow up the joint."

Billboard barely recognized it, swiftly commenting: "A fine performance of a straightforward lyric over a rumba backbeat." The market ignored the song as well. At the end of 1953, Hayes recorded "Take Me Back" with "Yours for the Asking," this time with Munroe Tucker and his band. It scored well regionally, first charting in New Orleans and the Washington, DC–Baltimore market before working its way nationally. The tune climbed to #10 on the R&B charts.[20]

Once again, the follow-up failed, so Hayes went back to her most successful formula, the answer record. This time she tried to piggyback on Hank Ballard's successful "Annie" records. Hayes's answer was titled "My Name Ain't Annie." *Billboard* wasn't enthused, writing: "Tune is fine, the beat is solid, and so is the performance, but the lyrics are dirty, and the disk is not recommended for deejay use."[21]

Hayes toured to support her records, never quite getting to the top of the marquee. In February 1954, she was to appear in Phoenix, and a large top-of-the-page to bottom-of-the-page promotion was run in the local African American newspaper. The headliner was Pee Wee Crayton followed by Linda Hayes. Whoever put together the advertisement clearly didn't know who Hayes was. Her section read: "Linda Hayes, song stylist, catapulted to national prominence with the recordings of 'Blues after Hours' and 'Texas Hop,'" two songs that Crayton recorded, not her.[22] In March, "Theatrically Yours" reported: "Eddie Boyd is now heading out for the first swing through the East. He will play one-nighters with thrush Linda Hayes."[23] Once again, she was the B-card. Linda Hayes, as a solo act, was back in Arizona in August, playing at the Elks' Home. The promotion issued an explanation as to who she was: "The sensational West

Coast vocal artist. . . . She will vocalize all her blues hits."[24] She had two hits, but apparently the *Arizona Sun* didn't know what they were.

Linda Hayes recorded very sporadically through the 1950s and then faded away. Interestingly, one Linda Hayes discography shows King Records later issuing a record with Annisteen Allen's "Baby I'm Doin' It" on one side and Hayes's "My Name Ain't Annie" on the other.

In April 1954, *Billboard* spotlighted the R&B market, with a lengthy story on the success of the independent labels. The story's author concluded, "Any major label would consider itself a mighty important factor in the business if it could consistently rack up the business in rhythm & blues records done by independents." The columnist also observed that male vocalists continued to dominate the genre as they had "for many years" before naming the women who were "hitting steadily" or rising in recent months: Dinah Washington, Ruth Brown, Faye Adams, Linda Hayes, Lulu Reed, Willie Mae Thornton, Big Maybelle, Varetta Dillard, Mercy Dee (who was a man, not a woman), and Christine Kittrell.[25]

A Cuban dance called the mambo first came to prominence in the 1940s and swept across Latin America and into the United States by the early 1950s. For songwriters, the mambo's moment arrived in 1954. On the pop charts, Rosemary Clooney's "Mambo Italiano" was a Top Ten hit (and #1 in the UK market). In an odd coincidence, Cuban bandleader Pérez Prado, the king of mambo, on June 20, 1954, appeared at the Cavalcade of Jazz concert in Los Angeles. Also on the bill were the Flairs (or Flares), founded by Richard Berry and Cornell Gunter.

The R&B world slowly came around. The "Rhythm 'n' Blues Reviews" column in the October 9, 1954, issue of *Cash Box* featured a tune by Linda Hayes and the Platters called "I Just Wanna Mambo." The review was tepid: "A pleasant mambo that should make a good buy for those interested in the hot kick." The song evaporated in the marketplace. That same week, the "Award o' the Week" went to another mambo cut, Ruth Brown's "Mambo Baby." The reviewer was overjoyed to say the least: "How much better than #1 can you get? Ruth Brown, currently sitting astride the rhythm & blues lists with 'Oh What a Dream,' has a delirious mambo item that should rocket through the nation's charts in record-breaking time. . . . Just to make sure that record sales have been nailed to the mast, the deck has a 'crazy' handclap effect that lends the arrangement individuality." The reviewer declaimed the song as a must for R&B radio stations and a wholehearted recommendation for any pop location.[26]

"Mambo Baby" became a #1 hit on the R&B charts. Whatever potential the song had for the pop charts was diminished when Mercury Records rushed to the market Georgia Gibbs's cover of the song. It didn't do much except blunt Ruth Brown from having a crossover hit.

"Mambo Baby" was the fifteenth best-selling R&B tune in 1954, and it wasn't even Brown's best effort. The top song by a female on the R&B charts for the year was Ruth Brown's "Oh What a Dream," also a #1 song and the seventh best-selling R&B platter of the year.

"Oh What a Dream" was written for Ruth Brown by singer-songwriter Chuck Willis, who is best known for his #1 R&B tune from 1957, "C.C. Rider," which was also a crossover hit, rising to #12 on the pop charts. Chuck Willis wrote many great songs, including "My Story," his #2 R&B hit in 1952, and "It's Too Late," his #3 R&B hit in 1956. The irony about "C.C. Rider" was that he didn't write it. The original version of the song, "See See Rider Blues," was by Ma Rainey in 1924, with numerous versions in the 1920s and 1930s by bluesmen such as Blind Lemon Jefferson, Big Bill Broonzy, and Leadbelly. Wee Bea Booze had a #1 R&B hit in 1943 with the song and actually crossed over to the pop charts. Chuck Willis got his chance at the tune fourteen years later.[27]

In the spring of 1954, Brown and Chuck Willis were at the Atlantic offices discussing new material. Brown turned to Willis and half-jokingly said, "When are going to write a song for me?" Willis was surprised. He stuttered, "Are you kidding? Do you really want a song from me?" Ruth quickly responded, "Of course, I do. I've never been more serious about anything."

Willis had been working on a soft ballad at the time. It was definitely something Ruth Brown could handle, and he told her he might have something "perfect" for another record. A few weeks later, Willis showed her the lyrics written out on a yellow legal pad and hummed a slow, bluesy tune called "Oh What a Dream." In May, Jesse Stone came up with a great arrangement, and the song was recorded.[28] The moody ballad jumped up the R&B charts with enthusiasm, not stopping until it hit #1. Writer Larry Birnbaum wrote that the song was "a slow ballad featuring a soulful tenor sax solo by Arnett Cobb and a . . . base line sung by a doo-wop group."[29]

If there was a chance of crossover appeal, that was killed quickly when Patti Page covered the song as "What a Dream," which became a Top Ten hit on the pop charts.

On September 11, 1954, with "Oh What a Dream" #1 in New Orleans and New York and #2 in the far-flung cities of Chicago, San Francisco, Newark, and Memphis, the gossipy "Stars Over Harlem" column in *Cash Box* reported that Atlantic Records' Ahmet Ertegun and Miriam Abramson had stopped by the magazine's offices "to keep us posted on the activities of Ruth Brown, whose 'Oh What a Dream' etching has caused the dynamic singing miss to once again take to the open roads for engagements from border to border and coast to coast."[30]

After a slow start to the year for female R&B singers, on November 6, 1954, they could boast five of the top fifteen R&B songs in the country. "Oh What a Dream" was still on the charts at #2, and newcomer "Mambo Baby" had already reached #8. Stubbornly at #1 was Faye Adams's "Hurts Me to My Heart." Joining the party was Dinah Washington with two songs: "I Don't Hurt Anymore" at #4 and "Dream" at #15.

"Dream" was indeed a dream record, climbing all the way to #9 on the R&B charts. It was outdone by "I Don't Hurt Anymore," which rose to #3. As good as those songs were, they were outclassed by what was one of the best, if not classic, tunes of any genre in 1954, Dinah Washington's own "Teach Me Tonight." It rose to #4 on the R&B charts, but Washington's version of the tune was so strong and iconoclastic that it crossed over the pop charts, rising to #23, despite a dense pack of competitors, including the very hot at the time Jo Stafford, whose version rose to #15 pop.[31] The Dinah Washington version was voted into the Grammy Hall of Fame as a tune of qualitative and historical significance.

The song is a hummer and a bit unusual in that there is no musical prelude. The first sound heard is Washington's exquisite voice. She's into the song before the orchestra wakes up: "Did you say I got a lot to learn? / Oooh, teach me tonight . . . / Let's start with the A-B-Cs of it / Roll right down to the X-Y-Zs of it."

The coy but sensual lyrics are from the pen of Sammy Cahn, one of the premier lyricists of the twentieth century. He wrote so many classic songs, it would take pages to list, so we'll just mention the four that won Academy Awards: "Three Coins in the Fountain," "All the Way," "High Hopes," and "Call Me Irresponsible." His main writing partners were Jule Styne and Jimmy Van Heusen. For "Teach Me Tonight," he hooked up with the lesser-known Gene de Paul. Although not of the first tier of mid-twentieth century American pop composers, de Paul did boast one really good tune from 1942, a jazzy western novelty confection called "Cow Cow Boogie (Cuma-Ti-Yi-Yi-Ay)." The original recording was by Freddie Slack and his orchestra, which featured vocalist Ella Mae Morse. They would team up again for the hipster-rap classic "The House of Blue Lights" in 1946.

By 1954, Washington was still referred to as the "Queen of the Jukeboxes" because her songs were so popular on the machines, but she was bridging into another form of stardom. The *Detroit Tribune* called her "America's foremost blues and ballad stylist."[32]

The "Stars Over Harlem" column in the November 1954 issue of *Cash Box* couldn't help itself, declaring the ". . . staffmen working like champions filling the many orders pouring in for copies of the new 'Teach Me Tonight' sizzler, which stars the Dinah of Washington. This baby is also showing signs of being the greatest yet for the wailing jukebox queen."[33]

Cash Box's "Rhythm 'n' Blues Ramblings" column one month later noted that Bob Shad, A&R man at Mercury, "was clicking like train wheels moving at 100 MPH." The reason for Shad's excitement: "His Mercury-Dinah Washington releases are riding merrily in the charts with two big sellers at the same time.

Dinah, who was really hot with 'I Don't Hurt Anymore,' has another torrid item in 'Teach Me Tonight.' Both items are selling like pizza pies in Coney Island."[34]

There are probably as many anecdotes about Dinah Washington and her cussing mouth as there are about her kindness to other singers. Singer Patti Austin told what is probably the only tale about Dinah Washington in which she helps a mere tyke climb her way to stardom. Austin was a four-year-old going with her mother and father to see Washington at the Apollo Theater. Her father, Gordon Austin, was an old friend of Washington's, and as a special treat, they went to meet the singer backstage before the show. After introductions by Gordon Austin, Washington leaned down to the very young Patti and said, "Hi, I'm Dinah Washington, and I'm a singer." The little girl replied, "Well, I'm Patti Austin, and I'm a singer, too." After everyone stopped laughing, Washington told Patti, "Well if you're a singer, you're going to sing tonight." That was just fine with Patti. When asked what she was going to sing, Patti responded, "I'll sing 'Teach Me Tonight' in B flat."

As she retold the story years later, Patti said, "It was a big hit for her [Washington], and that's how I knew it, from hearing it at home."[35]

In a year on the pop charts when Perry Como's "Wanted," Eddie Fisher's "Oh My Papa," the Gaylords' "The Little Shoemaker," and Frank Weir's "The Happy Wanderer" were all major hits, Dinah Washington's "Teach Me Tonight" was pure bliss and the only classic tune to emerge out of the detritus of pop music in 1954.

This isn't to say some mighty interesting things weren't happening in America's music world, especially on the distaff side. You wouldn't find it on the pop charts, and there was just a hint of it on the R&B charts; but the future was coming.

In 1976, *Rolling Stone* magazine published a softcover coffee table book called *The Rolling Stone Illustrated History of Rock & Roll*. Squeezed between chapters on Buddy Holly and the rise of Top Forty AM radio were eight pages dedicated to doo-wop. Of all the picture pages in this chapter, there is one aggregation of twenty mid-1950s doo-wop groups, everyone from the El Dorados to the Rivingtons to the Monotones. In all of those pictures there isn't one female. The Platters were the first big-time doo-wop group to add a woman, when Zola Taylor joined the boys. Even with the addition of a strong singer like Zola, the Platters' distinctive voice emanated from lead singer Tony Williams. From its beginnings, which some date back to the late 1940s recordings of the Orioles and the Ravens, doo-wop was a male province.

It took a half decade, until 1954, before young ladies came on the scene, and it was only for a brief moment, but that was long enough to point the way for the earliest, strongest period for female singers in the rock 'n' roll canon, the girl group sound of the early 1960s.

In the annals of popular American music, the concept of a girl group was like a slow train running—but never getting to the station. Outside of hillbilly music, which became country & western, the idea that three or four women should get together to form a professional singing group never really gelled except in the odd case of sister acts—and that was generally in the popular music genre. Sister acts in what was once called "race" music and then R&B were rarer than a white rhinoceros on the African plains.

The Duncan Sisters were a white vaudeville act at the turn of the twentieth century sometimes appearing in blackface. They segued into early motion pictures and along the way recorded a few tunes, some of which were quite popular. However, the real pioneering girl group act of the twentieth century was the Boswell Sisters. The young women began recording in the early 1930s and became extremely popular as they came to prominence during a period of increasing record sales (capitalizing on the new electrical disc-playing machine, heavily marketed at the end of the 1920s) and their success on the second (after the phonograph) of one of the great new media technologies of the early twentieth century: radio. The Boswell Sisters were stars of the airwaves. Eventually, they even made appearances in motion pictures. Most importantly, they were a very successful and imitated musical act. From 1931 to 1938, the Boswell Sisters charted twenty Top Twenty records, including their biggest hit, a 1934 #1 record "The Object of My Affection."

The Boswell Sisters consisted of three ladies, Martha, Connee, and Hel-vetia (Vet) Boswell, who were brought up in a middle-class family in New Orleans, which was very important because in the early twentieth century, New Orleans was the original laboratory of a new sound in America, jazz. The girls all received classical musical training, but oddly enough, their mother was an enthusiast of the endemic New Orleans sound and regularly took her three girls and older son to hear local jazz and blues musicians swing out. The girls from a young age heard some of the best jazz players of the day as they were growing up in the 1910s and 1920s (they were born between 1905 and 1911).[36]

America's first popular girl group owed some of its success to jazz and blues that definitely tinged their best recordings. Bits and pieces of their music borrowings were obvious, such as recordings of "Darktown Strutters' Ball" or "St. Louis Blues," but they made some strangely prescient records as well. In 1931, the girls picked up a song called "Shout, Sister, Shout" written by African American jazz pianist and composer Clarence Williams and really swung the syncopation, doing their New Orleans heritage proud. In 1931, the girls moved to New York and signed with the CBS Radio network. They sang with the Dorsey Brothers, and one can hear them scatting on their hit record "Roll On, Mississippi, Roll On."

To top it off, in the 1934 film *Transatlantic Merry-Go-Round*, the Boswell Sisters sang a tune flat-out called "Rock and Roll." While the melody was not rock 'n' roll in the modern sense, the song was perky and had a chorus of "the rolling rocking rhythm of the sea." It was a Top Ten record in 1934, according to music historian Joel Whitburn.

"The Boswell Sisters were one of the most innovative American vocal groups ever," exclaimed musicologist Larry Birnbaum. "They anticipated rock music by adopting jazz rhythms and African American inflections with an authenticity that few other white artists could match."[37]

The Boswells can also be credited with starting a trend that continues today, the girl group break-up. After five years on the charts, the Boswell Sisters went their separate ways in 1936. They were quickly replaced in the hearts, minds, and ears of the American public with an even more popular girl group, another sister act, the Andrews Sisters.

The Andrews Sisters came along quickly after the Boswells, first recording in 1937. They were so successful right out of the gate and for a decade beyond that the Boswell Sisters have been all but forgotten except among the most dedicated musicologists. The Andrews Sisters' first big hit was a straight-up swing tune called "Jammin'," and it was for its time a jammin' record. As good as it was, the song that put the Andrews Sisters on the musical map was their next platter, the 1937 #1 recording of "Bei Mir Bist Du Schön" (Means That You're Grand)". The ladies had their final #1 record in 1950 with "I Wanna Be Loved" just as the group began to evaporate, with Patty going her own way.

LaVerne, Maxene, and Patricia (Patty) Andrews were born between 1911 and 1918 and started their career imitating the Boswell Sisters before becoming who they really were, the Andrew Sisters of swing. During their years together, the three women sold seventy-five million records and were the most successful girl group of the first half of the twentieth century.[38] There are probably a dozen records one can pick out as the quintessential Andrews Sisters recording, but most people would say their greatest record, which still sounds as fresh today as when it was when it was released in 1940, is "Boogie Woogie Bugle Boy."

For a twenty-five-year period, the girl group concept continued to be dominated by sister acts, with the last of the successful sister combos recording through most of the 1950s. Again a threesome, the last big go-round for the sibling concept was the McGuire Sisters: Christine, Dorothy (Dottie), and Phyllis (all born between 1926 and 1931). By the time the McGuire Sisters began recording, the world had changed substantially. If the Boswell Sisters and Andrews Sisters were given kudos for being early adapters of African American rhythms, by the 1950s it was felt that white groups such as the McGuire Sisters were now stealing from African American musicians through what were called "cover records." In the mid-1950s, radio playlists were not fully integrated, and records by African American singers that became popular on the R&B charts would be "covered" by white singers for the pop charts, thus diminishing record sales for the original artist.

The success of these three individual girl group/sister acts in the 1930s, 1940s, and 1950s masked what was really happening on the female side of popular music, where the greatest achievement came with individual recording acts, both on the mainstream and R&B charts. Oddly, as the 1940s slid into the 1950s, an unusual bifurcation happened in song booths, radio stations, and eventually on the music charts as well. In the early 1950s, mainstream radio stations were playing a lot more female recording acts, resulting in considerable chart success for the ladies. On the R&B scene, the exact opposite was happening. The success of the doo-wop group sound pushed female singers off the charts because the girl group concept didn't yet exist (except for sister acts who were white).

Looking at *Billboard*'s mainstream chart listings, we can discern a pattern. In 1949, of the top thirty songs, very few were by female artists, just two individual efforts: Evelyn Knight's "A Little Bird Told Me" and Dinah Shore's "Buttons and Bows." In addition, Margaret Whiting, the Andrews Sisters, Jo Stafford, and the Fontane Sisters (another three-sister act, Bea, Geri and Marge Rosse) all had big hits teaming up with a male singer. At the start of the 1950s, the women did a little better, with Teresa Brewer, Eileen Barton, Kay Starr, and Patti Page (two songs) all charting Top Thirty songs in 1950. The Andrews Sisters and Kay Starr also teamed up with male counterparts for big hits.

In 1952, female singers had really become a force as the top thirty songs of that year included hits by Kay Starr, Jo Stafford (two hits), Vera Lynn, Rosemary Clooney (two hits), Patti Page, Georgia Gibbs, Ella Mae Morse, and Doris Day.

In comparison, *Billboard* reported that of the twenty songs that reached #1 on the R&B charts in 1948, only two were by women: Julia Lee and Her Boy Friends' "King Size Papa" and Dinah Washington's "Am I Asking Too Much." The next year, there were only a dozen #1 songs on the R&B charts, and all but one, Dinah Washington's "Baby Get Lost," were by men.

By the early 1950s, the first doo-wop songs began to dominate the R&B charts, so if we skip ahead to 1951, we see the emergence of such classic doo-wop numbers as "The Glory of Love" by the Five Keys and "Sixty-Minute Man" by the Dominoes. Also released in that year was what some people consider the first true rock 'n' roll song, "Rocket 88" by Jackie Brenston and his Delta Cats. That year, there were thirteen #1 records on the R&B charts, none by women.

From 1952 through 1955, the only women to have #1 songs on the R&B charts sang in the classic R&B vein and not in what was proving to be the more progressive music movements of doo-wop and pre-rock 'n' roll. Breaking through in that four-year period were Ruth Brown with "5–10–15 Hours," "(Mama) He Treats Your Daughter Mean," "Oh What a Dream," and "Mambo Baby"; Willie

Mae "Big Mama" Thornton with "Hound Dog"; Faye Adams with "Shake a Hand," "I'll Be True," and "It Hurts Me to My Heart"; Etta James with "The Wallflower"; and Priscilla Bowman, who sang "Hands Off" with Jay McShann and his orchestra—just enough women to form a basketball team.

The time was ripe for the women to make the dual jump—to doo-wop and forming girl groups—just as the men had done, singing these intricate vocal group harmonies that emerged from the big cities.

In the doo-wop hothouse of South Central Los Angeles, the kids were having their day. Those who grew up there in the early 1950s generally went to either Jefferson or Fremont high schools. In 1954, Fanita James (Barrett), a student at Fremont, teamed up with five other girls to form a sextet called the Dreamers. One of their friends was another student, Dexter Tisby, who sang with the Penguins of "Earth Angel" fame.[39] According to writer John Clemente, Tisby introduced the Dreamers to his friend, up-and-coming singer/songwriter Richard Berry. Fanita James remembered it differently, that Johnny Otis introduced them, which is possible because, again from Clemente, Otis spotted the girls at a local talent show and began using them as backing vocalists. By this time, two of the girls dropped out, and the lineup was now Fanita, Gloria Jones, and sisters Nanette and Annette Williams.[40]

In 1954, Richard Berry and the Dreamers recorded two singles for Flair Records, "Bye Bye" and Savannah Churchill's "Daddy, Daddy," and in 1955, one more song, "Together." Not much came out of these records, but the group continued their session work, backing up another local girl, Etta James. "I didn't know her personally," said Fanita James. "We just met in the studio, but she was real nice, a hard worker." By 1957, the quartet became the Blossoms when they signed with Capitol Records. In 1958, when Nanette left the group, she was replaced by Darlene Love (Wright). In the early 1960s, Fanita and Darlene joined with Bobby Sheen to form Bob B. Soxx and the Blue Jeans, who had a hit in 1963 with "Why Do Lovers Break Each Other's Heart." As a Bob B. Soxx, Fanita toured with LaVern Baker, who she remembered as "very demanding."

Also making their way into recording studios in 1954 were two pioneering R&B groups, the Hearts to record "Lonely Nights" and Shirley Gunter with the Queens to record "Oop Shoop." In the race to be the first girl group to make the best-seller list in the doo-wop world, Shirley Gunter and her girls got into the studio quicker and received the little amount of glory that came with that distaff distinction of being first. The song's catchy doo-wop chorus went something like this: "Oop shoopy dooby dooby, Oop shooby-dooby dooby, Oop shoopy-dooby dooby, Oop shooby dooba."

There were so many South Central LA singers and songwriters in the 1950s, they caromed against each other like bumper cars. Gaynel Hodge remembered one afternoon when Arthur Lee (who fronted the rock group Love in the mid-1960s) came over to his house with Johnny "Guitar" Watson and Curtis Williams (the third cowriter of "Earth Angel"). They were all sitting around when Cornell Gunter showed up, bringing his sister Shirley Gunter with him.[41]

Pop music history books, if there is any mention at all of a female doo-wop group, always give a nod to Shirley Gunter and the Queens as the only significant all-girl doo-wop group in the mid-1950s because of their 1954 hit record "Oop Shoop."

Shirley signed with her brother's record company, Flair, and like other R&B singers, went out on her own. With no success as a solo artist, Shirley then formed the Four Queens with Blondean Taylor, Lula B. Kenney, and Lula Mae Suggs in late 1953 or early 1954. Blondean and Shirley sat down together and scratched out the nonsensical "Oop Shoop," which writer Tony Rounce called the first record to be written and performed with any degree of success by young Black women.[42]

"Oop Shoop" was a surprise hit, so, in the tenor of the times, it became imperative for a white group to cover it for the pop market—and the winner was the Crewcuts, who made a career out of covering R&B tunes. They took "Oop Shoop" to #13 on the pop charts in 1954, "Ko Ko Mo" to #6 in 1955, "Earth Angel" to #3 in 1955, and "Sh-Boom" to #1 in 1954.

At the start of September 1954, *Billboard* covered the "Oop Shoop" moment: "This tune had kicked off a lot of excitement since its release, and now that the Crewcuts have stimulated interest further with their powerful pop version of it, Shirley Gunter's original recording is edging closer to the national charts. Already on the Los Angeles territorial charts for two weeks, it is also reported to have strength in St. Louis, Nashville, Detroit, Cleveland, Pittsburgh, and New England."[43]

In November, a *Billboard* survey of the Most Promising R&B acts had Shirley Gunter tied for the ninth position.[44]

When "Oop Shoop" hit, Shirley Gunter and the Queens were such an anomaly that they made the cover of *Cash Box*. Author John Clemente labeled Shirley Gunter and the Queens as the first female group with a chart hit and "the first female group in R&B."[45]

Shirley Gunter and the Queens quickly garnered the support of Alan Freed. Even after traveling the long and hard road of many a rock 'n' roll package tour, the group never attained any other recording success.

CHAPTER SIX

TWEEDLE DEE (1955)

ZELMA "ZELL" SANDERS—IKE AND BESS BERMAN—
MACY LEE AND CHARLES HENRY—MIRIAM AND HERB
ABRAMSON—LOUISE HARRIS MURRAY—REX GARVIN—
SOL RABINOWITZ—ETTA JAMES—BARBARA HAWKINS—
REGGIE VINSON—LAVERN BAKER—WINFIELD SCOTT—
GEORGIA GIBBS—DINAH WASHINGTON—RUTH BROWN—
ELLA JOHNSON—PRISCILLA BOWMAN—JOHNNY ACE—
VARETTA DILLARD—CLYDE MCPHATTER—GENE & EUNICE

The revolutionary "Oop Shoop" from 1954 and "Lonely Nights" from 1955 performed similarly in that these records attained strong but not outsized success. Even so, there was one major difference between the two songs: one harkened back to the R&B sound from which doo-wop emerged, while the other pointed forward to what would become known as the girl group sound.

"Oop Shoop" is a bit of novelty song. It opens with a bluesy piano riff, a chorus of doo-woppy sounds, and then Shirley Gunter on lead with the Queens filling in behind. The structure is very much like the early 1950s group sound, upbeat but tinged with a bluesy lead, including a very good sax break in the middle. "Lonely Nights" by the Hearts begins with a sax/piano introduction, and then the tenor lead vocal of Joyce West comes in with three other girls behind her. Louise Murray's alto does the talk-break: "Lonely days, lonely nights / I'm so lonely / Please come home, you great big lump of sugar."

For 1955, the sound was modern, shedding the structural limitations of doo-wop. It could have been rereleased in 1961 and no one would have known it was different from any of the other girl group songs on the radio at that time.

"Lonely Nights" was a good seller, but even more important, it had a huge effect on the direction of music itself; the humorous and sometimes salacious jump sounds that had led the way in the past were quickly giving ground to romantic group-harmony ballads.

The creation of "Lonely Nights" was a youthful combination of the right singers (all of the Hearts were teenagers), the right arranger in Rex Garvin (another teenager), and Zelma "Zell" Sanders, an amazing and unusual record producer and music entrepreneur. In 1956, Sanders attempted to go where Berry Gordy went when he founded Motown Records in Detroit three years later: a music boss with total control over talent and full oversight of song creation from beginning to end.

Like the song "Lonely Nights," Sanders was ahead of her time as an African American woman in the music business. Unfortunately, for all her skills, ambition, and aspirations, she was equally greedy, overworked, and understaffed, showing little regard for the talent she was always endeavoring to find on the mean streets of Harlem and the Bronx.

Sanders wasn't the first female music mogul. A smattering of entrepreneurial women first appeared in the American music world starting in the mid-1940s when the married couple Ike and Bess Berman formed Apollo Records along with Herman "Hy" Siegel and Sam Schneider. The Bermans bought out their partners, and in 1948, Bess took charge of the business, recording gospel and R&B singers such as Mahalia Jackson and the early doo-wop group the Larks.

From 1949 to 1951, Macy Lela Henry and her husband Charles ran Macy Record Distribution in Houston, and among the artists their label Macy's Recordings introduced was country singer Jim Reeves. More successful was Lillian McMurry, who in 1950 founded Trumpet Records/Diamond Recording Company in Jackson, Mississippi. She recorded such great blues musicians as Elmore James and Arthur "Big Boy" Crudup.

One year before Bess took over Apollo, another married couple, Miriam and Herb Abramson, joined Ahmet Ertegun to form Atlantic Records, which became one of the premier labels for R&B and soul music in the 1950s and 1960s. Miriam took on the duties of finance and production and stayed with the company until the early 1960s, when she sold her stake to Ertegun.

Prior to 1960, the number of women who founded successful record companies, no matter how small, could probably be counted on two hands. To understand how that happened, one has to go back in time to the mid-1940s, just a decade before.

Employing the dance bands so popular in the 1920s and 1930s to do radio work was expensive, so in the mid-twentieth century there was a subtle shift to using recorded music, which, in the form of a disc (sometimes called a platter), could also be dropped into jukeboxes (another profit source for record producers). Swing dance bands were already facing tough times during the World War II years as members were drafted and it became too expensive and difficult to tour—especially with rationing of raw materials such as rubber (for tires) and gasoline (for automobiles). The American Federation of Musicians went on strike in 1942 to protect its musicians from the expanding use of recorded music. The strike lasted two years.

Oddly, the recording ban, a consequence of the strike, was only for instrumental music, so small groups of singers were allowed to record and did so. The emergence of the compact group (generally four to six singers) would affect the direction of popular music in the postwar years. That was just one of the strike's numerous unintended consequences. Author Philip Ennis explains the other: "Another result was that shoestring operations . . . took the risk of ignoring the AFM to produce 'bootleg' records. . . . This occurrence was especially prevalent in the Black pop stream, which was given a boost and thus positioned for a great post-war expansion."[1]

Skipping ahead to the early 1950s, when white teenagers began to follow R&B stations and the African American population had money to spend on records and live performances, being in the R&B business could actually be profitable.

Billboard on May 23, 1951, reported new labels were appearing on the order of two or three per week, even though R&B only accounted for 5.7 percent of the entire record business.[2]

"Over a hundred labels were slugging it out in the marketplace, even though the rewards were slim—over 40,000 copies were considered a hit, and 100,000 a big hit," according to music writer and historian Ed Ward. "For the most part these new companies were fly-by-night. They could record with minimal accompaniment a singer or small group, pay the artists a one-time session fee, take the publishing rights, and cut the record."[3]

Into this hot mix came Sol Rabinowitz, who in 1953 founded Baton Records, and Zell Sanders, who created J&S Records in 1956.

The Hearts' story begins with a Harlem girl named Louise Harris Murray, who won two Amateur Night contests at the Apollo, the first when she was eight years old and the second when she was twelve or thirteen. A year or two later Louise, now a real street kid, met up with a friend who told her, "There's a girl I know who joined a singing group, and they are looking for other singers."

Louise still loved to sing, so she took down the address, made contact, and went to audition for the girls' manager, a woman named Zell Hicks (she hadn't changed her name to Sanders yet), who, when not trying to put together a singing group, was a security guard.

Zell had heard three young Harlem singers (Joyce West, Forestine Barnes, and Hazel Crutchfield) at the Apollo Theater, probably at Amateur Night, liked the way they harmonized, and thought she could produce a record with them. The girls were excited by the interest, even though Zell preferred they record as quartet, not as a trio. Zell put out feelers in the neighborhood about auditioning for a singer, and one of the people who came in was Louise.

"I did the audition for Zell, and she liked me," says Louise. "I was 12 but looked older. The other girls were young as well. This would have been 1951 or 1952."[4]

Considering when "Lonely Nights" was recorded, which seems to have been in late 1954 (the song charted in early 1955), the year Louise met Zell Sanders was probably late 1953 or 1954, when she would have been at least fourteen years old.

The appearance of Louise Harris at an audition was a godsend for the group Zell Sanders was putting together. Zell already had in mind a sound that she wanted the girls to produce, and what was missing was a good female alto. Sopranos were easy to find, but an alto wasn't. Louise was just what Zell had hoped for but had not yet found, a young woman who could sing in harmony but with a voice deeper than the average girl.

Louise remembers meeting with three other girls, Hazel, Joyce, and Forestine, and everyone got along well.

Not part of the all-girl group but present at all rehearsals (and in some group photos) was a young boy from the neighborhood, Rex Garvin, who played the piano.

Rex was a year younger than Louise. He was born in Harlem in 1940 and raised by foster parents in the Bronx. At some point, his family appears to have taken him back, and in the mid-1950s, he lived in Harlem with his mother and possibly grandmother. When he was eight years old, he started taking piano lessons, as his mother had aspirations for him to a classical pianist.

Rex would have a long career as a singer, songwriter, musician, and arranger, but that was in the future. At Zell's place, he was just another teenager with talent that Zell recognized.

"Rex was young, and his grandmother didn't want him to play doo-wop because the family was religious," said Louise. "He would come to rehearsals and then leave because he had to be home. He used to stutter, and all of us girls would laugh at him. He didn't hang out with us. He was like a little boy."[5]

Zell had a network of talent in Harlem and either heard of, or heard, Rex's piano playing. At the end of 1953 or early 1954, Zell asked Rex's mother if she would allow him to play piano for a group of girls she was training to sing.

Rex recalled, "My mother said, 'Okay, but I don't want no stuff from you,'" indicating that she didn't want to hear about him playing that "gutbucket" music, which, of course, was what Rex wanted to play.

Rex went to visit Zell Sanders. "She was a policewoman," he remembered. "Well, actually, more a store detective, and she used to carry this gun around. She was a big woman and very threatening. She reminded you of Pearl Bailey. Everybody was scared of her. I wasn't. She was real strict. She wanted her singers to sing in key. She would shout at them, 'You're not singing this right. You're not singing this right. What's wrong with you?'"[6]

Rex was sharp, with a good sense of song. During the early rehearsals for "Lonely Nights," all of the girls were sitting around waiting for Zell to come to some conclusion about a break in the song when Rex realized the best the way to do it was to have Louise do the song-rap, telling Zell, "Let Louise do that part because she has a deep, deep voice."[7] And that's Louise with the talk-break in the middle of the song, including the lugubrious phrase, "please come home, you great big lump of sugar."

Playing on the recording were some fine musicians, including Big Al Sears on tenor sax and Mickey "Guitar" Baker, the premier session guitarist on the East Coast. In 1956, Baker teamed up with Sylvia Vanderpool (later Sylvia Robinson) to record the hit "Love Is Strange" as the duo Mickey and Sylvia.

It was the girls' first time in the studio, and to celebrate, Zell brought in food for everyone. Time was money, so Zell made sure she got the right sound quickly. Then it was the B-side, "Oo-Wee," and probably one other cut. The session was over quickly. After all, recording time costs money. For the teenage girls, it was just another fun day, a lark. For Zell, recording the girls was serious business.

Zell liked the final results and told the girls she was taking the demos to Baton Records, a local record label. The first response from Sol Rabinowitz, the record label owner, was "never in a million years will we get these girls to do a record." Doo-wop was a man's world, and Rabinowitz, who had just started his label, found success almost immediately with a male group, the Rivileers. Their first hit was "A Thousand Stars," which was revised by Kathy Young and the Innocents in 1960.[8]

Zell was persistent, and finally Sol relented, probably because he realized if he was going to succeed in the record business, he needed a stable of reliable artists, which he didn't have.

AM radio was on the rise as teenagers in increasing numbers started listening to the R&B sounds. For music producers, getting the attention of deejays was important. A little gift here and there didn't hurt the cause. Sol not only made the rounds in New York, but also contacted R&B deejays in other cities like Alan Freed in Cleveland, which turned out to be fortuitous because Freed would eventually move to New York to join WINS radio. At one point, two Baton records, the Rivileers' "Sentimental Reasons" and the Hearts' "Lonely Nights," were #2 and #3, respectively, on the Alan Freed show, probably the most important AM radio show in the country.[9]

"Lonely Nights" broke on the East Coast early in 1955, and the "Rhythm 'n' Blues Ramblings" column in *Cash Box*, which focused on three cities, New York, Chicago, and Los Angeles, took notice. At the very end of the New York entry on February 19, 1955, the unnamed columnist noted, "Baton Records has come up with what looks like another 'strongeee' in 'Lonely Nights' by the Hearts, a group of young girls who look like real comers."

Throughout the early 1960s, young "teen" singers would get their first exposure as performers being shuffled to high school gymnasiums for record hops or singing at local charity events. *Cash Box*'s "Rhythm 'n' Blues Ramblings" columnist was keeping an eye on the Hearts, probably through the earnest efforts of Rabinowitz and Sanders, the latter learning the music game from her associate. On February 26, 1955, a blurb in the column read: "Another B'nai Brith dance for the kids to prevent juvenile delinquency took place last Thursday at P.S. 118 in Manhattan. Dick Sugar [WEVD-New York] again M.C.'d the affair with . . . the Hearts of Baton and 'Lonely Nights' providing the vocal calisthenics. The Hearts are a group of teenage girls, but you never know it to hear them belt."[10]

The February 26, 1955, issue of *Cash Box* gave "Lonely Nights" its first big endorsement. The "Rhythm 'n' Blues Reviews" picked it as the "Sleeper of the Week." The reviewer wrote: "A group of young girls, the Hearts, spin two enchanting sides that should spell success for the kids. The Hearts have an obvious, natural feeling for a tune, and they handle the upper deck 'Lonely Nights' with a sureness and flavor that comes through. It looks like a deck that could take off."[11]

The same column observed, in test airings in New York, that the song brought a "definite reaction."

Author John Clemente summed up the record's appeal this way: "The lyrics tell of the yearnings of uncertain love, exuding pent-up energies caused by roller-coaster relationships, sung with the insights of middle-aged dancehall molls, ironically delivered by 15-year-olds."[12]

Billboard was a little slower to catch on, finally choosing "Lonely Nights" as one of its three "This Week's Best Buys" in "Rhythm & Blues Records" on March 26, 1955. The column pointed out the song's rise, building "sizeable proportions" in New York, Philadelphia, Baltimore, and Washington, DC. The review added, "This disk is now achieving a good national spread of reports."[13] That week, the record climbed to the #14 spot on *Billboard*'s national R&B chart. It was coming on strong.

Over at rival *Cash Box*, the "Rhythm 'n' Blues Ramblings" columnist who first spotted the Hearts got a chance to crow and took it, writing on April 9, 1955, "Couldn't happen to a nicer bunch of kids. The Hearts on Baton zooming with 'Lonely Nights.' We tipped this tune so-o-o long ago and hope some of you distrib readers [distributors] came up with it."[14]

In the April 9, 1955, issue of *Cash Box*, the top fifteen R&B songs at that moment showed four woman acts also charting: Etta James's "The Wallflower" at #4, LaVern Baker's "Tweedle Dee" at #9, the Hearts' "Lonely Nights" at #12, and Varetta Dillard's "Johnny Has Gone" at #13.[15]

Rabinowitz told writer Arnold Shaw: "Our first truly national hit, and probably the biggest hit Baton had was 'Lonely Nights' by the Hearts—three [four] Bronx chicks [some from Harlem] and a cat named Rex Garvin—and it made Top 10 on *Billboard*'s Best-Selling R&B Singles."[16] It made it to #8 on *Billboard*'s R&B charts.

"Lonely Nights" was also listed as one of the Top Fifty best-selling R&B records for 1955 by *Billboard* magazine.

In some regards, the music business in the mid-1950s was no different than today. In order to sell records (stream songs, in today's vernacular), one had to go out on the road and perform live. The business wasn't so organized back then, but for young singers there were two approaches: local venues, clubs, and dances; and group shows as pioneered by Alan Freed.

Before "Lonely Nights" hit, Zell had them singing at storefronts in Harlem. One of the first places Murray remembered singing at was the Red Shield Club, which was a tiny bar behind a store on 124th Street. "I don't think it could fit more than ten people," Murray recalled. "The night the Hearts sang, no one was in there except my mother. That was our first gig, and the other girls' parents didn't even bother to show up."[17]

The song was released in January 1955, and after charting, the Hearts moved up to popular venues like the Apollo and Rockland Palace, both in Harlem.

JC Marion, who in 2015 wrote a brief history of the Hearts for a blog, noted: "Early in February of 1955, the Hearts make one of their first in-person appearances at a show at P.S. 188 for the city's B'nai Brith organization. The emcee was radio personality Dick Sugar, and the Cadillacs also appeared along with Alfredito's mambo band." By July, the little Baton label was doing well with the Hearts and the Rivileers and pushed ads in the trade press backing its records.[18]

In mid-March, "Lonely Nights" was listed as a top seller in New York City. Riding the crest of their first record's popularity, the Hearts appeared with Tommy "Dr. Jive" Smalls at Harlem's Rockland Palace, along with Roy Hamilton, the Cadillacs, Buddy Johnson's Band, and a surprise guest appearance by Billie Holiday.

In New York, the largest, brightest, and most renowned showcase for African American performers was the Apollo Theater in Harlem, and on April 8, 1955, the Hearts made it to the big time. On a show headlined by the legendary Louis Jordan, the Hearts made their first appearance at this venue. Of all the shows Louise did with the Hearts, the one she said she remembered was the first one at the Apollo.

The flyer for that show reads: "Harlem's High Spot, Apollo, Gala Easter Show beg. Friday. April 8." Then came the listing of performers with the headliner first: "Mr. Personality Louis Jordan his band and Big Revue, Ace Trombone Star Benny Green and his band, child star of the Star Time Show Sharon Porter; 'Lonely Nights' by the Hearts, Arnold Dover, and 'Crip' Heard."

"Everybody on that show treated us girls well," said Louise. "We got to meet Louis Jordan; he was very nice to us. Arnold Dover the comedian was good to me. As for Sharon Porter, I always wondered what happened to her."

The girls sang "Lonely Nights," "Blue Moon," "Money Honey," and—Louise's memory faltered—maybe "All My Love Belongs to You" as the final song. What she did remember was that she was excited, but not nervous on stage. In fact, she added, the girls were never nervous on stage, "not even Rex, our piano player."

Afterward, the girls went to get a bite to eat, walking across the street to a Nedick's, where you could get two hotdogs for a quarter. "None of us had any money," Louise said. "This was our celebration. Zell didn't treat us to anything. She was still a security guard at this point, so she had no money to take us girls out."

Louise Murray, just wanting to be a teenager, meet guys, and have free time instead of adhering to Zell Sanders's strict discipline, dropped away from the Hearts. Before she did, there was one story she recalled. The place was the Brad-dock Hotel in Harlem, which was located on the corner of 126th Street and 8th Avenue. As it was in walking distance to the Apollo Theater, the establishment was first popular with African American jazz musicians and eventually with the 1950s blues and pre–rock 'n' roll singers. On this particular night, Louise was sitting in a Braddock hotel room drinking steadily and heavily with Etta James and Johnny Tanner of the "5" Royales, a doo-wop group that had remained popular since hitting #1 on the R&B charts with "Baby Don't Do It" in 1952. They were five talented, handsome, and hard-partying guys from North Carolina. Group members Lowman Pauling and Ralph Bass wrote "Dedicated to the One I Love," which later became a big hit for the Shirelles, the most successful of the girl groups. At some point in the night, Louise and Johnny left Etta and went to Tanner's room, where "Baby Don't Do It" became "Baby I'm Doin' It."[19]

Toward the end of 1955, *Billboard* summed up the year in music by exclaim-ing it was the "Year R&B Took Over the Pop Field." Eschewing the phrase rock 'n' roll, the magazine asserted that R&B singers and songs virtually crashed the pop charts, having overcome many obstacles. The article declared: "Despite covers by top pop artists, more and more original versions of tunes by R&B artists are making it in all markets."[20] The pacesetter was "Pledging My Love," the soft ballad by the recently deceased Johnny Ace. It was the most played R&B record of the year and a crossover hit despite a strong cover by popular songstress Teresa Brewer. Songs that would be declared seminal rock 'n' roll hits, such as Chuck Berry's "Maybellene," Ray Charles's "I Got a Woman," Bo Diddley's "Bo Diddley," and Fats Domino's "Ain't It a Shame," were huge R&B

hits in 1955. It wasn't just the men who benefited by the country's teens turning
to the new rock 'n' roll sound. Two female singers, Etta James and LaVern Baker,
burst onto the music scene in 1955 with their own slant on the new music. Both
would end up in the Rock & Roll Hall of Fame.

It's easy to see why 1955 was a vanguard year for R&B or incipient rock 'n' roll.
So many classic songs tumbled down to deejays, it was like a California gold
strike. Among the transformative and timeless tunes of 1955 (in addition to the
previously mentioned rock 'n' rollers) were the Platters' "The Great Pretender,"
the Penguins' "Earth Angel," Al Hibbler's "Unchained Melody," the Moonglows'
"Sincerely," and the Cadillacs' "Speedo." That was a problem for the women; all
of those songs were by men. Of the Top Twenty songs of the year, only Etta
James's "The Wallflower" broke through, checking in as the #9 best-seller. If
the list expands to the Top Twenty-five, three more made the cut: Shirley and
Lee's "Feel So Good" at #25 and LaVern Baker with two songs, "Tweedle Dee"
at #22 and "Play It Fair" at #23. Of the Top 100 R&B tunes for the year, LaVern
Baker would snag four positions, as would Ruth Brown. Dinah Washington
would take two slots. The Hearts, Varetta Dillard, and white singer Gale Storm
covering the Fats Domino song "I Hear You Knocking" would add their singular
hits as well. Three male-female duets would also chart.

Etta James (Jamesetta Hawkins), who had two major hits in 1955, was born
in 1938 in Los Angeles. Her mother was fourteen years old when Jamesetta was
born and her father was unknown, although he was rumored to be Minnesota
Fats (Rudolf Wanderone Jr.), the legendary pool player. As with most African
American singers of her generation, Etta James got her start singing in church.[21]

Like Fanita James of the Dreamers, Etta James was lucky enough to grow
up in the musical greenhouse of South Central Los Angeles. Except Etta went
to the other school, Jefferson High, which was where Big Jay McNeely, Dexter
Gordon, Barry White, Johnny "Guitar" Watson, Gaynel Hodge, and Richard
Berry had all gone to school. This is how James remembered her youth: "I was
10 or 11 when I met Alex Hodge and his brother Gaynell Hodge. Along with
Eugene Church [who scored a big hit in 1956 with "The Girl in My Dreams"],
another close chum of mine, they formed the Fellas and the Turks . . . Richard
Berry, who wrote and sang 'Louie, Louie' was also part of our crowd. We all
went to Jefferson High—that was the hip school."[22]

When Etta James was fourteen, she joined two sisters Jean and Abye Mitchell
to form the Creolettes, eventually renamed the Peaches. Johnny Otis discovered
them at an amateur night contest and recruited the girls to sing backup. As
an answer song to Hank Ballard and the Midnighters' big hit "Work with Me,
Annie," James wrote "Roll with Me Henry." Both the words "work" and "roll"
were long established in the African American community as hip-talk for sex.
During the song "Roll with Me Henry," when Richard Berry questions on the

talk-break "Hey baby, what do I have to do, to make you love me too?" James answers, "You got to roll with me, Henry." That response could have numerous meanings depending on one's point of view.

As with other answer records, the melody was lifted from the original song, in this case Hank Ballard's "Work with Me, Annie," but the words belonged to Etta James. The song was recorded on Thanksgiving Eve 1954.

Johnny Otis had the recording printed the next day so he could play it at his record store on Western Avenue, across from the Red Hut, a hangout where Otis also did a record show. As James recalled, "It was from that funky shop that Johnny broke the record and launched my career."

Otis also did a number of other things to get that song to the public. He created a professional name for Jamesetta Hawkins, turning her forever into Etta James. Although all of the Peaches were part of the recording, on the record Otis credited the performers as Etta James and the Peaches. When Modern Records decided to issue the record, Otis listed Etta James as the songwriter along with his wife Phyllis.[23] Not that she had anything to do with creating the song, but Otis wanted to pull some royalties out of the song for himself.

King Records owned the song's original rights and had to come to terms with Modern Records, which was going to distribute the record on its own label. The song had inherent issues. Some deejays and listeners understood the double entendre meaning of the words and wouldn't play the record because it was "dirty." When the record came out, it had a new name, "The Wallflower," signifying that the song was about dancing. The song arrived on the desks of deejays in January and as late as March the "dirty record" issue had not died away. For example, in early 1955, WJW was the only radio station in Cleveland that didn't go along with a local ban on the "The Wallflower" record. *Billboard* interviewed station manager Jack Kelly, who pioneered playing R&B disks with Allan Freed's revolutionary *Moondog* radio show. Kelly maintained that he decided to play "The Wallflower" only after surveying local teenagers, who told him they didn't think the lyrics were dirty and that their primary interest in R&B was the beat.[24]

The January 22, 1955, issue of *Billboard* ran a brief review of the song, noting: "Here's a wild one. On it, thrush Etta James tells her dream man that he'll be a wallflower if doesn't learn to dance. It swings and it moves all the way, sparked by thrush's outstanding vocal. This could be a big one."[25] And it was—a monster hit and a career-maker for Etta James.

The song was a #1 tune on the R&B charts. Although it had the potential to cross over to the pop charts, that didn't happen, mostly because popular pop singer Georgia Gibbs covered it, cleaning it up once more and changing the name to "The Wallflower (Dance with Me, Henry)." That version of the song shot all the way to #1 on the pop charts and was a Top Ten song of the year.

With "The Wallflower" stomping all over the R&B charts, Modern quickly got James on the road, placing her in one of the big R&B extravaganzas that would be touring later in the year. Called the Big Ten Review, it was put together by impresario Lou Krefetz. According to press reports, the review would tour the East, Midwest, and South and was being sold for $3,000 (about $30,000 in 2021 dollars) on weeknights and $3,500 for weekends, which might seem like a lot, but this was a big show, so the artists weren't making much money per performance. Faye Adams was given the top female slot. This was to be a great show with performers Joe Turner, the Clovers, Bo Diddley, Bill Doggett, Gene and Eunice, Etta James and her Peaches, Charlie and Ray, the Paul Williams Band, Al Jackson as emcee, and the Drake Trio as a dance team.[26]

Modern rushed (perhaps too quickly) a follow-up song, a brainless piggy-back to "The Wallflower" ("Roll with Me Henry") called "Hey! Henry." Hank Ballard had milked "Annie" for four songs, and there was also the answer song by Etta James, so one more in the canon was superfluous to say the least. *Billboard* gave it short shrift, in fact liking the B-side tune "Be Mine" better: "This is Miss James' first since her 'Wallflower' smash was released, and it looked like a two-sided winner. The 'Be Mine' side is an appealing ballad convincingly wailed, while 'Henry' is the jump side, and the obvious follow-up to 'The Wallflower.'"[27]

James dismissed the song, writing, "after 'Roll with Me, Henry,' the Biharis [Saul, Jules, and Joe Bihari, who founded Modern Records] wanted to cash in with a follow-up, but 'Hey! Henry' didn't do it."[28] The song that did "do it" was "Good Rockin' Daddy," a tune that bridged the gulf between a traditional blues shuffle and rock 'n' roll. The songwriter, James's old friend Richard Berry, understood the future was coming quickly because in the heart of the song he scribed: "They stood around with a great big smile / When we start to rock 'n' roll, they all went wild."

The songwriting credits read Richard Berry and Joe Bihari. Like other independent label owners, for all the good they did recording R&B, they were equally exploitive of the talent they signed. The Bihari brothers had one of the worst reputations. Or as James said, "Sometimes the Biharis got a little greedy and took more than just the publishing share. Joe couldn't write a song any more than I can pilot a plane."[29]

The Biharis weren't the only ones to exploit young talent. One of James's first tours in 1955 was a Johnny Otis extravaganza. When someone from the show asked her how much she was getting paid, she frankly answered $30 a night. The person responded, "A star like you should be making lots more."[30]

"Good Rockin' Daddy" shot to #6 on the R&B charts and was James's second major hit of 1955. James said of the song, "'Good Rockin' Daddy' is another primitive example of strong early rock."[31]

Barbara Hawkins, one of the original singers in the Dixie Cups, who sang the #1 hit "Chapel of Love," recalled that Etta James was one of the first singers she ever met: "Long before we started singing as the Dixie Cups, Etta James was to appear at a concert in my hometown of New Orleans. My uncle was a police officer, and he would handle crowds at R&B shows. He got my mom and me in to see the show. After the performances, he took us backstage to meet Etta James. At that moment, she was waiting for her ride. After my uncle introduced us, she leaned down and asked me if I had a piece of gum. I did and I gave her a stick. We talked a little bit about where she had been and where the show was going. I told her I liked her singing." Hawkins was too shy to tell her she was trying to become a singer, so she didn't extract any morsels of wisdom from James. Nevertheless, Hawkins remembered the meeting warmly, saying, "She was very nice, very much a real lady."[32]

Rockabilly singer and songwriter Reggie Vinson also had wonderful memories of Etta James, with whom he toured. They met in Detroit around 1970. Vinson was twenty years old.

"One rainy night, I was playing with blues singer Jimmy Reed when Etta James walked in. She walked up to the bar and said, 'Hey white boy, can I sing with you tonight?'" Vinson thought, "Oh my God, it's Etta James." "The bartender brought her drink, which she downed immediately. She got another and walked onto the stage. She sang 'Dance with Me Henry' and 'Tell Mama.'" Vinson recalled, "I knew all these blues songs because they only had three chords. She also sang 'I'd Rather Go Blind,' which was one of my favorites."

Afterward, she told Vinson, "I'm staying at this hotel, come over tomorrow. I'm looking for a guy to play guitar for me, and you look like the right one. How does that sound to you, white boy?" Vinson took umbrage at the appellation, and James added, "You are long and skinny and white as a whale. I'm going to call you white boy."

The next day, Vinson drove over to the hotel at about noon or one in the afternoon. He knocked, and James yelled to come on in. She was lying on a bed with two men. They were half naked and she was wearing lingerie. Vinson reintroduced himself. James replied, "I remember you. I'm looking for a guitar player to play with Joe Swift, who was the bass player for Stevie Wonder." Vinson replied that he knew Joe. James handed him a bunch of songs and an eight-track tape. Later that night, Vinson and James sang some old blues songs, and Vinson said, "We hit it off real good. Those other two guys were still there smoking joints and drinking whiskey. Etta would take a big shot of whiskey and instead of getting drunk would sing even better. Every time she took a swig, it would blow my mind how great she was."

About a week later, they began the tour. It was five people jammed into a van that was pulling an equipment-laden trailer. For three weeks, they toured throughout the Midwest, doing fourteen shows. She paid Vinson $100 to $150 for each gig.

"The last time I saw her was in Los Angeles," Vinson said. "She was performing at the Whisky a Go Go, and I went to see her. She hugged me and asked how I was doing. She still called me 'white boy.' When I was about to leave, she said to me, 'Don't forget who I am.'"[33]

Toward the end of 1955, *Billboard*'s survey of the most promising new R&B artists found Etta James in fourth place. Number one on the list was somebody named Chuck Berry.[34] It's hard to say whether the survey was a good predictor or not. "Good Rockin' Daddy" was the last charted song in the 1950s for Etta James. Her time would come with the next decade; rock 'n' roll and the coming soul music genre would have to catch up to Etta James.

The year 1955 was a great one for two newcomers to the pop charts, Etta James and LaVern Baker. James's success came out of the blue, but a lot had been expected from Baker, especially after she signed with Atlantic Records in 1953. The record company quickly got her into the studio, and her first recording to be released as a single was an unusually powerful ballad called "Soul on Fire." With a deeper resonance than the popular Dinah Washington, Baker's "Soul on Fire" transcended traditional blues and foreshadowed many of the coming trends in music: rock 'n' roll, the girl group sound, and even soul music. "Her [LaVern Baker] rough-edged voice, at once earthy and refined, presages the soul singing of the following decade," wrote author Larry Birnbaum.[35]

It was a song ahead of its time. "Soul on Fire" scored in a few local markets but not enough to make the national R&B charts. It's a forgotten masterpiece.

By 1954, Baker was on the verge. She released another strong single, "I Can't Hold Out Any Longer," that featured just a tinge of Patsy Cline country. Music writers, long familiar with LaVern Baker, had been waiting for her to explode nationally. *Cash Box*'s "Stars Over Harlem" R&B column predicted, "LaVerne [*sic*] Baker and 'I Can't Hold Out Any Longer' could be the smasharoo the whaling [*sic*] miss has been long searching for."[36] It wasn't. Once again, she was just ahead of the trend line in popular music.

Her songs caught enough attention that she was added to the lineup of one of the big R&B extravaganzas at the Brooklyn Paramount Theater in the autumn of 1954. The lineup included Baker, Roy Hamilton, the Drifters, Faye Adams, the Spaniels, the Counts, Big Maybelle, Erskine Hawkins, and Rusty Bryant.[37]

When "I Can't Hold Out Any Longer" did not hold out, late in November, Atlantic released another single, a little number called "Tweedle Dee." Music critics, who had long ago recognized LaVern Baker's raw talent and were dismayed by her lack of popular success, finally saw that she would cross the finish line. *Cash Box*'s "Rhythm 'n' Blues Reviews" column chose "Tweedle Dee" as one of its coveted "Sleeper of the Week" songs, which meant a more in-depth commentary. The reviewer squealed in delight: "LaVern Baker has been making covetous eyes at the charts with her last few releases, and it is our opinion that she's about ready to crash with her newest, titled 'Tweedle Dee.' The gal swings out with a personality-packed vocal that rocks. She's vital, alive, and happy as she shouts out her enthusiastic vocal. This one's loaded."[38]

The song was written by African American songwriter Winfield Scott, who had a successful career during the early years of rock 'n' roll with songs for Bill Haley, Conway Twitty, Peggy Lee, Connie Francis, and Elvis Presley. Other than "Tweedle Dee," Scott's best-known song was "Return to Sender" for Elvis Presley. "Tweedle Dee" was a wonderful cross of novelty and R&B. The words were essentially meaningless ("Jiminy cricket, jiminy jack, you make my heart go clickety clack"), but they sure sounded like something important when Baker spat 'em out. The song was "delivered with all the guts and drive of her [Baker] chesty contralto to a Latin-inflected riff. How memorable and horny, her 'hompy-om-bom-bom' fill!" wrote author Arnold Shaw.[39]

"Tweedle Dee" chirped onto the charts in early 1955 and kept climbing until it landed at #4 on the R&B chart. Bill Haley and the Comets' huge hit "Rock around the Clock" pushed rock 'n' roll down the stuffed gullet of the pop charts in 1955, and "Tweedle Dee" was in the slipstream. It crossed over to the pop charts, rising to #14. It probably would have ended up as a Top Ten pop hit as well, but Baker, like Etta James, got the Georgia Gibbs treatment. She covered the song, and Gibbs's version was a #2 hit on the pop charts. In May 1955, Baker's "Tweedle Dee" passed the 500,000 sales mark. That would have been more impressive if Mercury Records, at almost the same time, hadn't announced the awarding of a gold record (designating one million in sales) to Georgia Gibbs.

Artists had been covering songs from different genres for decades, and jazz musicians often took a standard and reworked it as something completely new. In the mid-1950s, some record companies just took the easy path, appropriating everything from arrangements to lyrics to the musicians from the R&B record and replacing the lead singer with a white person. Second, covering a song was also a matter of economics. Baker claimed Gibbs cost her $15,000 in royalties (about $150,000 in 2021 dollars), which was a lot of money to an R&B singer at the time. Third, R&B singers didn't make as much money performing as headlining pop singers did. They also didn't have the same opportunities to sing at many of the most important clubs around the country due to blatant or de facto segregation. To have a record cross over to the pop charts could expand the opportunities for African American singers.

Baker was so angry about Gibbs covering "Tweedle Dee," she asked her congressman if something could be done about it. Ed Ward wrote, "All she got back was an envelope full of reelection materials." That wasn't exactly true. According to *Billboard*, she contacted Congressman Charles Diggs Jr., who introduced a bill in Congress that was designed to prevent such actions in the future. *Billboard* reported, "After having the situation probed, Diggs drew up his House of Representatives Bill 5366 to create a federal commission to study copyright laws and to make recommendations for their revision. It was referred to the Senate Committee on the Judiciary for further study."[40]

Nothing happened, and the cover phenomenon continued.

In July 1955, the *Jackson* (Mississippi) *Advocate*, perhaps using the wrong phrasing in the headline, reported all good things coming to Baker. The headline read, "'Tweedle Dee' Still Cash for LaVern Baker." The story said "Tweedle Dee" was rated as one of the most played tunes in the nation by the top disc jockeys; Baker "drew top honors" for being the singer that the platter spinners featured the most on their programs, and she was appearing at the Showboat Cafe in Philadelphia. The story concluded with the observation that LaVern Baker recently finished a successful tour with a package show that drew capacity audiences. The reviewer added, "When she left the theaters and auditoriums in which the show played, she was always mobbed at the stage door by autograph seekers."[41]

Not all was copacetic for Baker's live shows. In December, she was on a monster program at the Brooklyn Paramount with three white acts: Johnnie Ray, Bill Haley, and Art Mooney. Bill Haley was, at the moment, king of the new sound sweeping America, rock 'n' roll, Johnnie Ray's big moment had already passed, and while Mooney did have a big hit in 1955 with "Honey-Babe," he wasn't a teen attraction. According to the *Cash Box*, the week's show netted $68,000 and was a disappointment, especially compared to Alan Freed's recent record-breaking extravaganza that netted $160,000.[42]

Despite the lack of response to the December Brooklyn Paramount show, LaVern Baker did not have a blue Christmas. The year 1955 was extraordinary for the singer. While "Tweedle Dee" went to #4 on the R&B charts, it was outdone by "Play It Fair," which went all the way to #2, and "Bop-Ting-a-Ling," which went to #3. One more hit, "That's All I Need," rose to #6. The latter two songs were a two-sided hit single, which Atlantic should have seen and separated. As soon as it was introduced in April 1955, *Cash Box*'s reviewer sussed it out immediately: "If it is not a two sider . . . it's a double-barreled buy." Both sides broke nationally, again because each had that modern rock 'n' roll beat that soon would drown out everything else on the radio. Over time, "Bop-Ting-a-Ling" has been forgotten, especially as Baker's first novelty hit, "Tweedle Dee," has only gained in stature, but it is a fantastic early rock 'n' roller. As *Cash Box*'s reviewer averred, "Miss Baker is singing from the toes on both sides as she rocks along."[43]

In 1955, Etta James and LaVern Baker captured the zeitgeist of the moment, leaving the female R&B standard-bearers bluesy Ruth Brown and jazzy Dinah

Washington trying to play catchup. On the surface, it would seem that Brown and Washington could boast another amazing year, with Brown as a solo singer snagging four of the Top 100 R&B songs of the year and Washington two of the slots. Yet all those positions were in the middle to end of the annual tally.

From mid-1948 through 1954, almost every song that Dinah Washington pushed onto the R&B charts was a Top Ten tune. In 1955, Washington bagged five more R&B tunes that charted, but only one, "That's All I Want from You," broke into the Top Ten. "That's All I Want from You," a beautiful, traditional pop song, managed to climb to #8 on the R&B charts. What the industry didn't realize was that even a singer as highly regarded as Washington was being ghosted from the very start of the year by upstart rock 'n' rollers. In Washington's case, it was Etta James. In January 1955, *Billboard* spotlighted "That's All I Want from You" with a fine review: "Dinah comes through with a wonderful reading of the tune that is now a smash hit in the pop field, over another unusual backing by the ork [orchestra]." On the very same page was notification of a spotlight on "The Wallflower" by Etta James and the Peaches.[44] At the very end of the year, when *Billboard* put the spotlight on "You Might Have Told Me," calling it "a particular standout," again on the same page was a story about Etta James. Her "Good Rockin' Daddy" was a new entry on the national charts.[45]

Dinah Washington was still in demand for live performances. Early in 1955, she spent a week at the Apollo, four weeks at the Royal Nevada in Las Vegas, and at some point, played the Mocambo in Hollywood. That year, she also made her first appearance at the Newport Jazz Festival.[46]

Nevertheless, her label felt she was being stigmatized. Bob Shad at Mercury Records was convinced that Dinah deserved a wider audience than she was getting as an R&B artist. "I wanted to take her out of the R&B field," he asserted.[47]

Ruth Brown notched a stronger year than Dinah Washington, yet experientially it wasn't much different. Two of Brown's four big songs for the year were "Bye Bye Young Men," which climbed as high as #13 on the R&B charts, and "I Can See Everybody's Baby," which rose to #7. Brown's two biggest songs were the two No. 4 cuts: "It's Love Baby (24 Hours of the Day)," a bluesy tune that she delivered with mucho gusto, and "As Long as I'm Moving," another quick groove, this time with a Joe Turner rock 'n' roll beat.

While 1955 seemed fine to Brown, she too found herself haunted. In April, *Cash Box*'s "Rhythm 'n' Blues Reviews" column gave its "Award o' the Week" to "As Long as I'm Moving" and said the ditty was "in the 'Shake, Rattle, and Roll' vein, and Miss Ruth drives it with all the talent in her possession." Unfortunately, it had to share the "Award o' the Week" with the great Fats Domino tune "Ain't It a Shame," which has since become a classic.[48]

In August 1955, *Cash Box* recognized "It's Love Baby" as a standout, giving the song its "Sleeper of the Week" award, which it had to share with the Platters' future #1 record, "Only You." To add insult to injury, the #1 song that same week was Fats Domino's "Ain't It a Shame."[49]

All was not lost. At mid-year, *Cash Box* polled R&B disk jockeys, asking them a handful of questions, one of which was: "Which female vocalists did you program most?" First by a wide margin was Ruth Brown, followed by LaVern Baker, Dinah Washington, Faye Adams, Ella Johnson, and Etta James.[50]

The outlier on that list was Ella Johnson. Some deejays were getting a very handsome payola package from Mercury Records because few teenagers knew who Ella Johnson was, even though Mercury had put her under contract the year before. It's not that she was an unknown or without talent, she was just past her prime years.

Ella Mae Johnson was born in 1919 in Darlington, South Carolina. Her break came when she joined her brother Buddy Johnson's band as a teenager. Buddy led a group of swinging musicians that were popular at such New York nightspots as the Savoy Ballroom.[51] She bragged her first hit in 1940 with "Please Mr. Johnson." In 1945, she sang "Since I Fell for You," which became a big hit for Lenny Welch in 1963. Mercury issued one single, "It Used to Hurt Me" / "Well Do It" by Ella Johnson in 1954, and then two more singles in 1955.[52] None of them caught fire in a big way. In *Billboard*'s "Rhythm & Blues Notes" column on October 22, 1955, writer Paul Ackerman once again decried the lack of girl vocalists on the best-selling R&B charts, asserting: "Good chanting [singing] does not have to be a male commodity." He then mentioned the success of individual performers such as Ruth Brown, Dinah Washington, and LaVern Baker, adding "In the past couple of years, Faye Adams on Herald, Edda [*sic*] James on Modern, Varetta Dillard on Savoy, and Ella Johnson on Mercury have also shown strength."[53]

As to getting the word out about a singer, in 1955, the complete opposite happened to another fine performer, Priscilla Bowman. She received little notice although she was the vocalist on one of the top R&B songs of the year, "Hands Off." That's because the song was written and recorded by Jay McShann, a Kansas City bandleader. On the record label, artist credit went to Jay McShann's Orchestra. However, if one looks a little higher, to the right of the "hole" in the middle of the platter, in smaller type it reads: Vocalist Priscilla Bowman.

McShann was a respected and well-known bandleader. Among the alumni of his many band incarnations were Charlie Parker, Al Hibbler, Ben Webster, and Jimmy Witherspoon. He kicked off his first group in the mid-1930s, and the sound was less jazz and more of what came to be known as Kansas City blues.[54]

Priscilla Bowman (Priscilla I. Mills) was born in 1928 in Kansas City. She joined McShann's band in the early 1950s.

In 1953, two African American entrepreneurs, Vivian Carter and James Bracken, founded Vee-Jay Records in Gary, Indiana. Vivian's brother, Calvin Carter, was recruited as a singer, A&R man, and even talent spotter. Although the company already scored several hit records, Carter recalled "Hands Off" was "the big one" as the company's first #1: "Jay McShann was out of Kansas City. My brother-in-law [James Bracken] found him and brought the band to Chicago to record them. Priscilla Bowman was the vocalist with the band."[55]

On October 22, 1955, when LaVern Baker's "Play It Fair" was highlighted by *Billboard*, the magazine also turned its attention to "Hands Off." The "Review Spotlight" on the Jay McShann Orchestra read: "Vocalist Priscilla Bowman turns in an exciting performance, and the band produces some fine sounds on this catchy, upbeat opus."[56]

The melody might sound familiar as it was later reworked as the popular blues-rock 'n' roll tune "Got My Mojo Working" sung by Muddy Waters and many others. However, the original tune was recorded by Coot Grant and Kid Wilson in 1932 as "Keep Your Hands Off My Mojo." As unfurled by Jay McShann/Priscilla Bowman, "Hands Off" became a driving, bouncy rock 'n' roller. It was another song in the slipstream of the attack on the mainstream behind Bill Haley's "Rock around the Clock."

In the last week in December, "Hands Off" was #1 on *Billboard*'s Best-Sellers in Stores chart ("Play It Fair" was #9), #1 on the Most Played by Disk Jockeys chart ("Play It Fair" was #3), and #5 on the Most Played in Jukeboxes chart ("Play It Fair" was #2).[57]

The song was #1 on the R&B charts at the end of 1955, knocking out the prior top seller, "Only You (and You Alone)" by the Platters. The song snagged one other bit of ironic glory. According to music researcher Joel Whitburn, "Hands On" was the last single to reach #1 on the R&B chart without crossing over to the pop charts until 1976.

One of the first groups signed by Vee-Jay Records was a local Gary, Indiana, doo-wop group called the Spaniels. In 1954, they had one big hit, "Goodnight, Sweetheart, Goodnight," and it was a classic! Four years later, Priscilla Bowman walked into a recording studio to lay down tracks for a Vee-Jay subsidiary label called Abner Records. Trailing behind Bowman were her old friends the Spaniels, who were recruited to sing backup. The key song that day was "A Rockin' Good Way (to Mess Around and Fall in Love)." The song, cowritten by Brook Benton, Clyde Otis, and Luchi de Jesus, fell by the wayside, as did Bowman's career. On the other hand, Brook Benton's career was on the rise, and in 1960, he recorded the song as a duet with Dinah Washington. Their version went to #1 on the R&B charts and #7 pop. Priscilla Bowman had again been too early with a song that later would become a major hit.

The darkest phenomenon to affect all the music charts in 1955 was the lingering impact of Johnny Ace's death at the end of 1954.

Way before there was a Michael Jackson, even years before there was an Elvis Presley, the first teen idol of the pre–rock 'n' roll years was Johnny Ace, an African American singer out of Memphis. Born John Marshall Alexander Jr.

in 1929, he was a friend of B.B. King and a member the seminal R&B band the Beale Streeters. As a solo artist, Johnny Ace was a blues balladeer. This subgenre was the quiet offshoot of blues singing that enjoyed occasional popularity after Cecil Gant boasted a huge crossover hit in 1944 with "I Wonder." Popularized by Ace, the blues ballad sound would morph into the softer side of soul music by the 1960s. Johnny Ace's first effort in the recording studio as a solo singer produced "My Song" in 1952. The tune zoomed up the R&B charts to #1 and stayed there for almost two months.

On September 6, 1952, *Cash Box*'s "Jazz 'n' Blues Reviews" column chose a Varetta Dillard single "Them There Eyes" / "You Are Gone" as its "Award o' the Week,"[58] just about the time "My Song" was beginning to explode. (Johnny Ace's and Varetta Dillard's fates would be tied together again three years later). In a series of new song reviews on September 6, 1952, were two covers of "My Song" by R&B songstresses. The first was by Marie Adams, and she received, as part of her review, a summarization of the "My Song" phenomenon: "Johnny Ace started a race to cover this slow beat blues when his release turned into an instantaneous hit, and the diskerie [record company], in an attempt cover the market, waxed its number one gal singer on the item." What happened was that Johnny Ace's "My Song" had originally been released by Duke Records, which Don Robey acquired and combined with his own Peacock Records out of Houston. Peacock issued the Marie Adams cover.

Mercury Records, which attempted a cover of just about every popular record, brought Dinah Washington into the studio to also record "My Song." *Cash Box*'s review the same week reported: "Dinah Washington throws her hat into the ring with her stylized reading of the exciting slow blues and comes through with a version that is bound to please her legion of fans."

Cash Box was way ahead of its own reviewers regarding the "My Song" craziness. The buzz on the record was so strong that as early as August 1952, *Cash Box*'s gossip column "Rhythm 'n' Blues Ramblings" sniffed out the hottest R&B story of the day: "Four fem versions of 'My Song' are hitting the market at the same time in a wild dash to get the jump. Peacock [actually Duke], which started all the excitement with its Johnny Ace release, follows up with a Marie Adams version that Don Robey, Peacock proxy, feels will establish the thrush as a nationwide star in the pop as well as R&B fields. OKeh enters the ring with Hadda Brooks, and Danny Kessler feels this one is the big one. Bobby Shad of Mercury comes through with his entry by Dinah Washington . . . and from Hollywood comes the Modern platter with Mary Jones handling the vocal."[59]

From 1952 through 1954, everything Johnny Ace released was a Top Ten hit, including another #1 song, "The Clock." The difficulty for Ace was that Robey, who controlled every aspect of his singers' careers, preferred to keep them on road. Even the immensely popular Ace barely spent time in the recording studio, so when news of his latest recording toward the end of 1954 began to leak to the public, teens were astir. The word was that this Johnny Ace song, called "Pledging My Love," was going to be the definitive blues ballad and Ace's best effort since "The Clock." Deejays, the trade press, and record buyers were poised. Peacock's Robey put Ace on the road with his other big singer Big Mama Thornton. Then tragedy struck. On Christmas day 1954 in Houston, Johnny Ace died of a self-inflicted bullet wound. Initially the press reported it was an accidental death, but even to this day, the myth has always been that Johnny Ace had been playing Russian roulette and lost.

The death started up a whole new Johnny Ace craze that manifested in two ways. "Pledging My Love" became a monster hit, dominating the R&B charts in 1955 for nine weeks. It even crossed over to the pop charts, climbing as high as #17, and probably would have gone higher if popular singer Teresa Brewer didn't cover the song and also take it to #17 on the pop charts.

In the annals of popular singers who died young, there probably has never been such a heartfelt combination of homage, exaltation, and eulogy as expressed musically through the tribute song. The record market was literally flooded with dedications. Linda Hayes and Johnny Moore's Blazers rushed out the two-sided extravaganza "Johnny Ace's Last Letter" with "Why, Johnny, Why"; Johnny Fuller warbled "Last Letter"; the Rovers went for "Salute to Johnny Ace"; and the Five Wings cried, "Johnny's Still Singing." Even Don Robey got into the act, tossing up Marie Adams to trill "In Memory (A Tribute to Johnny Ace)." Those records piled up on the desks of deejays and mustered little airplay in all instances except one. "Johnny Has Gone" by Varetta Dillard touched the souls of radio listeners and record buyers, climbing to #6 on the R&B charts and becoming one of the top R&B songs of 1955.

On February 5, 1955, Hollywood Records promoted "Johnny's Ace's Last Letter" and "Why, Johnny Why" in a vertical box-ad in *Billboard*. This was bad timing, as the magazine's "Review Spotlight" on the very same page as the ad focused on "Johnny Has Gone," saying: "Here's the first in what may well turn out to be a series of wax tributes to the late Johnny Ace. The canary [female singer] warmly sings the clever special lyrics written to include the titles of Ace's old hits."[60]

Two weeks later, the review spotlight focused on the Hearts' new entry, "Lonely Nights," but even that was secondary to the news about the launch of "Johnny Has Gone." As *Billboard* declared: "Varetta Dillard's reminiscences of Johnny Ace and his songs have taken off with formidable speed. Eastern sources, in particular New York, Philadelphia, and Baltimore, have been unusually enthusiastic over sales in their areas."[61]

When *Cash Box* jumped to commend "Johnny Has Gone" as its "Award o' the Week," the reviewer smartly turned the attention to singer Varetta Dillard:

"This gal has been threatening to break out into the real big time for a long time, and we think she has done it this time. She has latched onto a natural in the way of material and sentiment. Miss Dillard handles the item with soul and heart. She really feels the lyrics."[62]

The first line of the review accurately summed up Dillard's career; she was always on the verge of the limelight, but never made it to the Promised Land.

Dillard offered up a pliable range, often vacillating between Ruth Brown's bluesiness and Dinah Washington's jazz vernacular. Dillard was a Harlem gal, born and bred. Her birthday was in February 1933. As a youngster, she suffered a congenital bone problem in her right leg, and for a time, it was thought the leg would have to be amputated. To pass the time during the treatment process, she sang along to the radio. It turned out she was very good at it, winning two consecutive Amateur Night contests at the Apollo. In 1951, Dillard entered Amateur Night once again and this time went home without the top prize. Record executives and scouts always haunted these shows looking for new talent. That night, Lee Magid, then head of A&R at Savoy Records, was in the audience. He liked what he heard, went backstage to introduce himself, and invited Dillard to make a test recording for his label.[63]

This is how *Jet* reported the moment: "Varetta Dillard was discovered when she appeared at Amateur Night at New York's Apollo Theater. In the Dinah Washington tradition, she sings such adult numbers as 'Hurry Up,' which she wrote with Lee Magid of Savoy Records. Magid says her keen musical ear was handed down from her Virginia-born grandmother."[64]

In September 1951, Dillard recorded her first four tunes for Savoy, none of which attracted much deejay attention.

Or so it seemed. One deejay who liked what he heard was the soon-to-be most influential disc jockey on the planet, Alan Freed. He was toiling at Cleveland's WJW radio in 1951 when he began a night show for the teenage market, playing R&B records by Black singers and musicians. As a marketing gimmick, Freed organized a huge March 1952 concert, the Moondog Coronation Ball, at the Cleveland Arena. The concert, which attracted a reported 20,000 teens to a venue that held half that many, was shut down almost immediately by the panicked Cleveland Police Department. The event has since gone down in history as the first rock 'n' roll concert. Who was on the lineup that night? The answer is just a handful of R&B performers: Paul Williams and his Hucklebuckers, Tiny Grimes and his Rocking Highlanders, the Dominoes, Danny Cobb, and the relatively unknown Varetta Dillard.

(In 1955, when Freed organized his first New York concert, the huge Rock 'n' Roll Jubilee Ball, among the talented invited to perform were Big Joe Turner, Clyde McPhatter and the Drifters, Fats Domino, Ruth Brown, the Clovers, the Harptones, the Moonglows, and Varetta Dillard.)

In 1952, Savoy, thinking it had the next Ruth Brown or Dinah Washington, unleashed six singles by Dillard. One struck gold, a bouncy blues cut with a pre–rock 'n' roll beat called "Easy, Easy Baby." The song, written by Rudy Toombs, went to #8 on the R&B charts and was covered on the pop charts by Eileen Barton. Dillard's next big hit, "Mercy, Mr. Percy" arrived the following year. That song went to #6 on the pop charts and has lived on in infamy because of its unfortunate lyrics that, in a sense, declare physical abuse as acceptable.

After "Mercy, Mr. Percy" came two dry years of good songs but no action. Finally, she broke through in 1955 with "Johnny Has Gone." She followed it up with "You're the Answer to My Prayer," which garnered the "Award o' the Week" from *Cash Box*. The reviewer expected big things: "Miss Dillard sings a romantic slow tempo with a touch of religious flavoring. It is a solid piece of material that the chantress sells . . . it is a strong wax both material-wise and in performance." It didn't find any interest from record buyers. Nor did the next offering, "I'll Never Forget You," about which *Cash Box* exclaimed: "Varetta Dillard chants a tender, romantic ditty with a 'Tennessee Waltz'-type appeal. Varetta should get a good reaction to this one."[65] She didn't.

After 1955 went cold for her, and she switched to recording with Groove Records, a subsidiary of RCA Victor. Nothing was working there in 1956, so out of desperation, she was pushed into recording another tribute record called "I Miss You Jimmy" after the death of James Dean.[66] It disappeared, and so did Dillard's career.

She continued to record with various labels. Her last live show was in 1964, reported musicologist Marv Goldberg.[67]

In the 1980s, her name came up in an odd story from European record producer Jonas Benholm. He had been frustratingly trying to arrange a recording deal with Screamin' Jay Hawkins, when he got a call from Varetta Dillard's apartment. Hawkins had been thrown out of his own home and was staying with Dillard. Benholm knew her well enough that she would occasionally consult with him on financial matters. "She called me about various things," said Benholm. "She had inherited a piece of land and wanted my advice and financial help to turn it into a trailer park."

Benholm, a fan, sent her a letter saying that a new Varetta Dillard compilation would make "everybody understand that she had been too long in the shadows of Ruth Brown." Unfortunately, Dillard, who was friends with Brown, showed her the letter, and Ruth took it personally. Said Benholm, "She probably thought I felt that Varetta was better than her—which I didn't."

Sometime later, Benholm got a call from Dillard explaining that Screamin' Jay Hawkins was no longer staying with her, and she was glad to be rid of him. Hawkins made a lot of phone calls from her phone, which he didn't pay for, and Dillard ended up having to foot the bill. They didn't part as friends.

In an interview with *Blues & Rhythm* magazine, Benholm recalled, "It almost sounded as if Varetta, who had been a rehabilitated alcoholic, had started drinking again."[68]

She died of cancer in 1993 at sixty years of age.

The unnamed gossip writer who produced the New York edition of *Cash Box*'s "Rhythm 'n' Blues Ramblings" began his October 15, 1955, column with these remarks: "This week found the reviewing department in a quandary. There were so many good disks ready for a rating that the reviewers found it difficult to make their choices." Among the many talents up for scrutiny that week were Ruth Brown and Clyde McPhatter together as a duo. Their new platter was called "Love Has Joined Us Together."[69] And in real life, this was a love story—of sorts.

Clyde McPhatter had been drafted in 1954, and for most of his time in the service, he was stationed in Buffalo, New York. After a promotion of their new record in New York City, they decided to give love a shot. Ruth met Clyde in Buffalo, and they stayed at a friend's house. The good news eventually coming out of this liaison was that Brown got pregnant. Their son Ronn David McPhatter became a singer as well. The bad news was that the handsome, idolized Clyde McPhatter was, as Ruth Brown surmised, bisexual. As a popular singer in the 1950s, Clyde couldn't come out as gay; it would have ruined his career. "He began drinking to drown the guilt and shame he felt, sinking his career into the doldrums," Brown said. "My friendship and regard never ended, though. It continued until the day the world lost Clyde."[70]

The oddest trend that bubbled to the surface in 1955 and would grow in importance into the early 1960s was the male-female duo. Besides Ruth Brown and Clyde McPhatter, the biggest duo hit of the year came from the consistent New Orleans hitmakers Shirley and Lee with their song "Feel So Good." And like all new trends, it began with a bit of unexpected insanity, in this case, but not with the previously mentioned performers. The biggest duo commotion arrived via chart rookies Gene and Eunice, who had two hit songs in 1955, "This Is My Story" and the phantasmagorically ubiquitous "Ko Ko Mo."

Although they were both born in Texas, Gene and Eunice each ended up in the same Los Angeles musical greenhouse as Etta James and the Dreamers. Forest Gene Wilson and Eunice Levy met in Los Angeles at an amateur song contest, and when they later decided to sing together, they chose the one-voice style popularized by South Central LA singers Marvin and Johnny and the Cliques (Jesse Belvin and Eugene Church). Two other things would make them different from subsequent male-female duos: they were married and wrote most of their own songs.[71]

Two things characterized Gene and Eunice's biggest hit, "Ko Ko Mo": the legal mess behind the recording and the massive number of performing acts who tried the tune. "This was probably the most extensively recorded rock 'n' roll song of that time," claimed music writer Charlie Gillett. Notice the wording: "Ko Ko Mo" was referred to as a rock 'n' roll song, not a blues or R&B cut. Gillett was not the only musicologist to make that leap. Writer Larry Birnbaum wrote: "'Ko Ko Mo,' with its habanera bass line and Caribbean lilt, has somehow been overlooked as a possible first rock 'n' roll record."[72] That's a huge statement, especially considering Perry Como got a hold of the song, whitewashed the R&B completely out of it, and ended up with a giant hit on pop radio.

Jake Porter, who in 1951 started his Hollywood-based Combo Records, first recorded Gene and Eunice. His recording studio was in the basement of his home, and that's where Gene and Eunice cut the song that they wrote and called "Ko Ko Mo." On the Porter-produced platter, the artists were listed as Gene and Eunice backed by Jonesy's Combo.

When the song began to blowup, the much larger Aladdin Records realized it had Gene under contract as a solo artist and claimed ownership of the team Gene and Eunice. In January 1955, Aladdin rushed Gene and Eunice into the recording studio. Backed by Johnny Otis's band, they recorded the song again.[73] In the Aladdin version, the duo is backed by Johnny's Combo. Aladdin claimed the publishing rights, which Porter had already sold. The whole legal scramble was eventually settled. *Billboard* solved its listing problem by combining the performance of the Combo and Aladdin issues as one unit. In this accounting, "Ko Ko Mo" rose to #6 on the R&B charts.[74]

While all that was getting sorted out, a panoply of recording artists of all genres and styles rumbled for chart supremacy with the song. Into the fray went the Charms, the Flamingos, the Crew Cuts, the Hutton Sisters, Perry Como, Louis Armstrong, Gary Crosby, Marvin and Johnny, Bill Darnel, Betty Clooney, Tony Bennett, Goldie Hill, Red Sovine, Jack Caldwell, Tito Rodriguez, and even actor Andy Griffith. On the pop charts, Perry Como ended up king of the hill. In the R&B world, no act came close to Gene and Eunice.

Even with all that notoriety, when Gene and Eunice began touring to support their records, they couldn't quite get the respect of the R&B public. In May 1955, they were appearing in Washington, DC, at the Howard Theater. The multitalent show featured first the Orioles and then Gene and Eunice.[75] That was understandable, as the Orioles were a known commodity in the R&B world. However, two months later, when they played the Riverside Ballroom in Phoenix, a newspaper advertisement promoting the concert read: "Gene Ammons and his orchestra, featuring Gene and Eunice, vocalists"[76]—as if people would know who Gene Ammons was but were clueless about Gene and Eunice.

The strangest story about Gene and Eunice was that they planned to open a marriage counseling clinic in Los Angeles. The happily married couple figured they had expertise in the espousal world and a few extra bucks in their pocket

from the success of "Ko Ko Mo." In September 1955, when the press got wind
of it, the couple was already trying to find staff and meeting with architects
about constructing a building.

Gene explained: "Too many of our friends seem to have marriage problems
because of little things that they could straighten out if they had some good
advice. Our marriage has been so great . . . our idea for a free clinic would fix
it so more people could be just as happy." Considering the many marriages of
Dinah Washington and the choice of lovers by singers such as Ruth Brown,
maybe Gene and Eunice were on to something.

"The clinic will be—in a little way—our way to show our appreciation for
our great, good fortune," said Eunice.[77]

While their good fortune as recording stars didn't last beyond 1955, "Ko Ko
Mo" may have changed music forever.

Perry Como's version of the song gave RCA Victor its first rock 'n' roll styled
hit. Nevertheless, it was becoming clear to the big record companies that rock
'n' roll "had its own particular idiom, which needed talents different from those
possessed by crooners," wrote author Gillett. Major recording company Columbia Records opted to sidestep this realization, but RCA Victor decided to find
somebody who could do rock 'n' roll properly. Toward the end of 1955, nine
months after Como's "Ko Ko Mo," RCA Victor bought Elvis Presley's contract
from Sun Records.

CHAPTER SEVEN

LET THE GOOD TIMES ROLL (1956)

BILLIE HOLIDAY—HADDA BROOKS—JULES AND JOE BIHARI—
EDDIE HEYWOOD—DENVER FERGUSON—DINAH WASHINGTON—
JOE GREENE—RUTH BROWN—LAVERN BAKER—
LINCOLN CHASE—SHIRLEY AND LEE—THE TEEN QUEENS—
THE SIX TEENS—LOUISE HARRIS MURRAY—ZELL SANDERS—
JUSTINE "BABY" WASHINGTON—CLIFF DRIVER

With the arrival of New Year's Day 1956, the decade was now heading into its second half. Rock 'n' roll, which was the coming thing since the start of the 1950s, had finally conquered. On the pop charts, white female singers such as Doris Day and Patti Page, who began their careers in the 1940s, were still putting out hit records, but in the jazz/R&B world, the older generation of African American songbirds now graduated to album recordings, live performances at better (or best) venues, and even the occasional television appearance.

For two singers who created successful careers for themselves going back to the 1930s and 1940s, 1956 was significant, but in different ways. In the 1940s, both these singers boasted lucrative, prodigious, or interesting careers, albeit in separate cultural channels. In 1956, they were at a crossroads, and each reacted to what options were available and in accord with their own personal inclinations. The portents were positive.

In the introduction to this book, Lillian Walker-Moss exclaimed that her parents thought Billie Holiday was the best singer on the planet. Many would have agreed with them. And there are music enthusiasts today who would still be in accord with that assessment. Like Ella Fitzgerald, almost everything Holiday recorded in the 1930s and 1940s went straight to the pop charts. In 1937 alone, Holiday, or Lady Day as she was known, boasted sixteen Top Twenty hits. That was after eleven Top Twenty hits in 1936. Then that part of her career slowed down significantly, and she charted just three more records from 1941 through 1945. In a normal world, this drop-off in both output and radio play would be the death of a career, but in Holiday's case, the esteem never crumbled, and by the mid-1940s, she earned $250,000 over a three-year period. That constituted an amazing income for an African American in those years (the median wage for "non-white" workers in 1947 was $1,279). In the 1950s, the new album format was quite amenable to a singer like Holiday, and she created some wonderful music on the new format, including *Billie Holiday Sings* in 1952 and *An Evening with Billie Holiday* in 1953.[1]

Holiday (Eleanora Fagan) was born in Philadelphia in April 1915. She overcame a very difficult and impoverished childhood, rape at a young age, and brutal discrimination. During the height of her career when she could have been at the top of the world, hard drugs took her to the dark side. She spent time in jail and lost her cabaret card, which meant she couldn't sing in any venue that sold liquor.

These troubles were probably inevitable. Touring for Black performers was, literally and metaphorically, a hard road to travel. A stretch of one-nighters could mean twenty-five stops in a month's time. In some parts of the United States, due to segregation there were few to no places to stay the night or order food. Sleeping in a car was not unusual, and bathroom breaks were often in the woods by the side of the road.

The pay was miserable. When Holiday went on her first tour with the Count Basie Band, she quit her job at the Uptown House in New York that was paying $35 a week for a chance to make $14 a day on the road. As Holiday wrote: "Nobody bothered to tell me I'd have to travel five hundred to six hundred miles on a hot or cold ragged-ass Blue Goose bus; that it would cost me two or three bucks a night for a room; that by the time I was through having my hair fixed and gown pressed—to say nothing of paying for pretty clothes to wear—I'd end up with about a dollar and half a day. Out of that I had to eat and drink and send home some loot to mom."[2]

Lady singers were on their own with the band—almost always men. Downtime amusement for musicians on the road was often sex, alcohol, or drugs. There also were the traps set by police and segregation laws that were different in every town, especially in the South. In many places, whites and Blacks could not by law be in the same entertainment establishment. In some cities like New Orleans, the music in the Black clubs was so good that white folk would chance breaking the law to hear great bands. The police were on the take and let integrated businesses slide until the day they decided it was time to bust a club. As previously noted, when "Wacko" Wade Wright, a white drummer, began playing with Black performer Huey "Piano" Smith in New Orleans, he was scared all the time that he would get busted.[3]

The law did just as it pleased when it came to Black performers. Probably the most capriciously galling bust in the mid-1950s involved Ella Fitzgerald, Dizzy Gillespie, and Illinois Jacquet. Jazz impresario Norman Granz had organized a tour called Jazz at the Philharmonic with a large group of musicians, including white performers such as Buddy Rich. In October 1955, the tour landed in Houston to play the Music Hall. After the first set, Ella and her assistant Georgiana Henry were drinking coffee in her dressing room. Also there were Gillespie and Jacquet, who, to pass the time, were in the corner of the room tossing dice. Out of nowhere and for no reason at all, five plainclothes members of the city's vice squad burst into the room with guns drawn. It was suspected that the vice squad wanted to plant drugs, but Granz made sure that didn't happen. Everyone in the dressing room including Granz was arrested anyway—on a gambling charge because Gillespie and Jacquet had dice.[4]

Holiday faced many "cracker" sheriffs from one tour to the next. Eventually, she decided to record it all, the bad times, the good times, and the hard times. The resulting memoir, which she wrote with author William Dufty, was published in 1956 by Doubleday. *Lady Sings the Blues* remains a cultural touchstone to this day.

To illustrate how different Holiday's memoir *Lady Sings the Blues* was, let's compare it to a book Patti Page authored in 1960 called *Once Upon a Dream*, which was part memoir and mostly advice to teenagers on how they could live a better life. Here's an early paragraph:

> But let's hope you are lucky enough to have a room all your own. We've a lot of serious talking to do, you and I, and it's nice not be interrupted. That's where I'm writing the book, by the way, in my own room. Only nowadays that room of mine is likely to be almost anywhere. Chiefly it's a room with a view of Park Avenue, for I think of my New York apartment as home.[5]

Compare that to Holiday's stick-in-the-eye approach. Here's the fourth paragraph of her book:

> It's a wonder my mother didn't end up in the workhouse and me as a foundling. But Sadie Fagan loved me from the time I was just a swift kick in the ribs while she scrubbed floors. She went to the hospital and made a deal with the head woman there. She told them she'd scrub floors and wait on the other bitches laying up there to have their kids so she could pay her way and mine. And she did. Mom was 13 that Wednesday, April 7, 1915, in Baltimore when I was born.[6]

In November 1956, a concert was staged at Carnegie Hall in New York that paid tribute to Holiday and the book. It featured Gilbert Millstein, a writer from the *New York Times* who read excerpts from the book in between musical performances by Holiday. The concert was sold out.[7]

Holiday released three albums that year: *Solitude*, *Velvet Mood*, and to support the book, *Lady Sings the Blues*. The latter album, on the Verve label, included the well-known Holiday cuts "Strange Fruit," "God Bless the Child," and "Good Morning Heartache."

Creatively, Holiday was still at her peak. Physically, she was quickly wearing down. She would die three years later at age forty-four. The book *Lady Sings the Blues* would only grow in stature—becoming as legendary as the singer herself, with motion pictures and theater productions all based on a slim volume of raw, hard memories.

Hadda Brooks used to frequent the blues clubs on Central Avenue in Los Angeles, and on one particular night, she had to remove herself from her table to visit the john. She was sitting in the stall, one might say minding her own business, when she was shocked to see the door swing open. A handsome woman leaned in to offer her a hit from a marijuana joint. The lady was Billie Holiday. They became fast friends.

Brooks (Hattie L. Hapgood) was one year younger than Holiday. The closeness in age, beauty, musical talent, and unexpected success were things the two had in common. Every other way their lives were different. Brooks was born in Los Angeles in October 1916 to a middle-class family. Her father was a law enforcement officer, and her mother was a physician. Instead of the school of hard knocks, Brooks graduated from Vocational Polytechnic High School and went on to the University of Southern California.

Musically, Brooks had begun taking piano lessons at the age of four, and as an adult played the ivories in a popular dance studio frequented by Hollywood luminaries Gene Kelly, Fred Astaire, and Shirley Temple.[8]

By the mid-1940s, South Central Los Angeles was so crowded with musical talent, any turn could land you in the face of someone who was an up-and-comer or aspiring mogul. That was Brooks's tale as well. According to one story, she was noodling around on the piano keys at a Los Angeles music store when a jukebox repairman named Jules Bihari was in the room.

Bihari operated jukeboxes in all-Black locations, and in 1945 it was difficult to obtain R&B records. His frustrations were crystallized by one particular record, Cecil Gant's "I Wonder." It was a monster hit, and Bihari couldn't get enough of the platters to feed all his machines. He said to his three brothers, let's make records. The result was Modern Records. Joe Bihari recalled what happened next: "The first record that Jules cut was just a girl playing the piano

and 'Swingin' the Boogie' as we called it. The girl was Hadda Brooks . . . and
Jules had her swing the boogie to the accompaniment of bass and drums."

Joe Bihari had a different story of how Hadda and his brother met: "Jules got
to know Hadda because she ate in a restaurant the Bihari brothers owned in
the Little Tokyo neighborhood on San Pedro Street. She worked as a rehearsal
pianist at a nearby dance studio."[9]

"Swingin' the Boogie," an instrumental, became a hit in 1945. It was Jules
Bihari who changed her name. Not only were Brooks's first records basically
all boogie tunes, but she also had a nifty trick of taking a classical melody, such
as "Polonaise," and remaking it in boogie style.

According to the Black press: "The sepia lovely became an instant hit with
her Modern discs 'Polonaise Boogie,' 'Hungarian Rhapsody in Boogie,' and
others. She was the originator of doing the classics in boogie-woogie, and the
idea clicked big."

Eventually, Brooks became known as the "Queen of the Boogie." That, however, was not her real success. She was equally adept at ballads. Her recording
of "That's My Desire" peaked at #4 on the R&B charts in 1947.

Perhaps because Brooks was based in Los Angeles and demurely attractive,
she was lucky enough to appear in five Hollywood films between 1947 and
1952, including such esteemed productions as *The Bad and the Beautiful*. In
1957, she became the first female African American singer to host a television
show, *The Hadda Brooks Show*.

An unknown journalist wrote about her: ". . . Hadda Brooks, a pretty sepia
song stylist, [was] known as the 'Queen of the Boogie' off her many movie
and recording hits and personal appearances in America's leading theaters
and nightclubs."

"Moviegoers throughout the world will recall the hit she made in the 1950
Humphrey Bogart film *In a Lonely Place*," the *Arizona Sun* reported. "Her rendition of the Ray Noble song, 'I Hadn't Anyone but You,' was one of the high
spots of that movie."[10]

It's ironic that her boogie piano style was very close to what would become
rock 'n' roll, yet she couldn't find herself a sinecure in the 1950s pop music
world. It wasn't for lack of trying. She even took a shot at recording Johnny
Ace's #1 R&B hit of 1952, "My Song," which the OKeh label teamed with the #1
pop tune by Patti Page, "I Went to Your Wedding." A 1953 release called "You
Let My Love Get Cold" got the cold shoulder from *Cash Box*, which opined:
"Hadda Brooks latches on the multiple voice and harmonizes with herself on
this deck. However, the gimmick falls flat."[11]

After releasing about a dozen singles from 1950 through 1954 and getting
little more than a shallow response in return, she didn't release any new cuts

in 1955. Although she was "between disk deals," Brooks was back in the news. What happened was, personnel changes involving the two big talent agencies that represented jazz and R&B artists fell into a war for talent. Shaw Artists was able to sign Hadda Brooks along with Bo Diddley, Jimmy Witherspoon, Lynn Hope, and Paul Williams.[12]

The Shaw agency did its job, because in 1956, Hadda Brooks signed with a new label, which was her old label. *Billboard* sorted it out: "Singer Hadda Brooks was reunited with the first recording company she waxed for . . . when Modern Records inked Miss Brooks to a term recording contract. Chirp [female singer] will cut both albums and singles and will not be confined to R&B material. One of the early mainstays of the Modern firm more than 10 years ago . . . she arrived her for recording sessions last week and later returned to Chicago, where she is currently appearing."[13]

Modern got Brooks into the studio as fast as could be managed, where she recorded one single, "Old Man River," on the A-side, with "Close Your Eyes" on the B-side. It got a warm reception from the trades. *Billboard* put the "Spotlight" on it, noting: "The thrush's [female singer] first disk in quite a while is also one of her best ever. The styling of this standard is in a jazz vein, but it is so swingy and kicky that it could easily go pop, jazz, and R&B."[14]

Alas, the song didn't cut it with the modern audience of 1956, and it technically was her last singles studio recording, although she did wax a couple of records on small labels in 1959 and then at the end of her career in the 1990s. She continued playing nightclubs, festivals, and cafes, more often than not overseas before coming back to the United States. She died in 2002 at the age of eighty-six.

With the arrival of Elvis Presley on the scene in 1956, the whole music world shook, rattled, and rolled. All the cards were reshuffled, and in the new deal, the winner was rock 'n' roll, which crashed the pop and R&B charts simultaneously. Things were so scattered that white singers like Elvis Presley and even the tepid Guy Mitchell dominated the R&B charts, while African American rock 'n' roll acts such as Little Richard and Frankie Lymon and the Teenagers crashed the pop listings.

This wasn't necessarily good for the female voices of the time, because rock 'n' roll was essentially a male province. Nevertheless, on the pop chart, numerous women, from newcomer Gogi Grant ("The Wayward Wind") to veteran Kay Starr ("Rock and Roll Waltz") roared their way onto the best-selling record charts. With the merger of R&B, doo-wop, and rock 'n' roll, the R&B charts looked strange, with Elvis Presley and Carl Perkins fighting it out with Fats Domino and the Platters for dominance. Except for Shirley and Lee's rock 'n' roller "Let the Good Times Roll," no song with a female singer made the Top Twenty of the R&B cuts in 1956. Still, it wasn't necessarily a bad year for the ladies, as those songbirds who were already singing in the rock 'n' roll vein such as Ruth Brown and LaVern Baker cut some swagger in 1956. The biggest surprise was the rise of the female group sound, especially with the classic doo-wop number "Eddie My Love" by the Teen Queens. Taking a back seat for the moment were the jazzy, soft balladeers such as Dinah Washington.

Early in October 1956, a group of old friends bumped into each other in Chicago and partied all night long—at least until Dinah Washington had to leave for a gig in Kansas City. Joining her in the reunion were Hadda Brooks and singer/songwriter Eddie Heywood. Of the three, Heywood was definitely having a better year. More a contemporary of Brooks than of Washington, Heywood was born in Atlanta in 1915. His father was a jazz musician, and when it was his time to shine, he moved first to New Orleans and then to Kansas City. He played backup to Billie Holiday in the early 1940s, and his sextet boasted a big hit in 1944 with their jazzy version of "Begin the Beguine." However, 1956 was his year to crow because Heywood and bandleader Hugo Winterhalter recorded Heywood's tune "Canadian Sunset" and took it to #2 on the pop charts. It was also the twentieth best-selling song for the year.

It's not that Dinah Washington had a bad year, but she had several distractions. While most were good, it slowed her recording pace. Mercury had her in the studio for just a handful of songs.

She was still a star and probably the best-known and beloved R&B singer in the mid-1950s. Those who knew Washington would say she was absolutely aware of her position in the hierarchy of Black female singers. She understood who she was and took no crap from anyone. Her wardrobe gal Ferris Kinbrough recalled that she was always "picking a fight with someone."[15] It was tough to stay on top, and Washington was on top. She was no longer "Queen of the Jukeboxes." She had become "Queen of the Blues," and the independent Black press adored her. In June 1956, when she moved to a new apartment in New York, the gossip columnists exclaimed, "Seventh Avenue Ticker Tape." The story reported, "Dinah Washington will be one of the first tenants to move into the lavish new apartment building recently opened by the Bowery Savings Bank on upper St. Nicholas Ave. and 145th Street in New York City."[16]

Two months later, the Black press, which always concerned itself with the size and weight of the female, but not male, R&B singers, noted: "Losing 40 pounds cost blues singer Dinah Washington a tidy sum in replacing the dresses and gowns in her wardrobe that she can no longer wear."[17]

All that dedicated adulation resulted in a big feature in the November 1956 issue of *Ebony* magazine that, in turn, developed into syndicated story for the Black press around the country. African American newspaper patrons were thrilled to read that "Dinah, who parlayed a sultry voice and a reputation for eccentricity into a $100,000-a-year personality, tells *Ebony* how she pulled a pistol on her frightened boss Lionel Hampton when he wouldn't let her sing the numbers of her choice." Of course, there were the immensely readable quotes from Dinah, who said, "I knew I was going to be the best singer in the business."[18]

The biggest diversion in 1956 was purely personal. Around the end of 1955 or the beginning of 1956, Washington met an old friend from high school, Eddie Chamblee, who was a sax player with Lionel Hampton's band. They fell in love and married in March 1957, seven years after her last trip down the aisle. None of Washington's marriages stuck, and years afterward she wrote, "He was living at the Alvin Hotel in New York, broke and disgusted. I loved him, so I lent him money to straighten himself out. To be near him, we booked his band with me as an act, and we traveled the country together."

Chamblee, in a later interview, recalled that Dinah said to him, "'Let's get married,' and we'd kind of gotten together anyhow, so she was just the one who first said it . . . She was warm and kind to me . . . under certain circumstances, she was a beautiful woman. And on stage, emoting, she could tear your heart out."[19]

Of her handful of recordings in 1956, Washington had two hits, "Soft Winds" and "I'm Lost without You Tonight." Both records went to #13 on the R&B charts. "Soft Winds" was a 1940 standard composed by Benny Goodman that Washington updated with a bouncy modern beat. Dinah was able to overcome a lame intro of background singers and then carry the whole thing on her inimical voice. As good as "Soft Winds" was, Washington had a near masterpiece with "I'm Lost without You Tonight." In any other the year, this would have been a Top Five song. When it hit the charts at the beginning of 1956, already dominating were such powerhouse tunes as the Platters' "The Great Pretender" and "Only You," Little Richard's "Tutti Frutti," and Jay McShann/Patricia Bowman's "Hands Off." Coming up quickly were the Cadillacs' "Speedo" and Clyde McPhatter's "Seven Days."

"I'm Lost without You Tonight" was written by Joe Greene, who, like Eddie Heywood, was born in 1915 and had his first brush of success in the 1940s. He had a big hit in 1946 with "Don't Let the Sun Catch You Cryin'" by Louis Jordan. (It's not the same song that became a 1964 hit for the English Invasion band Gerry and the Pacemakers—although they did steal the title.) Greene had a good year in 1956. Bandleader Nelson Riddle, who bagged a monster instrumental hit with "Lisbon Antigua," recorded Greene's "The Tender Trap."

Greene's big shot in the arm was having Washington sing "I'm Lost without You Tonight." When Washington eases into "shipwrecked without a desert island, hungry without an appetite / run without a place to run to, I'm lost without you tonight," you're already smitten, and the song has just started.

Although the loungy ballad had enough interest to keep it in play through early 1956, most teenage R&B record buyers were in the mood for doo-wop or rock 'n' roll, which was good for the decade's other steadfast R&B singer, Ruth Brown.

Just about the time Dinah Washington was tying the knot with Eddie Chamblee, Ruth Brown married musician Earl Swanson. The difference in the two marriages was that Washington's union to Chamblee slowly devolved, while Brown jumped into an explosive relationship. Swanson was an abusive husband, once beating Brown to the ground. That marriage didn't last, although the two had a child together who was named Earl Jr.[20]

Professionally, Ruth Brown was peaking. In mid-1956, a *Cash Box* poll of R&B deejays selected Ruth Brown as the most programmed female artist. It wasn't even close. She polled 38 percent of the vote, way ahead of LaVern Baker at 19.9 percent and Dinah Washington at 10.5 percent.[21]

Brown also became one of the first R&B artists to appear in a television advertisement. Bill Simon at *Cash Box* reported the story as a truly pioneering moment by a Black performer. He wrote: "A new, loot-laden era was opened up to R&B talent last week—that of TV commercials. The first important act to break the barrier was Atlantic's Ruth Brown, who got the word that her 'test' effort for Lucky Strike had been accepted. It has taken the big agencies a long time to wake up to the sock-selling abilities of R&B talent, but now that Miss Brown has convinced 'em, look out!"[22]

Brown downplayed her break. "I was asked to do several television commercials, pretty unheard of for a Black lady at that time unless you happened to be Lena Horne . . . I was the Lucky Strike girl for a while, and when I did my jingle, 'Light up a Lucky! It's a light-up time,' the band behind was led by Paul Williams and included a young unknown named James Brown. I was also, so help me, the poster girl for Jax Beer."[23]

Mirroring Dinah Washington, Brown boasted two Top Twenty hits in 1956. Being as much a rock 'n' roll singer as she was an R&B act, Brown's offerings were in the same groove as the beat teenagers were digging that year. Her biggest hit was "I Want to Do More" with "Old Man River" on the B-side. In 1955, Brown had snagged a hit record by joining Clyde McPhatter as a duo. In 1956, she teamed up with his old group, the Drifters. The credits on "I Want to Do More" read Ruth and her Rhythmakers, which were in real life the Drifters. A good pairing to be sure, because the Drifters were coming off a #1 record, "Adorable," in 1955 and would have four more hits in 1956. "I Want to Do More" was straight-up rock 'n' roll because the songwriters were Jerry Leiber and Mike Stoller, who were the kings of that genre from the 1950s deep into the 1960s. "I Want to Do More" rose to #3 on the R&B charts.

Ruth Brown's other big hit of the year was "Sweet Baby of Mine," a fine tune with a keen electric guitar lead. Brown came down an octave for this swinger of a ditty, which had a hint of Peggy Lee's "Fever" in the melody.

Both Brown songs were strong entrees, but, like Washington, she ran into a maelstrom of male rock and doo-wop. When "Sweet Baby of Mine" hit the charts, the only other record doing well with a female voice was "Eddie My Love" by the Teen Queens. Otherwise, it was a deluge of terrific tunes by boys and men: "Why Do Fools Fall in Love" by the Teenagers with Frankie Lymon, "Corrine, Corrina" by Joe Turner, "Long Tall Sally" by Little Richard, "Drown in My Own Tears" by Ray Charles, "Church Bells May Ring" by the Willows, "Ivory Tower" by Otis Williams and the Charms, and "My Blue Heaven" by Fats Domino, not to mention incursions from Elvis Presley and Carl Perkins.

The best rock 'n' roll tune from a female soloist in 1956 and a song that could compete with anything from the boys was LaVern Baker's "Jim Dandy." Not only was it a #1 R&B tune, but in the year of rock 'n' roll, it crossed over to the pop charts, where it rose all the way to #17.[24] Part of the reason for its success in the pop world was that it was so deeply beat-driven and perfectly fit for the LaVern Baker treatment that it would have been tough for white songstresses to cover with any credibility. As author Gillett observed: "On 'Jim Dandy,' Baker displayed a rougher, deeper voice that successfully evaded imitation and established her name in the pop market."[25] Indeed, two other Baker songs, the #4 R&B tune "Still" and the #7 "I Can't Love You Enough," also crossed over to the pop charts.

Over the years, there have been two ways musicologists have considered the song "Jim Dandy." Author Birnbaum admitted that the lyrics were inane. Nevertheless, he calls the song "a rock 'n' roll landmark."[26] Marv Goldberg referred to "Jim Dandy" as "mindless" while adding it was given such "an infectious sound by LaVern that it was the one that made it to #1."[27] It stayed on the R&B charts for eighteen weeks.

"Jim Dandy" was written by songwriter Lincoln Chase, who in the early 1950s penned records for Big Maybelle and Ruth Brown. The Drifters had a hit with his song "Such a Night." His dandiest number was "Jim Dandy," which briefly turned him into a media star when a fawning, almost religious profile of him appeared in Black newspapers across the country. The opening paragraph read: "Lincoln Chase, God's gift of 'seven-in-one' is a true example of what to do with those talents God gave you since he is an accomplished writer, composer, arranger, coach, singer, musician, and specialist in material for personalities. His divinely blessed talent . . . his special material for such artists as Ruth Brown, Duke Ellington, Clyde McPhatter, Cab Calloway, LaVern Baker, Johnnie Ray . . . and others are all of such a personalized nature that only Chase could write such."[28] Whew!

Around 1959, Chase met singer Shirley Ellis and wrote or co wrote her big hits such as "The Nitty Gritty" in the early 1960s.

On December 8, 1956, a story in the *Miami Times* began this way: "Georgia Gibbs is at it again! And her special target, LaVern Baker, is the victim. Yes, the pop singer has stolen another hit tune from Baker, who sued for 'Tweedle Dee.' Georgia Gibbs uses the same style as the R&B vocalist, and it's destined to become a pop favorite. The tune, 'Tra La La.'"[29]

The B-side of "Jim Dandy" happened to be "Tra La La," which was getting play as a single. The odd thing was that Baker's version never made it to the R&B charts, but it did arrive at the lower regions of the pop charts. It might have done better if Georgia Gibbs hadn't covered the tune and turned it into a hit, taking it to #24 on the pop charts.

The story gets even weirder because in 1956, the Alan Freed film *Rock, Rock, Rock!* opened in theaters around the country. Among the rock 'n' rollers featured in the film was LaVern Baker, who sang "Tra La La."

Alan Freed had an abiding affection for Baker. In 1951, when Leo Mintz, who owned a record store in Cleveland, offered to "buy" Freed's radio show if it would be all R&B. Freed thought the man was crazy and exclaimed, "Those are race records." Mintz replied, "Not anymore."

Freed responded that he listened to LaVern Baker and Della Reese, "two girls with real contralto voices who know how to tell a story." Freed eventually acquiesced to Mintz's request and created his pioneering late-night R&B program. He eventually moved to WINS in New York City. But before he left town, Freed hosted his Second Annual Biggest Rhythm & Blues Show for almost ten thousand kids. Among the stars were LaVern Baker and Faye Adams. When Freed unleashed his Rock 'n' Roll Jubilee in April 1955 at the Brooklyn Paramount, LaVern Baker was again in the lineup.[30]

In May 1956, a huge extravaganza of a show appeared in Miami that was touted as the "biggest rock 'n' roll show" of the year. The preview commentary squealed in delight: "Here in one big show are all the greats of rock 'n' roll . . . including Bill Haley and his Comets, the Platters, LaVern Baker, Big Joe Turner, the Drifters, Bo Diddley . . ."[31]

On the lighter side, LaVern Baker didn't get quite the scrutiny of the Black press the way Dinah Washington did, but when it came to journalists' continued fascination with the body shape of female R&B singers, she got a few mentions. In May 1956, a wire service story that appeared in Black newspapers began: "Equally buxom Dinah Washington and LaVern Baker clashed in a vocal battle at a Brooklyn nitery with LaVern almost stealing Dinah's show with her house-rockin' 'Tweedle Dee.'"[32]

In 1956, when it came down to what was the best rock 'n' roll tune with a female vocalist on any chart in America, pop, R&B, or even country & western, the answer was Shirley and Lee's "Let the Good Times Roll," which not only went to #1 on the R&B charts, but crossed over to the pop chart, making a dent at #20. The duo of Shirley Goodman and Leonard Lee had been scoring hit songs since they met at Joseph Clark High School in New Orleans.

When Cosimo Matassa opened his J&M Recording Service in 1947, a lot of musical strands coalesced in New Orleans. First, the town and its environs, particularly Gretna across the Mississippi River from the Big Easy, were loaded to the fish gills with bars, nightclubs, and juke joints. Famous entertainers, blues singers from the Mississippi Delta, itinerant musicians, and even cross-dressing singers could find a place to play in New Orleans. That still wasn't enough to fill the bandstands every night, so local talent did the rest. New Orleans singer Clarence "Frogman" Henry, who boasted hits in the early 1950s with "Ain't Got No Home" and "But I Do," got his start in Gretna. "That's where I wrote my first song, playing in a club called the Joy Knocks Hot Club," said Henry. "A lot of guys from my time played there."[33]

Second, at the end of the 1940s, when blues and R&B began reaching into the world of white radio listeners and record buyers, independent record companies looking for talent started coming to New Orleans. The added benefit of being among so many singers and musicians was that they could record the prodigals right there at J&M. The first independent to score was De Luxe Records out of New Jersey at the end of the 1940s. After De Luxe's success with Roy Brown's "Good Rockin' Tonight," with that unique proto–rock 'n' roll beat, everyone else followed, in particular the Los Angeles independents such as Specialty, Aladdin, and Imperial. On Imperial Records president Lew Chudd's first trip to the city, he signed Fats Domino and David Bartholomew. It was a wild scene in New Orleans and sometimes it was tough to cut through the segregation and craziness. Johnny Vincent, who was a local A&R man for Specialty Records, not only had to bail Ray Charles out of jail when he was busted for weed, but also had to sell his boss Art Rupe at Specialty on Guitar Slim's recording of "The Things That I Used to Do." Rupe called the record a piece of shit, but it went on to sell millions. Vincent quit Specialty and formed his own label, Ace Records, in Jackson, Mississippi. Third, with a growing reputation as the place to make music, up-and-coming musicians by the hundreds gravitated to New Orleans. Early rock 'n' rollers such as Ray Charles, Little Richard, Lloyd Price, and Guitar Slim among many others all washed into town to record at J&M in the early 1950s.

This all leads back to Shirley (Mae) Goodman, who was born in 1936 in New Orleans. She was one of six children, and when her parents divorced, she was sent to live with her grandmother, who raised her. Goodman sang at her grandmother's Baptist church and anywhere else she could find space and friends. As she told New Orleans music historian Jeff Hannusch, "I'd be singing all the time with my friends in the streets. My favorite then was Dinah

Washington; she had a light and happy sound that appealed to me. She was the greatest singer I ever heard."

When Shirley was a freshman in high school (still thirteen years old), she was part of a large group of boys and girls who enjoyed singing together. They hung out at the house of one girl who had a piano, and together they all came up with a song called "I'm Gone," which Goodman said just "went on and on." They all liked "I'm Gone" and decided to record it. They went to J&M Records and asked Cosimo if they could record. He was a busy guy and didn't want to deal with a bunch of kids, so he gently shushed them away. They came back so often he finally relented, saying, "Bring me two dollars and y'all could make a record."

None of them had two cents, let alone two dollars, and it took a few weeks until the kids raised the money. Cosimo led a small group into the studio, where two great musicians, Earl Palmer and Lee Allen, were hanging out. That was the first lucky break, because Palmer and Allen helped on the recording. Soon afterward, the second big break arrived in town. Eddie Mesner, the owner of Aladdin Records, went to New Orleans scouting for talent. He was at the J&M Studio with Cosimo, and they needed a tape on which to record. Cosimo decided to use the one from the kids' recording, which he didn't need any longer. Before the old recording on the tape was erased, Mesner asked to listen to the song on it. He heard a girl's high-pitched voice dominating a tune called "I'm Gone." Mesner was blown away and told Cosimo, "Find that girl." Shirley Goodman was eventually located, and Mesner decided to record her with a male voice as a duo. He listened to all the boys who were in the recording studio that day and decided on Leonard Lee. The singing duo Shirley and Lee was born.[34]

In 1952, Shirley and Lee stepped into the studio to record "I'm Gone" with "Sweethearts" on the B-side. David Bartholomew produced the recording session, as he did with the duo's next two songs. The record label reads Bartholomew and Lee as the songwriters. Singing credits go to Shirley and Lee, and in smaller letters, Dave Bartholomew and his orchestra. "I'm Gone" was a #2 R&B hit in 1952.

Famous male and female singers often got together to sing, but there weren't many successful acts that were established primarily as a duo. In the early 1950s, Les Paul and Mary Ford, a husband-and-wife team, began a successful run the first year of the new decade. Between 1950 and 1954, the duo boasted sixteen Top Ten hits. The other big pop duo of the mid-1950s, New Orleans–born Louis Prima and Keely Smith, didn't get rolling until 1954.

In the R&B world, male singers did their thing and female singers did theirs. Occasionally, a Louis Armstrong would duet with an Ella Fitzgerald, but there was not a history of successful long-term duet acts. Shirley and Lee's triumphs would have a lasting effect on R&B, from Gene and Eunice to Johnnie and Joe to Mickey and Sylvia. By the early 1960s, rock 'n' roll would cave as well. Dick and Dee Dee had a big hit in 1961 with "The Mountain's High," Paul and Paula with "Hey Paula" in 1963, and Nino Tempo and April Stevens, also in 1963, with "Deep Purple." The Ike and Tina Turner Review formed in 1960.

Despite the success of "I'm Gone," Aladdin decided to make the B-side song, "Sweethearts," the duo's underlying theme. They were billed as the Sweethearts of the Blues and over the next two years released romantically themed songs such as "The Proposal" with "Two Happy People" on the B-side, "Shirley's Back" with "So in Love" on the B-side, and "Baby" with "Shirley Come Back to Me" on the B-side. Although none of these songs were big hits, teenager Louise Murray listened to these records, and decades later when she started singing with her husband Donald Gatling, they included "Shirley Come Back to Me" in their act as well as "I'm Gone."[35]

After a two-year drought, Shirley and Lee finally had another big hit with "Feel So Good," which soared to #2 on the R&B charts. Writer Birnbaum noticed that all their previous romantic-themed songs had similar bass lines. He thought "Feel So Good" succeeded because it was different: "'Feel So Good' . . . extends the romantic theme and responsive format of the preceding singles but with a different descending bass line and in a more exultant mood."[36] Shirley squeals in orgiastic delight: "Feels so fine, know that I'm on your mind / Oh, what a feeling to know you're revealing / Feels so good now, please don't stop now, ooh."

Shirley and Lee were pitched to the public as a couple, and they would play that up in their stage act. Bobby Rush, who saw their show several times, said they were comedic like Sonny and Cher: "They weren't die-hard singers, but good entertainers. They would pick on each other. If he sang, for example, 'it takes two, honey,' there would be a break and then she would say 'it takes more than two of you to satisfy me.' They could be ribald."[37]

The public believed Shirley and Lee were married. Years later, Shirley laughed about it, saying, "People thought that because we sang those songs about each other. We didn't have time for each other . . . I got married and so did Lee. We were real good friends, but that was all."

The 1960s girl group the Dixie Cups emerged out of New Orleans, and in their act over the years, they often sang tunes from other New Orleans performers such as Fats Domino, Jessie Hill, and Shirley and Lee. They sang "Let the Good Times Roll." New Orleans wasn't that big a city, so most musicians knew or heard of each other. The Dixie Cups' Barbara Hawkins couldn't recall meeting Shirley and Lee in New Orleans, but she did remember that Leonard Lee was married to a lady on her block who they used to call Aunt Geri. Barbara and her sister Rosa were friendly enough with Aunt Geri that she remembered Leonard was always gone, always on the road. The Dixie Cups' first manager, singer Joe Jones, would often talk about Shirley and Lee because before he sang his hit song "You Talk Too Much," he had a band that played back-up for the duo on one of their tours.[38]

In 1956, Huey "Piano" Smith, who would soon write and record such classic rock 'n' roll tunes as "Rockin' Pneumonia and the Boogie Woogie Flu," "Don't You Just Know It," and "Sea Cruise," had just signed with Johnny Vincent's Ace Records. To support his first single "Little Liza Jane," he went on the road that year as a supporting act and backup pianist for Shirley and Lee. The duo had just released "Let the Good Times Roll."

Also on the road was Leonard Lee's wife, which caused a whole lotta problems in the Shirley and Lee stage act because they couldn't do their flirtatious, quibbling patter. "It wasn't no harmony when Leonard's wife was out there," Huey remembered. "Leonard sitting there, talking, with blood in his eyes. Yeah, fire. The show didn't do too good. He's mad with his lips all stuck out because he can't give no attention to Shirley."[39]

What Goodman remembered from that tour was that her pianist (Huey Piano Smith) always "had a lot of ladies in his room."

A few bumps on a tour were small potatoes to Shirley and Lee in 1956, because more than any other R&B act with a female singer, they were at the top with two Top Five songs. "I Feel Good," went to #3 on the R&B charts, and the great "Let the Good Times Roll" settled at #1 R&B and in jukebox play in September of that year.

Leonard Lee got credit for writing the two songs, and both were strong, primordial rockers. What made the cuts work for the duo was the romantic frisson that was the underlying theme of their songs and their stage act. In "I Feel Good," Goodman sings, "When you're close to me, Hold me tenderly / Then the world can see, I feel good." On "Let the Good Times Roll," she sings, "Come on baby, just close the door / Come on baby, lets rock some more / Come on baby, let the good times roll / Roll all night long."

Author Birnbaum wrote: "'Let the Good Times Roll' borrows the introductory riff from 'Feel So Good' but uses it more extensively, along with a more conventional boogie bass line. With its rollicking Lee Allen saxophone solo, the record has a strong New Orleans feel, but the song has become more than just a Crescent City anthem, covered by everyone from Conway Twitty to Barbra Streisand to the Animals."[40]

The other major music genre besides rock 'n' roll to dominate the R&B world and encroach upon the pop scene at the same time was doo-wop. This harmonic sound had been growing in popularity since the start of the 1950s and had become a mature if not dominant form of musical expression. In the early days, it was almost exclusively a song-form performed by male groups, but after the trailblazing efforts of Shirley Gunter and the Queens and the Hearts, more females began pushing into the field.

In the mid-1950s, if you were a teenager in the Northeast, particularly in the New York metropolitan area, from Long Island to New Jersey to Connecticut, and went to a dance or basement party, you probably slow grooved to one of three songs: "In the Still of the Night" (1956) by the Five Satins, "Eddie My Love" (1956) by the Teen Queens, or "Tonight, Tonight" (1957) by the Mello-Kings.

A survey of top hits from an unnamed New York radio station (either WINS or WABC) for 1956 through 1962 showed how strong doo-wop was across the Big Apple in 1956. The #1 song according to this survey was "In the Still of the Night," one slot ahead of Elvis Presley's "Don't Be Cruel." The #14 record was "Eddie My Love," one position in front of Presley's "Hound Dog." *Billboard* would list Presley's "Heartbreak Hotel" and "Don't Be Cruel" as the two top songs of the year, with "Hound Dog" at #8.

The Five Satins and Mello-Kings were New York area boys, and their success reinforced the assumption that doo-wop was an urban sound, mostly popular in dense cities in the Northeast and Midwest, places like New York, Philadelphia, Washington, DC, Newark, and Boston.

"Eddie My Love" was different for two reasons. First, it was a song by two teenage girls, and second, it came out of the West Coast petri dish of R&B, South Central Los Angeles. In retrospect, in the early 1950s, with its clubs, homegrown talent, and cavalcade of independent record companies, Los Angeles—not the Northeast—was probably the epicenter of doo-wop in America. Classic doo-wop songs such as "Earth Angel," "Goodnight My Love," "Ko Ko Mo," and "Eddie My Love" were created by denizens of the Los Angeles music scene.

The genesis of "Eddie My Love" began with Aaron Collins, who sang with a gospel group called the Soul Seekers. In 1955, they approached Modern Records, run by the Bihari Brothers, about a record deal. The Bihari brothers' A&R man Maxwell Davis suggested they abandon the spiritual for secular music. The Biharis had plenty of brothers (Saul, Jules, Joe, and Lester) and plenty of labels (Modern, RPM, Crown, Kent, Flair, and Meteor). Due to complications among the labels, the old Soul Seekers became the Cadets, who recorded the popular novelty tune "Stranded in the Jungle" on Modern, and the Jacks, who recorded the big hit "Why Don't You Write Me?" on RPM. (Collins would also become a member of the Flares, which had a hit tune in 1961 with "Foot Stompin', Part 1.")[41]

In 1956, Aaron Collins brought his two sisters Rose and Betty Collins into the Modern Studios to record a song he wrote called "Eddie My Love." It was released on the RPM label. Collins was forced to share songwriting credits with Maxwell Davis, who played the mellow sax riffs on the tune, and Sam Ling. The latter name was a pseudonym for Saul Bihari, who had nothing to do with writing the song. In the sleazy world of independent labels, the Bihari boys liked to cut themselves some of the songwriting credits, which could be lucrative if the song became a hit. And "Eddie My Love" was a titan of a song, becoming a #3 best-seller on the *Billboard* R&B charts and the second best-selling R&B tune by a female that year. The song crossed over to the pop charts, climbing to #14. It might have done even better, but the song was covered by the Chordettes and Fontane Sisters, both of whom had Top Twenty hits with it.

John Clemente, who wrote *Girl Groups: Fabulous Females That Rocked the World*, said of "Eddie My Love": "The song's arrangement contains low blowing saxophones and slow, countering piano chords to introduce the song and ends just the same way. The pace of the tune is meant to evoke the sentiment of a funeral dirge. This arrangement would become a trademark in Teen Queens' recordings."[42]

What worked so well in "Eddie My Love" never gelled with new recordings. The Teen Queens recorded sporadically on different labels into the early 1960s without ever finding that winning formula again. For Rose and Betty Collins, life didn't treat them any better than the record world did. Rose died by her own hand in 1968, and Betty, who had drug problems, passed away three years later.

In March 1956, a gala tour was put together by promoter Irvin Feld. Among the acts in the lineup were Bill Haley and his Comets, the Platters, LaVern Baker, Clyde McPhatter, the Drifters, Joe Turner, Bo Diddley, Red Prysock, the Flamingos, the Colts, and the Teenagers (actually, the Teenagers with Frankie Lymon), and the Teen Queens. There was a little confusion at the end with those teen-named groups.[43] By April, the teen group label became a sludge pile. While the Teen Queens' "Eddie My Love" was still fighting with the Teenagers' "Why Do Fools Fall in Love" for supremacy on the record charts, a new "teen" entry was spotted by *Billboard*. Its "Review Spotlight On" focused on a group called the Six Teens with its single "Teenage Promise" on the A-side and "A Casual Look" on the B-side.[44]

As the reviewer shrewdly noticed, "On the flip, 'A Casual Look,' there's an equally strong bit that has beautiful harmony and a salable teenage love theme."

"A Casual Look," a surprise hit in 1956, was another doo-wop standard to come out of the Los Angeles music scene. The group behind the song called themselves the Six Teens because they were six teenagers. The oldest, Ed Wells, was seventeen and the youngest, Trudy Williams, was twelve. The other singers were Kenneth Sinclair, Darryl Lewis, Louise Williams, and Beverly Pecot. They originally organized in 1955 as the Sweet Teens, but when they signed with Hollywood-based Flip Records, which itself was just organized in 1955, they became the Six Teens. "A Casual Look" was the label's first big hit.[45]

The tune played out in the same fashion as a male-female duet, with the high-voiced female lead bouncing off the bass of the male lead. Song credits went to Ed Wells, and he really did a good job making it contemporary. The year 1956 fell between the Korean War and the buildup to the Vietnam War.

The draft was still in effect, and a lot of singers were getting drafted, from Elvis Presley to Clyde McPhatter to Los Angeles king of doo-wop Jesse Belvin. Perhaps at seventeen, Wells knew what would be coming. In the song, he implores, "Darling, can't you see that I'm going overseas / . . . So hear, hear my plea, and marry, marry me / Before it's too late."

The song was very strong in its hometown market of Los Angeles before busting loose across the country. One month after *Billboard* spotted the tune's commercial potential, the magazine put the spotlight on records by the Clovers, Little Esther, James Brown, and Big Maybelle, but its two up-and-comers were "Hallelujah, I Love Her So" by Ray Charles and "A Casual Look" by the Six Teens. Of the latter, the magazine commented on the song's journey: "For the past two weeks, the Los Angeles R&B territorial chart has been carrying this record, and this week, the Pittsburgh pop territorial chart lists 'A Casual Look.' Wherever it has been available, pop and R&B acceptance has been very good. Philadelphia, New York, and Baltimore have been among the cities that have been doing a good sales job."[46]

One month later, in June, the song was still #1 in Los Angeles. On June 16, Flip Records broke open its pocketbook and took a quarter-page ad in the trades to keep the momentum going. A *Cash Box* promotion read: "The Original Smash Hit! A Casual Look. The Six Teens. #1 in Los Angeles, Breaking POP Nationally."[47] In July, against stiff competition from Little Willie John's "Fever," Clyde McPhatter's "Treasure of Love," Little Richard's "Rip It Up," Chuck Berry's "Roll Over Beethoven," the Platters' "My Prayer," and Joe Turner's "Corrine, Corrina," "A Casual Look" hit #7 on the R&B charts, one spot ahead of the Cadets' "Stranded in the Jungle." It would also cross over, rising to #25 pop.[48]

Max and Lilian Feirtag operated the Flip label, but their background is obscure. Since they appeared to be rookies in the business regarding the label's first stars, the Six Teens, Flip's management made a beginner's error in marketing. Unfortunately, it was a death spiral type of mistake. In 1957, when the group should have been on tours across the continental United States, expanding its appeal in local markets, management signed the Six Teens to a lengthy stay in Hawaii.[49] In effect, they were isolated. In September 1956, the group's next release "Send Me Flowers" made the coveted "Sleeper of the Week" slot in *Cash Box*. The lengthier review read: "The Six Teens, who took the big jump upwards with their 'A Casual Look,' pair an intriguing coupling, 'Send Me Flowers,' a quick beat jump cutie, and "Afar into the Night," a pretty slow ballad. The 'Send Me Flowers' etching combines a swinging beat, a romantic lyric, and the vocal sound and reading of the Six Teens."[50]

Also written by Ed Wells, "Send Me Flowers" was a hyper-doo-wop number without charm. It was a #1 song in Hawaii and did *nada* everywhere else, which pretty much summed up what happened to the group. What can you do if one of your follow-up records is called "Stop Playing Ping Pong with My Little Heart?" The Six Teens somewhat modeled themselves on the Teenagers featuring Frankie Lymon, so it wasn't much of a surprise to see the 1957 offering "Arrow of Love" with a song credit reading the Six Teens featuring Trudy Williams. Although Flip kept recording the group into the 1960s, no other hits were forthcoming.

Weak secondary efforts and management mistakes weren't the only things to plague R&B groups in the mid-1950s. In the pop world, sister acts (the McGuire Sisters, the Fontane Sisters, and so on) were stable units, but the newly emerging female R&B groups were formed by girls who didn't have those family ties. It was tough keeping them all together. Some of the girls dropped out just to do teenage things, some married, and others got pregnant.

For Zell Sanders, members of the Hearts moving on was a problem until she realized fans didn't really know the individuals in the group; she could substitute new voices and no one would care. The leads in the early Hearts' recordings were either Joyce West or Louise Murray. By 1956, they were gone, so Sanders brought in Justine "Baby" Washington to be the new lead singer. Her first single with the Hearts was unleashed in March 1956. *Cash Box*'s review listed "Going Home to Stay" as the A-side with "Disappointed Bride" as the B-side. On "Going Home to Stay," the commentary read: "The Hearts . . . turn out a good side. Could be a hit." As to "Disappointed Bride," the reviewer wrote, "Another slow beat with a similar story pattern and a narrative-type vocal in parts. OK deck that could get a good reaction from the teeners."[51]

Zell Sanders wrote both songs. Each was more blues-oriented than "Lonely Nights," and the market was less appreciative.

Louise Murray said about Zell Sanders that she would just walk down the streets of Harlem, stopping girls and asking them if they could sing. It was more or less a broad commentary on Sanders's penchant for shifting girls in and out of her groups, a practice that would eventually get bizarre a few years later. Sanders didn't have to stop girls on the street, as she had a very good network of where to find talent.[52]

Justine Washington was born in Bamberg, South Carolina, on November 13, 1940. Her parents moved to Harlem when she was two. As she got older, Justine sang in church and was sent to Carr Studios, just down the street from the Apollo, for singing and dance lessons. Her only brush with fame was when a group of girls and guys from Carr Studios sang a jingle for one of the local radio stations.

In 1956, Sanders was looking for girls to replace all the recently departed Hearts. She went to the studio and after doing auditions, selected Justine and Anna Barnhill. The new Hearts were now Justine, Anna, Joyce Peterson, and Theresa Chatman. Even Rex was included in the group.

It was here that Washington acquired her famous stage name.

"When I was with the Hearts, they just called me 'Baby' because I was so young. It was kind of a nickname from the other girls," Washington remembered.

Washington joined the Hearts probably in autumn of 1955, which would have made her fourteen at the time. She had a pleasant, deep voice—not as solidly alto as Louise, but good for what Sanders wanted, and was quickly given the role of lead singer.

Justine, now more often referred to as "Baby," was thrilled to be a member of the Hearts and didn't mind Sanders's overzealous management of the girls. She said, "I just wanted to sing and wasn't intimidated by her. Sanders was a businesswoman. She wanted harmony a certain way. She had us do steps a certain way. She dressed us alike. She bought the shoes, the clothes, and had pictures taken."

Sanders was all business. She took care of the dates, had the Hearts record a theme song for deejay Georgie Hudson's radio show in New Jersey, backed other recording groups, and made sure the Hearts got to and from their engagements.

After the failure of "Going Home to Stay" / "Disappointed Bride," Baton tried once again in 1956 with the Hearts, releasing one more record that year, "He Drives Me Crazy," in July 1956. Once again, Zell put her name on the record as songwriter. The song was fast paced, with an El Dorados' "At My Front Door" beat and too much else going on. It was a real mess and went nowhere. Much better was the B-side, "I Had a Guy," which had intimations of the coming girl group sound and where Sanders was really headed musically.

In 1956, most of the Hearts' appearances were in the summer months, as they were all young and still in high school the rest of the year. If a gig was close by, they worked weekends as well. As a Heart, Washington remembers working a lot on Long Island, in Springfield, Massachusetts, and in theaters in Baltimore and Washington, DC. A lot of one-nighters were squeezed into their schedule.

There was still the Apollo, which was always happy to showcase the Hearts no matter who was in the group. For teenager Justine Washington, it was a thrill to be around other stars, who she would watch from the wings. There was always something to learn from other singers, plus watching others drove home the point of what Sanders was trying to teach them: to look professional, act professional, and sound right as a group.

The Apollo was not just a good time—it was hard work. Generally, a group was booked for a week, with as many as five or six shows a day. Sometimes on the weekend, if the take looked good, the Apollo would push in an extra show. As Washington recalled, "It was a work-out and so hard you would never think to yourself, 'Ah, look at me, I'm at the top.'"

Ironically, the Apollo was also the end of the line for Washington and the Hearts. One day, Sanders's secretary left Sanders's Apollo contract exposed where all the girls could see what the Hearts were earning for their week stay at the Apollo. They decided to ask for more money. Sanders called a meeting. When everyone was present, she fired all of the singers in the Hearts, keeping with her only the secretary and Rex—she couldn't do without Rex.

"We were on a salary. Whenever we worked, we would get $50 for the entire week [Louise remembered getting $75]. That was $50 for each person," Washington stressed. "Sanders was getting paid thousands for our appearances. We should have gotten more."[53]

Soon after leaving the Hearts, Justine met Cliff Driver, a blind piano player who fronted his own band. She started doing one-nighters in the New York area as Baby Washington. After one gig, a man came up to her and said he knew someone at a record label who should hear her sing. The man was Ben "Sweet" Fowler, who was working for a small label out of Newark, Neptune Records. Neptune decided to record her, with the first song being "The Time," which was written by Baby Washington.

As a coda to Cliff Driver, in 2015, a writer and friend Jacob Blickenstaff wrote: "Cliff took a young singer from the Hearts named Baby Washington into the studio and produced her first solo sessions. They would have a number of R&B hits together on Neptune Records, starting with a two-sided record 'The Time' with 'The Bells' in 1959." She would go on to record "Workout" and "Nobody Cares About Me" for Neptune, both moderately successful songs. In 1962, Baby split from Cliff and moved to Juggy Murray's Sue label.

Henry "Juggy" Murray and Bobby Robinson founded Sue Records (and numerous subsidiary labels such as Crackerjack and Broadway Records) in 1957. The two had a good ear for music and a fine eye for talent, signing Bobby Hendricks, who gave them their first big hit, "Itchy Twitchy Feeling," in 1958. Two years later, they signed Ike and Tina Turner to the label. Then two years after that, they signed Baby Washington. It was with Juggy that Baby made her two best-known recordings, "That's How Heartaches Are Made" in 1963 and "Only Those in Love" in 1965. Both songs were helped by an industry veteran named Bert Keyes, who did a good job arranging the Sue Records success "Mockingbird," by Inez and Charlie Foxx. He conducted and arranged "That's How Heartaches Are Made," while one of the songwriters for "Only Those in Love" was well-known orchestra leader Bert Kaempfert, who also wrote the music for "Strangers in the Night."

Baby Washington would have five Top Twenty records on the R&B charts, including the two Top Ten records "That's How Heartaches Are Made" and "Only Those in Love." Oddly, Baby Washington had little crossover appeal despite an assertive voice with a lot of melodic variation. The wonderful "That's How Heartaches Are Made" boasted a background of female singers, giving the song a real girl group sound. It was her best shot at white, female record-buyers, hitting #40 on the pop charts. Perhaps it had more soul than the lighter female songs of the time. Keyes, who worked with white and Black rock 'n' rollers, including female singers Eydie Gorme and Timi Yuro, gave "Only Those in Love" the overwrought orchestration of something from early Patti LaBelle and the Bluebelles.[54]

From the start, Washington switched personalities in the studio, recording as Baby Washington, Jeanette Washington, or Justine Washington. She plowed on, recording often through the 1960s and 1970s in the United States and UK. She never gave up on her quest for the golden ring of success, even recording as a duo with Don Gardner in the 1970s. She was still making inroads on the R&B charts, but mainstream success eluded her; that's too bad, because she had a killer voice.

CHAPTER EIGHT

LOVE IS STRANGE (1957)

ZELL SANDERS—FREDDIE SCOTT—JOHNNIE AND JOE— MICKEY & SYLVIA—THE TUNE WEAVERS—FRANK PAUL— ANNIE LAURIE—PAUL GAYTEN—LAVERN BAKER— RUTH BROWN—JERRY LEIBER & MIKE STOLLER— DINAH WASHINGTON—THE BOBBETTES

Louise Harris and Baby Washington never met in the 1950s, which was odd because they were both very friendly with Zell Sanders's daughter Johnnie.

Johnnie Louise Richardson, born in 1935 in Montgomery, Alabama, by all accounts had a bubbly personality and no really strong desire to be a famous singer. However, she ended up in a special place anyway as part of the successful doo-wop duo Johnnie and Joe, who had a big hit in 1957 with "Over the Mountain, Across the Sea."

When Louise was still with the Hearts, she, Johnnie, and Joyce West would hang out almost every day. Even after leaving the Hearts, Louise remained buddies with Johnnie, forever visiting at her house, where, after the turmoil of the Hearts, she remained friendly with Zell as well. As Louise recalls, "Zell Sanders always liked me," and it was so much easier to like Sanders once Louise was no longer part of her grand ambitions.

And Zell Sanders had aspirations, big ones. She wanted to dive deeply into the music business, but to do that she needed to create a label of her own. In May 1956, Zell decided to start a new record company, J&S Records, which she ran from her home in the Bronx.[1] What great timing, because 1956 was the year rock 'n' roll burst across America.

This isn't to say other record company executives were wearing permanent blinders and that they didn't see the teenage buyer market was growing by fantastic leaps and bounds.

Philip Ennis in his book, *The Seventh Stream: The Emergence of Rocknroll in American Popular Music*, writes about that amazing year of 1956 this way:

Record sales in the United States had been growing explosively. The Recording Industry Association of America reported total record sales in 1956 increased by $100 million to a figure of $331 million. This was an increase of 43% over the previous year, a huge jump in a growth rate that had averaged, over the previous decade, just over 4% per year. Though the LP record and the hi-fi craze were surely accountable for the stimulation in sales, the industry believed it was the youth market responding to the rhythm & blues efforts of the independent labels that was largely responsible.[2]

Zell, who kept an ear to what radio stations were playing and what records were selling, couldn't help but notice the Teen Queens' chartbuster "Eddie My Love." This only confirmed her intuitive, entrepreneurial concept that there was a market for the girl group sound. She knew she could create a hit record, but she also wanted to control her own destiny instead of relying on bigger labels to control her product. Besides, independent record labels were bursting out of the firmament like dandelions in an abandoned lot in the Bronx. Why not a record label by Zell?

With the creation of J&S Records, Sanders eschewed the Hearts for the moment and instead unleashed a strange collection of new groups, including a trio under the age of ten years that she called the Pre-Teens.[3] Then there was the religiously implied Pilgrim Pioneers, with a gospel-sounding record "The Wooden Church," and finally the Shytone Five with a song called "Disc Jockey Kick Off." There it was, recording acts with three of the worst names for singing groups ever, all with songs of no interest to the radio-listening public.

After shooting herself in the foot, Sanders finally got back on track, doing what she did best, finding great novice talent on the street. First off was a young man named Freddie Scott, who in 1963 would have a Top Ten hit with "Hey, Girl." He would chart once more in 1967 with "Are You Lonely for Me." That was all in the future.

Scott was born in 1933 in Providence, Rhode Island. His family moved to New York, and he attended Cooper High School. In an interview published on soulexpress.net before he died in 2007, Scott told Heikki Suosalo: "I had three sisters: one twin sister, and two other sisters. My mother played a little piano. We used to sing and write songs. My mother had a great voice." It was through his grandmother, Sally Jones, that Freddie got more seriously involved in music. "She was a gospel singer. I sang with her [Sally Jones and the Gospel Keys] when I was 11 and 12. At 12 years old, I went with her to Europe."[4]

In his late teens, he attended Paine College in Augusta, Georgia, where he became a member and lead singer for the Swanee Quintet Juniors. That's where he felt the lure of a life in music.

In 1956, at the age of twenty-three, he was back in New York, another young man with talent looking for entry into the music world. Freddie didn't say whether he sought out Sanders or she found him, but in his interview, he said, "I met Zell Sanders, who was someone that I liked very much. I started out with them [J&S Records] as a writer. I wrote a song for Johnnie and Joe, 'Turn the Lamps Down Low,' and it just didn't happen. Sanders said, 'Why don't you do it,' and I did it. We sold over 100,000 records."[5]

About the same time, Rex Garvin penned a song called "I'll Be Spinning." Radio play on the song caught the attention of Chess Records, which put it into national distribution. As part of the deal, Chess issued all subsequent issues of "I'll Be Spinning" on its own label. The singers were a duo put together by Sanders: her daughter Johnnie and a local boy named Joe Rivers.

Being such good friends with Johnnie, Louise recognized that she was a harmonizer and not a lead singer, so when Louise heard Sanders had teamed her up with a male singer and the duo was doing well, she was surprised. Like Sanders, Louise, for all her personal shortcomings, had good instincts for song. Sanders could have put Johnnie in the original Hearts, although at the time she was still young, so she held her back. Now she saw an opening for her daughter where she could hide Johnnie's lack of power and play to her strengths, which was to be part of the harmonizing whole. Joe Rivers was a very strong singer, and in their most successful songs, Joe is in the forefront and Johnnie is singing the background.

As Garvin told an interviewer, "My best friend was Joe Rivers. Mrs. Sanders lived in 222, I lived in 224, and Joe Rivers lived in 230. Mrs. Sanders asked Joe if he could come to her apartment to rehearse with her daughter. I wrote a song for Joe called 'Over the Mountain, Across the Sea.' Joe sang the lead, and Johnnie sang the background. They were called Johnnie and Joe."[6]

The Hearts, with Baby Washington as the lead, used to rehearse in the basement of Sanders's home in the Bronx, and then, because some of the girls were young teenagers, they had to wait for either Sanders or a friend of Sanders to drive them home to Harlem. While waiting, they used to watch Johnnie and Joe rehearse "Over the Mountain." Baby Washington's concluding memory of that time: "Her mom used to give Johnnie at lot of static because it didn't seem like she wanted to sing."

But Johnnie did sing and did a very good job of it. "Over the Mountain, Across the Sea" begins with Joe singing the title line with only Garvin on the piano and no other instruments behind, then a straight blues shuffle with Johnnie doing what she does best, using her sweet voice against Joe's deep

intonation. Johnnie doesn't really sing but mixes her voice as part of the orchestration. She is really very good, and it's a beautiful song. The only oddity is that
Zell couldn't quite give up on her patented talk-break, except she pushed it to
the end of the song where Johnnie coos, "Darling, here I am over the mountain
/ But all the mountains in the world, couldn't block your love from my heart."

"The record begins to sell locally in New York, then steamrolls into Philadelphia, where it catches the ear of Dick Clark, who plays it on his nationally
televised *American Bandstand* show," wrote J. C. Marion. "The record explodes
across the country, and once again Chess Records picks up the distribution
and issues further copies on their label. It is one of the biggest sellers of the
entire decade."[7]

The record broke nationally, but not everywhere. On July 13, 1957, *Cash
Box* magazine's survey of top-selling records by R&B retail outlets in selected
markets showed "Over the Mountain, Across the Sea" charting in just three
of the nine cities featured: Norfolk, Virginia, New Haven, Connecticut, and
the Bronx, New York. A similar survey of R&B Disk Jockey Regional Record
Reports again showed "Over the Mountain, Across the Sea" charting in three of
nine featured cities in Massachusetts, Arizona, and Colorado.[8] Two weeks later,
a *Cash Box* survey of what was "hot" on the R&B charts in selected cities noted
"Over the Mountain, Across the Sea" charting in three of six selected cities: #4
in Philadelphia, #1 in Los Angeles, and #4 in San Francisco, but missing the
charts in Detroit, Atlanta, and Memphis.[9]

Nevertheless, *Cash Box*'s end-of-year "Final Count" listed "Over the Mountain, Across the Sea" as the eighteenth Best R&B Record of 1957, one spot
behind "Mr. Lee" of the Bobbettes. At the top of the list were "School Day" by
Chuck Berry at #3, "C.C. Rider" by Chuck Willis at #2, and "Searchin'" by the
Coasters at #1.[10]

"Over the Mountain, Across the Sea" was also one of the few songs with a
female voice that made the Top R&B tunes of the year.

With the machismo of rock 'n' roll steamrolling across the radio waves, it was
a difficult year for the women. Rock 'n' rollers LaVern Baker and Ruth Brown
each had one big new song for the year, but they were low in the annual listings.
"Jim Dandy" continued to sell into 1957, which gave LaVern two hits in 1957.
If "Jim Dandy" is not considered, then only seven records with a female voice
made it to the Top 100 R&B songs of that year. Again, without "Jim Dandy," no
female performer had two songs that were hits. Of the five remaining songs,
four were by duets or groups, leaving the final song to a soloist who was back
on the R&B charts after being away for almost a decade.

In 1957, Shirley and Lee managed another Top Twenty record with "When I
Saw You." It would be the duo's last big hit, although they would chart records
into 1961. Nevertheless, the former New Orleans teenybopper sensations did
their job, making the R&B world safe for duets.

In addition to the superb "Over the Mountain, Across the Sea," one other duet-made song stormed the R&B charts, nestling in at #1 and crossing to the pop charts, where it would climb all the way to #11. It would prove to be one of best records of the year on any chart, sell more than a million copies, and, over time, become a classic. The tune has been featured in numerous motion pictures and recorded by everyone from Paul McCartney to the Everly Brothers. In 2004, it was inducted into the Grammy Hall of Fame.

The song is "Love Is Strange," and the singers were Mickey and Sylvia.

Bob Rolontz, the *Billboard* gossip columnist who always seemed to be deeply tapped into the R&B world, was hired by RCA Victor for its subsidiary label called Groove. The idea was to turn Groove into an R&B mecca. In 1955, Rolontz went to Nashville to record a blues singer named Piano Red. Out of the session came "Jump, Man, Jump," which was Groove's first taste of success. The record sold about 60,000 copies.

Rolontz next signed the duet Mickey and Sylvia, and their first release was "Walkin' in the Rain," with "No Good Lover" on the B-side. The tune was written by the singers Mickey Baker and Sylvia Vanderpool and looked like it was going to take off when Johnnie Ray came out with his song, "Just Walkin' in the Rain." It was a totally different song but a pop sensation. The end result was that Mickey and Sylvia's "Walkin' in the Rain" stumbled, lost momentum, and faded away.

Groove recorded one other single in 1956 with Mickey and Sylvia: "Love Is Strange" with "I'm Going Home" on the B-side.[11] In mid-March 1957, "Love Is Strange" climbed to #1 on the R&B charts, knocking out LaVern Baker's "Jim Dandy." LaVern and Sylvia were the only two female leads to have #1 songs in the first half of 1957. "Jim Dandy" supplanted Fats Domino's "Blue Monday," but the big man got his revenge. His "I'm Walkin'" took the #1 slot back from "Love Is Strange."

Teaming Mickey (McHouston) Baker and Sylvia Vanderpool (later Sylvia Robinson) was a record producer's dream. The two were excellent musicians and singers and two of the smartest people in the music business. Baker was ten years older than Sylvia. He was a southern boy, born in Louisville in 1925; she was a New York gal, born in Harlem in 1935.

They both had a journey to travel, although Baker's was longer and harder. At eleven years old, he was caught stealing and sent to an orphanage. On the plus side, he picked up an interest in music, playing either the trumpet or trombone. On the negative side, he couldn't abide the orphanage's structure and repeatedly ran away. Baker was sometimes called Mickey "Guitar" Baker, and the legend behind the shift in instruments goes like this. By the early 1940s, Baker made his way to New York, where he hit the pawnshops looking to buy an instrument. The only thing he could afford was a guitar. He had an ear for music, and in a few years, turned himself into a very fine guitarist. On a gig in California, he met Pee Wee Crayton, who seemed to be making a pretty good living playing blues-style guitar. Baker took note, came back to New York, and by the early 1950s was the supreme session guitarist for R&B on the East Coast, backing everyone from Joe Turner to the Drifters. He played behind Big Maybelle on "Whole Lotta Shakin' Goin' On." He also played with Ruth Brown, Little Esther, and LaVern Baker. How good was Mickey "Guitar" Baker? He was one of the session musicians when Screamin' Jay Hawkins recorded "I Put a Spell on You." During that session, the musicians were so drunk they could barely stand, yet they pulled off one of the great recordings of the 1950s.

Sylvia Vanderpool's journey was shorter and quicker. As a teenager, around 1950, Vanderpool had been singing bluesy duets with "Hot Lips" Page for Columbia Records. At some point, Herman Lubinsky signed her for his Savoy label. Lubinsky already had Little Esther under contract, so he created the recording personality Little Sylvia. With nothing happening at Savoy, Vanderpool approached Baker about giving her guitar lessons. He backed Little Sylvia at a 1953 recording session for the Cat subsidiary of Atlantic. This is where the genesis stories differ slightly. The oft-told tale is that Baker, looking to emulate Les Paul and Mary Ford, asked Sylvia to join him as a duet.[12]

Rolontz had different memory: "After a time, she [Sylvia] got the idea that by working together, something might happen for them. They went to Rainbow Records, and Eddie Heller signed them and made six sides with them. Nothing happened, but some of their sides got aired around New York. Disk jockeys got to know them. At one point, Bob Astor, who started as a bandleader and then became an agent, approached me about them—and that's how I got them."[13]

The songwriting credit on "Love Is Strange" reads Ethel Smith, who was Bo Diddley's wife. She didn't write the song. It's complicated.

Singer Billy Stewart signed with Bo Diddley's label Chess Records in 1955, and Diddley and his band backed Stewart on the recording of a song called "Billy's Blues," a regional hit in Southern California. The songwriters for "Billy's Blues" were listed as Billy Stewart and Jody Williams, who played in Bo Diddley's band. Williams's guitar riff in "Billy's Blues" is basically the same one heard in "Love Is Strange." Officially, the latter song was written by Bo Diddley. He used Williams's guitar riff and then gave songwriting credit to his wife. Baker gave a nod for his version of the song to Bo Diddley. As could be expected, there was a lawsuit to sort it all out.[14]

"Love Is Strange," with its feint to Caribbean rhythms, works for a number of reasons. First, Baker's nifty guitar playing gets an early workout and continues strongly throughout the three-minute song. Second, even when the two voices coincide, Sylvia's stronger, higher range is given prominence. Third, the talk break, or repartee, is pure gold.

Bobby Rush, who remembered Mickey and Sylvia, said their stage act was just like the song, a teasing playfulness. They were a fun duo to watch.[15]

In the early 1960s, when Rosa Hawkins, Barbara Hawkins, and Joan Marie Johnson, who would become the Dixie Cups, were discovered by former singer Joe Jones, the first thing he did was call Sylvia Vanderpool in New York. Before he had his own hit "You Talk Too Much," his band had backed Mickey and Sylvia on a tour. Jones thought the three girls had talent and wanted to take them to New York. He had no money, so he called Sylvia to front him. The plan was to also have Sylvia find them a place to stay. He would become their manager and split any commission with her. "We met Sylvia when we arrived. She introduced herself. I, of course, knew her songs. She was very pretty. But after the introductions, we never saw her again," Barbara Hawkins remembered. That was probably because Jones stiffed her. When asked if Sylvia got reimbursed for lending money to Jones, Hawkins exclaimed, "Hell no, he didn't pay her. He never paid anybody."[16] For Sylvia, it was a lesson that would come in handy in later years.

In 1978, Rolontz summed up the duo this way: "I don't regard Mickey and Sylvia as an R&B team; they really made pop records with a touch of blackness that made sense for the time period. They were not R&B as Shirley and Lee were. They could be, but they weren't. They were one of the big cross-over groups. 'Love Is Strange' is today still an up-to-date record because it was a cross-over, and not ethnic."[17]

"Love Is Strange" arrived on the music scene at a time when a Caribbean rhythm, called calypso, attained popularity in the United States. The peak year was 1957, when three calypso tunes made the annual best-seller list: the Tarriers' "Banana Boat Song," Harry Belafonte's "Day-O (Banana Boat Song)," and the Easy Riders' "Marianne." Gillett argued that most calypso songs were novelty tunes with a lilting rhythm, adding, "the only one with an enduring quality was the charming 'Love Is Strange,' recorded by Mickey and Sylvia for RCA's R&B market subsidiary Groove. Apart from an entertaining lyric, the record featured an ingenious extended blues-influenced guitar break by Mickey."

The message of the duo's follow-up, "There Ought to Be a Law," should have been heeded. There should have been a law against the follow-up song sounding too much like the preceding hit tune. Just enough guitar breaks and calypso in "There Ought to Be a Law" gave Mickey and Sylvia a Top Ten tune on the R&B charts and a song that crossed over to the midlands of the pop charts. The B-side tune, "Dearest," never made it to the R&B charts but did scrape by on the pop charts.

In September 1957, Mickey and Sylvia were one of the featured performers at Alan Freed's Third Anniversary Show at the Brooklyn Paramount. After the brochure was printed, Freed added another group to the show, the Tune Weavers, who were red hot with their "Happy, Happy Birthday Baby" platter sweeping across the country. On September 14, the record appeared on the R&B best-seller chart for the first time, coming in at #11. Freed liked to keep his show *au courant*.[18]

The song climbed all the way to #4 on the R&B charts and #5 pop. It was one of the top R&B tunes of 1957 and one of just a handful with a woman's voice on the lead.

The ascension of "Happy, Happy Birthday Baby" was a very slow process, akin to watching paint dry; the same could be said for the Tune Weavers, who were like an accident waiting to happen.

The story of this African American vocal group starts in Woburn, Massachusetts, when Margo Sylvia (Lopez), who was born in April 1936, started singing jazz and pop tunes at local clubs with her older brother Gilbert Lopez, born in July 1934. In 1956, they formed a quartet, adding Margo's husband John Sylvia and a cousin, Charlotte Davis. As to the name of the new group, take your pick of two tales. The first bit of mythology claims the band was originally called the Tone Weavers, but when an emcee mistakenly announced the Tune Weavers, the name stuck.[19] The other version of the name formation story is that Charlotte's fiancée suggested the group call themselves the Tune Weavers because that was what they were doing, weaving tunes.

Margo Sylvia sang lead with Charlotte Davis as obbligato, Gil Lopez as tenor, and John Sylvia as baritone.

In late 1956, they came to the attention of Frank Paul when he heard his brother-in-law rave about the group. Paul was a former bandleader who founded a small record label called Casa Grande. With his interest piqued, he went to his brother-in-law's home to hear the group. Not much was interesting to Paul until they sang a tune Margo originally wrote four years before called "Happy, Happy Birthday Baby." Paul's eyes opened wide, and he bellowed, "That's the one we're going to record!"[20]

In March 1957, with Margo eight months pregnant, the Tune Weavers recorded the song, with "Old Man River" on the B-side. On March 23, 1957, Paul splurged for a column ad in *Billboard*: "Watch for the smash hit by the Tune Weavers: Happy Happy Birthday Baby?" The ad mentioned the label, Casa Grande Records at 6 Carter Place, Woburn, Massachusetts.[21] (Note that the song title is different, with no comma between the two "Happy" words and a question mark at the end.)

The record did very well locally at first but nowhere else. Then success jumped to Philadelphia, where not only did local disk jockeys pick up the song, but Dick Clark played it on his show *Bandstand*. Suddenly, it was headed to hit record territory. Frank Paul's little label couldn't keep up with demand, so he signed a distribution deal with Chess. The song was rereleased on Chess' Checker label.[22]

"Happy, Happy Birthday Baby" would eventually sell over two million copies, which is a testament to the song's strength and not Chess/Checker's slipshod, perhaps sleazy, practices.

When "Happy, Happy Birthday Baby" was first released on Casa Grande, the group was listed as the Tune-Weavers. When Checker took over, the official group name was then two words, the Tune Weavers. At some point, Checker decided the B-side song, "Old Man River," was strong enough to stand on its own, so it slyly substituted a different song on the B-side, "Yo, Yo, Walk," an instrumental by Paul Gayten. The label tried to fool the public by listing the artists as the Tune Weavers/Paul Gayten, although the Tune Weavers had nothing to do with the song.

In November 1957, Frank Paul took out a full-page ad in *Billboard* promoting the Tune Weaver's follow-up record "I Remember Dear" with the B-side tune "Pamela Jean." The promotion prominently highlighted that national distribution was by New York's Ember Records (not Chicago's Chess/Checker Records).[23]

Checker would get its revenge. On November 30, 1957, *Cash Box* chose for its coveted "Sleeper of the Week" two Tune Weavers tunes. The first was "I Remember Dear" with "Pamela Jean" on the Casa Grande label. The second on the Checker label was the formerly discarded Tune Weaver song "Old Man River" on the A-side paired with another instrumental, "Tough Enough" by Paul Gayten and his Small Tone Weavers.[24]

The review by *Cash Box* read: "The Tune Weavers, who skyrocketed into the disk spotlight with their huge best-seller 'Happy, Happy Birthday Baby,' are represented this week with new releases on two different labels—one on the Casa Grande diskery, the label for which they now record, and the other on the Checker label, which carried the 'Birthday' hit into the Top Ten. The big side under the Casa Grande banner is a tune tagged 'I Remember Dear,' a slow, dramatic romancer with a pretty melody displaying some wonderful R&R harmony . . . On the Checker label, the polished group hands in an exciting new R&R treatment of a great standard . . . The Tune Weavers backing on Casa Grande is a jump item. The Checker flip [B side] is an R&R instrumental featuring Paul Gayten of 'Nervous Boogie' fame."

Billboard didn't catch up with the new releases until December 2, 1957, and it only featured what it called the "Ember-Casa Grande platter." The reviewer quickly wrote: "The group [Tune Weavers] is riding high with 'Happy, Happy Birthday Baby.' This side is similarly styled. It has strong potential in both pop and R&B."[25]

Alas, the song didn't succeed in either genre. Despite some heavy touring with rock 'n' roll shows, the Tune Weavers never had another hit record.

Without overusing the word "irony," the resurgence of Paul Gayten in 1957 coincided with the extraordinary comeback of singer Annie Laurie. Ten years before, the two recorded a couple of tunes in New Orleans that helped jump-start the transition of R&B to rock 'n' roll and put the Crescent City on the map as one of the birthplaces of the new musical format.

In 1957, Annie Laurie's "It Hurts to Be in Love," a moderate-tempo rock 'n' roller, climbed to #3 on the R&B charts, crossed over to the pop charts, and ended up as one of the top R&B songs of the year, on some lists outselling "Happy, Happy Birthday Baby."

It all started a decade earlier for Annie Laurie. In 1947, Jules Braun went to New Orleans from New Jersey for his De Luxe label and recorded Roy Brown singing "Good Rocking Tonight." That was happenstance. Braun arrived in New Orleans specifically to record local musician Paul Gayten and his band, including female vocalist Annie Laurie. Braun recorded Laurie singing "Since I Fell for You," which had been a hit song for Ella Johnson in 1945. Laurie's version became a major record in 1947, reaching #3 on the R&B charts and #20 pop. (Lenny Welch had another hit with the song in 1963.)

During the summer of 1947, Gayten was hosting a concert in New Orleans' Hardin Park. Among the singers and musicians with Gayten were sax player Lee Allen and "svelte singer Annie Laurie." At one point, he made an announcement: "We have a special guest in the audience, a young man who really plays the piano, Antoine Domino. Antoine, can you come up and play us a tune?" The boy who would become known as Fats Domino came on stage and played "Swanee River Boogie." The crowded whistled and cheered, giving the young man his first taste of fame.[26]

Annie Laurie (Annie L. Page) was born in Atlanta in 1924. She got her big break when she began touring with Snookum Russell, whose band, starting in the 1930s, primarily worked the Chitlin' Circuit throughout the Southeast. Preston Lauterbach, who wrote about the Chitlin' Circuit's history, called Laurie "a big-league beauty."[27] Singer/songwriter Billy Vera, who was long-time friends with Gayten, said Laurie's first recording was probably when she was with Snookum Russell, who recorded on the Trilon label in 1946.

The success of "Since I Fell for You" by Laurie, with Gayten backing her in the studio, changed the music scene in New Orleans. One old-time disk jockey told Lauterbach, "Most of the clubs had a lot of the out-of-town acts that came to New Orleans . . . It seemed like when Paul Gayten and Annie Laurie had 'Since I Fell for You' and started working the Robin Hood, it was like the beginning of a brand-new day here. It made people know that there was talent in New Orleans, and they started coming out to see it."

In that 1947 recording session with Annie Laurie, Gayten recorded a single called "True," which became a hit before "Since I Fell for You." Vera called it the first hit record to come out of New Orleans; Birnbaum said it was the first national R&B hit by a New Orleans artist.[28]

Gayten was born in the Big Easy. He began playing piano in Kentwood, Louisiana, before landing in Jackson, Mississippi. He was fourteen when he began touring with a local band. In 1949, he wrote a tune called "For You, My

Love" for a young singer named Larry Darnell, who had moved to New Orleans from the Midwest. It was a #1 record. He also helped Chubby Newsom on her 1949 hit, "Hip Shakin' Mama." That year, Laurie released another Top Ten R&B platter, "Cuttin' Out." Laurie, Newsom, Gayten, and others toured together as a group on the Chitlin' Circuit.[29]

In 1950, Laurie and Gayten as a duo cut a tune called "I'll Never Be Free" that was first recorded by Lucky Millinder. They weren't alone. It was a real free-for-all time. Laurie and Gayten's tune went to #4 on the R&B charts, Dinah Washington's version climbed to #3, and Louis Jordan and Ella Fitzgerald's recording managed #7. They were all outsold by Tennessee Ernie Ford and Kay Starr, who took the tune to #2 on the pop charts.

Laurie didn't chart again until "It Hurts to Be in Love" in 1957. (Gene Pitney's 1964 hit "It Hurts to Be in Love" is a different song.)

Said Vera, "To me, she was one of the greatest of all R&B singers, although her fame is not as renown as many of the other female singers. She had an incredible voice."[30]

As noted, Laurie's "It Hurts to Be In Love" was definitely in the rock 'n' roll vein, which was when pop and R&B finally combined. Many of the big songs in 1957 were straight-up rock 'n' roll, such as "All Shook Up" by Elvis Presley, "School Day" by Chuck Berry, "Peggy Sue" by Buddy Holly, and "At the Hop" by Danny and the Juniors. This should have been good news for the rockin' and rollin' ladies LaVern Baker and Ruth Brown.

The year 1957 was expected to be another strong year for Baker, but either she herself or Atlantic took the wind out of her career sails. She only recorded three singles in 1957, and one of those was the old chestnut "St. Louis Blues" with "Miracles" on the B-side. That certainly wasn't the right song for 1957.

Neither was "Humpty Dumpty Heart," which rolled on with a pop/country melody that was already a cliché by 1957. The R&B world skipped it entirely, although it did manage to creep onto the lower regions of the pop charts. The song was way too juvenile for Baker.

That left Baker with her follow-up tune to "Jim Dandy." Atlantic Records was so pleased with the results that songwriter Lincoln Chase was called back to do the follow-up, which became "Jim Dandy Got Married." It climbed to #7 on the R&B charts and crossed over to the pop charts, where it inexplicably didn't do as well as the unforgivable "Humpty Dumpty Heart."

Like Baker, Ruth Brown didn't do much recording in 1957. Her big ditty for the year, "Lucky Lips," was recorded in 1956 but not released until the next year. While the song was a mid-level hit on the R&B charts at #25, it climbed to #6 pop. Atlantic Records claimed it sold a million records. The bouncy, countryish tune charmingly began, "When I was just a little girl with long and silky curls / my mamma told me honey, you got more than other girls / You may not be good looking, but you'll soon wear diamond clips / And you'll never have to worry, because you got lucky lips."

The rumblings on "Lucky Lips" began on February 9, 1957, in *Cash Box*'s gossip column "Rhythm 'n' Blues Ramblings." The New York portion of the lengthy column began with a story about New York's Paramount Theater closing out its Nat King Cole, Ella Fitzgerald, Count Basie, and Joe Williams concert, which ran for a week and grossed $145,000 ($1.4 million in 2021 dollars). Here was the kicker: Fitzgerald took ill in the middle of the gig and was replaced by Eileen Barton, the Mills Brothers, Dinah Washington, and Ruth Brown. Dinah did four shows, and Ruth Brown did eight. The columnist noted, "From what we hear, Dinah and Ruth were sensational, and while the management regretted the absence of Ella, they were elated with the way the two gals sold themselves to the large audiences. . . . Ruth Brown is currently moving skyward with her biggest in some time, 'Lucky Lips.'"[31]

The song became something of a mania for the unknown columnist, who the very next week reported, "Now that the excitement over calypso has subsided somewhat, it seems that R&B is not yet to be replaced with the pop buyer. A look at the Top 50 shows Mickey and Sylvia's 'Love Is Strange' . . . LaVern Baker's 'Jim Dandy' . . . and coming up like a house afire, Ruth Brown's 'Lucky Lips.'"[32] The next week was more of the same, with this note, "Ruth Brown, working one-niters out East, calls to report 'Lucky Lips' among her top requests."[33]

The lucky circumstances that created the song, which would eventually prove unlucky for Brown, began the year before, when the songwriters Jerry Leiber and Mike Stoller wrote a song for a group called the Robins. The tune was "Smoky Joe's Café," which was released on a tiny independent label, Spark Records. Nesuhi Ertegun brought the record to Atlantic, which leased it for national distribution on its Atco label. Leiber and Stoller were hired by Atlantic, and the Robins' Carl Gardner and Bobby Nunn followed, forming a new group called the Coasters.

The next year, Leiber and Stoller wrote "Lucky Lips" for Atlantic's recording star Ruth Brown.[34] Ahmet Ertegun, who was then vice president of Atlantic Records, had specifically asked Leiber and Stoller to write a "good, up-tempo, swinging number" for Brown. The songwriting team knew what Ertegun meant, and the result was enthusiastically greeted. Arranger Ray Ellis ordered up a big-band arrangement, which was unusual because hits at that time rarely used anything larger than a small orchestra to back up a singer. Brown took to the song immediately, and either the fourth or fifth take was used for the single.[35]

Leiber and Stoller would also work with LaVern Baker. In an interview, Leiber said, "LaVern Baker was tough, but Ruth Brown was a sweetheart."

Ken Emerson, who wrote about the Brill Building songwriters, said that the song "was an uncharacteristic attempt by Leiber and Stoller to pen a formulaic pop song."³⁶ Really! After "Lucky Lips," Leiber and Stoller traveled to California to write songs for an Elvis Presley movie.

In 1957, Brown toured on her own and joined Alan Freed's supershows, where numerous entertainers would appear for one or two songs and then quickly be replaced by the next act. Sometimes the shows would run repeatedly all day and night. As Brown commented, "On one of Alan's extravaganzas, I sang 'Lucky Lips' seven times in one day. And nothing else. It was a fiasco, a rock 'n' roll circus, but it was a huge business."

She added, doing so many "supershows" had a bad effect on her throat. She ended up at the Harlem Eye, Nose, and Throat Hospital having a tonsillectomy under a local anesthetic. One result was that it changed her sound, "deepening it a fraction to a Marian Anderson contralto, but not so's anybody noticed."

Decades later, when Brown was in a battle royale, actually a battle-royalties, over money due her from Atlantic Records, the song "Lucky Lips" came to the fore. Trying to hold back from paying its former star any royalty money, Atlantic Records maintained that "Lucky Lips," which in 1957 the company told *Billboard* and *Cash Box* had sold a million copies, in the 1980s reported that the song only sold 200,000 copies.

From 1955 to 1961, Atlantic boasted to *Billboard* that Ruth Brown had three million-selling singles. Brown wrote, "A five percent royalty on just one of them, 'Lucky Lips,' would have yielded $40,000 on its own. As for the 200,000 copies they now said were sold . . . they were either lying to the trades and public back then or they were lying to the artist now. Challenged with this kind of irrefutable logic, Atlantic chose the line of least liability. They had, they now maintained, originally 'misrepresented' sales to *Billboard*."³⁷

Dateline Hollywood, Florida: In March 1957, according to a police report, someone sent a box of chocolates to singer Dinah Washington. If she had eaten the tasty snippets, it "could have proven fatal." The chocolates contained slivers of glass. The local press reported that "the 32-year-old Negro singer appearing at Zardi's" learned about the chocolates the day after she arrived. Washington received a 1.5-pound box through the mail and gave it to a friend, who bit into one of the chocolates, discovered the glass, and returned the box to Washington, who called the police. The enclosed note read: "My tail is short as you can see, good-bye to you from me, Yasha."

US postal inspectors were called in on the case. Jack Gordon, Zardi's manager, declared there was no discrimination at his club, which hosted "white and Negro jazz musicians and singers. Audiences also are mixed." Gordon scoffed at any idea that the plot was aimed at Dinah Washington because of her race.³⁸

Washington wasn't intimidated and did her show at Zardi's. *Billboard* covered the performance and announced: "In the best show must go on tradition, Mercury recording star Dinah Washington belted out the blues at Zardi's . . .

despite the fact that she'd just been apprised a box of candy she'd received was spiced with ground glass."

Despite the threat to Washington's life, not even *Billboard* could avoid talking about her physical appearance. The reporter noted, "trimmed down to about 150 pounds, Miss Washington presented a chic appearance."[39]

It was that kind of an uneven year: a few highlights and myriad problems. With rock 'n' roll taking over the music world, Washington didn't help herself by going negative on the trend. She was quoted as saying: "The big audience for it is kids, and when they grow enough to understand what it is, they won't like it. It's like the Susie-Q used to be: something to make their mothers mad. It'll die out: after a while, even the FBI won't be able to find Elvis Presley."[40]

She recorded a bunch of singles in 1957, none of which charted, which was the first time that had happened to Washington in the 1950s. She also recorded three albums, two of which were strictly non-rockers, including *Dinah Washington Sings Fats Waller*. She did an album with Quincy Jones that was mostly standards such as "I Get a Kick Out of You."

In 1957, Washington made her first major television appearance, with Rex Harrison on CBS-TV's *DuPont Show of the Month*. In November of that year, Dinah Washington placed third in *Billboard*'s "Favorite Female Artists of R&B Jockeys." The results were heavily biased to the jazz side and much less to the R&B songstresses. The two singers who polled ahead Washington were Ella Fitzgerald and Sarah Vaughan. One behind was LaVern Baker. Washington's old friend, comedian Slappy White, would marry LaVern Baker in 1961.[41]

As for Dinah Washington's marriage, it was under duress. By 1957, she was traveling a tremendous amount with a seven-piece band led by her husband Eddie Chamblee. As biographer Jim Haskins wrote, "She [Washington] was still on the road almost constantly and being on the road hadn't gotten any easier as the years went on. She had money worries, troubles with Eddie over who was in charge of the band. On New Year's Eve 1957, she passed out on stage."[42]

The year 1957 was more or less a blur. Washington was working harder than ever without the usual popular success. If she would have taken her old hit "TV Is the Thing (This Year)" and rewrote it as "Rock 'n' Roll Is the Thing (This Year)," the year might have been different. Instead, Washington doubled down on the standards.

She should have been reading the Black press. A story in the *Jackson* (Mississippi) *Advocate* in September 1957 screamed "Rock and Roll Ain't Dying." The wire service story, which was datelined Pittsburgh, began: "Those critics who are crying loudest that rock and roll music is dying out should have been here at the Syria Mosque auditorium to see for themselves how wrong they are. For three solid hours, top-notch performers . . . gave a standing room audience something to scream and cheer for . . ." Labeled the Biggest Show of Stars for '57, the tour included Clyde McPhatter, Fats Domino, Chuck Berry, Paul Anka, the Drifters, the Spaniels, and the Crickets. Females on the tour included LaVern Baker, Ruth Brown, and the Bobbettes. The article noted the economics of the huge extravaganza. It grossed $19,000 ($182,000 in 2021 dollars) for one night in Pittsburgh. The tour traveled in "two super deluxe buses" and sometimes in planes when the jumps were over 400 miles. More than fifty people were on the $47,000 ($443,000 in 2021 dollars) weekly payroll.[43]

It's easy to see why Washington felt threatened. The trend line was moving away from her. Not just with rock 'n' roll, but with female R&B singers. Ever since female doo-wop groups such as Shirley Gunter and the Queens, the Hearts, and the Teen Queens had broken through the glass ceiling, teenage girls became more and more excited about the concept that if they organized in groups of three, four, or five, they too could make beautiful music. There was a stirring among musically talented teenage girls of America away from becoming a soloist such as a Dinah Washington or Ruth Brown and instead being like the Drifters, Frankie Lymon and the Teenagers, or the Del-Vikings and sing in close harmony with a few others. As Lillian Walker-Moss notes in this book's foreword, she always wanted to be a soloist until she heard her friends practicing in group harmony, and then she wanted to start her own group.

The confirmation of all that occurred in 1957, when the biggest selling record by female voices that year was "Mr. Lee" by the Bobbettes. The song went to #1 on the R&B charts, where it sat for four weeks and then leapt over to the pop charts, where it slid all the way to #6, thus making the Bobbettes the first girl group to have a #1 R&B song that also was a Top Ten pop tune.[44]

With rock 'n' roll men smashing everything in sight, it was a terrible year for ladies on the pop charts. Only four female acts had songs that made Billboard's Top Fifty best-sellers list for the year: Debbie Reynolds with "Tammy," Gale Storm with "Dark Moon," Patti Page with "Old Cape Cod," and the first African American girl group to do so, the Bobbettes with "Mr. Lee."[45]

Even on the R&B charts, the Bobbettes were overcoming the rock 'n' rollers. On September 14, when the Tune Weavers' "Happy, Happy Birthday Baby" first became an R&B best-seller, hitting the chart at #11, the only other females around were the Bobbettes, who were at #2. A month later, nothing changed; it was still the Tune Weavers and the Bobbettes versus the boys on the R&B chart.[46]

The earliest origin story of the Bobbettes, a 1957 wire service report from the Black press, has the girls coming together while attending P.S. 109 in New York. John Clemente, who interviewed original member Emma Pought, wrote that they all met at I.S. 155 on 99th Street in Harlem. The only reason any of that would be of importance was that the original version of "Mr. Lee" was about their teacher or their principal, depending on which origin story one might read.[47]

The five girls who made up the Bobbettes, Emma Pought, Jannie Pought, Reather Dixon, Laura Webb, and Helen Gathers, were born from 1941 through 1945, meaning they were twelve to possibly fifteen years of age. The old wire service story from 1957 claimed they were twelve to fourteen, while writer Gillian Garr, in *She's a Rebel: The History of Women in Rock & Roll*, had them at eleven to fifteen.[48]

All writers agree that the girls attended the same school, where they began singing. Originally, the group included eight members, and when things became more formal they organized as the Harlem Queens. Eight was far too bulky, and eventually they became a quintet, which in the doo-wop world was a popular group size. They sang at school functions, local shows, and Amateur Night at the Apollo. Along the way, they hooked up with a talent manager named James Dailey, who thought they had potential and took them to Atlantic Records. Journalist Harry Bacas, who wrote the original story on the Bobbettes, put it this way: "Getting bigger ideas, they acquired a manager, James Dailey. Mr. Dailey took them to Atlantic, in New York, for an audition. One of the songs they sang for the audition was 'Mr. Lee.'"[49]

While most of these early girl groups are remembered only as singers, a handful, such as the Chantels and Shirelles, wrote their own songs at the start of their careers. This was the case with the Bobbettes. "Mr. Lee" was their own composition, as were three other songs they sang at the audition. Garr, who interviewed Reather Dixon, wrote that the song originally derided the "Mr. Lee" of the title, but Atlantic, which liked the ditty, wanted to thematically change it into a resemblance of a love song. "Instead of 'He's the ugliest teacher I ever did see,' we changed it to 'the handsomest teacher ['handsomest sweetie' on the record] I ever did see,'" recalled Dixon.[50]

After the Bobbettes were signed, Atlantic ordered an arrangement from Ray Ellis. He gave the tune a "bongo beat" that was played not on the bongos but on a snare drum. The unusual rhythm accents were assigned to Joe Marshall on the guitar. The girls were backed by the Reggie Obrecht Orchestra. Songwriting credits on the record went to the Bobbettes in their entirety, although author John Clemente wrote that Obrecht took some writing credits as well.[51]

Atlantic's Ahmet Ertegun and Jerry Wexler liked the tune, although they might have been unsure of its marketability because they didn't bring in their big guns to back the girls. The Reggie Obrecht Orchestra appeared to be rookies in the studio just like the girls. Even so, the record was well conceived and arranged. It was quirky and infectious, with a sound very different from anything else on the radio at that moment. Emma Pought and Reather Dixon were the dual leads, and the chorus of "Mr. Lee, Mr. Lee . . ." was always startlingly broken by an assertive yelp. The fast-paced tune boasted an attractive groove.[52]

Clemente interviewed Emma Pought, who told him: "Along 125th Street, they played records outside. You could hear the music. I heard this song and I kept saying 'that sounds like me . . . nah, that's not me.' I went up to the store and they played it louder and louder. I said, 'That's us!' I started running . . . by the time I got to the building where we lived, my mother and everybody in the building knew about it."

"Mr. Lee" was released in June 1957, and Atlantic, feeling somewhat more confident, took a small one-column ad in *Billboard*. It read "Swingin'est Record of the Year; Mr. Lee; The Bobbettes; The New Teenage Sensations . . ."[53] The next week, *Cash Box*, with a full page of R&B reviews, made a couple of poor decisions. One of its "Award o' the Weeks" went to a Mickey and Sylvia platter that would end up being poorly received; "Two Shadows on Your Window" was the A-side, and the ridiculous "Love Will Make You Fail in School" was the B-side. Fourteen mini-reviews made up the rest of the page. Only one became a hit: "Mr. Lee" by the Bobbettes. The review hit it nicely: "The Bobbettes make exciting music as they swing out the quick beat novelty bouncer. The young group has a wonderful sound and a saucy, infectious quality that attracts. Watch this deck [record]. The Bobbettes initial try could be a big seller."[54]

The song wasn't an instant hit. It moved slowly but steadily up the record charts. *Cash Box*'s gossipy "Rhythm 'n' Blues Ramblings" divined that the song's success caught Atlantic unaware. It read: "Atlantic's 'Mr. Lee' continues to surprise but elate the indie as it moves steadily up into an important national best-seller. The Bobbettes, five young females, made it on their first recording. With such a power-packed lineup as Clyde McPhatter, LaVern Baker, Ruth Brown, Ray Charles, Joe Turner, the Drifters, the Clovers, and Chuck Willis—all established hitmakers—it is quite a switch for these kids to come along and perhaps turn in Atlantic's best-selling record to date—if it keeps up its present progress."[55]

"Mr. Lee" saved Atlantic's year. In September, the label already had three songs in the market: "Humpty Dumpty Heart," which was struggling; Clyde McPhatter's "Long Lonely Nights," a much bigger hit for Lee Andrews and the Hearts; and "Mr. Lee." It then unleashed four new releases by Ruth Brown, the Clovers, Ray Charles, and Joe Turner. None of these new cuts scored with record buyers or deejays.[56]

In November, feeling a lot more confident in the Bobbettes, Atlantic took a large, two-column ad in *Billboard* to promote the group's next song. The tune was called "Speedy" with "Come-A Come-A" on the B-side. The odd promotion began with thick script that read "Bobbettes Back with a Bigger Hit" and then three paragraphs written in tiny type. In part it read, "Frankly, we didn't think that we would be able to find as strong material for the Bobbettes second read as 'Mr. Lee.' Then the girls themselves came to our rescue. They brought in two tunes that they had written. . . ."[57]

No rescue for Atlantic. The Bobbettes did not come back with a bigger and better song. "Speedy" wasn't even a hit.

On the good news front, the end of the year wasn't a total loss for the group. In *Billboard*'s poll of disk jockeys regarding their "Favorite Small Vocal Groups," the Bobbettes were the only females on the list, coming in fifth behind the Del-Vikings, Coasters, Moonglows, and Five Satins.[58]

Oh, Mr. Lee, thank you very much.

CHAPTER NINE

MAYBE (1958)

JULIA LEE—MARIE ADAMS—THREE TONS OF JOY— MICKEY & SYLVIA—BILLY & LILLIE—DIANE RENAY— BOB CREWE—THE QUIN-TONES—RUTH BROWN— BOBBY DARIN—THE SHIRELLES—THE CHANTELS— GEORGE GOLDNER

On December 7, 1958, Julia Lee played her usual gig at the Hi-Ball Lounge on 12th Street in downtown Kansas City. The Hi-Ball had been something of a jazz mecca when the Missouri city was wide open and all booze and blues. As usual, Lee would spotlight one of the club's patrons. She listened patiently as the brunette, or possibly blonde, would explain about her marriage or dating woes. Then in a voice warped by years of blues singing, would whisper that everything was going to turn out all right, "for you honey." After her first set, she concluded with these words to the audience, "let's drink it over."

After her show, Lee went home and fell asleep on her divan. She never woke up. Her long-time maid, Gladys Dillum, discovered her where she had ended her night. Julia Lee had a history of heart issues, yet it never slowed her down—until the very end.[1]

Julia Lee, who recorded as Julia Lee and Her Boy Friends, saw her career blossom in the late 1940s, with bluesy, double-entendre tunes such as "King Size Papa." Some of her boogie melodies like "Gotta Gimme Whatcha Got" were proto–rock 'n' roll, putting her right on the verge of the coming wave. The 1950s should have been rockin' for her, but her good fortune played out. After 1951, her recording pace slowed drastically and then sputtered to a close, although in 1957, the tiny Foremost label released "Bop and Rock Lullaby" with a B-side of her old standby "King Size Papa." *Cash Box*'s review noted: "A slow blues introduction leads into a swinging rocker featuring Julia Lee with a spirited reading. Jumpin' dance item."[2]

Julia Lee was born in Booneville, Missouri, in 1902 (some biographies list 1901), and grew up in Kansas City during the 1920s, when it was one of the best jazz and blues towns in the country. In 1918, at sixteen years of age, she started playing in nightspots, in particular Kansas City's Novelty Club. After two years, she joined her brother George E. Lee's band and stayed with the group for fourteen years. After surviving a car crash while touring with her brother, Lee preferred to stay back home in Kansas City, often refusing to tour in support of songs. In 1948, she made an exception.[3] Lee traveled to Washington, DC, to play at the White House Correspondents' Dinner at the White House. President Harry Truman sat down next to her on the piano bench and asked her to teach him to play boogie-woogie, admitting "I have trouble playing that eight to the bar with my left hand."[4]

At the end of the 1920s, she made her first recordings with her brother's band on the local Merritt label. Brunswick discovered her, and she recorded a couple of singles. In 1930, Brunswick released "He's Tall, Dark, and Handsome," with credits going to Julia Lee with George E. Lee's Novelty Singing Orchestra. Then she was back in Kansas City playing Milton's Tap Room and didn't record again until the mid-1940s.[5] David Dexter, a journalist, was working at Capitol Records, punching out corporate news and recording performers. He had a good eye for talented females and brought to Capitol stand-out singers Peggy Lee, Kay Starr, Nellie Lutcher, and Julia Lee.[6]

Lee recorded with Jay McShann on Capitol and then one issue with Mercury before launching her solo recording career in 1946 with "Gotta Gimme Whatcha Got," which went to #3 on the R&B charts. Author Birnbaum called the song a "12-bar verse and refrain hokum song done in a jazzy style with stop-time verses, a boogie piano bass, and a light backbeat." In other words, it was rock 'n' roll before there was rock 'n' roll.[7]

Then came a string of hits under the Julia Lee and Her Boy Friends format, including "Snatch and Grab It" and "King Size Papa," two R&B tunes that were #1 for twelve and nine weeks, respectively, in 1947 and 1948. At the end of 1949, "You Ain't Got It No More" broke into the Top Ten of the R&B charts, and Julia Lee was ready to burst open the new decade. But the target moved.

She recorded ten cuts (five singles) in 1950 without catching fire. Capitol wasn't deterred, getting her back in the studio the next year for twelve cuts (six singles). In March 1951, her "Ugly Papa" / "I Know It's Wrong" had to face down Savannah Churchill's "And So I Cry" / "Wedding Bells Are Breaking Up That Old Gang of Mine" in *Billboard*'s "Rhythm & Blues Record Reviews." Both evaluations were tepid. Of the "Ugly Papa" cut, the reviewer wrote: "Julia states her preference for an ugly papa so she can have him to herself. There are at least a few Kansas City blues fanciers who would pay to find out." [8]In October 1951, a *Billboard* review of "If You Hadn't Gone Away" / "Scream in the

Night" received a mixed commentary. This time the reviewer liked the A-side and hated the B-side. About "Scream," the reviewer wrote: "Wretched novelty material hinges on Miss Lee's screaming at regular intervals. She displays little relish for the chore."[9]

In February 1951, *Cash Box* gave its "Award o' the Week" long-form review opportunity to Hadda Brooks for her new single "Vanity" with "It Hadda Be Brooks" on the B-side. The magazine passed over "Pipe Dreams" / "Lotus Blossom" by Julia Lee, which got a short review. "The second side ['Lotus Blossom'] is a slow tune with a beat on which Julia gets some good instrumental backing." Five years later, Johnnie Ray on *The Big Beat* album recorded Lee's "Lotus Blossom" along with tunes by Faye Adams, Savannah Churchill, and Ruth Brown.[10]

In 1952, Julia Lee recorded just a couple of singles for Capitol. "Last Call" / "Goin' to Chicago Blues" got reviewed by *Cash Box*, which said, "Julia Lee runs through a cute bouncer with Her Boy Friends in the backdrop to make some zestful listening out of a rhythm & blues type." In the bouncy tune, Julia sings "This is the last call for alcohol this evening / drink up, drink up and order again."[11] That's a little different from Semisonic's 1998 hit "Closing Time" where they sang, "Closing time, one last call for alcohol." Except for a few sporadic recordings over the next few years, it was the last call for Julia Lee as a singles artist.

The death of Julia Lee, a Kansas City favorite, who started with such greats as Count Basie, Bennie Moten, and Andy Kirk in George Lee's ragtime band, "is a great loss to show business," her onetime manager, Milton Morris, mourned at Lee's passing in 1958. "A few years from now, people will start missing her, and she will become a legend."[12]

Just when Julia Lee's career began to sputter back in 1952, Marie Adams broke big with her delightful "I'm Gonna Play the Honky-Tonks." While it looked as if the two singers were heading in opposite directions, it turned out that Adams's big moment was just that, a moment. She recorded sporadically in the early to mid-1950s, which wasn't her fault. Her label, Peacock, was owned by Don Robey, who, as already noted, preferred his performers be on the road, which meant a steady income for him via his subsidiary management and tour companies.

The year 1955 looked like it was going to be comeback time for Adams when she recorded one of the many tribute songs about Johnny Ace after his death in December the year before. The song was called "In Memory" with "Boom Diddy Wa Wa" on the B-side. *Cash Box* chose the song for its "Sleeper of the Week" with these indifferent comments: "'In Memory' is another tribute to her former label mate, Johnny Ace. While late in the eulogy derby, it will undoubtedly satisfy many buyers, who snatch up any and all Johnny Ace memorial records."[13] Not exactly a ringing endorsement. In fact, the reviewer liked "Boom Diddy" much better, saying "Marie Adams comes up with her strongest piece of material in several years . . . strong assist comes from the Johnny Otis orchestra."

The record didn't take off, so Peacock, in a rare moment of generosity, released a second single by Marie Adams, "The Shape I'm In" / "My Destination," in 1955. Once again, the review, this time by *Billboard*, was so-so. Of "The Shape I'm In," the reviewer wrote: "With backing in a Deep South groove, the thrush really belts this meaningful slow blues." Of the B-side, the reviewer added: "Potent chirping by the thrush; the material isn't too unusual."[14]

Nothing much happened with either single released by Marie Adams in 1955, but all was not lost because, the year before, she had begun touring with Johnny Otis. A big advertisement that ran in numerous Black journals where the tour would stop showed a picture of Johnny Otis, who was the featured performer, and then the copy read: "Featuring Marie Adams, Dynamic Vocalist; Hit Tunes: 'Sweet Talking Daddy,' 'He's My Man,' 'My Song,' and 'Alone.'"[15]

In 1954, the year before Adams started touring with Otis, *Jet* reported "hefty blues chirpers [singers] Marie Adams, Willa Mae (Big Mama) Thornton, and Big Maybelle were considering forming a trio, and each weighed more than 250 pounds."[16]

The magazine might have been onto something because Marie recruited two of her sisters Sadie and Francine McKinley to form Three Tons of Joy, as the girls together weighed eight hundred pounds. Johnny Otis took the ladies on tour and in 1957 signed with Capitol Records. One of its first Otis releases was the 1921 comedic chestnut "Ma (He's Makin' Eyes at Me)" attributed to the Johnny Otis Show with Johnny Otis and his orchestra with Marie Adams and Three Tons of Joy. Tom Morgan, who produced the record, overdubbed snippets of a wild audience reaction that the Johnny Otis Revue received while playing LA's Orpheum Theater and added the sounds to the studio recording by Three Tons of Joy. The record didn't chart in the United States, but in 1958 it was a #2 best-seller in the UK.[17]

"Ma (He's Making Eyes at Me)" was so strong in the UK that Capitol rushed out a follow-up, a duet between Marie Adams and Johnny Otis called "Bye Bye Baby." That song also made the Top Twenty across the pond. When, in January 1958, "Ma (He's Makin' Eyes at Me)" peaked in England at #2, "Bye Bye Baby" appeared on the charts at #23. By the next month, as "Ma (He's Makin' Eyes at Me)" began to slide, "Bye Bye Baby" stubbornly held its position. In mid-February, the "London Lowdown" column in *Cash Box* covered the Johnny Otis conundrum: "Johnny Otis, whose waxing of 'Ma (He's Makin' Eyes at Me),' which, although not a hit in the U.S., has been a smash over here, is considering coming over here for a concert tour with Marie Adams."[18]

In March 1958, both "Ma (He's Makin' Eyes at Me)" and "Bye Bye Baby" were still on London's chart. Capitol tried to keep it all humming in the UK by releasing a fine rock 'n' roller called "A Fool in Love" combined with another chestnut, "What Do You Want to Make Those Eyes at Me For." Neither song stirred up much interest either in the UK or the States.

Around 1960, Marie Adams and Three Tons of Joy left the Johnny Otis show. About a decade later, she got together with Johnny Otis once again for a tour in Great Britain. Then she disappeared—literally. As Dik de Heer, in his review of Marie Adams's career, concluded, "It is unclear how she spent the last two decades of her life."[19]

"I'm Gonna Play the Honky-Tonks" was Adams's only US-charted song. She passed away in 1998 at the age of seventy-two.

In 1958, the best-selling record chart in the UK represented a mishmash of genres, from American rock 'n' roll to local favorites singing American tunes to Frank Sinatra to Louis Prima. Although the songs were different, the American charts were fundamentally as mishy-mashy as they were in the UK. The R&B chart for the year was completely invaded by white rock 'n' rollers and pop singers. Even Domenico Modugno's "Nel Blu Dipinto Di Blu (Volare)" made the R&B charts, and it was in Italian. Absolutely none of this helped the revered women of song, who traditionally had some of the finest R&B songs of the year, or the novices, who punctuated the best-seller list with some of the best new tunes in the genre.

Rock 'n' roll still did not give much expression to female singers. On the pop charts, not one lady managed a best-seller in the Top Twenty-Five songs of 1958. On the annual R&B list, only one song by a woman managed to crash the Top Twenty, and it was performed by a white singer, Connie Francis, who sounded a long way from R&B. Of the Top 100 R&B tunes, only four were by African American female soloists, female groups, or mixed groups with a female lead—and those songs were toward the bottom of the list.

Part of the problem was the market, with Black and white teens buying up anything that was rock 'n' roll or doo-wop. Some of it was also stupidity by the labels, or just the same old self-inflicted wounding of one's own career.

Take, for example, Mickey and Sylvia, who stormed the country's radio stations with their duet, "Love Is Strange." The follow-up tunes in 1957 were weak, and they only recorded three singles and one EP in 1958. At first, it was the record company's fault. In 1957, RCA decided that it had too many labels and combined a number of acts, including Mickey and Sylvia, onto a label called Vik. Although a few really good musicians like King Curtis were brought in to back Mickey and Sylvia, Bob Rolontz, who was switched from Groove to Vik, exclaimed, "The Vik label was probably the worst collection of talent in the history of the world . . . I did my best to buy out their contracts . . . Some I actually had to record. Diahann Carroll was on the label—a lovely person, but in my opinion, she couldn't sing on records."[20]

In 1958, only one Mickey and Sylvia song, "Bewildered," charted, and it was at #57 on the pop charts. It didn't make the R&B chart.

The duo started to fall apart. Rolontz recalled, "They began to have quarrels of their own. Mickey couldn't care less about money or being a star. Sylvia wanted both. The first moment he could get away, the happier he was. Sylvia was the driver. Mickey did whatever he did only because she was on him all the time. There was no love interest."

RCA decided to discontinue Vik. Mickey and Sylvia flirted with Atlantic, but wanted too much money, so they continued on at RCA into 1960 with middling success. In the 1960s, Baker finally escaped, moving to Europe. Vanderpool was still striving—and she would eventually have her way.

With the evaporation of Mickey and Sylvia, for a brief moment in 1958 the R&B duo concept was saved by a new arrival on the scene: Billy and Lillie.

The successful pairing of Billy Ford and Lillie Bryant had a lot to do with another fortunate duo, the songwriting and record producing team of Bob Crewe and Frank Slay, who wrote Billy and Lillie's hits of 1958, "La Dee Dah" and "Lucky Ladybug." The story begins two years before with the founding of Cameo Records in Philadelphia. The company scored its first two successes in 1957 with "Butterfly," a rock 'n' roller by Charlie Gracie, and a doo-wop standout, "Silhouettes" by the Rays. The latter song was written by Crewe and Slay, who also did the production.

That same year, Bernie Binnick and Tony Mammarella founded the Swan label in Philadelphia, using the freelance talents of Crewe and Slay. There was also the matter of Dick Clark, impresario of television's popular *Bandstand*, owning a one-third piece of Swan—all of which would be sorted out in the payola hearings of 1960.[21] Swan's first hit of 1958 was a song called "Click Clack" performed by Dicky Doo and the Don'ts. (Dicky Doo was the nickname of Dick Clark's young son.) Right on the heels of "Click Clack" came "La Dee Dah" by Billy and Lillie.

Lillie Bryant was born in February 1940 in Newburgh, New York. Her partner Billy Ford was a much older veteran of the music industry. Billy (William T.) Ford, born in Bloomfield, New Jersey, fudged his birth date as 1925, although blues researchers have pinpointed his true birth date as 1919. Having a singing partner who was fifteen years younger looked a lot better than twenty years younger.

"I got started singing in church. I also began playing the piano, but I didn't go forward with it," Lillie Bryant recalled. "Basically, singing was my great love; that was my concentration. I did the Apollo Theater's Amateur Night, where I won second place for singing Ruth Brown's 'Mama, He Treats Your Daughter Mean.' My mother owned a club that had musicians play on the weekends. As a teenager, I began performing."[22]

In a convoluted way, that was also how Bryant came to meet Billy Ford. One evening at her mother's club, the piano player said to Lillie's mother, "Wow, Lillie had a nice sound. When she gets older, contact me, I'll see what I can do to help." Sure enough, when Lillie turned eighteen, she contacted the piano player, who got her booked at a club in New Jersey. A shake dancer at the show heard Lillie sing and said to her, "I like your style. I have a friend, his name is Billy Ford, and he usually goes on tour with two female vocalists in his band, but one of the singers left. I'm going to tell him about you."

Bryant didn't know it, but right about then Billy Ford and his group, the Thunderbirds, were booked to entertain the troops in Greenland. After not hearing from Billy Ford, Bryant returned to Newburgh a bit depressed by not hearing from anyone. About six weeks later, she received a phone call. It was Billy Ford inviting her to Manhattan for an audition. When Bryant arrived, good fortune also walked in the door. Songwriters Bob Crewe and Frank Slay had come to see Ford because they had written a song for a duo and knew Ford usually worked with female vocalists. That particular day, Ford's vocalist was ailing.

Ford told Crewe and Slay bad luck for them because his singer was sick and stayed home. They turned to Bryant and asked, "Then who is she?" Ford demurred: "It's someone I'm going to interview after you all leave." But Crewe and Slay were hot to introduce their song and inveigled Ford to let them hear her sing. Bryant got to trill, and the two songwriters were overwhelmed. "We like her sound," they declared before poking into a briefcase and pulling out sheet music to a song called "La Dee Dah." They said to Ford, "Let's hear you two sing together." The piano player started playing, and Billy and Lillie crooned. Crewe and Slay looked at each other and swooned. "Yeah, we got our duo."

"Billy and Lillie really started out in a bad way, because Bob and Frank were the ones who told us to do the recording," Bryant said. "Whether Billy liked me or not, he was stuck with me. He had nothing to do with hiring me."

Lillie Bryant more or less became part of the Thunderbirds' entourage. Right after recording "La Dee Dah," the group again was booked to entertain the troops in far-off Greenland and Labrador. Bryant was all of seventeen years old. While there, Ford got a call from Crewe, who told him that Billy and Lillie had a hit record.

"When we got back to the States, my husband picked me up at the airport, and as soon as I got in the car and turned the radio on, the first song I heard was 'La Dee Dah,'" said Bryant, still amazed many decades later. "That was the first time I heard it on the radio. It was mind-blowing."[23]

Although mostly known for his work with the Four Seasons, Crewe had a good touch for female voices.

Diane Renay, who sang the Top Ten hit "Navy Blue" in 1964, owed her career to Crewe. When she was signed by Atco, her first release did well in Philadelphia but nowhere else, so the label asked Crewe to come in and produce her next recording session. "For my second release, I went to Crewe's five-story walk-up apartment," Renay recalled. "My father dragged up a tape recorder as he had cowrote a song called 'Tender.' We recorded it, and Atco released it. The song was #1 in some local markets, spotty elsewhere around the country, but none of that was big enough for Atco, which dropped me."[24]

Bob Crewe believed in Renay and put her under contract to himself. He told her father, "She has a lot of talent, and I can get a hit record for her." Renay went back to the studio where she cut three singles. "Navy Blue" was the last single she did, and it was the B-side of a record called "Unbelievable Guy." A deejay in Worcester, Massachusetts, flipped the record and played "Navy Blue," which took off like wildfire.

"I came home from high school, and the phone rings," Renay remembered. "It is Bob Crewe, and he says, 'I have something to tell you, you better sit down.' So, I sat down. He said you have a hit record, and you're never going to believe what song it is. It's 'Navy Blue.'"[25]

The rock 'n' roll wave that started in 1955 and 1956 showed no signs of ebbing at the start of 1958. On January 20, the Latin beat–flavored "La Dee Dah" broke into the R&B best-seller chart, jumping all the way to #9 in its premiere showing. It was a considerable accomplishment considering the best-seller chart was loaded with rock 'n' rollers such as "At the Hop," "Peggy Sue," "Great Balls of Fire," and "Jailhouse Rock." Also on the chart for the first week was "Silhouettes" by the Rays. It was Crewe and Slay versus Crewe and Slay.

The cute, bubbly tune with lyrics like "la dee dah, oh boy, let's go cha-cha-cha" was sung in two-part harmony. The songwriters snuck in a few song titles, including one self-reference: "You're my special angel, be-bop baby, my little bitty pretty pet / you send me a lot of lovin', lips of wine, just want baby to be my silhouette."

Despite, or because of, the song's success, all was not copacetic with Billy and Lillie. "What happened was that I wasn't being treated fairly," said Bryant. "Billy was the one getting most of the money. I had met Sylvia Vanderpool and called her. I went to her house, explained what was going on, and she contacted her lawyer. He got my contract straightened."[26]

In October 1958, the press reported that, with "La Dee Dah" reportedly selling a half million copies, Bryant received just $200 in royalties. Her lawyer was able to wrangle an additional $500 in payment. Her partner Billy Ford was paid $5,000 in royalties.[27]

"I was a young girl and didn't know what I should have known," she said. The question is, who was working for whom, because Billie and Lilly's manager, Noel Kramer, didn't take care of Bryant in the deal. "Truthfully, I didn't have a manager," said Bryant. "He wasn't my manager. Noel Kramer was Billy's manager, and Billy and Lillie somewhat fell under Ford and his Thunderbirds act."[28]

There were other issues as well. Kramer was also managing the Rays and would place the two acts together. In April 1958, Kramer put both acts on the stage at a fundraising concert in East Orange, New Jersey.[29]

In the end, neither group received the attention that was needed and the career paths of the two Kramer acts ended up similarly. The Rays recorded "Silhouettes," which went to #3 on the pop and R&B charts in 1958 and then a had couple of records at the start of the 1960s that placed low on the pop charts. Billy and Lillie had two hits, "La Dee Dah" and "Lucky Ladybug," in 1958 and one other song in 1959 that placed very low on the pop charts.

"Lucky Ladybug" made the "Sleeper of the Week" spot in *Cash Box* on November 15, 1958. The review was optimistic: "Save a high spot on the charts again for Billy and Lillie. Because the team that hit it big with 'La Dee Dah' has a tremendous new novelty item that could hit hard. The side that could bring the team back is 'Lucky Ladybug,' a cute cha-cha beat novelty with a daffy but delightful romantic lyric. Most pleasant arrangement, harmony, and beat."[30]

By the end of the month, *Cash Box*'s gossipy "Rhythm 'n' Blues Ramblings" observed that Billy and Lillie were in Chicago, where a distributor squired them around the town as they were plugging "Lucky Ladybug." The duo also had been appearing at Bill McLaughlin's Club Laurel for a five-day run.[31]

The song caught on, and in early 1959 rose to #14 on the pop charts. Billy and Lillie's only other charted song was "Bells, Bells, Bells (The Bell Song)," which barely touched the charts at #88 in 1959.

The whole issue of management and contracts proved to be the end of the line for Billy and Lillie. Crewe and Slay recorded Lillie Bryant on her own as a single act. The Swan label released Bryant's "Smoky Gray Eyes," with a classic stroll (a popular line dance in the 1950s) melody. The record left the gate strongly before petering out. The problem was Billy wouldn't allow Lillie out of her Billy and Lillie contract. She couldn't go out as a singles act in support of the record. "He said to me, 'You are booked with Billy and Lillie, so I can't let you go do that,'" said Bryant. "I couldn't even promote my own song." Lillie Bryant walked away from the music business in the latter part of 1959. "I felt abused and misused," she said.[32]

No tears for Lillie Bryant, because she went home to Newburgh, raised six kids, and became a well-known politico in her hometown, serving on numerous boards and the housing authority. She even ran for mayor, winning the primary but losing the general election. One of her sons is now on the Newburgh city council and another is vice president of the school board.

In the August 9, 1958, issue of *Cash Box*, the "Sleeper of the Week" designation was shared by four different singles. The first was Mickey and Sylvia's "It's You I Love" / "True True Love." The fourth chosen single was by newcomers the Quin-Tones for "Down the Aisle of Love" / "Please Dear." The reviewer presciently concluded about the latter record: "The Hunt label should have its biggest money-maker in a fascinating new rock and roll ballad effort by the Quin-Tones under the title 'Down the Aisle of Love.' The use of an organ gives the side an unusual, yet appropriate sound for the wedding setting of the lyric. The group creates an attractive teenage blend and has a wonderful lead voice that sells the romantic love story in a grade 'A' fashion."[33]

Two weeks later, the "Rhythm 'n' Blues Ramblings" column in the same magazine caught up with Larry Newton of the ABC-Paramount label, who chatted about three records he thought were worth calling attention to. One of the three was "Down the Aisle of Love" by the Quin-Tones.[34]

Despite the good notices, the trip down the aisle for "Down the Aisle of Love" probably seemed endless for the quintet of singers that formed the Quin-Tones. The song was one of those surprises that came out of the blue simply because the teenage audience took to it and the small label that distributed the record didn't have the infrastructure to get it out to radio stations quickly enough. "Down the Aisle of Love" was a best-seller in stores a week before it was one of the most played tunes by R&B disk jockeys.

At the end of the 1940s, another group called the Quin-Tones had worked the Midwest and South, playing everywhere from Hot Springs, Arkansas, to Duluth, Minnesota. The two groups were unrelated.[35] The Quin-Tones who sang "Down the Aisle of Love" were five sixteen- and seventeen-year-old teenagers (four girls and one boy) who attended William Penn High School in York, Pennsylvania. They were Kenny Sexton, Phyllis Carr, Jeannie Crist, Carolyn "Sissie" Holmes, and lead singer Roberta Haymon. Because they sounded so good together, they decided to form a group called the Quinteros, which played teen dances.[36]

Paul Landersman, a disk jockey at Harrisburg's WHGB, often worked the local dance hops because his station promoted these events. He was so impressed with the Quinteros' performance he decided to become their manager. To win over the teenagers, he promised they would eventually sing on Dick Clark's *Bandstand* in Philadelphia. In February 1958, he brought the teenagers, now called the Quin-Tones, to Philadelphia's Reco-Art Studio, where they recorded several songs. The group's first single, "Ding Dong," was issued by Chess Records. While it didn't come close to becoming a hit, having a record out meant Landersman was able to get them better bookings. As the Quin-Tones traveled a short tour loop, they wrote some songs, one of which was "Down the Aisle of Love." When Landersman was able to get them another studio session, that was one of the tunes recorded. What made the song noticeable, if not memorable, was that the recording tricked-up the lead-in with an organ playing "Here Comes the Bride." Landersman was so pleased with the recording session he rushed the demo across town to the Red Top label. The song took off, but Red Top couldn't handle the demand, so Hunt Records took over distribution.[37]

Besides being a good song, "Down the Aisle of Love" arrived in a swirl of heavily romantic records aimed at the teen market. Other popular tunes in the autumn of 1958 included "Tears on My Pillow," "Ten Commandments of Love," "Little Star," and even "Nel Blu Dipinto Di Blu (Volare)." The song made *Billboard*'s charts the third week in September. It wound up as a #5 R&B hit and rose to #18 pop.

As promised, the group appeared on *Bandstand*; at the Apollo with the Coasters, Danleers, Olympics, Spaniels, and Bobby Hendricks; and at the Howard in Washington, DC, with Jerry Butler and the Impressions, the Spaniels, Bobby Hendricks, Ray Peterson, and Doc Bagby.[38]

Subsequent releases included a remake of Edna McGriff's "Heavenly Father," but the fickle teenage market moved on, and the songs attracted little attention. To make matters worse, after selling almost a million records, the Quin-Tones received no royalties. Somebody made lots of money off "Down the Aisle of Love," but not the teenagers from York, Pennsylvania—and they wrote the darn song.

The Quin-Tones didn't realize it, but they were being chased up and down the charts by one of the great R&B veterans of the decade, Ruth Brown. In September 1958, as "Down the Aisle of Love" was beginning to gain traction, already ahead of it on the charts was Brown's "Why Me." For example, in St. Louis, when "Down the Aisle of Love" moved up to #6 on the local chart, "Why Me" was already at #3. But Brown had an ace up her sleeve. "Why Me" was part of a two-sided hit record, with the stronger song, "This Little Girl's Gone Rockin'," being introduced soon after the first. By mid-October, the durable "Down the Aisle of Love" was three weeks on the chart of songs Most Played R&B by Jockeys, settling at #3. Just two spots behind was "This Little Girl's Gone Rockin'," its second week on the chart.

A major review of the Ruth Brown single came on August 30, 1958, in *Cash Box*, which gave it the "Award o' the Week" slot. The lengthy review got it perfect: "Ruth Brown, who has had a healthy share of two-market hits to her credit, comes up with what could turn out to be her biggest to date. It's a sensational, fast-moving entry dubbed 'This Little Girl's Gone Rockin',' which has the quality, novelty, and charm to bust wide open on the rock 'n' roll scene. Ruth sparkles as she leaves a note for her momma tellin' her that she's completed her household chores and now it's time to rock. Under deck [B-side] is a steady tear-jerker, tagged 'Why Me,' on which Ruthie sadly reflects that when anything goes wrong, she's the one who suffers. Howard Biggs' ork [orchestra] attractively showcases the thrush on both ends."[39]

Billboard made the single its "*Billboard* Pick" and gave it a short review: "Spins of the chick's latest platter should prove a real threat for both adult and teen listeners. She's at her best on the swingin' rocker penned by Bobby Darin. 'Why Me,' the flip, is a gospel-flavored tune that can also please."[40]

The two songs were Brown's only hits in 1958. "Why Me" went to #17 on the pop charts. "This Little Girl's Gone Rockin'" shot to #7 on the pop charts and #24 R&B.

"This Little Girl's Gone Rockin'" is pure 1950s rock 'n' roll, including a tinge of rockabilly. It showcases all of Brown's skills as a singer with pacing skips, voice modulations, inflections, and pure pleasure of song.

The record got made because Ahmet Ertegun and Jerry Wexler at Atlantic slightly changed the company's direction. The label was known for its roster of R&B talent, from Ruth Brown and LaVern Baker to Ray Charles to the Drifters; when it signed the white singer/songwriter Bobby Darin it was signaling a shift to rock 'n' roll. Darin had been a Brill Building songwriter and had recorded on Decca without success. When he came to Atlantic, he was assigned to the Atco label and quickly rewarded his new team with the novelty rocker "Splish Splash," which went to #1 on the R&B charts and #3 pop.

One of the Atlantic performers who took to the young man was Ruth Brown, and they became good friends. Brown told what happened next: "I often came across him in the studio, trying out little things on the piano. 'I hear you're a songwriter,' I jived him one day. 'Why don't you write me a song?' He did, and the record was produced by two other ex-Brillers [Brill Building denizens], Jerry Leiber and Mike Stoller."[41]

In 1958, *Billboard* magazine ran a multi-page story on the rise of Atlantic Records. Ruth Brown's name came up a few times, and each time was noteworthy:

> Ruth Brown was Atlantic's first star. An unknown in 1949, she cut "So Long" on her first date and skyrocketed to fame. She has been associated with the company ever since and is gratefully recognized by Atlantic for being responsible for a major share in establishing the new company on firm commercial ground in its early years. . . .

> A glance at Atlantic's books reveals that the company has at least 14 artists who, even on flips, never sell less than 50,000 of a release. These include Ruth Brown, LaVern Baker, and the Bobbettes. . . .

> Ruth Brown and LaVern Baker have been frequent visitors to the charts—and are rare repeaters among girl vocalists in the R&B or pop charts.[42]

A story in *Cash Box* on June 7, 1958, noted, "Ruth Brown cutting her first Atlantic LP is emphasizing the torchy ballads." In all the years Brown had been with Atlantic, she had never done an album designed and performed just by her. Her songs had appeared in compilations but that was not the same. It was a bit of a battle to get there, as Brown reported: "I really had to fuss and fight to get *Late Date with Ruth Brown* off the ground. It was my vehicle to take me back to the ballads and standards I loved."[43]

After all that fussing and fighting, Atlantic did do Brown a big favor: Bobby Darin was assigned to be the album's arranger.

On April 12, 1958, a small item in *Cash Box*'s "Rhythm 'n' Blues Ramblings" column mentioned that Dinah Washington and her husband Eddie Chamblee were booked into the Palm Supper Club in Hallandale, Florida, for a gig. Chamblee, who was interviewed by Dinah Washington's biographer, said it was literally at that show when his marriage shattered.[44]

Things started off badly when Washington and the band had to drive all night to make the booking. They finally got on stage. At some point, Washington was singing "Drowning in My Tears," and, Chamblee recalled, he must have hit the wrong note or a lot of wrong notes. Washington, extremely short of patience, picked up Chamblee's brand-new Selmer-Mark IV tenor saxophone and threw it against a concrete wall. On impact, it exploded into bits and pieces. Chamblee walked off the stage and never came back to the concert or Dinah Washington.[45]

It was that kind of year for Washington. She released an album called *Dinah Sings Bessie Smith*. A *Billboard* reviewer slammed it, writing: "One would think that if anyone could do Bessie Smith, it would be Dinah Washington. But her recent album falls short. It's neither good Dinah nor good Bessie."[46]

To top it off, Bobby Shad, who had joined Mercury Records in 1951 and worked closely with Dinah over the years, left the company. In the end, that might not have been a negative for Washington. In his years with Mercury, Shad kept Washington in the jazz and old-style pop side of the market.[47] He would be succeeded by Clyde Otis, who was one of the first African American executives at a major record label. His orientation, while still pop, was much more in synchronicity with the record market at the time. Otis's pop, with an R&B flavor, fit well with the rock 'n' roll world.[48]

Washington only recorded two singles in 1958. The one that looked like it was going to be a hit was "Never Again" with "Ring-A My Phone" on the B-side. Despite a loungy-pop feel, the omens weren't good. On June 9, 1958, *Billboard* listed a full page of record reviews. Almost forty new songs were treated to quick reviews, including a new Johnnie and Joe record, "Where Did She Go" / "Why, Oh Why," and Dinah Washington's "Never Again." For the latter platter, the reviewer succinctly wrote: "Ballad has the Washington touch and good choir backing. Nice thrushing for the gal."[49] It really was a list of losers because not one of those songs made it.

Three weeks later, *Cash Box* gave four songs its "Sleeper of the Week" treatment, including "Born Too Late" by a new group called the Poni-Tails. Among the four was also "Never Again." This time, the reviewer, an obvious Dinah Washington fan, was enthusiastic, scribbling: "The Great Miss 'D' has in her latest Mercury release a number that'll splash her name all across the circuits once again. Titled 'Never Again,' it's the canary's most beautiful effort in years and her most commercial offering in ages. Superb romantic opus with great choral accompaniment."[50]

There was no helping the song, which was a bit out of touch with the market. While it did not make the US pop or R&B charts, it did reach the lower rungs of the Canadian chart.

Washington's other single, "Make Me a Present of You" with "All of Me" on the B-side, was an updated, 1940s, big-band kind of number. The lyrics were strong: "I don't need a desert of rubies / Or an ocean of pearls to swim through / But if you wanna make me happy / Just make me a present of you."

Again, it was a song that did not lead but rather lagged the market, which had totally integrated R&B and rock 'n' roll. There were still enough Dinah Washington fans out there that it made it to #27 on the R&B charts.

In April 1958, Louis Jordan appeared at the Howard Theater in Washington, DC, with four relatively unknown supporting acts. Three of the four—Wiltshire and Brooks, Juanita Monroe, and the Frank Motley Band—stayed relatively unknown. The fourth supporting act would have a wonderful future. They were four teenage girls who called themselves the Shirelles.[51]

Beverly Lee laughed when recalling the Shirelles' first time on a tour bus. They boarded all dressed up for a performance with high heels and crinolines under the skirts. Those bus rides were long and uncomfortable and you had to dress comfortably. "We were green," said Lee. "We knew nothing about touring. Ruth Brown, who was on the bus, took us aside and said, "Young ladies, for traveling, you need to do this, that, or the other. Get some jeans, bring a pillow, and be comfortable. We eventually learned to bring food because we couldn't stop and eat in many restaurants unless we happened upon a Black facility. You always needed to bring cans of something, whether it was Vienna sausages or sardines. Ugh, one of the Drifters always ate sardines."

The Shirelles, Lee added, "got on-the-job training from Ruth Brown, LaVern Baker, and Etta James. They kept an eye on us. LaVern would help us do our hair. Etta and Ruthie used to tell us to watch out for the guys. In particular, they said be careful of Al Hibbler and Ray Charles, who were blind, because they would try to get a sense of who you were by touching your face and then cop a feel. We were so young that Etta told us if one of the other performers wanted to take one of us out, another Shirelles needed to go along. I did that for a long time."[52]

The female group wasn't an unusual phenomenon in the pop world. Since the 1930s with the success of the Boswell Sisters, and in the 1940s with the Andrew Sisters, the ladies had their days, if not months, at the top of the charts. The only oddity, as one can detect in the name of the groups, was that the most successful of these aggregations were sister acts. In the R&B world, females who climbed to the top of the best-seller chart were soloists. Female groups were extremely rare. In the early 1950s, the rise of doo-wop, a group sound, eventually gave space to the pioneering female aggregations of Shirley Gunter and the Queens and the Hearts. This was followed by other successful acts such as the Bobbettes.

Then came 1958, one of the most transformative years for the female voice in the history of pop music. During those twelve months, two groups of teenage girls unleashed tunes that slightly altered the basic doo-wop construction, which often consisted of novelty lyrics or harmonic remakes of the American songbook. As reconfigured by the Chantels and Shirelles, existing doo-wop became increasingly more teenage romantic, more lushly produced, and built around a very strong female lead. This disturbance in the force would eventually create the girl group era of the early 1960s, the first great wave of female ascendancy in pop music.

In 1958, the Chantels were key players with the earliest arrival, better songs, and puissant chart runs. Over time, the Shirelles would become the most influential and successful girl group until the coming of the Supremes from Motown.

The Shirelles consisted of four teenage girls: Shirley Owens, who was born in Henderson, North Carolina; Doris Coley, born in Goldsboro, North Carolina; Addie "Micki" Harris, born in North Point, North Carolina; and Beverly Lee, born in Passaic, New Jersey. Harris was first swaddled in 1940, while the three other girls greeted the world in 1941. They met at Passaic High School and premiered their first song, "I Met Him on a Sunday," at the school gym. A fellow student heard the song that day, liked it, and shortly afterward introduced the four students to her mother, Florence Greenberg, who created a new company called Tiara to record the girls.

Greenberg was a real go-getter, and in February 1958, the Shirelles got probably their earliest press coverage in *Cash Box*, when the trade magazine blessed the girl group twice. In the "Rhythm 'n' Blues Ramblings" column, two lines read: "Tiara Records pitches a new group at the trade named the Shirelles. The team offers two goodies in 'I Met Him on a Sunday' and 'I Want You to Be My Boyfriend.'" In the "R&B Reviews" section, which took up a whole page, the magazine featured seventeen new songs by the likes of the Coasters, Moonglows, Midnighters, Bobby Blue Bland, and James Brown. Not one became a hit except for a little song called "I Met Him on a Sunday" by the Shirelles.[53] It wasn't a major hit, climbing only as high as #49 on the pop charts.

Nevertheless, it was a good, fun song written by all four of the girls and might have done better if the record had been originally released by a major label. The song proved so successful at the start that tiny Tiara couldn't handle the distribution, so Greenberg sold the song to Decca (one might say she sold the group to Decca for $4,000). Decca didn't really know what it had with the Shirelles. The label released two more Shirelles singles in 1958.

In June, Decca released "My Love Is a Charm" with "Slop Time" on the B-side. The record was up against new releases by Billie and Lillie, "The Great Spoon" / "Hangin' on to You," and Sarah Vaughan, "Too Much Too Soon" / "What's So Bad About It." No luck at all for the women that month.

In November, the Shirelles released "I Got the Message" with "Stop Me" on the B-side. *Cash Box*'s reviewer preferred the B-side: "The Shirelles, who made the grade with their 'I Met Him on a Sunday' clicker, bid fair to follow with another chart item. The artists hand in a teen-appealing vocal treatment of a catchy, romantic rock-a-cha-cha."[54] The A-side tune, which had more charm, was cowritten by Shirley Owens of the group. Neither scored, not at all like one other song debuting that same week, "I Cried a Tear" by LaVern Baker.

Disenchanted with the Shirelles, Decca decided to drop the group, which was great news for Florence Greenberg, because she welcomed her girls back with open arms, creating another label, Scepter, to record them anew. The Shirelles' future hits would be on Scepter.

There was other good news for the group. "I Met Him on a Sunday" was not a huge hit, but the girls made an impact. A June poll of disk jockeys by *Cash Box* included the question, "Which Up-and-Coming Vocal Group Do You Think Is the Most Promising?" The Shirelles were listed as one of a dozen new groups chosen by deejays. Also on the list were the Chantels, Bobbettes, and Johnnie and Joe.[55]

Three months earlier in the same magazine, a small set of goodies was listed as "R&B Sure Shots." Along with future hits "Book of Love" by the Monotones and "To Be Loved" by Jackie Wilson were "I Met Him on a Sunday" by the Shirelles and a song by the "5" Royales called "Dedicated to the One I Love."[56]

After appearing on stage with the "5" Royales, the girls adopted "Dedicated to the One I Love" and would sing it all the time around Scepter's offices. Greenberg assumed the girls wrote the song because they sang it so often, but they didn't. Nevertheless, she had them record it. The Shirelles' version of "Dedicated to the One I Love," now a pure girl group song, came to market in 1959. It failed to make the R&B charts and only touched the lower rungs of the pop charts. It was just too soon for that kind of sound. Two years later, with the girl group sound in full blossom, Scepter reintroduced the song, and it shot to #2 on the R&B charts and #3 pop. The girl group sound was ascendant.

In early January 1958, the Howard Theater in Washington, DC, promoted its first concert of the year under a screaming banner that read "Blasting Off 1958." The two headliners were Al Hibbler and Bo Diddley. Listed in the number three slot was an act called the Chantels, which, next to the group's name, was a reminder that it had sung "He's Gone."[57]

The year before, the unknown Bronx quintet released its first single "He's Gone" / "The Plea" on George Goldner's End label. It was a minor hit, managing to climb to #71 on the pop charts.

Goldner was one of those brilliant, talented record producers and auteurs of the pop music world in the 1950s and 1960s but was also a bit shady. This wasn't so unusual back in the days when the mob had infiltrated not only the recording industry, but the New York club scene. Goldner, who reportedly was an inveterate gambler, had to repeatedly sell his successful labels to pay off his debts. He also wasn't above the usual sticky-fingers practice of attaching his name to the songwriting credits to snag a piece of those royalty checks. Both "He's Gone" and "The Plea" were written by teenager Arlene Smith, but on the record, songwriting credits go to both Smith and Goldner.

Despite his dark side, Goldner had an ear for pop music and was a sorcerer in the studio, producing wonderful doo-wop recordings such as "I Only Have Eyes for You" by the Flamingos and rock 'n' roll hits like "Why Do Fools Fall in Love" by the Teenagers with Frankie Lymon.

"He's Gone" did well enough that Goldner, figuring the Chantels had momentum, at the very end of 1957 released the group's next single, a song called "Maybe." It would prove to be not only one of the best songs of 1958, but in the historic canon of pop music, one of the most revolutionary tunes ever. It changed the direction of the music stream and opened the entertainment business to masses of young women with beautiful voices and an urge to be heard. It would take a couple of years, but after "Maybe," the radio and record worlds were pearls to be plucked not only by men, but also by women.

Alan Betrock, author of *Girl Groups: The Story of a Sound*, in a wholly understated summation, wrote, "Not only was 'Maybe' one of the biggest selling records of its time, but its sound greatly influenced musicians and producers for years to come."

The Chantels were five friends who grew up in the Bronx, New York: Arlene Smith (lead singer), born in 1941; Sonia (Millicent) Goring, born in 1940; Renée Minus, born in 1943; Jackie Landry, born in 1941; and Lois Harris, born in 1940. The girls had been singing together since second grade choir. By the time they were older teens, they were all attending St. Anthony of Padua School in the Bronx. Inspired by Frankie Lymon and the Teenagers, Smith, who had trained as a classical singer and performed solo at Carnegie Hall when she was twelve, decided to organize a group of her own. The name Chantels was borrowed from a rival school, St. Francis de Chantal.[58] As always, there are variations to the myth of how high school teenagers made the leap from schoolgirls to stars. According to writer Gillian Garr, the girls finagled their way backstage at a

Teenagers concert and met their manager, Richard Barrett, a renaissance man of pop music (performer, songwriter, producer, and manager). He brought the group to George Goldner, who initially was not interested, as he didn't believe that girl groups were "saleable." Barrett, who had discovered the Teenagers, was a sharp judge of talent and threatened to withhold his songs from Goldner's vast conglomeration of labels. Goldner needed Barrett's array of skills and decided it was in his best interest to record the Chantels.[59]

Charlotte Greig, who wrote *Will You Still Love Me Tomorrow: Girl Groups from the 50s On*, quoted Smith directly: "When the group [Teenagers] came out, they were mobbed by girlfriends and fans. We caught up with one of the members. I said I wanted him to hear my group, but he said he was really too busy. When Richard [Barrett] came out, I did the same thing again, and he listened; we sang 'The Plea,' a song that I'd written. Richard was impressed and took my number . . . He took 'The Plea' and another song of mine, 'He's Gone,' and arranged them. Then we went down to George Goldner at 1650 Broadway and stood in his office. We sang 'The Plea.' He jumped up and said, 'I have a contract for you.' In a month or so, we were in the studio."[60]

Arlene Smith, whose amazing voice was, as author Ed Ward noted, "capable of soaring over the other four girls' voices,"[61] had also written a song of unrequited teen love called "Maybe." With Goldner, you always got the excellence and the pathetic, or the bad and the good depending on your perspective. He liked the song so much he not only stole the songwriting credits, but also decided he would produce the record himself. Legend has it that Goldner coaxed, some might say terrorized, teenage Arlene Smith take after take until her voice reached utter desperation—just right for the pleading theme of the song. Ed Ward noted, "She [Smith] sings with a noticeable sob in her voice, and decades later, 'Maybe' remains a riveting performance."

The best synopsis of the song's complex attractiveness comes from Betrock: "Barrett kicks off the record with a series of piano triplets, a wailing vocal chorus jumps in, and then Arlene tears your heart out with one of the most searing and honest vocal performances ever. It all came together here; the churchy-gospel influences meshed with a commercial R&B sensibility."[62]

"Maybe" climbed to #2 on the R&B charts and #15 pop. It could have done better, but the sudden burst in the record's popularity overwhelmed Goldner's production capabilities. If you swim with sharks, you might get eaten, and that's what happened to Goldner with his hot new platter. Word got out of about his production woes, and bootleggers quickly moved in, selling thousands of counterfeit records—unofficially.

Goldner released five Chantels singles in 1958 with varied success. "Every Night (I Pray)" went to #16 on the R&B charts and #39 pop, and "I Love You So" climbed to #12 on the R&B charts and #42 pop.

Despite their success, it would come as no surprise that the Chantels weren't making any money and Smith was getting zero royalties. Later on, Smith would say, "We were five little girls, and they were rippin' us off. That's exploitation."[63] She would be gone from the Chantels by the coming year.

CHAPTER TEN

WHAT A DIFF'RENCE A DAY MAKES (1959 AND BEYOND)

The Soloists

LAVERN BAKER—RUTH BROWN—DELLA REESE—
SARAH VAUGHAN—NINA SIMONE—DINAH WASHINGTON—
ARNOLD SHAW—CLYDE OTIS—ANNIE LAURIE—
SHIRLEY GOODMAN—SYLVIA VANDERPOOL ROBINSON—
JOE JONES—LEZLI VALENTINE—ETTA JAMES

Rock 'n' roll took a breather in 1959. Gone from the charts were the early pioneers, Chuck Berry, Little Richard, Jerry Lee Lewis, and Fats Domino. Only Elvis was still pumping out hits, but his big number for the year, "A Big Hunk o' Love," didn't even make the Top Twenty-Five best-seller list for 1959. Indeed, the #1 song for 1959 was the novelty country tune, "The Battle of New Orleans," which nosed out Bobby Darin's "Mack the Knife," a pop remake of a 1928 tune from the German musical *Die Dreigroschenoper* (*The Threepenny Opera*). Also in the Top Twenty that year was "The Three Bells" by the folk-country group the Browns and the instrumental "Quiet Village" by Martin Denny. Of the Top Forty tunes in 1959, only two females boasted hits. The reliable Connie Francis came through with "My Happiness" and the novelty tune "Lipstick on Your Collar." The best-selling song by a woman in 1959 was another novelty cut, "Pink Shoe Laces" by Dodie Stevens.

Gone from the pop charts were the female groups and duos that were, more or less, an entity as opposed to two recording stars getting together for one or two songs. Just considering the latter type of duet, two songs made the Top 100 for the year. Youthful television stars Edd Byrnes and Connie Stevens got together to record yet another novelty cut, "Kookie, Kookie (Lend Me Your Comb)." Country singer Tommy Dee joined Carol Kay and her group the Teen-Aires to sing "Three Stars," a tribute to Buddy Holly, Richie Valens, and the Big Bopper, who died in a plane crash early in 1959.

The R&B charts were even more severe. Not only were girl groups gone from the top R&B best-seller lists, but so were the great duos of Shirley and Lee, Mickey and Sylvia, and Billy and Lillie. No new duo stepped up to take their place.

Lady rock 'n' rollers such as Ruth Brown and LaVern Baker still found their rightful spots on the R&B charts. Indeed, the really big song by an African American woman in 1959 was "I Cried a Tear," which was the best of the many great songs LaVern Baker had sung over the course of a decade. Introduced the prior year, it was the only Top Ten R&B best-seller by a female in 1959. The song climbed all the way to #2 on the R&B charts and #6 pop. In the annual tally, "I Cried a Tear" was only the sixty-third biggest best-seller for the year. It would have done much better, but "I Cried a Tear" was introduced in 1958 so some of its sales occurred the prior year.

This classic LaVern Baker tune had a very obscure beginning. The songwriting credit on the record goes to Al (Alfred?) Julia, which could have been a pseudonym as the cognomen doesn't appear again for another song. Credit is now given to Al Julia and Fred Jay. The latter was a prolific songwriter born Friedrich Alex Jacobson in Linz, Austria. He was Jewish and fled the Nazi invasion of Austria, making it to France in 1938. When the Nazis invaded France he was held in a camp until fleeing a second time, ending up in New York. His first hit in America was "What Am I Living For," recorded by Chuck Willis. Then LaVern Baker sung his "I Cried a Tear."[1] The sultry sax on the recording is by King Curtis.

LaVern Baker (Deloris Evans or Deloris Baker or Delores Baker) was born in 1929 in Chicago. Musicologist Marv Goldberg tried to track down her roots, but it was so confusing that he was left with more mystery than certainty. In some stories, she is related to blues singers Memphis Minnie (Lizzie Douglas) and Merline Johnson (the Yas Yas Girl), although there is no proof thereof. The most accepted history is that Baker grew up singing in the local church choir. When she was seventeen, she began performing at nightspots in Chicago, appearing as Little Miss Sharecropper (at the time, there was a popular singer known as Little Miss Cornshucks). Although the name was just a gimmick, it stuck. When she moved on to the Club DeLisa, she met bandleader Fletcher Henderson, who wrote her a song. By the end of the 1940s, Baker had recorded for RCA Victor as Little Miss Sharecropper, but with nothing happening, she was back singing in Chicago nightclubs. In the 1950s, she moved to Detroit, where she sang at the Flame Show Bar. That's where she met her manager Al

Green, which was also about the time she decided to retire the Little Miss Sharecropper act. It was in Detroit that she first tried out a new name, Bea Baker.[2] It didn't last long.

LaVern Baker caught a career uplift in 1953, not only appearing at the Apollo for the first time, but also signing with Atlantic Records. Her first single for the new label was "Soul on Fire." While it wasn't a big hit, the song was a slow groove, pre–rock 'n' roll number that really showcased that great LaVern Baker voice.

In 1955, "Tweedle Dee" rolled out, and Baker was on her way. Four years later, she was at a creative peak with "I Cried a Tear." She was also very busy on and off the circuit.

In July 1959, Atlantic Records boasted the best month in its history and its second month grossing more than $1 million. The company was really on a roll with Ray Charles's "What'd I Say," the Drifters' "There Goes My Baby," the Coasters' "Poison Ivy," Bobby Darin's "Mack the Knife," and LaVern Baker's "So High, So Low."[3] While many tears of happiness flowed for "I Cried a Tear," it wasn't Baker's only hit of the year. She charted four other records as well. "So High, So Low," went to #12 on the R&B charts and #52 pop; "I Waited Too Long" rose to #5 on the R&B charts and #33 pop; "Tiny Tim" was #18 on the R&B charts and #63 pop; and "If You Love Me" climbed only to #79 pop.

Before the year was over, a grateful Atlantic Records re-signed Baker to a new contract even though her present pact had not yet expired. Jerry Wexler at the time indicated, "the contract was of a long-term nature."[4]

The alternatively generous and cantankerous Baker always made for good press. When a female heckler interrupted her rendition of a song at New York City's Apollo Theater, she cast an evil eye on the woman and loudly declared, "I hope that you never grow to be as old as you look, so shut up while I earn my living."[5]

In 1959, she was even a part of a Kansas City show that was closed by police. When over 12,000 teenagers showed up for a Dick Clark tour that included Paul Anka, Lloyd Price, Annette Funicello, and Baker, and the crowd got too rowdy, a police riot squad halted the performances.[6]

On the bright side, she became something of a media star. In February 1958, she appeared on the *Ed Sullivan Show* and in 1959 on *Bandstand* as well as local shows like Mitt Grant's in Washington, DC.[7]

In February 1959, when she headlined at the Howard with Little Anthony and the Imperials, comedian Slappy White was on the undercard. That was no coincidence, as the two were married later in the year.[8]

The coming nuptials didn't attract much attention in the general press, but the Black press stayed as close as possible, including this inside report that LaVern Baker had difficulty removing a "huge" dinner ring from her third finger, left hand, to make room for a wedding band. Of course, when Slappy

White bought Baker an early Christmas gift—a $35,000 home in Westchester, New York—that was big news.[9]

Baker continued to wed and record throughout the 1960s. The closest she came to another major hit was in 1962 with her recording of "See See Rider," which went to #9 on the R&B charts and #14 pop.

Baker left Atlantic Records in 1965 and switched over to Brunswick, but her days as a singles champ were over. The odd story about her is that around 1972, Baker was appearing at the Subic Bay Naval Base's Marine Corps nightclub in the Philippines when her divorce from Slappy White came through, her manager split, and she became seriously ill. A friend recommended that she stay on as the entertainment director at the nightclub. She did—for almost twenty years. Toward the end of her life she suffered from diabetes, which claimed both of her legs. She died in 1997.

And what about Ruth Brown, Atlantic's other great rock 'n' rolling female? She too had a bit of a renaissance in 1959, although nothing like LaVern Baker. There were no standout songs such as 1958's "This Little Girl's Gone Rockin'," or even "Lucky Lips" from 1957, but 1959 proved to be her most productive year since the mid-1950s.

But, let's first jump all the way back to 1953, when Ruth Brown was touring with the Billy Eckstine and Count Basie orchestras. The tour was in Roanoke, Virginia, and Eckstine and Brown took the stage together to sing a comedic version of Willie Mabon's very popular "I Don't Know." The repartee was right-on, or as Brown used to say, "it never failed to bring the house down." "I Don't Know" was a deep bluesy, talk-sing bit of hokum, which was a lot different from the "I Don't Know" Brown unleashed in 1959. Despite the same name, this one was a sophisticated, lushly produced, Peggy Lee–esque performance, with wonderful choral backing and sharp orchestration. It was cowritten by Brook Benton (red hot in 1959 with the million-seller "It's Just a Matter of Time") and Bobby Stevenson, who was also sharp as a tack in 1959, having written Dee Clark's "Hey Little Girl."

The song was a long way from Willie Mabon's "I Don't Know" and even "This Little Girl's Gone Rockin'," but Ruth Brown fans didn't care. The new "I Don't Know" shot all the way to #5 on the R&B charts, her best showing since 1956. It also crossed over to the pop charts, settling in at #64.

Another singer/songwriter came through for Brown in 1959. She recorded Chuck Willis's "Don't Deceive Me," a pleading ballad with a country backbeat. Again, not necessarily a Ruth Brown–type song, yet she conquered it. This one went to #10 on the R&B chart and did slightly better than "I Don't Know" on the pop charts, coming in at #62.

Her final charting number brought Brown back to her rock 'n' roll roots. Prolific songwriters Jerry Leiber and Mike Stoller wrote the rollicking "Jack o'

Diamonds," which Brown recorded with a rockabilly bounce in her voice. The fun cut was a modest hit, making it to #23 on the R&B tabulation but barely touching the pop charts.

It would be the last hurrah for Ruth Brown. One of the most successful R&B soloists of the 1950s would not have another hit record in the next decade. After a golden groove, Brown's life would tarnish due to a combination of poor personal decisions and the not-unexpected shady accounting practices of her record company. At some point, she would be so impoverished she had to do domestic work to provide for her family.[10]

Unlike LaVern Baker and Dinah Washington, two tough women, Brown was considered one of the nicest people in the R&B world. She was friendly, accepting, and generous, and some say a soft touch for boyfriends, family, and acquaintances.

After her former manager left her heavily in debt, it took her years to get out from under. Finally in 1959, Brown completely paid off her IOUs.[11] Without taking another breath, she made a $9,000 payment on a New York apartment. Also in 1959, she became part owner of the House of Weston, a barbershop that opened in Portsmouth, Virginia, by her brothers Benny and Leroy Weston.[12]

The next year, the press reported Brown financed her boyfriend Danny Moore's new band to the tune of $3,500 for uniforms and music.[13] In 1961, Brown and her manager George Treadwell slugged it out in the courts over $2,100 he claimed was due to him in commissions.[14]

Sure, one might accuse Brown of profligacy, but her records had sold millions of copies. For awhile, Atlantic Records was known as "the House that Ruth Brown Built." She assumed she was making good money from royalties, but not by the record label's arcane accounting. For example, between 1955 and 1961, Atlantic paid Brown less than $30,000, which by the company's calculations was $20,000 more than she should have gotten once recording expenses and commissions were paid out. At one point, Atlantic declared Brown owed the company $30,000.

As the *Washington Post* noted, "Atlantic's royalty system did not favor artists, with its low royalties and family bookkeeping. Many artists left the studio owing money for production costs, which Ms. Brown said was a way to discourage attempts to collect payment when a studio reissued material."[15]

Again, no tears for Ruth Brown, who staged an extraordinary career comeback, eventually earning a Grammy Award for Best Jazz Album, a Tony Award for Best Actress in a Broadway musical (*Black and Blue*), an induction into the Rock and Roll Hall of Fame, and finally, a payment of $20,000 from Warner Communications (eventual owner of Atlantic Records), with an addendum that all debts (hah!) to the company were "forgiven."

She died in November 2006 at the age of seventy-eight. Ruth Brown explored life to the fullest.

Skipping back to 1959, in the midst of Brown's last glory year as a hitmaker, it is interesting to scan *Billboard*'s chart listings of R&B songs. It was then called the *Billboard* Hot R&B Sides and included the Top Thirty R&B songs in the country. For the week ending November 15, 1959, the #1 tune was Brook Benton's "So Many Ways." What makes this particular chart so fascinating is the female representation. At #3 was "Don't You Know" by Della Reese, #8 "Smooth Operator" by Sarah Vaughan, #9 "I Don't Know" by Ruth Brown, #16 "I Loves You, Porgy" by Nina Simone, and #30 "Unforgettable" by Dinah Washington.

Sure, Ruth Brown and Dinah Washington were no strangers to R&B best-seller charts; they were two of the most successful African American performers of the decade. The oddities were the jazzy, album-oriented cabaret acts of Sarah Vaughan, Della Reese, and Nina Simone. While these were some of the great voices of the 1950s and 1960s, their particular talents didn't attract teenagers of the 1950s, who were more inclined to buy doo-wop, R&B, or rock 'n' roll records and listen to the deejays who played those kinds of songs.

The year 1959 was a kind of bridge year for music. The pioneer days of rock 'n' roll were coming to a close. The rambunctiousness and noise abated as 1950s teenagers had grown up and the question for each of them as an individual was what would they listen to going forward: rock 'n' roll, jazz, bebop, pop, R&B, folk, or country? The 1959 generation of rock 'n' rollers—Paul Anka, Frankie Avalon, Ritchie Valens, Dion and the Belmonts, the Fleetwoods—were youthfully sweet, and for older teens it was a good time to listen to what adults were putting down. Into this space came female singers best known for their work in other genres and venues.

When Della Reese died in 2017, almost all of the news sources that carried the story used a headline that read something like this: "Touched by an Angel Star Dies at 86." After decades of appearing on television and in motion pictures, people had forgotten Della Reese began life as a singer. Not just any old pop singer, but a well-respected and adored jazz-blues soloist. Talented and embracing, she operated in a different arena from that of Ruth Brown or LaVern Baker. When others were doing one-nighters across the South, she was performing in Las Vegas. By 1959, the year she scored her biggest hit, "Don't You Know," she was already a popular television guest and news item in the Black press.

"Don't You Know" came along toward the end of the year, and this was her schedule at the beginning: second week in January, a guest appearance on *The Jimmy Dean Show*; end of January,[16] an announcement that Reese would be doing two February TV spectaculars in London;[17] third week in April, an appearance on *The Ed Sullivan Show* (she would appear again on the show in 1961 with Erroll Garner).[18] Somewhere in between, the gossip columns reported she was in a hot romance with musician Larry Wrice, who was once Dinah Washington's husband.[19]

Della Reese (Delloreese Patricia Early) was born in 1931 in Detroit, Michigan. At the age of six, she began singing in church. As a teenager, she was hired to sing with Mahalia Jackson's gospel group. Her big break came when she won a song contest; the prize was a week of appearances at the Flame Show Bar. The owners liked her so much they kept her on. Despite everything going on in popular music in the early 1950s, Reese modeled her act on jazz singers like Billie Holiday and Sarah Vaughan. In 1953, she signed a recording contract with Jubilee Records in New York. One of her first recordings in 1955 was an old song from 1937 called "In the Still of the Night."[20] It quickly disappeared without a trace. Or did it? Reese brought back the old chestnut, and the name of the song alone inspired a young Connecticut teenager named Fred Parris to write "In the Still of the Nite," a doo-wop song released in 1956 that since has become one of the defining songs of the doo-wop era.

Reese's first big hit, "And That Reminds Me," arrived in 1957. The jazz-pop tune assertively sung by Reese was based on an Italian instrumental, "Concerto D'autunno," and the original pop version in 1956 was in Italian. The English-language lyrics were written by Paul Siegel and Al Stillman.[21] The latter gentleman was one of the most prolific and successful pop songwriters of the 1950s and 1960s, with songs such as "Chances Are" for Johnny Mathis, "Moments to Remember" for the Four Lads, and "I Believe" for everybody.

Reese recorded the first English version of the song, taking it to #12 on the pop charts. That was truly an accomplishment because the song was a real scrum, with other female singers such as Jane Morgan and Edna McGriff taking on the tune. The big competition came from Kay Starr, who took a renamed "My Heart Reminds Me" to #9 on the pop charts. As *Cash Box* noted in its review of the Reese song: "Beautiful theme adapted from 'Autumn Concerto' has also been done by Kay Starr. Version here will probably come second to Miss Starr's disk, which carries the title 'My Heart Reminds Me.'" Jubilee fought. On August 5, 1957, the label took a full-page ad in *Billboard* to boast about its star singers. The top half of that whole promotion was dedicated to Della Reese, including a sexy photo.[22]

One of the first big stories on Della Reese was in the November 1957 "After Dark," a syndicated column for the Black press written by Harry MacArthur. He began this way: "Della Reese is a girl with a most unusual voice who further embellishes a song with precise and individual diction. This is not news to you, of course, if you have recently been within range of a radio or a jukebox, where her 'And That Reminds Me' is getting quite a spin."

MacArthur had caught up with Reese when she was appearing at a night-club. He would become a lifelong fan after being blown away by her performance. He wrote, "She has an infectious smile that lights up a room and a 50-kilowatt personality that instantly warms an audience . . . you'll pay attention when Della Reese is out there singing with more voice than one slim girl should have."[23]

Two years later, when she became a star, MacArthur caught up with her again, this time at the Champagne Room in Washington, DC. Still smitten, he wrote, "Having started out as a gospel singer, Miss Reese endows every song that can use it with a wonderfully exultant quality. It's a pleasure to have her back in town . . . Miss Reese, tall and attractive . . . is something of a rarity among popular singers. She has an individual style that is distinctively hers alone. When she sings, the only singer she sounds like is Della Reese."[24]

Maybe only Della Reese could have pulled off the surprise of the year, "Don't You Know." In 1959, with rock 'n' roll now in the vanguard of pop music, Reese's old-school waltz, a full-throttled, speaker-rattling attack that sounds like it could have been a theme song from a motion picture melodrama, was hugely popular and the biggest hit of her career. "Don't You Know" was #1 on the R&B charts and #2 pop. It was the forty-third best-selling song of the year, the best performance by a Black female.

On August 8, 1959, *Cash Box* published a photo of Reese sitting between executives from RCA Victor because she had just signed with the bigger label. The announcement was made by Hugo Peretti and Luigi Creatore, the company's pop song producers who were known in the industry as simply Hugo and Luigi. The producing duo promised to get Della Reese into the studio before the month was over.[25] And they did.

The underlying tune for "Don't You Know" was lifted from "Musetta's Waltz," which opera buffs know came from Puccini's *La Boheme*. The story is that Hugo and Luigi were not very enthusiastic when Reese first sang the tune for them. Reese responded, "Let me take it home and learn it." Three or four days later, Reese sang the song for Hugo and Luigi, and suddenly all was right in the world. Hugo sketched out the arrangement using trombones, a rhythm section and a dozen violins. According to one news story out of Washington, DC, "Disc jockeys who heard the new record were captivated. They thought the record makers showed a lot of enterprise in trying to crack today's rock-and-roll market with a waltz."[26]

The first public crumbs about the song were in *Cash Box*'s September 5, 1959, "Rhythm 'n' Blues Ramblings": "Since svelte Della Reese was *pacted* by Hugo and Luigi for their RCA Victor, H&L Productions, Stan P. spends his evenings leading the cheering section at the swank Cloister Lounge [Chicago], where Della is holding forth currently. Stan tells us he's already making the deejay circuit with La Reese's Victor debut, 'Don't You Know.' He assures us it will be the biggest H&L have yet released on RCA."[27]

It was a slow build. "Don't You Know" finally hit that #2 spot in *Billboard* on November 30, 1959.

Della Reese would have one more hit record, "Not One Minute More," in 1960 (#16 on the pop charts, #13 R&B). She would continue to record throughout the 1960s without ever experiencing the exultation of 1959. That type of thrill would only come again for her with acting.

However, some fans never forgot what a fine singer she was. Columnist Harry MacArthur caught up with her once again in 1962. Clearly in a bit too deep, he wrote, "It will be good to have the tall, trim, and eminently talented Miss Reese back again. She has not merely a talent for singing, but a flair for doing it excitingly."[28]

In 1953, a story in *Jet* spotlighted Sarah Vaughan, who the publication felt was no longer getting the accolades she deserved: "There is little doubt, despite the heavy volume of 'plays' given jukebox recordings by Dinah Washington, Ella Fitzgerald, and Billie Holiday, that actually there is a 'Big Four' among Negro jukebox queens. In the group, Sarah Vaughan has been a serious factor to contend with. Whereas Dinah and Billie are 'switch' singers, jumping with ease from gritty blues to classic popular songs . . . Sarah Vaughan remains supreme in one field, the sentimental ballad."[29]

Nice try, but Vaughan, often grouped with Ella Fitzgerald and Billie Holiday as one of the great jazz voices of the twentieth century, did not have that kind of popular, jukebox-playing teenage appeal in the 1950s. While Vaughan had been the goddess of bebop at the end of the 1940s and has often been referred to as "the Divine One," she was not a singles act—although she had been issuing records (and was moderately successful at it) since the mid-1940s. Then in that weird year of 1959, when teenagers were experimenting with more adult sounds, she had her biggest hit ever, "Broken-Hearted Melody." The ditty rose to #7 on the pop charts and #5 R&B. It was also a #7 song in the UK. The same-year follow-up, "Smooth Operator," was another great cut, topping out at #8 on the R&B chart and #44 pop.

Sarah Lois Vaughan was born in March 1924 in Newark, New Jersey. At age seven, she began taking piano lessons that continued for the next eight years. She also sang in church, eventually becoming the organist and choir soloist at Mount Zion Baptist. On a dare, she entered Amateur Night at the Apollo Theater, and with a sizzling version of "Body and Soul," took first place. Promoters, talent scouts, and bandleaders would attend Amateur Night looking for new talent, and on that particular night, singer Billy Eckstine was sitting in the audience. He would soon join the Earl Hines band and take Vaughan along with him.[30]

In Hines's band were the seeds of the bebop revolution. In 1942, Charlie Parker joined the group, which at one time or another would include Dizzy Gillespie, Budd Johnson, Bennie Green, Billy Eckstine, and, as second pianist, Sarah Vaughan. According to writer, playwright, and poet Amiri Baraka (LeRoi Jones), the first real bebop orchestra was created in 1944 when Billy Eckstine organized his own band, which at one time or another included Miles Davis, Gene Ammons, Dexter Gordon, Charlie Parker, Art Blakey, Budd Johnson, and, on vocals, Sarah Vaughan.[31]

Vaughan began her recording career in 1945 with small independent labels. Her breakthrough as a singles artist came in 1947 with "Tenderly," which rose to #27 on the pop charts. Through the end of the decade, Vaughan would boast Top Twenty hits including "Nature Boy," "Black Coffee," and "That Lucky Old Sun (Just Rolls Around Heaven All Day)."

One song that didn't make it big was the 1948 recording of "The One I Love (Belongs to Somebody Else)" with the B-side cut "What a Difference a Day Made," an overlooked jazzy but up-tempo ballad.

In 1949, Vaughan jumped to a major label, Columbia, where she recorded "That Lucky Old Sun." With Columbia, Vaughan moved solidly into the pop music world. Some jazz purists never forgave her.

Jazz pianist Cecil Taylor, when recalling his early days in the music world, told an interviewer: "Of course I had heard Bird [Charlie Parker] before on records, but man, like you've really never heard him until you've dug him standing in front of the audience and sweating. I also heard Sarah [Vaughan] for the first time during that period. That was young Sarah, before she adopted all the mannerisms she is known for now. In '51, when she was sitting in with Dizzy [Gillespie] in Boston, she was at her best, she broke it all up. She cut Ella Fitzgerald, who was the established singer at the time and was on the same bill."[32]

From 1950 through 1953, Vaughan boasted a handful of Top Twenty hits, but nothing in her pantheon. Then in 1954 and 1955, two releases, "Make Yourself Comfortable" and "Whatever Lola Wants," climbed as high as #6 on the pop charts. "Make Yourself Comfortable" rose to #4 R&B.

There was not much to brag about in terms of hit records over the next three years. Part of her success and lack thereof had to do with moving to Mercury Records in 1954. Mercury was very good at middle-of-the-road and having its important female singers remake popular and Broadway tunes. That worked for the label into the mid-1950s, but with R&B and rock 'n' roll coming on strong, that strategy got stale.

In that odd year of 1959, however, Mercury's old-school tactics were the right approach for just that moment in time.

Vaughan's lackluster performance as a singles artist is perhaps meaningless, as she was one of the most highly regarded singers of her time. If pop artists had to endure a trunk tour with fifteen other performers sharing a bus to catch thirty different stops along America's byways, Vaughan operated on a different plane. In 1958, she accepted an invitation by Princess Grace and Prince Rainier to star in a three-day concert in Monaco. She would also make an appearance at the Brussels World's Fair as part of a three-month tour of Europe, which her manager, George Treadwell, estimated would gross more than $75,000 ($700,000 in 2021 dollars).[33]

In 1960, Vaughan appeared for the first time at the Waldorf Astoria's Empire Room in Manhattan. A reviewer wrote, "Miss Vaughan hit the high spot of the evening with an a cappella rendering of the spiritual 'Walk with Me.' Here Vaughan vocally unclothed with not a whisper in the audience to interrupt her revelry. It was a jewel."[34]

In between all the grandeur was Vaughan's 1959 reentry into the pop world, when most of the female competition (except for Ruth Brown) were the jazzy balladeers. On October 17, 1959, Cash Box's "Regional Record Reports" for Los Angeles listed Vaughan's "Broken-Hearted Melody" at #5, Della Reese's "Don't You Know" at #7, and Dinah Washington's "Unforgettable" at #10. In Chicago, Ruth Brown's "I Don't Know" was #1, immediately followed by "Don't You Know" at #2, and "Unforgettable" at #3. The #5 song was "Broken-Hearted Melody."[35]

Make no bones about it "Broken-Hearted Melody" is pure pop. Connie Francis or even Dodie Stevens could have taken on this song without a blink of an eye. Whether they could have made it a hit is another story. The song was written by two very talented songwriters who were graduates of the Brill Building era. The less known is Sherman Edwards, who might easily be written off as a purveyor of superfluous pop with co-ownership of songs such as "Dungaree Doll" for Eddie Fisher, "Flaming Star" for Elvis Presley, and "Johnny Get Angry" for Joanie Sommers. Edwards also cowrote "Wonderful Wonderful" for Johnny Mathis and "See You in September" for the Tempos. His crowning achievement was writing the music for Broadway's 1776, which won the Tony award for best musical.

Edwards's collaborator on "Broken-Hearted Melody," Hal David, is best known for his work with Burt Bacharach, including almost everything that made Dionne Warwick a star in the 1960s. Along Hal David's long journey, he also wrote movie theme songs such as "Alfie" and the Oscar-winning "Raindrops Keep Falling on My Head." Even with all that good stuff, left out of the packet are great country and western–tinged songs such as "To All the Girls I've Loved Before" and "Sea of Heartbreak."

While "Broken-Hearted Melody" was pop, it had a pedigree. An anonymous song reviewer at Cash Box got everything right: "'Broken-Hearted Melody' is the tune that's sure to turn the Top Ten chart trick for Sarah Vaughan. The thrush hands in a tantalizing vocal job on the sentimental romancer set to a rock-a-cha-cha beat. Ear-arresting choral and musical backdrop rounds a real winner."[36]

She would score once more in 1959 with "Smooth Operator" (not Sade's 1984 song of the same name). The tune rose to #8 on the R&B charts and #44 pop.

Sarah Vaughan was more an album artist than a purveyor of singles, and in 1959, Mercury released her *Great Songs from Hit Shows, Vol. II*. It was one of twenty-nine albums Mercury scattered to the market in the month of November.[37]

It was a banner year for Mercury, and company vice president Art Talmadge bragged: "Contributing greatly to our total score this year was the signing of Brook Benton, who has hit the top on every cross-the-country charts with each of the four singles we have released . . . top selling singles are habitual with the Platters and Patti Page, but this year has been unusually rewarding in view of the smash breakthrough of Sarah Vaughan and Dinah Washington into the pop favorite circles."[38]

The next year, Vaughan changed labels to Roulette.[39] She would continue her glorious career, but not as a hit singles artist, barely charting in the years ahead. She died of lung cancer in 1990.

In 1959, Vaughan was in midcareer, while one of her competitors on the charts was just getting started. Nina Simone, who would go on to become one of the most important singers of the twentieth century for her forays into jazz, pop, blues, folk, and protest, was beginning her ascent.

Her surprise hit of 1959, "I Loves You, Porgy," from the 1935 George Gershwin opera *Porgy and Bess*, shot to #2 on the R&B charts and #18 pop. It was more of an accident than a planned campaign.

After playing a couple of years in clubs and bars from Atlantic City to Philadelphia to New England, Simone was earning a reputation as a fine pianist and singer. Around 1958, she was playing the New Hope Playhouse Inn in New Hope, Pennsylvania, where she made a demo tape. It quietly made the rounds of record labels before catching the attention of Syd Nathan.

Nathan, the founder of King Records, one of the pioneering R&B labels of the 1940s and 1950s (it recorded James Brown's first single "Please, Please, Please"), had in 1958 signed a distribution deal with jazz-oriented Bethlehem Records. When Nathan heard the demo tape, he realized what a natural fit Nina Simone would be for his new association. He was so excited about the possibilities for this new singer he personally traveled to Pennsylvania to sign her. Simone, even as an up-and-comer, could be intransigent and headstrong, and when Nathan told her he had a bunch of songs for her to record, she said no.

Simone recalled, "It was difficult for a man like Syd Nathan to understand that an unknown girl who made a living playing small clubs would turn down a record deal without thinking twice about it. He came back to the house later in the afternoon and said I could do whatever I wanted so long as I left with him the next day to go to the studio. I spoke with Jerry [Simone's agent], and he said the money they were offering was fine, so I agreed."

Simone recorded a full album, *Little Girl Blue*, in fourteen hours. It was released in 1958. A few music publications said good things about the album, but that was the extent of its market penetration, as there was no promotion or supporting tour. Then an R&B deejay from Philadelphia, who used to sit in when Simone worked the local clubs, began playing the album, in particular the song "I Loves You, Porgy." Soon other deejays were playing the song as well. Nathan recognized the signs and quickly issued a single with "He Needs Me" on the B-side.[40]

"I Loves You, Porgy," really all piano and Simone's exquisite voice, was an outlier. It sounded nothing like anything on the radio at that time. It went to #2 on the R&B charts when the competition was Dee Clark's "Hey Little Girl," the Isley Brothers' "Shout," Lloyd Price's "I'm Gonna Get Married," and the Drifters' "Dance with Me."

Nina Simone (Eunice Kathleen Waymon), born in 1933 in Tryon, North Carolina, would remain an outlier all her life. She would always go her own way, including becoming a warrior for civil rights. Among the songs she penned were "Mississippi Goddam" and the anthemic "To Be Young, Gifted, and Black." The latter was one of her few hit singles, in 1969 going to #8 on the R&B charts and #76 pop. Oddly, as a single act, she was more popular in the UK. In 1968, on the British charts, her version of "To Love Somebody" went to #5 and "Ain't Got No, I Got Life" (from the musical *Hair*) and "Do What You Gotta Do" both went to #2. The next year, her sultry reimagining of "Screamin' Jay" Hawkins's "I Put a Spell on You" climbed to #28 on the British chart. It has since become her most defining song, and *I Put a Spell on You* was her memoir's title.

She lived in France for the last ten years of her life, passing away in 1998.

During her life, Nina Simone was honored by many organizations for her contributions to music. After her death, she was inducted into the Rock and Roll Hall of Fame, and her song "Mississippi Goddam" was selected by the Library of Congress for preservation in the National Recording Registry. In 2000, she also was honored with the Grammy Hall of Fame Award for her interpretation of "I Loves You, Porgy."

The interregnum in the rock 'n' roll music vanguard that created an opportunity for wonderful jazz-cabaret singers to have pop hits also became a bonus for Dinah Washington, who refused to change her style to meet the times. She didn't have to. With the arrival of Clyde Otis as Mercury's A&R director (in 1959, the only Black in such a position in the entire industry), different kinds of tunes were brought in for her to record. Although these songs appeared middle-of-the-road-ish with violins and chorus, the arrangements were modern. A white or Black teenager in 1959 who would buy "Smoke Gets in Your Eyes" by the Platters or "16 Candles" by the Crests would not be embarrassed to also pick up a copy of something new by Dinah Washington.

Amidst the juvenile dross of "Kookie, Kookie (Lend Me Your Comb)," "Pink Shoe Laces," and "Lipstick on Your Collar," many fine songs were introduced in 1959, from "Mack the Knife" by Bobby Darin to "There Goes My Baby" by the Drifters to "Sleep Walk" by Santo and Johnny to "Stagger Lee" by Lloyd Price. Somewhere in that latter group—certainly one of the essential, if not classic, tunes of the year on both the pop and R&B charts—sits Dinah Washington's reclamation of "What a Diff'rence a Day Makes."

The song had a long history, beginning life as a beautiful Spanish ballad, "Cuando Vuelva a Tu Lado" ("When I Return to Your Side"), written and recorded by Mexican singer Maria Grever in 1934. It was such an attractive melody that New York songwriter Stanley Adams (a member of the Songwriters Hall of Fame) rewrote the tune in English, and numerous big bands took a shot at recording it. The Dorsey Brothers Orchestra was the most successful, taking the tune to #5 on the pop charts in 1934.[41]

Ten years later, Andy Russell (born Andres Rabago), who was of Mexican descent and knew the Grever record, opted to croon an English version of the song under the title "What a Diff'rence a Day Made" backed by the Paul Weston Orchestra. It was a moderate hit, rising to #15 on the pop charts in 1948. Sarah Vaughan's jazzier version in 1948 used a similar title, "What a Difference a Day Made."

Dinah Washington would turn thirty-five years old in 1959 and had been stuck in a rut. Mercury kept her locked in an R&B cage, noted writer Arnold Shaw: "Her versatility proved a besetting limitation. Because of it, Mercury Records used her to reach Black record-buyers with songs they normally might not buy. As soon as a disk showed promise of becoming a hit—country song, film theme, show tune, Tin Pan Alley ballad—Dinah was rushed into the studio to make a cover for Black listeners."[42]

Before becoming a respected writer about music history, Shaw had been the creative head of Edward B. Marks Music Corporation, a music publishing company. He was a fan of Dinah Washington and would often tell the execs at Mercury that Washington could sell to pop audiences. He was dismissed because the Mercury people were happy with what Washington had been doing for the label. Then Clyde Otis became head of A&R at Mercury and Shaw smelled opportunity, bringing in the song "What a Difference a Day Made" for Washington. Otis bit.

At the recording session, Washington was backed by the Belford Hicks Orchestra. Oddly, the one big alteration Washington made to the song was changing the tense of the titular verb. The title became "What a Diff'rence a Day Makes."

Traditionally, Mercury sales executives limited their Dinah Washington efforts to R&B disk jockeys and Black sales outlets.

"I was so excited when Otis cut the Marks [Edward B. Marks] standard with her that even though field record promotion was the province of other members of my staff, I went on the road," wrote Shaw. He spent nine weeks visiting disk jockeys—not R&B jockeys but "pop platter spinners." He was having no difficulty getting her record programmed and called the Mercury execs to tell them about the enthusiastic reaction of the white deejays, but they were so hidebound, the company wouldn't widen its promotion, even telling Shaw he was "misguided."

Not even the trade magazines were getting excited by the new Dinah Washington record. In April 1959, *Billboard* barely gave the song any notice. The brief, unenthusiastic review read: "Effective rendition of the lovely oldie."[43] *Cash Box*'s review was slightly better: "A solid entry for deejay play from the great stylist, who tenderly surveys the fine oldie, backed by a subtle teen-directed beat. Strings and chanting chorus give the deck a legit look."[44]

Yet something was happening. At the beginning of May 1959, Washington was booked for a two-week engagement at the Village Vanguard, which was located in New York's Greenwich Village, the most in-spot in the country for new music, whether it was folk, pop, or jazz—and definitely not an exclusive R&B enclave.[45] On May 23, a column in *Cash Box* observed: "'What a Diff'rence a Day Makes' featuring Dinah Washington on Mercury looks like it could be the one Dinah has been looking for."[46]

In June, the Mercury exec who told Shaw that he was "misguided" had to eat crow, calling Shaw to tell him the song crossed to the pop charts. The song climbed to #8 on the pop chart and #4 R&B, where it stayed for seventeen weeks. It was also one of the Top Fifty best-sellers of 1959. Over the years, it has been used in more than a dozen films.

In Dinah Washington's world, there were always some rough patches on the road to Never-Never-land. On the good news front, in 1959, she was back touring in Europe. She married for the sixth time on a boat off the coast of Sweden.[47] There was also a story in the Black press that a St. Louis tavern owner was awarded $1,000 in a five-year-old assault case against Washington, who also faced a disorderly conduct charge filed by cops who claimed she verbally abused them.[48]

Washington was no shrinking violet, and with her success came the usual law enforcement abuse of Black performers such as experienced by Ella Fitzgerald and Billie Holiday—except Washington could never go quietly. She had a mouth and knew how to use it. One can't blame her.

In 1960, she was taken to the Los Angeles police narcotics bureau to answer questions about a large bottle of pills officers found in her Los Angeles apartment. Why was the narcotics squad raiding her apartment? No reported reason, and that's probably because it was just the usual harassment. Washington was permitted to leave after it was discovered the pills contained no narcotics. An angry Washington explained, "They took my reducing and sleeping pills. I gained four pounds."[49]

With a chance to become a mainstream star, Washington changed her look, featuring a sleek new hairstyle with a straight ponytail, lots of glitter, gowns, white mink, and "exuding glamour." As biographer Jim Haskins wrote, "She may have grown tired of being identified always as a blues singer, but she had never minded the 'Queen' part."[50]

In November 1959, Mercury ran a full-page ad in *Cash Box* promoting its stars of the moment, mixing Patti Page, Johnny Preston, and country singer George Jones with Brook Benton, Sarah Vaughan, and Dinah Washington. Each of the performers listed had their hit song written underneath their name. For Dinah Washington, the song was "Unforgettable."[51]

"What a Diff'rence a Day Makes" was such a great song that it overshadowed "Unforgettable," her other terrific cut unleashed in 1959, which rose to #7 on the pop charts and #15 R&B.

Clyde Otis then came up with the brilliant idea of teaming Washington with Mercury's other hot R&B singer, Brook Benton. In 1960, the duo's "Baby (You Got What It Takes)" stormed the charts, rising to #1 on the R&B chart and #5 pop. The follow-up, "A Rockin' Good Way (To Mess Around and Fall in Love)," did almost as well, shooting to #1 R&B and #7 pop.

The year 1960 was some kind of year for Washington, as she would introduce one of her finest songs, "This Bitter Earth." Washington dug deep into her soul for this elegiac lament written by Clyde Otis: "Lord, this bitter earth, yes, can be so cold / Today, you're young, too soon, you're old / And this bitter earth, ooh, may not, oh, be so bitter after all."

Over the next two years, Washington would record steadily, including such fine songs as "Love Walked In" and "September in the Rain."

Then the unthinkable happened. On December 14, 1963, her husband found her dead. Washington had accidentally killed herself, mixing a lethal combination of diet pills, sleeping aids, and alcohol. She was thirty-nine years old.[52]

Dinah Washington wasn't the only former R&B singer to chart records into the 1960s. New Orleans's favorite daughter Annie Laurie did so as well, only she never left her R&B roots. In 1960, Laurie snagged her last charted song, "If You're Lonely." Recorded on the De Luxe label, the Dinah Washington–styled tune went to #17 on the R&B charts. Although her recording career began in 1947, Laurie only recorded twenty-five records over the years, the last in 1962 on the Ritz label. Afterward, the only singing she did was for the Lord, as she devoted herself to religion. She died in 2006 at the age of eighty-two.[53]

Fellow New Orleans singer Shirley Goodman didn't get her start singing in the 1940s, but her first big hit performing with Leonard Lee arrived in 1952—close enough!

Goodman would be lucky enough to get a career revival at the start of the seventies disco era. Oddly enough, Goodman's late-career success had a lot to do with another duo survivor, Sylvia Vanderpool of Mickey and Sylvia. But, before talking about Shirley, we need to delve into Sylvia's unusual life.

In 1964, when Rosa Hawkins, Barbara Hawkins, and Joan Marie Johnson, who would become the Dixie Cups, were discovered by former singer Joe Jones, the first thing he did was call Sylvia Vanderpool in New York. Except she was no longer a Vanderpool, having married Joseph (Joe) Robinson in 1958 and changing her surname to his.

Before Jones became a solo act, his New Orleans–based band had backed Mickey and Sylvia for a tour. Sylvia returned the favor by producing Jones's hit record "You Talk Too Much" in 1960 (without getting production credit).

By the early 1960s, Mickey Baker immigrated to Paris and the Robinsons moved to the not-quite-as-exotic Englewood, New Jersey, where they founded Soul Sound recording studio and All Platinum Records.[54] As with the Mickey and Sylvia act, in this married duo, Sylvia Robinson was the driving force, finding talent and producing records. All Platinum's first hit record was "I Won't Do Anything" by singer Lezli Valentine, who first recorded with the Hearts in the 1950s and the Jaynetts in the 1960s. The arranger was Bert Keyes. Sylvia Robinson took cowriting song credits.

Robinson knew the record business, including when and where to snag songwriting credits. In 1968, Valentine recorded a single, "The Coward's Way Out," with a tune she cowrote for the B-side called "Love on a Two-Way Street." The songwriting credits iced Valentine and went to Robinson and Keyes, which probably wouldn't have amounted to much except the song was recorded two years later by the Moments and became a huge hit.

Robinson, as a solo act called Sylvia, had a #3 pop hit in 1973 with "Pillow Talk." The songwriting credits were Michael Burton and Sylvia Robinson.

That brings us back to Shirley Goodman. The Shirley and Lee act broke up in 1963. Shirley moved to Los Angeles, staying active as a recording session backup singer and occasionally forming duets with other singers such as Brenton Wood to record new music. In late 1974, Sylvia Robinson contacted Shirley and persuaded her to record a dance track with a group of studio musicians to be called "Shame, Shame, Shame." In 1975, the newly released song jumped to #1 on the R&B charts and #2 pop. According to author Birnbaum, the song "spurred the nascent disco craze."[55]

The record, which was released by an All Platinum subsidiary label Vibration, lists the singers as "Shirley (and Company)" and the songwriter as Sylvia Robinson. This was the last hurrah for Shirley Goodman (two minor chartings in 1975 and 1976 with "Cry Cry Cry" and "I Like to Dance," respectively). She died in 2005 in California but was buried in her beloved hometown of New Orleans.

As for Soul Sound, things started going to south around the middle of the 1970s, and the company was in financial trouble. One night, Sylvia Robinson was in a Harlem dance club and heard the deejay "rapping," which, she noticed, excited the crowd. According to her son Joey Robinson, she turned to him and said, "Joey, wouldn't this be a great idea to make a rap record." On a tip from a friend, Joey traveled to a New Jersey pizza parlor, where Henry "Big Bank Hank" Jackson was making pies. He grabbed Guy "Master Gee" O'Brien and the two auditioned for All Platinum in the back of Joey Robinson's car. Adding one other person, they became the Sugar Hill Gang. In September 1979, the group released "Rapper's Delight," which is credited as the first record exposing hip-hop music to the greater public.[56] The rap sat on a riff created by the band Chic for its song "Good Times." The label read "Sugar Hill" and in fine print, "A Sylvia Inc. Production." In 1982, Robinson produced another landmark hip-hop recording, "The Message" by Grandmaster Flash and the Furious Five. With that feat, music executive Sylvia Robinson earned the sobriquet "The Mother of Hip-Hop."

Most of the Robinsons' labels quietly were put to sleep in the early 1980s. Sugar Hill followed in 1986. The Englewood recording studio burned down in 2002, two years after Joe Robinson died.[57] Sylvia passed away in 2011 at the age of 76. Love is strange and so is the music business.

Indeed, the strangest career for any of the 1950s soloists belonged to the highly celebrated Etta James. That's because after the #1 hit, "The Wallflower (Dance with Me, Henry)," James hit the road touring and it seemed she never left. After 1955, she didn't chart another song in the decade. So, when one considers Etta James's Rock and Roll Hall of Fame worthiness, it's not about the 1950s. It's about the next decade. The great Etta James songs that most people remember, from "At Last" to "All I Could Do Was Cry" to "I'd Rather Go Blind," all happened in the 1960s.

Nothing came easy to James. She suffered through a severe drug problem in the 1960s and that was after blowing up her budding career in the 1950s. Her revival was not a given or a gift. It was hard-earned.

James's boyfriend at the end of the 1950s was Harvey Fuqua of the Moonglows, who then was recording for Chess Records in Chicago. James at the time was opening for Jackie Wilson in the Midwest. After a St. Louis show, the promoter stiffed James on payment, but Wilson forked over the money out of his own pocket. James took the cash, which paid for a bus to Chicago. James's plan was to sign with Chess, but after arriving in the city, Fuqua was on the road, and she couldn't get to see anyone of importance at the record company. With money running out, she had the good fortune to meet a fan named Greg Harris, who said, "If you let me manage you, I'll get you a deal with Chess." In 1959, he did both, but first he had to get James a release from her old label, Modern, owned by the infamous Bihari Brothers. Of course, they claimed that, with all James's recording expenses, she actually owed them money. Harris queried, "How the hell can she owe you money when you never paid her a cent of royalties?" James wrote, "They asked for $8,000 to nullify our contract but took $3,000. Leonard [Chess] offered me $5,000, and by the time I paid my back bills, I wound up with $500."

In 1959, James's first recordings for Chess were duets with Harvey Fuqua. They called themselves Etta and Harvey and rolled out "I Hope You're Satisfied" that year. Other duet recordings were released in 1960, including "I Can't Have You," which rose to #6 on the R&B charts and #52 pop, and "Spoonful," which made it to #12 on the R&B chart but just #78 pop.

Leonard Chess, who founded Chess Records with his brother Phil, had a good relationship with an up-and-coming songwriter in Detroit named Berry Gordy. The man who would soon start the Motown label had cowritten a song with his sister Gwen and Billy Davis called "All I Could Do Was Cry."

In 1960, the song as performed by Etta James went to #2 on the R&B charts and #33 pop. That year also produced "My Dearest Darling," which reached #5 on the R&B chart and #34 pop.

"Professionally, Harvey and I got closer," James wrote in her memoir. "Chess packaged us as duo and had us singing 'I Just Want to Make Love to You' and 'If I Can't Have You,' songs close to my true feelings about Harvey, who couldn't have cared less. What he did care about was money—and so did I. We weren't making much at Chess. 'All I Could Do Was Cry' would turn into a big R&B hit—my biggest since 'Roll with Me, Henry'—but it didn't come out for a long time."[58]

Harvey Fuqua would soon move to Detroit to help Berry Gordy with his new record company. James would stay at Chess, recording for its subsidiary labels such as Argo.

Etta James would swim deeply and successfully in the R&B pool for most of the 1960s, recording ten top R&B singles between 1960 and 1964. These records would have only modest success in the pop world, the most successful being "Pushover," which went to #25 on the pop charts in 1963. James's best performance on the pop charts in the 1960s was the 1967 hit "Tell Mama," which reached #23 on the pop charts and #10 R&B. The B-side, "I'd Rather Go Blind," has come to be regarded as an Etta James classic.

Guitarist and songwriter Brian Ray was Etta James's musical director for fifteen years and spent another fifteen years writing songs and recording with her. He also wrote a hit song for Smokey Robinson and has played backup to Paul McCartney. He and Etta remained very close over the years, so much so that Ray was godfather to James's youngest son. "We had an abiding, deep relationship," Ray said. "I knew her mom, her two husbands. She knew my dad, my sister, my story. She was like a second mom to me."

Offstage, James was very funny, smart, perceptive, and empathetic, but she could be hotheaded and adversarial and got screwed over so often in the music business that she had a tough time with trust. But on stage, "there was something about Etta," Ray still recalls with wonderment. "She was an outstanding performer who owned every set of ears in every house she played. She won people's hearts. People who sought her out in concerts were never disappointed. She had a particular talent of making you feel what she felt."

Ray started working with James in 1974, the year after he graduated high school. How that happened is a long and winding story.

He got a leg up in the music business early in life because his half-sister Jean Ray was half of the well-known folk duo Jim and Jean. The male part of the duo, Jim Glover, taught folk singer Phil Ochs how to play guitar. As a lark, Jean was singing backup with novelty act Bobby "Boris" Pickett, who sang "Monster Mash" in 1961. At a gig at the amusement park Six Flags Over Texas, she was one of Pickett's Crypt-Kickers and brought her half-brother Brian on as the band's guitarist.

That seemingly inconsequential gig turned out to be important because in 1973, when singer Gram Parsons died, his friend, road manager Phil Kaufman, stole Parsons's body from Los Angeles International Airport and transported it away in a borrowed hearse. As per Parsons's wish, Kaufman attempted to immolate the body at Joshua Tree National Park. He was arrested and subsequently held a fundraiser at his house to help pay for his legal expenses. To entertain the throng, and as an inside joke, one of the acts was Bobby "Boris" Pickett and his Crypt-Kickers. Ray played that night, and oddly enough, he and Kaufman bonded. Kaufman was also friends with Etta James, and one night she had a gig in Long Beach and needed a guitarist. Kaufman recommended Ray. "I thought, this is going to be fun, I'm going to play with Etta James," said Ray. "But then I didn't hear from her for a long time. One night I get a call. 'Brian, its Etta James. I'm up in Ventura County and I'm going on in an hour and a half, can you get up here?' I said, 'I'm on my way.' I packed my Les Paul and my amp and drove up the highway. That was the start of a thirty- to forty-year friendship."[59]

What made Etta James great? "She had an incredible voice and full command of that incredible instrument," said Ray. "She was the product of all her pain and struggles, some of which were self-inflicted. She survived a heroin addiction. She really sang from such a deep place that like so many Black singers comes from a shared experience that goes back hundreds of years."

In the waning years of her life James suffered from leukemia, dementia, and kidney problems. "I came to Etta's house in Riverside, California, because I was told her dementia had taken a turn for the worse," said Ray, summoning back sad memories. "She was in bed. Clearly, she was on the last pages of the chapter of her life. I sat beside her, and it took awhile for her to recognize me. Then she started to say my name loudly and excitedly. She grabbed my hand hard and wouldn't let go. She loved me and expressed that."[60]

Etta James died in 2012 at the age of seventy-three.

CHAPTER ELEVEN

SALLY GO 'ROUND THE ROSES (1959 AND BEYOND)

The Groups

THE BOBBETTES—RICHARD BARRETT—THE CHANTELS—
THE BLOSSOMS (THE DREAMERS)—PHIL SPECTOR—
THE SHIRELLES—LUTHER DIXON—THE JAYNETTS—
ABNER SPECTOR—JIMMIE RAYE—ZELL SANDERS—
ARTIE BUTLER—LOUISE MURRAY—LEZLI VALENTINE

Girl groups began to successfully invade the best-seller charts in the mid-1950s with moderate success. These young women didn't know it at the time, but they were pioneering a sound that would blossom at the start of the 1960s like tulips in springtime. It would take too long to happen for some groups such as Shirley Gunter and the Queens, who would fade away after the success of "Oop Shoop."

For other aggregations and individual singers, time was no obstacle. They would enter the 1960s still in the game. Some would quickly lose, some would slowly fade away, and some would have a late burst of circumstance before disappointment came roaring back, but many would find huge success, especially during the girl group era from 1960 to 1964.

Outside of Dinah Washington and Ruth Brown on the R&B charts or Patti Page, Teresa Brewer, or the McGuire Sisters on the pop charts, there seemed to be an almost universal plague among female singers in the 1950s. Boom! They would chart with a masterpiece and then nothing they sang would ever come close to being a hit record again.

The Bobbettes, even at powerhouse Atlantic Records, struggled to find success after "Mr. Lee." In 1959, the group released a single "Don't Say Goodnight" with "You Are My Sweetheart" on the B-side. As with the three other singles the Bobbettes released after "Mr. Lee," it failed to dent the record charts.

In 1960, with the young ladies now at a smaller label, Triple-X, they issued a follow-up record, "I Shot Mr. Lee," with hit potential. Whatever the real-life Mr. Lee had done to one of the Bobbettes, he was now getting his comeuppance. The song begins this way: "One, two, three, I shot Mr. Lee. Three, four, five, I got tired of his jive."

This follow-up record looked like it was going to be a winner, but outside circumstances would doom it. Writer Jason Ankeny explained: "The group left the label for the Triple-X imprint. There, 'I Shot Mr. Lee'—a song recorded but rejected by Atlantic—began to climb the charts, forcing Atlantic to release its own version and effectively killing the single's momentum."[1]

With Atlantic going against them, the Bobbettes' "I Shot Mr. Lee" failed to crack *Billboard*'s Top Fifty, topping out at #52. The Bobbettes would continue recording into the 1970s, residing in the bottom rungs of the charts just twice more with "Have Mercy Baby" at #66 on the pop charts in 1960 and "I Don't Like It Like That, Part 1" at #72 in 1961. The group officially disbanded in 1974.

Richard Barrett was a singer, record producer, songwriter, and talent scout. He discovered the Chantels and brought them to record producer George Goldner, who would own or co-own numerous labels over the years including Roulette, Rama, Gee, Gone, and Red Bird. When Goldner recorded the Chantels, he issued their records under the newly formed End label.[2] Meanwhile, Barrett, who had sung lead for a doo-wop group called the Valentines, decided to go behind the microphone once again. In 1959, with the Chantels reduced to doing backup, Barrett covered the Fleetwoods' big hit "Come Softly to Me" with "Walking Through Dreamland" on the B-side. This single was on Goldner's Gone label, and the credits read "Richard Barrett" in big letters above "with the Chantels" in smaller font. Not much happened with that record.

That year, Barrett and the Chantels also recorded a second single "Summer's Love" / "All Is Forgiven," which did slightly better, making it to #29 on the R&B charts and a lowly #93 pop. The credits were the same as on "Come Softly to Me."

In 1959, on their own, the Chantels only released one new record, "I'm Confessin'" / "Goodbye to Love," which disappeared without a trace.

About this time, Goldner's panoply of labels drifted into bankruptcy, and he sold his controlling interest in the whole rickety structure to Roulette Records.[3] As author John Clemente tells it, the Chantels and their parents were told that End Records would be no more and that they were released from their contracts.[4]

Goldner, who discovered (with Barrett's help) such groups as the Crows, Frankie Lymon and the Teenagers, and Little Anthony and the Imperials, had a real affection for the music American teens wanted to hear. None of that made him a saint. He was a gambler and gamboled with mob-related record men such as Morris Levy of Roulette. Levy notoriously exploited the talent who recorded for him, and Goldner wasn't much better. The Chantels weren't making any money despite having hit records. According to writer Gillian Garr, in 1959 Arlene Smith left the Chantels "due to frustration over the group's finances, and Lois Harris left at the same time."[5]

When Smith and Harris departed, Annette Smith (no relation) joined the Chantels as the lead singer. The Chantels would continue as a quartet. The group recorded straight through the 1960s, charting five more records. The only big hit by the Annette Smith–led group came in 1961 with "Look in My Eyes," which climbed to #6 on the R&B charts and #14 pop.

The Chantels' last recorded single, "Love Makes All the Difference in the World," arrived and departed quickly in 1970.

The Dreamers, who formed in 1954 and first tasted success backing the likes of Richard Berry and Etta James, finally got signed to a major label, Capitol Records, around 1956. The one hitch was that the company's A&R man didn't like the group's name, Fanita James recalled. "Noticing our different skin tones, he said we looked like a bouquet of flowers in bloom. That's why we went to Capitol as the Blossoms."

In 1957, Capitol released the Blossoms' first single, "He Promised Me" / "Move On." By the next year, the lineup changed. "As the Blossoms, we were myself, Gloria Jones, and the twins Annette and Nanette Williams," Fanita James explained. "The latter twin married and became pregnant, so she dropped out of the group." James knew of another girl, Darlene Wright (soon to be Darlene Love), from her old Los Angeles neighborhood. Although she was only sixteen at the time, Darlene Wright joined the Blossoms. In 1958, Capitol unleashed two more singles by the Blossoms. By the second release, "No Other Love" / "Baby Daddy-O," Darlene Wright had moved into the lead singer spot.

Starting in 1959, it became difficult to keep up with the group. They began recording under different names depending on the needs of different labels. In 1959, recording as the Playgirls on RCA, they issued a single, "Hey Sport" / "Young Love Swings the World." Also that year, on the Colpix label, a 45, "Angel Face" / "I Don't Wanna Lose Ya," was released by the Blossoms with Jimmy Darren (soon to be James Darren).

The Blossoms, because of their harmonic skills, were also building a reputation as the finest session singers on the West Coast for whoever needed help in the recording studio.

The individual Blossoms would all marry and have children. Around 1961, Annette would drop out, leaving the group a trio. "Then we met Phil Spector," James remembered with emphasis.[6]

In 1962, Spector encountered singer/songwriter Gene Pitney, who at the time was working out of the Brill Building. As Pitney remembered it, Spector had come to the Brill Building looking for material. Pitney's manager Aaron Schroeder played him a song Pitney wrote called "He's a Rebel." Spector wanted it, and Schroeder said he could have it as an exclusive, but Spector knew Schroeder gave out exclusives like candy at Halloween. There indubitably would be competition, so time was the essential factor if Spector was going to make a hit from Pitney's song.

In 1961, Spector had formed his own record label called Philles Records and was already having success with a girl group called the Crystals. Spector was very specific about things and wanted to record "He's a Rebel" in Studio A at Gold Star Studios in Los Angeles. The trouble was, the Crystals, who were on the East Coast, didn't want to fly to Los Angeles, so he needed to find a group of girls on the West Coast who could do the song. Anyone in Los Angeles knew the go-to group for harmonic singing was the Blossoms. In the Spector biography *He's a Rebel: The Truth About Phil Spector—Rock and Roll's Legendary Madman*, author Mark Ribowsky wrote: "While Gene Pitney intended 'He's a Rebel' to include strings, the stringless demo was so good as it was that Spector cut the song as pure, jazzy-licked, blues-rock."[7]

While cutting the master, Spector heard of another version of the song being done by Vicki Carr. Spector's "He's a Rebel" was released in the later part of 1962, jumping to the #1 slot on the pop charts on October 6 and staying there for two weeks. Although the Blossoms recorded the song, the record that was released on the Philles label was credited to the Crystals.

Spector would make amends, somewhat, by recording Fanita James, Darlene Love, and Bobby Sheen as Bob B. Soxx and the Blue Jeans, which had a Top Ten hit in 1962 with "Zip-A-Dee-Doo-Dah" and in 1963 with "Why Do Lovers Break Each Other's Heart?" Spector would also record Darlene Love as a solo act. As for the Blossoms, they would become television stars. *Shindig!* the musical variety show that premiered in 1964, employed the Blossoms as backup singers for just about anyone and everyone who appeared on the show. They also continued to provide their talents to a slew of star performers (Ike and Tina Turner, Elvis Presley, and many others) in the studio and onstage. In 2013, the group was featured in the Oscar-winning documentary *20 Feet from Stardom*.

Like the other groups that first began recording in the 1950s, the Shirelles (Shirley Owens, Beverly Lee, Doris Coley, and Addie "Micki" Harris) ended the decade's final year with a very small output, just one single, and it didn't exactly the set the world on fire.

The song was called "A Teardrop and a Lollipop" with "Doin' the Ronde" on the B-side. Although it didn't cause much of a thrill with deejays or record buyers, the single remained a favorite for the group because, as with "I Met

Him on a Sunday," the Shirelles wrote the B-side song while "A Teardrop and a Lollipop" got worked into their stage act.

"Around the time we were doing the recording of 'Dedicated to the One I Love,' when Florence was still leaning on us for creativity, we recorded a couple of songs that became the follow-up record to 'Dedicated,'" Beverly Lee reminisced. "I'll start with the B-side, a song called 'Doin' the Ronde,' which was another number the Shirelles wrote. It was a bit of mash-up in that it was about a dance called the ronde. I'm not sure where we picked it up or saw it . . . we might have discovered it in Jamaica, at least that's what we told the audiences. The song begins with a Creole call: 'Jambalaya.' A response: 'Jambalaya boys.' Then we sing, 'It came from Jamaica.' Eventually, the song turned on a rock 'n' roll beat. In the end, it was in the same vein as the other songs we wrote."[8]

The A-side was different. "A Teardrop and a Lollipop" was written by Jack Hammer, who the Shirelles didn't know. Florence Greenberg found the record for the group. Doris took the lead, singing, "Last night at a party, my baby said goodbye / Ran off and left, oh how he made me cry / A teardrop and lollipop, that's all that's left of my love." At live shows, Beverly Lee would proclaim, "And I won a lollipop!"

The song continues, "I saw them dancing together, and prayed the music would stop / But they won the dancing contest." At that point, on the Chitlin' Circuit, Lee would lean into the mic and alter the lyrics, to exclaim, "And I won a damn lollipop!" The audience would always find this funny. Later, when the group sang "Foolish Little Girl," Lee, who would always play the put-upon girl, would say the line, "But I still love him."

After sending the Shirelles off to Decca Records, Florence Greenberg took them back, forming a new label to record them. "A Teardrop and a Lollipop" appeared on Scepter, which on the earliest pressings even published on the label its address at 1674 Broadway in New York City. The sub-credits underneath the Shirelles read "Arranged and conducted by Stan Green," who was Florence Greenberg's son.

No slight to Stan Green, but Florence Greenberg needed help and she knew it. There were many things she was good at such as promotion and getting records into the hands of people who could be helpful. Greenberg was also good at discovering talent. Her weakness was at the technical end, particularly the studio work of organizing arrangements and conducting recordings.

In 1959, she got the break she needed. Sometime early in the year, Greenberg bumped into Luther Dixon in the elevator at 1650 Broadway. As Lee explained it, "he was twenty-seven years old, handsome, a successful songwriter, musician, and veteran of the music industry—all of which appealed to Florence."[9]

Dixon began his music career as a singer in the doo-wop group the Four Buddies, which eventually passed through the Decca stable as did the Shirelles.

He was more successful as a songwriter, penning tunes for Bobby Darin and Elvis Presley. His big success came in 1958, when he cowrote "16 Candles," a major hit for the Crests.

"There didn't seem to be an upside for Dixon to tie himself to a tiny record label with no history," Lee said, but Greenberg turned him around. Essentially, she offered him a lucrative package that Lee assumed included a piece of Scepter and a deal with his own music publishing company called Ludix. Greenberg and Dixon would also have an affair, but that didn't seem to help anyone.[10]

In the history of pop music, sometimes there is such a close relationship between the songwriters or record producers and the star that they seem to be the only ones on the same planet. For example, for Scepter, the songwriting duo of Hal David and Burt Bacharach appeared to have a direct channel into the mind, soul, and vocal cords of Dionne Warwick. Almost all her 1960s hits—from "Don't Make Me Over" to "Walk on By" to "Do You Know the Way to San Jose"—were from the songwriting team of Bacharach and David.

The same held true for the Shirelles. Once Luther Dixon came on board at Scepter and began producing the group's records, everything turned from tin to gold for the four young ladies. For four years, from 1960 through1963, the Shirelles were the dominant girl group of their time, creating such standards as "Will You Still Love Me Tomorrow" (#1 in 1960) to "Soldier Boy" (#1 in 1962) to "Dedicated to the One I Love" (#3 in 1961) to "Foolish Little Girl" (#4 in 1963). In those four years, the Shirelles boasted a dozen Top Forty records.

Then Luther Dixon moved on. With his departure, the Shirelles lost their mojo and, some might say, their respect for each other. Lead singer Shirley Owens attempted a solo career. Doris Coley dropped out for awhile to raise a family. Beverly Lee was kicked out of the group twice before being invited back. After Addie "Micki" Harris died in 1982, each of the remaining Shirelles hit the oldies circuit with their own "Shirelles Show." Doris Coley died in 2000. In the final summation, Shirley Owens, as lead singer, would earn recognition and respect for her distinctive voice, but Beverly Lee ended up with the rights to the group's name.

What is the best girl group recording ever? Some people go with "Will You Still Love Me Tomorrow" by the Shirelles or "Be My Baby" by the Ronettes or "Da Doo Ron Ron" by the Crystals. As to the most memorably mysterious and reluctantly beloved of the girl group canon, without debate that distinction usually falls to "Sally Go 'Round the Roses" by the Jaynetts. It's even been called one of the most discussed records of all time.

In Dave Marsh's book *The Heart of Rock & Soul: The 1001 Greatest Singles Ever Made*, at #377 is "Sally Go 'Round the Roses," which Marsh called the "spookiest and most exotic of all girl group discs." He writes: "Superficially, Sally's friends are just warning her against going downtown, because there she'll find the 'saddest thing in the whole wide world,' her baby with another girl. But the mix and arrangement and the odd metaphor of the endlessly repeated chorus ('Sally, go 'round the roses / They won't tell your secret') lend the entire production an ominous air, as if some deeper tale waits to be told."[11]

Take your pick. The deepest, darkest tale about the "Sally Go 'Round the Roses" is either its origins or the aftereffects of two key singers. Let's start with the song's genesis, which vocally had a lot to do with Zell Sanders's greatest successes: two key singers, Lezli Valentine and Louise Harris Murray, from the Hearts of "Lonely Nights" fame, and her daughter Johnnie Louise Richardson of Johnnie and Joe, who sang "Over the Mountain, Across the Sea."

In 1959, the Hearts with Lezli Valentine singing lead released a single called "My Love Has Gone" / "You or Me Has Got to Go."

Also in 1959, Murray recorded a single for Zell called "A Prisoner to You" with "From a Cap to a Gown" on the B-side, which was released on the obscure record label Argyle. Sonny Moore was listed as the songwriter. As Louise remembered, Zell called her into the studio to record the songs, but the record was to be released under the Enalouise and the Hearts group name for "tax purposes." Enalouise was a combination of Louise's name and that of her mother. The heart of the Hearts at that point was Lezli Valentine and Marie Hood—a combination that would soon reappear under another name. "She had me sing these songs, and nothing happened with the record, so I just let it go," says Murray.[12]

The two singles went nowhere; both were released in the middle of a long stretch of musical strikeouts by Zell Sanders that would extend into the early 1960s. By that time, her J&S Records was more an enterprise in need of rehab than a fully functioning corporate entity. By one account, only Zell's long-standing contracts with Chess Records of Chicago were keeping it afloat. It was certainly looking like the end of the line for Zell's little recording enterprise. Then, out of the blue, or, as one might say, during the time of the "Blue Moon," one last adrenalin shot of redemption came her way—and she certainly made the most of it.[13]

Let's begin with the very lengthy back-story. After World War II, Abner Spector (no relation to Phil Spector) was working at his family's business in Chicago while writing songs on the side. By the late 1940s, a singer named Lona Stevens performed one of his songs on the radio, which was his first taste of success (he would later marry Lona). As the 1940s rolled into the 1950s, Spector was writing and promoting songs full-time for Mellin Music. That brought him into the orbit of Chicago-based Chess Records, where he began working with Leonard Chess. In 1960, Spector moved to New York to start a new label, Tuff Records. By some accounts, this wasn't a truly independent new company but actually a Chess venture, with Spector reporting to Leonard Chess. Jimmie

Raye, who came to Tuff Records as a singer, remembered that Spector not only had Chess Records distributing for his company, but he often did a lot of recording in Chicago.[14]

Raye, who had sung with a group called the Collegians while in the service, ended up in Washington, DC, where he helped create a local label inexplicably called Satan Records with Don Covay, Eddie Floyd, and Billy Stewart, all of whom would become successful recording acts. Raye's first recording was "Hey, Let's Dance" on Satan Records. It caught little traction with radio stations as all the important studio action and promotion infrastructure was still in New York, where Raye eventually wandered. A friend introduced him to Abner Spector.

"I was living on 52nd Street and Broadway, and right nearby were all the offices of the entertainers and music writers," Raye said. "Abner had a studio at 1519 Broadway, and the Tuff Record offices were across the street."[15] Tuff Records did eventually release a Jimmie Raye record, "Look at Me Girl (Crying)," in 1964, two years after Spector's first success, with a song called "Smoky Places" by the Corsairs, which rose to #12 on the pop charts in January 1962.

Chess Records was a strong R&B label that had early success in the 1950s with doo-wop groups. It needed diversification, and Tuff Records was set up. It was in New York to tap into the whole zeitgeist of production and songwriting coming from the Brill Building and 1650 Broadway. Music writer Dave Marsh reported that Spector was sent to New York specifically to hook up with Zell Sanders. If Chess Records was considering doing girl group music, it already had that Zell connection, so it was only natural that Spector and Sanders would meet and try to get something together.[16]

Some music historians claim Spector wrote "Sally Go 'Round the Roses," although on the record credit is given to Zell Sanders and Lona Stevens. Dave Marsh gives a lot of impetus to the song's origins to Zell, who, in desperate need of a break, told Spector she not only had a girl group ready to go, but the outlines of a song as well.[17]

While the song certainly seems as if it evolved out of the playground singing game "Ring around the Rosie," Zell never said that it did or didn't, leaving the metaphor murky and creating one of the most talked-about songs of the early 1960s.

If the song's genesis remains opaque, the same can be said of the performances on the record. One account says five singers made up the Jaynetts: Zell's daughter Johnnie, Ethel Davis, Mary Sue Wells, Yvonne Bushnell, and Ada Ray Kelly.[18] Author John Clemente agrees about Ethel Davis and Ada Ray Kelly but says the other Jaynetts during the time period when "Sally Go 'Round the Roses" was recorded were either Selena Healey, Marlina Mars (Mack), Mary Green Wilson, or Iggy Williams. Initially, any combination of these names could have been true, but those aren't the singers on the record.[19]

One memory of the recording session by Johnnie Louise Richardson was that Spector sequestered the girls in the studio on a Friday and didn't allow them to leave until the following week when the recording was completed. But it remained a troubled recording, not quite the song that anyone wanted or expected. Zell and Spector threw everything at it, trying to get it right. Johnnie was quoted as saying, "Anybody that came in the studio that week, he [Spector] would put them on [the track]. Originally, I think he had about 20 voices on Sally."[20]

"Abner was a creative person with strange recording habits," said Jimmie Raye. "He would invite a lot of people into the studio, put down tracks, and then he would go get different people to sing. If he liked anything, he might make a recording but under different names than they had. A lot of people did recordings, and people can't find out who they were because he might just choose his own name for them."[21]

Zell could be something of a perfectionist with a song she really believed in and was not happy at all with the recording by the new Jaynetts, whoever they were, so she brought in the A-team of her girl network, Lezli Valentine, Marie Hood, and Louise Murray, all of whom sang for her before in the various iterations of the Hearts.

"Zell calls me up and asks if I would sing on this song she had called 'Sally Go 'Round the Roses,'" Murray remembered. "Ms. Sanders had some other girls in there at first, and they couldn't do it the way she wanted it done. That's why she had us sing." Louise was married with three children and an abusive husband. She jumped at the chance. "I didn't even care if it was going to be a hit or not. I just did it for fun," she said. "We practiced and then went into the studio."[22]

Some stories about the recording of "Sally Go 'Round the Roses" note that there were as many as eight girls on the recording. There were five girls originally, but it was the three new singers who are the ones mainly heard on the record.

Other than being in the vicinity of the Brill Building, Murray didn't remember where the studio was or what it looked like. When she, Lezli, and Marie went to record a new version of "Sally Go 'Round the Roses," there were a number of musicians in the studio, although the only one she remembered was Artie Butler.[23]

There would be no "Sally Go 'Round the Roses" without Butler, who created the melody, arranged the song, and even played most of the instruments.

As Artie Butler wrote on his online biography, he was working at Bell Sound Studios as a setup man, getting the studios ready for recording sessions and assisting the engineers during the sessions. The songwriting team of Jerry Leiber and Mike Stoller was one of Bell Sounds' biggest clients. "One day, they were recording with a large orchestra, and the piano player couldn't play the part properly," he wrote. "I offered to overdub once they dismissed the orchestra.

After I played it, they asked me to work for them." Soon afterward, he was also working for Jeff Barry and Ellie Greenwich, becoming the arranger and pianist of many of their hit records.[24]

"I wasn't at the recording session for the Jaynetts," Raye said. "But I remember Abner told me how he put it together. First, he took the rhyme, with Louise Murray doing a lot of the talking on the record. Then he recorded the music. He layered the vocals onto the music. He was a different kind of producer." Raye also maintained that Abner leaned heavily on a small group of musicians for session work, including Richard Tee, drummer Bernard Lee "Pretty" Purdie, and Van McCoy (who would have a #1 instrumental hit, "The Hustle," in 1975).[25] While they might have been in the recording studio with the singers, none of them were in the recording studio when Butler put the record together.

In 1963, Butler found himself at Tuff Records as the arranger of "Sally Go 'Round the Roses."

"Abner Spector called me with this song," Butler recalled. "He found me because I was starting to get busy in New York; I was one of the new young guys in the industry coming up. Abner said to me, 'I want to do something with this, and I have these girls to sing it.' He wanted me to listen to it. It was just a little ditty, and my immediate response was, 'It's pretty trite.' I felt it was circular and trite like a nursery rhyme, which is okay when you're seven years old."[26]

Being a young man on the make with an opportunity to create a record, Butler didn't tell Abner that it didn't appear to be a very exciting song. Instead, he told Abner he would take a tape home with him and listen to it again in private and maybe he could pump some fairy dust into it. He left Abner's office saying, "Let me see what I could come up with."

Butler played the tape in his Brooklyn apartment, listened to it, and eventually found inspiration. "I called up Abner and said, 'I hear something, but it isn't what you have.' He said, 'Go into the studio, I'll pay for the studio time.' 'Okay,' I told him, 'I'll play all the instruments myself,' which I did, except for the guitar. I played the piano, bass, drums, organ, and tambourine. There was nobody in the studio but me."

The recording was done at the old Broadway Recording Studio in the Ed Sullivan Studio building. The engineer was Pat Jacques, who operated the studio. Artie did it all on two Ampex AG-350 mono recorders because that is what they had—it was a demo studio. "I went from one mono machine to the other, back and forth, back and forth, and that's what made the eerie sound, the loss of audio quality going from one track to the other," Butler said. "I compensated for it by changing the EQ [treble/bass equalization], adding highs and echo with each subsequent layer."

He added, "There were rumors afterward that I racked up a studio bill of $60,000 for three days—that's absurd. And there were also rumors that Buddy

Miles played. Believe me, there was no Buddy Miles back then—and if there was, who ever heard of him?"

Butler didn't have the girls in the studio when he did the instrumentation. His memory of the girls doing the vocals is sketchy because he wasn't in the studio when they did their recording. "I think I showed them what I needed to show them because my treatment was completely different from what the song was originally," he said. "They didn't know what I was going to do, so they couldn't just go into the studio and sing. I'm sure I told them what I had in mind. It went a whole different track than they were used to."

Fifty years after the record was made, the only girl's name Butler remembered was Ada (Ada Ray Kelly), while the only musician that Murray remembered was Butler, so he might have addressed both groups of girls, although he asserted that he was not at any of the vocal recording sessions.

When it was complete, Butler proudly played the track for Abner, who just flat-out hated it. Abner stood up and screamed at Artie, "You are supposed to be one of the wonder kids in this town and you give me this piece of shit!"

Laughing about it, Butler also recalled, "He spelled it out, S-H-I-T. I looked around to see who he was talking to. I said, 'I beg to differ with you Abner,' but he continued, 'This is garbage. I'm in the record business—you're not. Who is going to buy this? It's a piece of crap. You're supposed to be talented.' I was reduced to Jell-O. I said, 'You're wrong, it's just different, you haven't heard anything like this.'"

Abner continued ranting, telling Butler that no disc jockey was going to play it. So Butler took a copy of the song and went back to Jerry Leiber and Mike Stoller, playing it for them. Jerry jumped off the sofa in his office and exclaimed to Artie, "You go back to Abner and tell him that Leiber and Stoller will buy this record and reimburse him for all of his expenses. I will write him a check right now." Butler picked up the phone in Jerry's office, called Abner, and told Abner everything Jerry just told him. Leiber and Stoller were red hot at the time, and hearing that they were interested turned Abner's thinking on the record 180 degrees.

"I remember driving down the West Side Highway in Manhattan, and Murray Kaufman, aka Murray the K, the biggest disc jockey in New York at the time, saying 'Whoever you are, wherever you are, pull over because once in a while, all of us who play records for you agree on one record that we all are going to lay on you, and this is one, it's called 'Sally Go 'Round the Roses' by the Jaynetts," conjured up Butler. "I almost drove into one of the ships at the docks alongside the highway. I said to myself, 'I wonder if Abner is listening.' When I got to home to Brooklyn, I called Mike Stoller and said that the record is on the radio, and he said, 'I'm sorry he didn't sell it to us.'"

The key to the record, Butler said, was his influences at the time, a lot of deep R&B via the likes of Ray Charles, Jimmy Reed, and Joe Williams.

"I just heard something," he added. "I sat down at the piano in my home and started singing. I said to myself, 'Whoa, Whoa. I got something here.' I knew I could make a very different sounding record. I felt it in my guts. I knew it was going to be a different sound with an R&B touch. As I was making it, I knew it had this ethereal R&B touch because that's what I was going after. After the record came out, I read articles that there was a hidden message that people were coming back from the dead, all kinds of *mishigas*. I just made the record, there were no hidden secrets. It was just a creative thing that I did and a flow that I was going after. I was in the moment."[27]

Early in 1969, journalist Richard Goldstein's book *The Poetry of Rock* was in bookstores for the first time. Among the songs he reviewed in his discursive prose was "Sally Go 'Round the Roses," to which he scrawled this preamble:

> You're about to encounter one of the most mystifying lyrics in rock. Its ambiguous refrain almost seems cribbed from an obscure corner of *Waiting for Godot*. Those who like to ponder meaning can choose between a gaggle of interpretations, including one which alleges that Sally experiences a religious epiphany, another which asserts that the whole thing is about a lesbian affair. But it's far more meaningful to grasp the song's sensual sadness than to clutch at interpretive straws. Sally's situation is the oldest cliché in rock, but the melancholic lyricism in which her scene is set is unique. It is that quality of despair that attracted all the explicators in the first place.[28]

There are several mysteries that have revolved around the song. What is the song about? At the time the song was popular, kids thought it referred to what eventually would be called urban legends, or grave-robber ghouls who steal cemetery flowers, or a tale of two lesbians, or a simple breakup story. Take your pick.

Who wrote the song? The record label credits Zell and Lona Stevens. Zell had many talents, but she wasn't a great songwriter. Back in the 1950s and 1960s, producers would pressure the real songwriters to share songwriting credits to be able to take 50 percent of the royalties. It was a very lucrative steal. This is probably the back story here as well. Clemente adds to the mix George David Weiss, a songwriter who had been around since the 1940s and who often worked with Claude A. "Bennie" Benjamin. However, the real second or third songwriting credit should have gone to Lezli Valentine, who even Clemente asserts wrote some of the song's lines.[29] If so, that would be the first but the not last time Lezli would lose writing credits on a hit song.

Who sang on the song? Butler appears to have layered Louise, Lezli, and Marie's vocals over an earlier group recording. Two sets of original singers have been noted, but those were not the final two choices. An Internet string turned up this surprising line from "Sheila in Batesville, Arkansas," who claimed that her mother, Mary Sue Wells, was one of the singers on "Sally Go 'Round the Roses." Sheila wrote: "Sadly, she passed away about four years ago. I asked her about the lesbian aspect of 'Sally,' and she said that the song was never about lesbians but a song about boyfriend cheating on girlfriend. Really, an innocent song that people tried to overanaly[ze]. I believe she was around 17 when she started singing with the Jaynetts. I loved hearing about the touring and shows when I was growing up. I will always miss her, but I will always have 'Sally' when I want to hear her singing again."

Who are the three women pictured on the Jaynetts album cover? We know two are Lezli and Ethel Davis, but the third has always been an unknown. However, Sheila from Batesville also wrote, "My mother was Mary Sue Wells. She is in the top left corner of the cover pic."[30]

Abner gave Butler arranging and conducting credits on the record but stiffed him on payment, so they never worked together again. At some point, Zell took the same "Sally" track and used it for another Jaynetts record, "Snowman, Snowman, Sweet Potato Nose."

"The saddest thing was, I was plugged into those girls," Butler said. "I could have made another hit record with them. Those girls are the ones that suffered. To be truthful, I was looking forward to working with them; they were nice girls. Zell Sanders was a tough lady. I liked her. She was a businesswoman with a good sense of humor. I was looking forward to continuing."

Butler went on to write, arrange, or produce dozens and dozens of hit records, from Neil Diamond's "Solitary Man" to Janis Ian's "Society's Child" to Louis Armstrong's "What a Wonderful World" to Barry Manilow's "Copacabana." He contributed keyboards to one other beautiful, ethereal, perfectly arranged and executed girl group song of note, the Shangri-Las' "Remember (Walking in the Sand)."

After listening to the song one more time, Louise Harris Murray was adamant that the lead is unmistakably Lezli and she and Marie are on the harmony.[31]

So difficult were the "Sally Go 'Round the Roses" sessions that Zell only got one recording out of it. No other songs were cut. To issue a single, Zell simply put an instrumental version of the song on the B-side.

In the autumn of 1963, "Sally Go 'Round the Roses" hit #2 on the pop charts, although it had a strange climb because it sold better on the pop charts than in the R&B market.

Louise, Lezli, and Marie cut one other song for Zell, a follow-up record called "Dear Abby," which, of course, refers to the famous advice column. Or did they? The single on Tuff Records is credited to the Hearts. According to the record notes, the song was created by the same team behind "Sally Go

'Round the Roses": arranged and conducted by Artie Butler, produced by Abner Spector, and written by Lona Stevens (the wife of Abner Spector). It too had an instrumental version on the B-side, which read "Sing Along without the Hearts"—"Instrumental Background to Dear Abby." Despite the credits, which suggest a 1963 recording, Murray can be heard on this song, so it could have been an earlier recording by the Hearts. Murray couldn't recall if they sang it anew or Zell just distributed the oldie as a new song.

Lezli Valentine hung in with Zell, while Murray and Hood disappeared. A Jaynetts album appeared with three singers, and aside from Lezli, Murray didn't even recognize the other two young women. Nor did she ever hear the other songs on the album beyond "Sally" and "Dear Abby," the two she helped cut in the studio.

"Sally Go 'Round the Roses" was Zell's third attainment of greatness and her third post-success inability to maintain momentum. This time, the fall was precipitous and unforgiving despite throwing everything but the kitchen sink into the mix. There was a wild bunch of horrendously titled songs—"Snowman, Snowman, Sweet Potato Nose," "Who Stole the Cookie from the Cookie Jar," "Chicken Chicken Crane or Crow" ("Chickama Chickama Craney Crow" was an old children's rhyme)—by new aggregations of Jaynetts, which were all attempts to milk something more from the success of the nursery rhyme–ish "Sally."

Zell also released songs by the Clickettes (including Lezli Valentine), the Poppies, the Z-Debs, and the Patty Cakes (their song "I Understand Them: A Love Song to the Beatles" was an obvious attempt to cash in on the Beatles phenomenon of 1964).

Zell was facing a battle she didn't realize she couldn't win. Musical styles don't last forever, and the girl group sound that began in 1958 had begun to peter out by 1964 as new music trends invaded the pop charts. Obviously, the big noise in 1964 was the Beatles, which ushered in the British Invasion sound.

Alan Betrock, in *Girl Groups: The Story of a Sound*, summed it up this way: "The girl-group sound eventually vanished from the charts. It was not due to any single event, but rather to a series of events that, when linked together, resulted in the demise of not only the sound, but the artists and producers as well."

Betrock made two important points. First, the girl group sound with its sunny, hopeful, ever-romantic lyrics matched the tenor of the times, those bright hopeful years of John F. Kennedy's new presidential administration. By the mid-1960s, America's mood turned darker and more rebellious, and songs of that period were harder, message-laden, and reflective of the changing values of young people.[32]

Second, by the mid-1960s, important writers and producers "dropped out of the scene," and many of the songwriting teams that sustained the girl groups broke up or were soon to break up. Zell couldn't break up her company because she was the whole company. Zell Sanders died in 1976.

In the late 1970s, Johnnie Louise Richardson contacted Murray to see if she and Baby Washington would be in a show that she was doing. Nothing ever came of it, but it was weird to hear from Johnnie because, as far as Murray understood, Johnnie was no longer in the music business. She had an office in Harlem's Hotel Theresa (where Fidel Castro stayed when he visited the United Nations) because she was running an ambulette service called Johnnie on the Spot.

Murray continued her self-destructive pattern. Just as she did as a Heart, she walked away from the Jaynetts when things were at peak. "I didn't want to be bothered no more," said Louise. "I didn't sing anymore with the groups, and I never went back with Zell after that."

If there was one good thing that she got from her Jaynetts venture, it was the urge to sing again, so she started going back to the Apollo for its amateur nights. "I thought I could make it by myself," she said.

And she almost did. One night at the Apollo, jazz organist Jimmy Smith was in the audience and was impressed by her voice. At the time, Smith was working with Clarence Avant, who had once managed R&B singer William Edward "Little Willie" John (who sang the original "Fever" in 1956) and Sarah Vaughan. Avant was then collaborating with record producer Tom Wilson (an African American who would work with some of the best white folk-rockers of the 1960s, including Bob Dylan and Simon and Garfunkel).

Smith gave Murray a business card with Avant's name and said she should give him a call and mention Smith's name. Murray did as suggested and was told to come down to chat. It was around 1965 or 1966 when she went back into the studio with Avant, even though she was pregnant with her fourth child. "They had two songs for me to record, 'The Love I Give' on the A-side, and 'For Some' on the B-side. The record went out on the Verve label." She added, "Friends who came back from England told me the record was #1 there."[33]

"The Love I Give" was never #1 on the UK's main pop charts, and a check with BBC deejay Spencer Leigh, who is an expert on British popular recording history, revealed a blank in radio play as well. Leigh couldn't even find if the record charted. He did suggest it may have been a standout in something called Northern Soul, a music and dance movement that emerged in Northern England in the mid- to late 1960s and to some extent continues to this day. Habitués of Northern Soul record shops and most importantly clubs and dance halls preferred harder soul music than that of, for example, Motown Records, which was popular in the United States during the mid-1960s. Dancehall and club deejays had their own playlists and charts, and apparently "The Love I Give" was the right kind of song for Northern Soul. It is still associated with the movement.[34] At the time, Louise had never heard of Northern Soul and assumed that the record was as dead as her career.

Unfortunately, Murray was not the only member of the Hearts/Jaynetts to have her career come to a heartbreaking halt despite recording one of the best unheard songs of the 1960s. Louise's friend and fellow Heart/Jaynett Lezli Valentine met the same fate.

This story also begins in the 1950s, but not with Valentine, Murray, or even Zell Sanders. It started with another entrepreneurial lady, Sylvia Vanderpool, who in 1954 teamed up with everyone's favorite session guitarist Mickey Baker to form the duo Mickey and Sylvia for a little song called "Love Is Strange."

Around the same time Sylvia was cooing "your sweet loving is better than a kiss" to Mickey and he was countering with "Sylvia, how do you call your lover boy," Lezli Valentine came into Zell's orbit. The year was 1957.

Throughout 1957, Zell mostly used Joyce West and then Baby Washington as the lead singer for the Hearts, sometimes inserting other leads such as Louise, Anna Barnhill, or Betty Harris. Then she found Valentine, who had already graduated high school and gotten her first job, so Zell hoped she was more mature than the first group of restless teenagers who had become the Hearts. Once again, Zell was able to find a gold nugget in a wide and fast-moving stream. Valentine was a fine singer with a strong voice, much in resemblance to Joyce West, but a little higher on the soprano range. Starting in 1958 and for the next two years, Valentine's voice was the lead sound of the Hearts. Over time, she would prove valuable in one other way, in that she remained loyal to Zell for a much longer time than the Hearts' prior key players.

But this is also a story of the Jaynetts, and in 1958, when Zell was looking to form a second girl group, she turned to the teenage gal next to her, who happened to be Valentine, and said, "Give me a good name for a group." The story Valentine told John Clemente goes like this: "I said, J for J&S and Aynetts for my middle name, Anetta. I had no idea she would use it."[35]

Zell tested the name in 1958 by issuing the record "I Want to Be Free" with "Where are You Tonight" on the B-side. The Jaynetts were the listed singers. The record, on the J&S label, was actually recorded the prior year with Baby Washington in the lead and Valentine as one of the other singers.

As noted, the Jaynetts didn't consist of singularly identifiable individuals. When a group had to be formed for touring and promotion, Zell created numerous entities, one of which included Valentine. Zell also promoted another female group, the Clickettes, which had been recording on a subsidiary label, Dice. At some point, Valentine found herself recording as a Clickette for a song called "I Just Can't Help It." By 1960, the Hearts were pretty much over, although Zell would continue to push out a few sporadic releases every now and then.

Meanwhile, for Sylvia Vanderpool life was getting interesting. She had married Joe Robinson and formed All Platinum Records. In 1966, Sylvia (now Sylvia Robinson) hired Lezli Valentine.

Valentine had been in the wilderness for a couple years, and when she came onboard at All Platinum, she did so as Joe Robinson's secretary, plus singer and songwriter. Two years later, Lezli Valentine gave the tiny label its first successful release, a song called "I Won't Do Anything" with "I've Got to Keep on Loving You" on the B-side. Sylvia Robinson cowrote "I Won't Do Anything," and Bert Keyes coproduced the record.

Then things went off the rails for Valentine. Her follow-up song was "The Coward's Way Out," with "Love on a Two-Way Street" as the B-side. The irrepressible Bert Keyes arranged and produced both songs. As fate would have it, the B-side was the most important tune, mostly because of its catchy, intriguing lyrics: "I found love on a two-way street, and lost it on a lonely highway." The record's B-side reads that "Love on a Two-Way Street" was written by Bert Keyes and Sylvia Robinson. However, it has since been revealed that Valentine was one of the song's principal writers.

This wouldn't have made much of a difference for the B-side of a record, but in that same year Sylvia Robinson brought into the studio a local New Jersey trio called the Moments to record an album on the All Platinum subsidiary label Stang. The album was titled *Not on the Outside, But on the Inside, Strong!* One of the songs was "Love on a Two-Way Street." Sylvia released the song as a single and it was a monster hit, rising all the way to the #3 best-selling record in the country and staying on the pop charts for fourteen weeks.

Years later, in a courtroom trying get her just desserts, Valentine explained why she should have gotten cowriting credits. According to her version of events, Sylvia came into the All Platinum office one morning and said that she had a dream but that the only thing she remembered were the words "love on a two-way street, lost it on a lonely highway." Then Sylvia and Valentine went into Bert's office, where Sylvia asked him to play what he felt could be a potential melody. (What he played actually became the melody!) At the same time, Valentine began to write the storyline: "True love will never die / so I've been told but now I must cry / it is finally goodbye, I know . . ." Sylvia added, "He held me in desperation / I thought it was a revelation / and then he walked out." The next lines came from Valentine: "How could I be so blind / . . . to be fooled is a hurting thing." Sylvia followed: "To be loved and fooled is a crying shame." Valentine's final lines concluded the story: "While I bear the blame / as he laughs my name." After it all came together, Valentine recorded the song. The lead sheets were hand delivered by one of the original Moments, John Morgan, who lived in Washington, DC.[36]

Valentine claimed the original application was altered without her knowledge and for good reason—she was dropped as one of the songwriters. Joe Robinson apparently knew what had happened, and when confronted by Valentine, he placated her, saying that he would rectify it. He never did. On the record, songwriting credits went to the other two people in the room that day, Sylvia Robinson and Bert Keyes.

For promotional purposes, All Platinum used a black-and-white glossy of a cat-ate-the-canary Bert Keyes holding Valentine close. She doesn't appear all that enthralled. Perhaps she already knew the game was afoot because she also asked Keyes to remedy the problem. He too said he would take care of it, but, like Joseph Robinson, he didn't feel compelled to compromise potential royalties, although many studio people knew that Valentine had cowritten the lyrics.[37]

Recognition eventually came her way, but legally, Valentine never got the credit nor royalties for such a major song. The duress of the lengthy legal battles fought and lost took its toll on Valentine, which she called "nerve-wracking." Valentine broke down under the stress, and as she admitted, it all "resulted in hospitalizations." Valentine eventually retired to Columbus, Ohio, and as Murray noted, she remained "very bitter" about the whole music business.[38]

In the 1990s, Louise Murray formed a group called the Super Girls with four other girl group veterans: Margaret Williams of the Cookies, Lillian Walker-Moss of the Exciters, Nanette Licari of Reparata and the Delrons, and Beverly Warren of the Raindrops.

The group still sang together until the COVID-19 pandemic. Murray and her husband became ill from the disease in 2020. They both survived.

EPILOGUE

When I began *All I Want Is Loving You: Popular Female Singers of the 1950s*, my first book about the wonderful female singers of the 1950s, my focus, at first, was only on white singers. I knew some of their great songs from "Tennessee Waltz" to "Why Don't You Believe Me" to "Let Me Go, Lover," but didn't really follow any of the singers. Indeed, as a youngster growing up in the 1950s, I couldn't even listen to their songs. If something like *Tammy*, a #1 song by Debbie Reynolds, came on the radio, I would rapidly, if not madly, change channels. A Rosemary Clooney or Patti Page tune was an assault to my ears, which were keenly attuned to the latest doo-wop or rock 'n' roll hit.

Then as I got older, far beyond my years of buying albums, then cassettes, then CDs, and then Internet downloads, I rediscovered some of those songs and realized how great they were. As I researched a song such as "Music! Music! Music!" or "The Wayward Wind," I realized that, in the early 1950s, the women of pop music were way ahead of the men, who were still trying to recreate the swing sound of the 1940s.

So initially my great idea was to write about these forgotten and underappreciated white female singers from the 1950s, to give them their due, although almost all have passed away at this point in the twenty-first century. Still, it was time get their reevaluation in print.

When the book was completed I was very happy with the result except for this nagging feeling that I wasn't telling the whole story of the 1950s. For a while, I was so lost in the editing, rewriting, and correcting of the book that I couldn't think beyond "Que Sera Sera." Finally, all concluding work slowed and the University Press of Mississippi, which had done such fine job publishing my book *Chapel of Love: The Story of the Girl Group the Dixie Cups*, decided to take this book as well.

If I boasted to friends and family about this latest tome, they made the usual felicitous comments. However, if I told anyone who knew music or other writers about the industry about my good fortune, they asked: What about the Black female singers from the 1950s? Aha, I thought, that's what I was missing: the other half of the 1950s story. Who were the African American success stories of the decade other than names I already knew, singers such as Dinah Washington, Etta James, LaVern Baker? I soon realized there were so many more great female singers from the period that I didn't know about or, frankly, had never heard of. It was a comeuppance. I eventually discerned I knew quantitatively less about R&B in the 1950s than my conceit would consider.

Once I started my research, it became apparent almost from the initial leap, that the African American experience was very different from the pop singers' universe of the same period. It was a Jim Crow world in the United States during the 1950s and segregation reigned supreme over the land, not just in the South but almost everywhere else in the country. Of course, the record indicators reflected this, with a separate R&B construct that in no way looked anything like the pop charts of the same time. The music industry itself, from top to bottom, from inside to outside, was equally segregated; venues, tours, publicity, representation, management, and anything else one can think of was color-of-skin separate and definitely not equal.

From the 1930s through the 1940s, just a handful of female acts, mostly jazz or smoky-lounge oriented chanteuses, made it to the pop charts. An Ella Fitzgerald or early Billie Holiday found a place on the pop charts, sometimes shooting all the way to having the #1 record in country. For blues and R&B females, the pop record charts were not so accommodating. Then, in the 1950s Black audiences began turning to this other pre–rock 'n' roll sound and the women R&B singers began to claim space on the radio dial and in record sales. The pop world, adrift and lacking in creativity, took notice of what was happening with doo-wop and R&B, and began covering those records. White singers adapted R&B hits for the pop world. This wasn't a good deal for the Black singers, whose potential record sales were cut off by cover versions. However, in the long run, teenagers who listened to pop music discovered that the original versions of these songs that sounded vaguely interesting were better than what was being aired on the pop music stations. It was time to turn the dial to stations that played R&B.

The slow evolution resulted in two different arcs of progression for the white pop singers and Black vocalists of the 1950s. Music was still a man's world. In a good year, the number of white females in the Top Fifty songs of the year, as per *Billboard* magazine, would number less than a dozen—and most years weren't that good. It was no different on the R&B charts (as per Playback.fm): few female stars would crack the list of Top Fifty charts. The big difference was that the white female singers boasted a lot better songs than the white males. In 1952, for example, it was a good year for mediocre crooners such as Eddie Fisher and Al Martino, but a great year for the women with strong tunes such as Kay Starr's "Kiss of Fire" and Jo Stafford's "You Belong to Me."

The early 1950s was the era of the woman soloist on the pop charts. Rosemary Clooney, Patti Page, Kay Starr, Teresa Brewer, and others outclassed the men. None of these ladies were beat singers, and with the coming of rock 'n' roll their recording careers began to fade. The experiential arc for the Black female singers of the 1950s was exactly the opposite. Many were R&B singers whose tunes were already proto–rock 'n' roll but had been ignored by the pop radio stations in the early 1950s. "Rock around the Clock" by Bill Haley in 1955 and the coming of Elvis Presley in 1956 swept away all pretensions about the advent of rock 'n' roll and who had been singing it since the start of the decade. Riding the train forward were such strong singers as Ruth Brown, Etta James, and LaVern Baker. When the careers of these ladies began to stumble in the late 1950s, the Black female group sound was pushing up the tracks right behind. Groups like the Chantels and Shirelles began their careers in 1958, eventually ushering in the Girl Group Era, pop music's second big moment for female singers.

As I write this in the first years of the 2020s, the female voice is in ascendance once again. The most exciting acts, the superstars of today's today, are the women vocalists, both white and Black.

There is an oft-quoted axiom by philosopher George Santayana that goes, "those who cannot remember the past are condemned to repeat it." Although I don't want to be a pessimist, I will leave you, the reader, with this bit of history. The first music era where the women ruled the pop charts was the early 1950s and that ended with the coming of Elvis Presley and the start of the first great revolution in the pop music world. The second time period where women singers flourished, dominating the record charts, was the girl group era of the early 1960s. That moment came to an end with the coming of the Beatles and the second great revolution in pop music. Today, women are again at the apex; does that mean another revolution in music is ahead of us? The omens are in place.

RESEARCH AND ACKNOWLEDGMENTS

The research behind this book relies on music trade publications, African American newspapers, general-circulation newspapers, magazines, music history books, and published biographies. In addition, I interviewed numerous individuals who supplied me with relevant, firsthand recollections of the personalities featured in the book.

References to yearly pop charts refer to *Billboard* compilations. All references to annual R&B charts are derived from https://playback.fm listings.

✦

About four years ago, Louise Harris Murray contacted me about doing a book about her life. At the time, I didn't know who she was. Even after she explained that back in the 1950s, she was in the pioneering female doo-wop group the Hearts and then in the 1960s sang "Sally Go 'Round the Roses" with the Jaynetts, I wasn't sure she would attract a big readership. After she told me the very long and sad story of her life, I gave the book a shot. She was so obscure a singer and her life was so grim, I couldn't get a publisher interested. I said to Louise, "Since your story coincides with the subject of this book I'm writing about Black female singers of the 1950s, let me use some of the interviews and research." She was kind enough to say yes. So, thank you, Louise Harris Murray.

As mentioned, I interviewed numerous entertainment sources for this book. And in various other encounters with artists and media, when the names of these singers or songs came up, I included their comments as well. A big thanks to:

Jonas Benholm
Lilly Bryant of Billie and Lilly
Artie Butler

Carlo Ditta
Barbara Hawkins of the Dixie Cups
Clarence "Frogman" Henry
Gaynel Hodge
Munyungo Jackson
Fanita James of the Blossoms
Beverly Lee of the Shirelles
Brian Ray
Jimmie Raye
Diane Renay
Bobby Rush
Billy Vera
Reggie Vinson
Lillian Walker-Ross of the Exciters
Justine "Baby" Washington
Jerry "Swamp Dogg" Williams Jr.
"Wacko" Wade Wright

NOTES

INTRODUCTION

1. Greg Patro, "Leon René," Allmusic, www.allmusic.com/artist/leon-rené-mn0000239164.

2. Marv Goldberg, "Mabel Scott," Marv Goldberg's R&B Notebooks, 2016, uncamarvy.com/Mablescott/mabelscott.html.

3. David Quirk, "Record Reviews," *Cash Box*, September 2, 1946, 10.

4. Billy Vera, interview.

5. Goldberg, "Mabel Scott."

6. "Race Record Reviews," *Cash Box*, January 1, 1949, 13.

7. Billy Vera, interview.

8. Larry Birnbaum, *Before Elvis: The Prehistory of Rock 'n' Roll*, Scarecrow Press, 2013.

9. "Hot in Other Cities," *Cash Box*, January 7, 1950, 14.

10. Jason Ankeny, "Sister Rosetta Tharpe," Allmusic, www.allmusic.com/artist/sister rosettatharpe-mn0000001351/biography.

11. Jessica Fisher, "Sister Rosetta Tharpe," Analog Revolution, July 30, 2015, www.analog revolution.com/sister-rosetta-tharpe-jessica-fisher.

12. Richard Williams, "Sister Rosetta Tharpe: The Godmother of Rock 'n' Roll," *The Guardian*, March 18, 2015.

13. "Never Before So Many Hits ... All Under One Roof! Decca," *Cash Box*, March 26, 1949, 13.

14. "Race Record Reviews," *Cash Box*, July 16, 1950, 13.

15. "Decca to Cut 'The Consul'. Firm Renews Sister Tharpe Pact," *Cash Box*, April 8, 1950, 10.

16. Billy Vera, interview.

17. Greg Prato, "Leon René," Allmusic, www.allmusic.com/artist/leon-rene'-mn0000239164.

18. Arnold Shaw, *Honkers and Shouters: The Golden Years of Rhythm & Blues*, Collier Books, 1978.

19. A Voice, "History of the Record Industry 1920s–1950s, Part Two: Independent labels, Radio, and the Battle of the Speeds," medium.com, June 8, 2014, https://medium.com/@vinylmint/history-of-the-record-industry-1920-1950s-6d491d7cb606.

20. Philip H. Ennis, *The Seventh Stream: The Emergence of Rocknroll in American Popular Music*, Wesleyan University Press, 1992.

21. Nelson George, *The Death of Rhythm & Blues*, Pantheon Books, 1988.

22. "Move on For Disk Dealers' Confab at NAMM Convention," *Billboard*, March 18, 1950, 16.

23. Ennis, *The Seventh Stream.*

24. Billy Vera, interview.

25. Brown and Yule, *Miss Rhythm: The Autobiography of Ruth Brown.*

26. Shaw, *Honkers and Shouters.*

27. "Jazz 'n Blues Review: Award o' the Week," *Cash Box*, April 8, 1950, 16.

28. "Atlantic Pacts Brown & McGhee Again," *Cash Box*, August 19, 1950, 16.

29. "Rhythm & Blues Record Reviews," *Billboard*, November 11, 1950, 21.

30. "Hot in Harlem, Chicago's South Side, New Orleans," *Cash Box*, November 18, 1950, 16.

31. "Pubs Bid for 'Teardrops,'" *Cash* Box, November 18, 1950, 19.

32. "Simon House Inc.," *Cash Box*, December 9, 1950, 12.

33. "Best Selling Retail Rhythm & Blues Records," *Billboard*, December 9, 1950, 28.

34. "Rhythm & Blues Notes," *Billboard*, December 2, 1950, 26.

35. *Cash Box*, December 23, 1950, 1.

CHAPTER ONE: I WANNA BE LOVED (1950)

1. "Aladdin Goes to LP," *Billboard*, November 11, 1950, 18.

2. "Jazz 'n Blues Reviews," *Cash Box*, June 3, 1950, 15.

3. "Jazz 'n Blues Reviews," *Cash Box*, July 15, 1950, 20.

4. "Jazz Singer Helen Humes Dies at 68," *Sarasota Herald-Tribune*, September 14, 1981, 10.

5. "Helen Humes," Discogs, https://discogs.com/artist/307298.

6. "Helen Humes," IMDb, https://www.imdb.com/name/nm0401793.

7. "Barnet Granted Pub Rights to 'Be-Baba,'" *Billboard*, January 26, 1946, 16.

8. "Gene Norman" (obituary), Ace Records, https://acerecords.co.uk/news/20151/gene-norman-obituary.

9. "Jazz 'n Blues Reviews," *Cash Box*, October 7, 1950, 17.

10. "Hot in Detroit, Los Angeles, in Other Cities," *Cash Box*, December 2, 1950, 15.

11. "Jazz 'n Blues Reviews," *Cash Box*, December 9, 1950, 20.

12. *Jet*, May 8, 1952, 62.

13. "Benny Carter, Helen Humes to Tour Europe," *Jet*, September 24, 1953, 57.

14. "Nellie Lutcher," All About Jazz, https://musicians.allaboutjazz.com/nellielutcher?width =1366.

15. Harry Levette, "Gossip of the Movie Lots," *Ohio Daily Express*, February 1, 1950, 3.

16. Peter Vacher, "Nellie Lutcher: Pianist and singer, she used risqué lyrics and mixed blues with a new bounce," *The Guardian*, June 13, 2007.

17. Vida Lutcher, *This Is Your Life*, December 31, 1952.

18. Darryl Munyungo Jackson, interview.

19. Dave Dexter, *This Is Your Life*, December 31, 1952.

20. Louise Harris Murray, interview.

21. "Record Reviews," *Billboard*, February 11, 1950.

22. Ralph Edwards, *This Is Your Life*, December 31, 1952.

23. Wil Stevens, "Vaudeville Reviews," *Billboard*, January 21, 1950, 46.

24. "It's Here," *Northwest Enterprise*, August 15, 1950, 1.

25. "'Round the Wax Circle," *Cash Box*, March 18, 1950, 9.

26. "Vaudeville Reviews," *Billboard*, March 11, 1950, 53.

27. "'Round the Wax Circle," *Cash Box*, January 21, 1950, 7.

28. "King Cole Receives '[the] Cash Box' Music Award," *Cash Box*, February 18, 1950, 13.

29. "MGM Moves Vs. ABC Air Ban of 'Can I Come In,'" *Billboard*, March 4, 1950, 20.

30. "The Cash Box Record Reviews: Sleeper of the Week," *Cash Box*, February 25, 1950, 8.

31. "Record Reviews," *Billboard*, February 18, 1950, 97.

32. "Here's A $$$ Secret," *Billboard*, December 2, 1950, 26.

33. "Nellie Lutcher's Sister Weds," *Jet*, October 1, 1953, 43.

34. "Nellie Lutcher Withdraws from Jack Webb TV Film," *Jet*, June 19, 1958.

35. Darryl Munyungo Jackson, interview.

36. Shaw, *Honkers and Shouters*.

37. Wade "Wacko" Wright, interview.

38. Shaw, *Honkers and Shouters*.

39. Jeff Hannusch, *I Hear You Knockin': The Sound of New Orleans Rhythm and Blues*, Swallow Publications, 1985.

40. Rick Coleman, *Fats Domino and the Lost Dawn of Rock 'n' Roll*, Da Capo Press, 2006.

41. Hannusch, *I Hear You Knockin'*.

42. "'Round the Wax Circle," *Cash Box*, February 4, 1950, 9.

43. "Hot in Harlem, Chicago's South Side, New Orleans, Central Avenues in Los Angeles, in Other Cities," *Cash Box*, February 25, 1950, 14.

44. "Imperial Records Presents," *Cash Box*, March 11, 1950, 24.

45. Coleman, *Fats Domino and the Lost Dawn of Rock 'n' Roll*.

46. Jim Haskins, *Queen of the Blues: A Biography of Dinah Washington*, William Morrow, 1987.

47. "The Year's Top Rhythm and Blues Artists," *Billboard*, January 14, 1950, 17.

48. "Top Artists on Juke Boxes," *Billboard*, March 4, 1950, 81.

49. "Dinah Washington Initiates New Policy," *Detroit Tribune*, March 18, 1950, 6.

50. "New Sunday Jazz Sessions May Hyp Nitery in D.C.," *Billboard*, March 18, 1950, 16.

51. "Dinah Washington Break Sabbath Rule," *Detroit Tribune*, March 4, 1950, 7.

52. "Café Chain Honors D'nh," *Detroit Tribune*, July 29, 1950, 13.

53. "Dinah Washington, Ravens Head Triple-Header Attraction at Paradise," *Detroit Tribune*, January 28, 1950, 7.

54. "Record Review," *Billboard*, February 11, 1950, 110.

55. "Jazz 'n Blues Reviews," *Cash Box*, June 17, 1950, 15.

56. "Rhythm & Blues Record Reviews," *Billboard*, November 11, 1950, 27.

57. "Record Review," *Billboard*, November 4, 1950, 38.

CHAPTER TWO: SMOOTH SAILING (1951)

1. Steve Walker, "Savannah Churchill," *This Is My Story*, www.tims.blackcat.nl.

2. "Savannah Churchill," *Jet*, January 12, 1961, 64.

3. Richard Koloda, "Ladies of R&B . . . Part Seven, Savannah Churchill," https://www.vocalgroupharmony.com/Icried.htm.

4. "Savannah Churchill," *Jet*, January 12, 1961, 64.

5. Shaw, *Honkers and Shouters*.

6. Walker, "Savannah Churchill."

7. "Celebrate with Champale," *Detroit Tribune*, March 3, 1952, 7.

8. "Genius of the 88 Coming to Paradise," *Detroit Tribune*, November 11, 1950.

9. "Jazz 'n Blues Review," *Cash Box*, January 20, 1951, 18.

10. "Jazz 'n Blues Review," *Cash Box*, March 24, 1951, 8.

11. "Savannah Churchill and Terry Timmons Signed by Victor," *Cash Box*, September 22, 1951, 20.

12. "'Sin' Breaks Wide Open Throughout Nation," *Cash Box*, October 6, 1951, 12.

13. "Disk Jockeys' Regional Record Reports," *Cash Box*, November 24, 1951, 12.

14. "Savannah Churchill," *Jet*, September 10, 1953, 60.

15. Hall Webman, "Paramount, New York," *Billboard*, February 3, 1951.

16. Birnbaum, *Before Elvis: The Prehistory of Rock 'n' Roll*.

17. Kate Hakala, "The Tragic Real-Life Story of Ella Fitzgerald," Grunge, www.grunge.com.

18. Stephen Holden, "Ella Fitzgerald, the Voice of Jazz, Dies at 79," *New York Times*, June 16, 1996.

19. "Record Reviews," *Cash Box*, May 12, 1951, 6.

20. "Sleeper of the Week/Record Reviews," *Cash Box*, May 26, 1951, 8.

21. "Kickin' the Blues Around," *Cash Box*, November 3, 1951, 8.

22. "Ella Signs for Five Years," *Jet*, November 1, 1951, 58.

23. "Ella Fitzgerald Signs New Decca Contract," *Cash Box*, October 27, 1951, 8.

24. Birnbaum, *Before Elvis: The Prehistory of Rock 'n' Roll*.

25. Holden, "Ella Fitzgerald, the Voice of Jazz, Dies at 79."

26. "Record Reviews," *Cash Box*, August 18, 1951, 8.

27. "Music Popularity Charts," *Billboard*, September 1, 1951, 31.

28. "Decca Data," *Billboard*, November 3, 1951, 19.

29. "Hwd. R&B Clubs Getting B.O.," *Billboard*, April 14, 1951, 41.

30. Larry Douglas, "Theatrically Yours," *Arizona Sun*, September 5, 1952, 6.

31. Holden, "Ella Fitzgerald, the Voice of Jazz, Dies at 79."

32. J. Henry Randall, "Ella Fitzgerald with Norman Ganz," *Ohio Daily-Express*, September 14, 1950, 1.

33. "Jazz 'n Blues Reviews," *Cash Box*, October 17, 1950, 17.

34. "Margie Day," www.discogs.com/artist/2050537=Margie Day.

35. "Hot," *Cash Box*, December 16, 1950, 15.

36. "Dot's Hot," *Billboard*, November 4, 1950, 38.

37. "Music Popularity Charts," *Billboard*, March 31, 1951, 35.

38. "Rhythm and Blues Notes," *Billboard*, March 3, 1951, 28.

39. "Battle of Bands," *Miami Times*, April 19, 1952, 11.

40. "Palace Theater," *Daily (Ohio) Express*, April 26, 1951.

41. *Miami Times*, October 20, 1951, 3.

42. "Kickin' the Blues Around," *Cash Box*, November 29, 1952, 21.

43. "Rhythm 'n Blues Reviews," *Cash Box*, December 6, 1952, 24.

44. "Rhythm 'n Blues Reviews," *Cash Box*, October 17, 1953, 24.

45. "Rhythm 'n Blues Reviews," *Cash Box*, May 22, 1954, 30.

46. "Margie Day," *Jet*, 1956.

47. Carlo Ditta, interview.

48. Brown and Yule, *Miss Rhythm: The Autobiography of Ruth Brown*.

49. "Paradise," *Detroit Tribune*, March 3, 1951, 10.

50. "Double Attraction at Riverside," *Arizona Sun*, April 6, 1951, 3.

51. Hal Werman, "Rhythm and Blues Notes," *Billboard*, April 21, 1951, 38.

52. "Willis Jackson's Scores at B'Way Club," *Miami Times*, November 17, 1951, 10.

53. Brown and Yule, *Miss Rhythm: The Autobiography of Ruth Brown*.

54. "Ruth Brown," *Detroit Tribune*, June 23, 1951, 11.

55. "Wanna Be a Singer? Read This First," *Detroit Tribune*, October 27, 1951, 16.

56. "Lombardo Plus Ames Bros to Gros Half-Mil," *Billboard*, March 31, 1951, 16.

57. "Jazz 'n Blues Reviews," *Cash Box*, July 21, 1951, 30.

58. "Rhythm & Blues Record Reviews," *Billboard*, July 7, 1951, 74.

59. "Jazz 'n Blues Reviews," *Cash Box*, July 21, 1951, 30.

60. "The Inquiring Candid Camera Man," *Billboard*, November 10, 1951, 41.

61. "Rhythm & Blues Reviews," *Billboard*, November 17, 1951, 35.

62. "Jazz 'n Blues Reviews," *Cash Box*, December 1, 1951, 20.

63. "The Final Count," *Cash Box*, December 8, 1951, 6.

64. "The Top 15 Rhythm & Blues Tunes for 1951," *Cash Box*, December 29, 1951, 30.

65. Haskins, *Queen of the Blues*.

66. "Queen of Jukeboxes, Milburn at Paradise," *Detroit Tribune*, February 17, 1951, 10.

67. "Dinah Washington," *Arizona Sun*, May 4, 1951, 4.

68. "Miss Dinah Gets 'Bird,'" *Detroit Tribune*, July 14, 1951, 11.

69. *Cash Box*, August 18, 1951, 1.

70. "Dinah Washington," *Detroit Tribune*, September 16, 1951, 16.

71. Hal Werman, "Rhythm and Blues Notes," *Billboard*, September 29, 1951, 42.

72. "Check List of Hits," *Billboard*, November 24, 1951, 37.

73. "Disc Jockeys All Over America Acclaim," *Billboard*, November 37, 1951, 31.

CHAPTER THREE: 5-10-15 HOURS (1952)

1. Shaw, *Honkers and Shouters*.

2. "Little Esther Phillips," Biography, https://imdb.com.

3. "Rockland Palace Proudly Presents," *Miami Times*, February 17, 1951, 16.

4. "Dance at VFW Hall," *Miami Times*, February 23, 1951, 14.

5. Ted Yates, "I've Been Around New York," *Miami Times*, September 8, 1951, 7.

6. Ted Yates, "Earl Bostic Seen as 'Perennial' Bandleader," *Detroit Tribune*, May 5, 1951, 10.

7. "Federal Signs the Youthful Queen of Jazz and Blues," *Cash Box*, February 17, 1951, 17.

8. "Rhythm & Blues Record Reviews," *Billboard*, December 15, 1952, 32.

9. Shaw, *Honkers and Shouters*.

10. "Rhythm & Blues Notes," *Billboard*, February 3, 1951, 28.

11. "Little Esther, Otis Switch," *Billboard*, December 1, 1951, 20.

12. "'Round the Wax Circle," *Cash Box*, January 5, 1952, 7.

13. "Little Esther & Savoy Settle Dispute by Arbitration," *Cash Box*, May 17, 1952.

14. Dik De Heer, "Little Esther (aka Esther Phillips)," *Tims This Is My Story*, www.tims
.blackcat.nl.

15. Jerry Williams Jr., interview.

16. "Dear Friends," *Jackson Advocate*, January 5, 1952, 7.

17. Marv Goldberg, "Wini Brown," 2015, www.uncamarvy.com/winibrown/winnibrown.html.

18. "Award o' the Week/Jazz 'n Blues Reviews," *Cash Box*, April 12, 1952, 18.

19. "Spinning with Sy," *Miami Times*, May 31, 1952, 16.

20. "Edna McGriff and Marie Adams, *Jet*, March 26, 1953, 61.

21. Dik De Heer, "Marie Adams," *Tims This Is My Story*, www.tims.blackcat.nl.

22. Sam Evans, "Kickin' the Blues Around," *Cash Box*, November 8, 1952, 21.

23. "Another Gem Dance," *The (Roanoke) Tribune*, May 9, 1953, 8.

24. Marv Goldberg, "Edna McGriff," Marv Goldberg's Yesterday's Memories, 2019, www
.uncamarvy.com/ednamcgriff/ednamcgriff.html.

25. "Edna McGriff," *Jet*, June 5, 1952, 15.

26. Hal Werman, "Rhythm and Blues Notes," *Billboard*, June 23, 1951, 33.

27. "There's No Stopping Jubilee Records," *Cash Box*, December 22, 1951, 15.

28. "Award o' the Week/Jazz 'n Blues Reviews," *Cash Box*, March 8, 1952, 18.

29. "No. 1 in the Nation in Rhythm & Blues," *Billboard*, May 10, 1952, 35.

30. "Edna McGriff," *Jet*, June 5, 1952, 15.

31. "Edna McGriff and Marie Adams," *Jet*, March 26, 1953, 61.

32. "Juke Operators Name 1952's Most Profitable R&B Records to Date," *Billboard*, September
13, 1952, 67.

33. Ria Darley, "Theatrically Yours," *Jackson Advocate*, May 24, 1952, 4.

34. Ria Darley, "Theatrically Yours," *Arizona Sun*, April 18, 1952, 3.

35. Larry Douglas, "Theatrically Yours," *Arizona Sun*, May 9, 1952, 2.

36. Goldberg, "Edna McGriff."

37. "Edna McGriff Hits Marriage Rumors," *Detroit Tribune*, November 15, 1952, 11.

38. "Edna McGriff," *Jet*, September 30, 1954, 64.

39. Goldberg, "Edna McGriff."

40. Haskins, *Queen of the Blues.*

41. "Rhythm & Blues Ramblings," *Cash Box*, March 8, 1952, 16.

42. Larry Douglas, "Theatrically Yours," *Arizona Sun*, October 10, 1952, 3.

43. Haskins, *Queen of the Blues.*

44. Ria Darley, "Theatrically Yours," *Jackson Advocate*, March 29, 1952, 4.

45. "Rhythm & Blues Reviews," *Billboard*, February 23, 1952, 37.

46. "Award o' the Week/Rhythm 'n Blues Reviews," *Cash Box*, December 13, 1952, 22.

47. "Rhythm & Blues Reviews," *Billboard*, February 23, 1952, 37.

48. "Stan Kenton Boff 8½ G Advance on Carnegie Date," *Billboard*, unknown page and
1952 date.

49. "Rhythm & Blues Ramblings," *Cash Box*, April 5, 1952, 18.

50. "Carnegie Hall Will Book Jazz Concert," *Billboard*, May 17, 1952, 31.

51. Larry Douglas, "Theatrically Yours," *Arizona Sun*, July 4, 1952, 5.

52. "Songsational Singing Star 'Solid,' Superb and Sparkling," *The Echo* (Meridian, Mississippi),
July 1, 1952, 1.

53. "Award o' the Week/Rhythm 'n Blues Reviews," *Cash Box*, October 26, 1952, 20.

54. Brown and Yule, *Miss Rhythm: The Autobiography of Ruth Brown.*

55. "Ruth Brown: Best Voice Since Vaughan," *Jet*, January 31, 1952, 64.

56. "Ruth Brown Robbed of Jewels & Music Valued at $10,000," *Cash Box*, February 23, 1952, 17.

57. Brown and Yule, *Miss Rhythm: The Autobiography of Ruth Brown*.

58. "Award o' the Week/Jazz 'n Blues Reviews," *Cash Box*, March 15, 1952, 18.

59. "Rhythm & Blues Ramblings," *Cash Box*, April 12, 1952, 16.

60. "Most Played Juke Box Rhythm & Blues Records," *Billboard*, June 14, 1952, 61.

61. "Rhythm & Blues Ramblings," *Cash Box*, May 24, 1952, 16.

62. "Spinning with Sy," *Miami Times*, June 21, 1952, 16.

63. "Award o' the Week/Jazz 'n Blues Reviews," *Cash Box*, August 9, 1952, 16.

64. "Best Selling Rhythm & Blues Records," *Billboard*, October 11, 1952, 42.

65. Larry Douglas, "Theatrically Yours," *Arizona Sun*, November 14, 1952, 2.

66. Sam Evans, "Kickin' the Blues Around," *Cash Box*, November 8, 1952, 21.

CHAPTER FOUR: HOUND DOG (1953)

1. Peter Guralnick, *Last Train to Memphis: The Rise of Elvis Presley*, Little, Brown, 1994.

2. Joel Whitburn, *Top Forty Hits*, Billboard Books, 1989.

3. Albert Goldman, *Elvis*, McGraw-Hill, 1981.

4. Nelson George, *The Death of Rhythm & Blues*, Pantheon Books, 1988.

5. Ken Emerson, *Always Magic in the Air: The Bomp and Brilliance of the Brill Building Era*, Penguin Books, 2005.

6. Tina Spencer Dreisbach, "Willie Mae 'Big Mama' Thornton," Encyclopedia of Alabama, www.encyclopediaofalabam.org/article/he-1573.

7. Michael Sporke, *Big Mama Thornton: The Life and Music*, McFarland, 2014.

8. Emerson, *Always Magic in the Air*.

9. "Hound Dog Top Selling Blues Record," *Jet*, April 30, 1953, 61.

10. "Theatrically Yours," *Jackson Advocate*, August 8, 1953, 4.

11. Ed Ward, Geoffrey Stokes, and Ken Tucker, *Rock of Ages: The Rolling Stone History of Rock & Roll*, Rolling Stone Press, 1986.

12. Birnbaum, *Before Elvis: The Prehistory of Rock 'n' Roll*.

13. Big Maybelle, Discogs, www.discogs.com/artist.412899-Big-Maybelle.

14. Preston Lauterbach, *The Chitlin' Circuit and the Road to Rock 'n' Roll*, W.W. Norton, 2011.

15. Birnbaum, *Before Elvis: The Prehistory of Rock 'n' Roll*.

16. Lauterbach, *The Chitlin' Circuit and the Road to Rock 'n' Roll*.

17. Jo Ann Botts, "Disc Digging," *The Voice* (Lincoln, Nebraska), April 9, 1953, 4.

18. "Rhythm 'n Blues Reviews," *Cash Box*, August 8, 1953.

19. Jerry Williams Jr., interview.

20. "New York Beat," *Jet*, November 25, 1954, 65.

21. Bob Rolontz, "Rhythm and Blues Notes," *Billboard*, January 31, 1953.

22. "Reviews of This Week's New Records," *Billboard*, February 7, 1953.

23. "Philadelphia, Charlotte," *Billboard*, February 1953.

24. Bobby Rush, interview.

25. George R. White, Robert L. Campbell, Tom Kelly, and Dr. Robert Stallworth, The Chess Label Part II (1953–1955), campber.people.clemson.edu/chess2.html.

26. Robert L. Campbell, George R. White, Tom Kelly, Dr. Robert Stallworth, Jim O'Neal, Armin Bitter, The JOB Label, campber.people.clemson.edu/chess2.html.

27. White et al., The Chess Label Part II (1953–1955).

28. Dik De Heer, "Annisteen Allen," Tims This Is My Story.

29. Larry Douglas, "Theatrically Yours," Arizona Sun, February 13, 1953, 5.

30. Beverly Lee, interview.

31. "Answer to Answers: Pubbers Train Legal Guns on Trail-Riding Indie Labels," Billboard, April 4, 1953.

32. Eartha Kitt, IMDb, www.imdb.com/name/nm0457755.

33. "Eartha Kitt," The Voice (Lincoln, Nebraska), May 7, 1953, 1.

34. Larry Douglas, "Theatrically Yours," Arizona Sun, December 4, 1953, 8.

35. "L.A. Politicians Protest Program Was Too Risque," Nome Nugget, November 18, 1953, 5.

36. "She'll Sing in Sanskrit Yet," Billboard, June 20, 1953, 23.

37. "Rhythm 'n Blues Reviews/Award o' the Week," Cash Box, June 6, 1953, 22.

38. "History of the Television," BeBusinessed, bebusinessed.com/history/history-of-the-television.

39. "Reviews of This Week's New Records," Billboard, October 3, 1952, 28.

40. "Stars Over Harlem," Cash Box, October 31, 1953, 22.

41. Haskins, Queen of the Blues.

42. "Theatrically Yours," Arizona Sun, September 4, 1953, 5.

43. Bobby Rush, interview.

44. "Rhythm 'n Blues Reviews/Award o' the Week," Cash Box, April 4, 1953, 22.

45. "Noble Sissle Rates Little Esther Tops Among Rhythm and Blues Singers," Arizona Sun, February 27, 1953, 5.

46. Haskins, Queen of the Blues.

47. "Dinah Washington and Universal Attractions Prexy Ben Bart," Jackson Advocate, March 28, 1953, 5.

48. "Rhythm 'n Blues Reviews," Cash Box, June 6, 1953, 22.

49. "Christine Kittrell," Biography, Allmusic, www.allmusic.com/artist/christine-kittrell-mn0000126209.

50. "Rhythm 'n Blues Reviews," Cash Box, February 7, 1953, 20.

51. "The Cash Box Hot," Cash Box, December 26, 1953, 22.

52. "Christine Kittrell," Soulful Kinda Music, www.soulfulkindamusic.net/ckittrell.htm.

53. "Rhythm 'n Blues Reviews," Cash Box, September 26, 1953, 26.

54. Richard Skelly, "Sarah McLawler," www.allmusic.com.

55. Colin Larkin, "Sarah McLawler Biography," www.oldies.com.

56. "Sarah McLawler," Discogs, www.discogs.com.

57. Brown and Yule, Miss Rhythm: The Autobiography of Ruth Brown.

58. "One Dime Blues/Blind Lemon Jefferson," Genius, www.genius.com.

59. "Dancer Sues, Says Singer Herb Lance Bit Her," Jet, May 21, 1953, 32.

60. Marv Goldberg, "Herb Lance," 2020, www.uncamarvy.com/herblance/herblance.html.

61. Brown and Yule, Miss Rhythm: The Autobiography of Ruth Brown.

62. Bob Rolontz, "Rhythm and Blues Notes," Billboard, April 1953, 48.

63. Marv Goldberg, "Faye Adams," 2018, www.uncamarvy.com/fayeadams.fayeadams.html.

64. "Riverside Park," Arizona Sun, April 4, 1952, 5.

65. Bob Rolontz, "Rhythm and Blues Notes," *Billboard*, August 1, 1953, 38.

66. Bob Rolontz, "Rhythm and Blues Notes," *Billboard*, August 1, 1953, 38.

67. "Rhythm 'n Blues Ramblings," *Cash Box*, August 22, 1953, 19.

68. "Top R&B Records," *Billboard*, September 19, 1953, 38.

69. "Record Companies Clash Over 'Shake a Hand' Thrush," *Jet*, September 24, 1953, 57.

70. "National Best Sellers/Most Played in Juke Boxes," *Billboard*, November 14, 1953, 49.

71. "Faye Adams into Another Category on 'Shake A Hand,'" *Detroit Tribune*, November 7, 1953, 4.

72. "District Theater/Virginia/Roanoke, Virginia," *The (Roanoke) Tribune*, Page 4, October 31, 1953.

73. Francis Palmer, "Key West: The Southernmost City," *Miami Times*, November 28, 1953.

CHAPTER FIVE: TEACH ME TONIGHT (1954)

1. Shaw, *Honkers and Shouters*.

2. Goldberg, "Faye Adams."

3. Larry Douglas, "Theatrically Yours," *Arizona Sun*, April 2, 1954, 3.

4. "The Billboard Music Popularity Charts/Rhythm & Blues Records," *Billboard*, March 13, 1954, 47.

5. "This Week's Best Buys," *Billboard*, August 21, 1954, 47.

6. Bob Rolontz, "Rhythm & Blues Notes," *Billboard*, August 21, 1954, 47.

7. Bob Rolontz, "Rhythm & Blues Notes," *Billboard*, September 25, 1954, 60.

8. "This Week's Best Buys," *Billboard*, August 21, 1954, 47.

9. "The Cash Box Hot," *Cash Box*, October 2, 1954, 23.

10. "The Cash Box Hot," *Cash Box*, November 6, 1954, 27.

11. "Rhythm 'n Blues Ramblings," *Cash Box*, November 6, 1954, 25.

12. Steve Huey, "Henry Glover," AllMusic, www.allmusic.com/artist/henry-glover-mn0000954906.

13. "Lula Reed," Soulful Kinda Music, www.soulfulkindamusic.net/lreed.htm.

14. "Lula Reed Called Musical Find of Year," *Jet*, January 22, 1953, 61.

15. Dave Penny, "Lula Reed," *Tims This Is My Story*, tims.blackcat.nl.

16. "Rhythm & Blues Record Reviews," *Billboard*, January 23, 1954, 40.

17. "Linda Hayes," Discogs, www.discogs.com/artist/479363-linda-hayes.

18. Gaynel Hodge, interview.

19. "New Records to Watch," *Billboard*, March 7, 1953, 28.

20. "This Week's New Territorial Best Sellers to Watch," *Billboard*, November 14, 1953, 49.

21. "Reviews of New R&B Records," *Billboard*, October 23, 1954, 45.

22. "Guitar Playing, Blues Singing," *Arizona Sun*, February 19, 1954, 8.

23. Larry Douglas, "Theatrically Yours," *Arizona Sun*, April 24, 1953, 3.

24. "Big Entertainment Night at The Elk's Home," *Arizona Sun*, August 27, 1954, 2.

25. Joe Martin, "Status Quo in R&B: Year's Been Good to Talent, Indies, Some Majors' Subsids," April 24, 1954.

26. "Rhythm 'n Blues Reviews," *Cash Box*, October 9, 1954, 24.

27. Birnbaum, *Before Elvis: The Prehistory of Rock 'n' Roll*.

28. Brown and Yule, *Miss Rhythm: The Autobiography of Ruth Brown*.

29. Brown and Yule, *Miss Rhythm: The Autobiography of Ruth Brown*.

30. "The Cash Box Hot," *Cash Box*, October 9, 1954, 22.

31. "The Nation's Top 15 Rhythm & Blues," *Cash Box*, November 6, 1954, 29.

32. "Dinah Washington Leads Big Stars to B'way-Capitol," *Detroit Tribune*, March 6, 1954, 5.

33. "Stars Over Harlem," *Cash Box*, November 27, 1954, 29.

34. "Rhythm 'n Blues Ramblings," *Cash Box*, December 18, 1954, 25.

35. Haskins, *Queen of the Blues*.

36. Kyla Titus, *The Boswell Legacy: The Story of the Boswell Sisters of New Orleans and the New Music They Gave to the World*, CreateSpace, 2014.

37. Birnbaum, *Before Elvis: The Prehistory of Rock 'n' Roll*.

38. "Last Surviving Andrews Sisters Member Dies at 94," Fox News, January 30, 2013.

39. Fanita James, interview.

40. John Clemente, *Girl Groups: Fabulous Females Who Rocked the World*, Krause Publications, 2000.

41. Gaynel Hodge, interview.

42. Tony Rounce, liner notes for Shirley Gunter, *Oop Shoop: The Flair and Modern Recordings 1953–1957*, CD, Ace Records, 2005, https://acerecordscol.uk/.

43. "This Week's Best Buys," *Billboard*, September 1, 1954.

44. "R&B Favorites/Most Promising," *Billboard*, November 13, 1954.

45. Clemente, *Girl Groups: Fabulous Females Who Rocked the World*.

CHAPTER SIX: TWEEDLE DEE (1955)

1. Ennis, *The Seventh Stream: The Emergence of Rocknroll in American Popular Music*.

2. *Billboard*, May 23, 1951.

3. Ward, Stokes, and Tucker, *Rock of Ages: The Rolling Stone History of Rock & Roll*.

4. Louise Harris Murray, interview.

5. Louise Harris Murray, interview.

6. "Interview: Rex Garvin," Othersounds.com/interview-rex-gavin.

7. "Interview: Rex Garvin," Othersounds.com/interview-rex-gavin.

8. Marv Goldberg, "Baton Records," www.uncamarvy.com/baton/baton.html.

9. Sol Rabinowitz, "The Story of the Baton Label," daremusic.com/story.htm.

10. "Rhythm 'n Blues Ramblings," *Cash Box*, February 19, 1955.

11. "Rhythm 'n Blues Sleeper of the Week," *Cash Box*, February 26, 1955.

12. Clemente, *Girl Groups: Fabulous Females Who Rocked the World*.

13. "This Week's Best Buys," *Billboard*, March 26, 1955.

14. "Rhythm 'n Blues Ramblings," *Cash Box*, April 9, 1955.

15. "Juke Box Report," *Cash Box*, April 9, 1955.

16. Shaw, *Honkers and Shouters*.

17. Louise Harris Murray, interview.

18. "My but the Baby Is Growing," *Cash Box*, July 2, 1955, 67.

19. Louise Harris Murray, interview.

20. "Virtual Surrender, 1955: The Year R&B Took Over Pop Field," *Billboard*, November 12, 1955, 126.

21. Dan DeLuca, "Etta James, the Husky-Voiced R&B Singer, Dies at 73," *Philadelphia Inquirer*, January 21, 2012.

22. Etta James and David Ritz, *Rage to Survive: The Etta James Story*, Da Capo Press, 1995.

23. James and Ritz, *Rage to Survive: The Etta James Story*.

24. "Cleve. DJ's Ban Randle's 'Firsts,'" *Billboard*, March 26, 1955, 22.

25. "Review Spotlight On ...," *Billboard*, January 22, 1955, 42.

26. Larry Douglas, "Theatrically Yours," *Arizona Sun*, July 29, 1955, 3.

27. "Review Spotlight On ...," *Billboard*, May 14, 1955, 48.

28. James and Ritz, *Rage to Survive: The Etta James Story*.

29. James and Ritz, *Rage to Survive: The Etta James Story*.

30. James and Ritz, *Rage to Survive: The Etta James Story*.

31. James and Ritz, *Rage to Survive: The Etta James Story*.

32. Barbara Hawkins, interview.

33. Reggie Vinson, interview.

34. "Most-Promising Newer R&B Artists," *Billboard*, November 12, 1955, 123.

35. Birnbaum, *Before Elvis: The Prehistory of Rock 'n' Roll*.

36. "Stars Over Harlem," *The Cashbox*, November 6, 1954, 29.

37. Larry Douglas, "Theatrically Yours," *Arizona Sun*, October 8, 1954, 6.

38. "Rhythm 'n Blues Reviews: Sleeper of the Week," *Cash Box*, November 27, 1954.

39. Shaw, *Honkers and Shouters*.

40. "LaVern Baker Complaint Brings Congressional Action," *Cash Box*, May 7, 1955, 25.

41. "Tweedle Dee Still Cash for LaVern Baker," *Jackson (Mississippi) Advocate*, July 9, 1955, 2.

42. "Rhythm 'n Blues Ramblings," *Cash Box*, December 19, 1955, 38.

43. "Rhythm 'n Blues Reviews: Award of the Week," *Cash Box*, April 9, 1955.

44. "Review Spotlight On .../Review of New R&B Records," *Billboard*, January 29, 1955, 67.

45. "Review Spotlight On .../Rhythm & Blues Notes," *Billboard*, November 5, 1955, 47.

46. "Music as Written," *Billboard*, January 8, 1955, 22.

47. Larry Douglas, "Theatrically Yours," *Arizona Sun*, January 21, 1955, 3.

48. "Rhythm 'n Blues Reviews/Award o' the Week," *Cash Box*, April 30, 1955, 26.

49. "Rhythm 'n Blues Reviews/Sleeper of the Week/Rhythm & Blues Top 15," *Cash Box*, August 6, 1955, 29.

50. "R&B Poll Results," *Cash Box*, June 18, 1955, 34.

51. "Ella Johnson," Biography, www.last.fim/music/ella+johnson/+wiki.

52. "Ella Johnson," Discogs, www.discogs.com/artist/343960-Ella-Johnson.

53. "Rhythm & Blues Notes," *Billboard*, October 22, 1955.

54. "Jay McShann's Orchestra with Priscilla Bowman," Way Back Attack, https://www.waybackattack.com/mcshannjay.html.

55. Mike Callahan, "The Vee-Jay Story," December 19, 2006, www.bsnpubs.com/veejay/veejaystory1.html.

56. "Review Spotlight On ...," *Billboard*, October 22, 1955, 46.

57. "The Billboard Music Popularity Charts," *Billboard*, December 24, 1955, 35.

58. "Jazz 'n Blues Reviews/Award o' the Week," *Cash Box*, September 6, 1952, 16.

59. "Rhythm & Blues Ramblings," *Cash Box*, August 23, 1952, 18.

60. "Review Spotlight On . . . ," *Billboard*, February 5, 1955, 46.

61. "Review Spotlight On . . ./This Week's Best Buys," *Billboard*, February 19, 1955, 53.

62. "Rhythm 'n Blues Reviews: Award of the Week," *Cash Box*, February 12, 1955.

63. Marv Goldberg, "Varetta Dillard," www.uncamarvy.com/varettadillard/varettadillard.html.

64. "Varetta Dillard," *Jet*, March 13, 1952, 64.

65. "Rhythm 'n Blues Reviews: Award of the Week," *Cash Box*, May 28, 1955, 24.

66. "Rhythm 'n Blues Reviews," *Cash Box*, September 18, 1955, 28.

67. Goldberg, "Varetta Dillard."

68. Jonas Benholm, interview.

69. "Rhythm & Blues Ramblings," *Cash Box*, October 15, 1955, 29.

70. Brown and Yule, *Miss Rhythm: The Autobiography of Ruth Brown*.

71. Ray Regalado, "Gene & Eunice: This Is My Story," September 21, 2003, www.electricearl.com.

72. Birnbaum, *Before Elvis: The Prehistory of Rock 'n' Roll*.

73. Regalado, "Gene & Eunice: This Is My Story."

74. Birnbaum, *Before Elvis: The Prehistory of Rock 'n' Roll*.

75. "Red Hot Rhythms Sizzling Songs," *Evening Star* (Washington, DC), May 28, 1955, B-16.

76. "Red Hot Rhythms Sizzling Songs," *Evening Star* (Washington, DC), May 28, 1955, B-16.

77. "Singing Lovebirds Gene and Eunice Invest in Romance," *Jackson (Mississippi) Advocate*, September 3, 1955, 3.

CHAPTER SEVEN: LET THE GOOD TIMES ROLL (1956)

1. *The Economic Situation of the Negroes in the United States*, Bureau of Labor Statistics, 1960.

2. Billie Holiday with William Dufty, *Lady Sings the Blues*, Penguin Books, 1956.

3. Wade "Wacko" Wright, interview.

4. Aimee L'Heureux, "Illinois Jacquet: Integrating Houston Jazz Audiences . . . Lands Ella Fitzgerald and Dizzy Gillespie in Jail," *Houston History* Vol. 8, No. 1, https://houstonhistorymagazine.org/wp-content/.

5. Patti Page, *Once Upon a Dream*, Popular Library, 1960.

6. Holiday with Dufty, *Lady Sings the Blues*.

7. David Johnson, "Late Lady: Billie Holiday on Verve in the 1950s," Indiana Public Media, https://indianapublicmedia.org/nightlights/late-lady-billie-holiday-verve-1950s.php.

8. Suzanne Herel, "Hadda Brooks, the 'Queen of Boogie,' dies," *San Francisco Chronicle*, November 23, 2002.

9. Shaw, *Honkers and Shouters*.

10. "Sepia Song Stylist, 'Queen of The Boogie' Gets Her Big Chance," *Arizona Sun*, June 20, 1952, 6.

11. "Rhythm 'n Blues Reviews," *Cash Box*, May 2, 1953, 24.

12. "Battle Looming for R&B Disk Artists," *Billboard*, July 16, 1955, 13.

13. "Hadda Brooks Back with Modern Label," *Billboard*, November 3, 1956, 52.

14. "Review Spotlight On . . . ," *Billboard*, December 15, 1956, 64.

15. Haskins, *Queen of the Blues*.

16. "Seventh Avenue Ticker Tape," *Miami Times*, June 16, 1956, 17.

17. Masco Young, "The Lowdown," *Miami Times*, August 25, 1956, 10.

18. "Headed to Be a Best Seller," *The Omaha Guide*, October 12, 1956, 3.

19. Haskins, *Queen of the Blues*.

20. Brown and Yule, *Miss Rhythm: The Autobiography of Ruth Brown*.

21. "R&B Poll Results," *Cash Box*, July 14, 1956, 28.

22. Bill Simon, "Rhythm-Blues Notes," *Cash Box*, June 9, 1956, 46.

23. Brown and Yule, *Miss Rhythm: The Autobiography of Ruth Brown*.

24. "Rhythm 'n Blues Disk Jocky Regional Record Reports," *Cash Box*, April 28, 1956, 33.

25. Charlie Gillett, *The Sound of the City: The Rise of Rock and Roll*, Outerbridge & Dienstfrey, 1970.

26. Birnbaum, *Before Elvis: The Prehistory of Rock 'n' Roll*.

27. Marv Goldberg, "LaVern Baker," Marv Goldberg's R&B Notebooks.

28. "Lincoln Chase 'Rolls' in Talent," *Jackson Advocate*, September 1, 1956, 4.

29. "A Date with Discs," *Miami Times*, December 8, 1956, 11.

30. John A. Jackson, *Big Beat Heat: Alan Freed and the Early Years of Rock & Roll*, Schirmer Books, 1991.

31. "Rock 'n Roll Show at Dinner Key," *Miami Times*, May 12, 1956, 8.

32. L. Masco Young, "The Lowdown," *Miami Times*, May 19, 1956, 11.

33. Clarence "Frogman" Henry, interview.

34. Hannusch, *I Hear You Knockin'*.

35. Louise Harris Murray, interview.

36. Birnbaum, *Before Elvis: The Prehistory of Rock 'n' Roll*.

37. Bobby Rush, interview.

38. Barbara Hawkins, interview.

39. John Wirt, *Huey "Piano" Smith and the Rocking Pneumonia Blues*, Louisiana State University Press, 2014.

40. Birnbaum, *Before Elvis: The Prehistory of Rock 'n' Roll*.

41. Marv Goldberg, The Jacks/Cadets, Marv Goldberg's R&B Notebooks, 2014, www .uncamarvy.com.

42. Clemente, *Girl Groups: Fabulous Females Who Rocked the World*.

43. "Rhythm 'n Blues Ramblings," *Cash Box*, March 17, 1956, 34.

44. "Review Spotlight On . . . ," *Billboard*, April 21, 1956, 54.

45. Andrew Hamilton, "Six Teens," Allmusic, https://www.allmusic.com.

46. "This Week's Best Buys" *Billboard*, May 24, 1956, 57.

47. "The Original Smash Hit! A Casual Look," *Cash Box*, June 16, 1956, 31.

48. "The Nations' Rhythm & Blues Top 15," *Cash Box*, July 14, 1956, 32.

49. Andrew Hamilton, "Six Teens," Allmusic, https://www.allmusic.com.

50. "R&B Sleeper of the Week," *Cash Box*, September15, 1956, 33.

51. "Rhythm 'n Blues Reviews," *Cash Box*, March 31, 1956.

52. Louise Harris Murray, interview.

53. Justine "Baby" Washington, interview.

54. Bruce Eder, "Bert Keyes," Allmusic, www.allmusic.com.

CHAPTER EIGHT: LOVE IS STRANGE (1957)

1. Louise Harris Murray, interview.

2. Ennis, *The Seventh Stream: The Emergence of Rocknroll in American Popular Music.*

3. J. C. Marion, "Zell Sanders and J&S Records," home.earthlink.net/~v1tiger/jands.html.

4. Heikki Suosalo, "Freddie Scott: The complete story with an interview," Soul Express, soulexpress.net/freddiescott.htm.

5. Suosalo, "Freddie Scott: The complete story with an interview."

6. Suosalo, "Freddie Scott: The complete story with an interview."

7. Marion, "Zell Sanders and J&S Records."

8. "R&B Retail Outlets/R&B Disk Jockey," *Cash Box*, July 13, 1957.

9. "The Cash Box Hot," *Cash Box*, July 27, 1957.

10. "The Final Count," *Cash Box*, December 7, 1957.

11. Shaw, *Honkers and Shouters.*

12. Birnbaum, *Before Elvis: The Prehistory of Rock 'n' Roll.*

13. Shaw, *Honkers and Shouters.*

14. Gillett, *The Sound of the City.*

15. Bobby Rush, interview.

16. Barbara Hawkins, interview.

17. Shaw, *Honkers and Shouters.*

18. "History," Tune Weavers Website, www.thetuneweavers.com/history/.

19. "The Tune Weavers," Brian Lee's Colorradio.com, www.colorradio/tuneweavers.html.

20. "History," Tune Weavers Website, www.thetuneweavers.com/history/.

21. "Watch for This Smash Hit," ad, *Billboard*, March 23, 1957, 75.

22. "History," Tune Weavers Website, www.thetuneweavers.com/history/.

23. "The Smash Follow-up to 'Happy, Happy Birthday Baby," *Billboard*, November 25, 1957, 71.

24. "Record Reviews/Sleeper of the Week," *Cash Box*, November 30, 1957, 12.

25. "Reviews of New Pop Records," *Billboard*, December 2, 1957, 52.

26. Coleman, *Fats Domino and the Lost Dawn of Rock 'n' Roll.*

27. Lauterbach, *The Chitlin' Circuit and the Road to Rock 'n' Roll.*

28. Billy Vera, interview.

29. Dik De Heer, "Paul Gayten," *Tims This Is My Story*, https://tims.blackcat.nl.

30. Billy Vera, interview.

31. "R&B Ramblings," *Cash Box*, February 9, 1957, 40.

32. "R&B Ramblings," *Cash Box*, February 16, 1957, 40.

33. "R&B Ramblings," *Cash Box*, February 23, 1957, 40.

34. Emerson, *Always Magic in the Air.*

35. "Top Teen Tunes: Ruth's Lucky Lips," *Evening Star* (Washington, DC), March 10, 1957, 4.

36. "Top Teen Tunes: Ruth's Lucky Lips," *Evening Star* (Washington, DC), March 10, 1957, 4.

37. Brown and Yule, *Miss Rhythm: The Autobiography of Ruth Brown.*

38. "Singer Escapes Candy Death," *Evening Star* (Washington, DC), March 13, 1957, A-5.

39. "Personal Appearances," *Billboard*, March 23, 1957, 23.

40. Haskins, *Queen of the Blues.*

41. "Favorite Female Artists of R&B Jockeys," *Billboard*, November 11, 1957, 126.

42. Haskins, *Queen of the Blues.*

43. "Rock and Roll Ain't Dying," *Jackson Advocate*, September 21, 1957, 3.

44. "R&B Best Sellers in Stores," *Billboard*, September 16, 1957, 58.

45. "R&B Best Sellers in Stores," *Billboard*, October 7, 1957, 68.

46. Henry Bacas, "Top Teen Tunes: Bobbettes Know 'Mr. Lee,'" *Evening Star* (Washington, DC), September 29, 1957, 3.

47. Clemente, *Girl Groups: Fabulous Females Who Rocked the World*.

48. Gillian G. Gaar, *She's a Rebel: The History of Women in Rock & Roll*, Seal Press, 1992.

49. Bacas, "Top Teen Tunes: Bobbettes Know 'Mr. Lee.'"

50. Gaar, *She's a Rebel: The History of Women in Rock & Roll*.

51. Bacas, "Top Teen Tunes: Bobbettes Know 'Mr. Lee.'"

52. Clemente, *Girl Groups: Fabulous Females Who Rocked the World*.

53. "Swingin'est Record of the Year," *Billboard*, June 24, 1957, 55.

54. "R&B Review/Award o' the Week," *Cash Box*, June 29, 1957, 50.

55. "R&B Ramblings," *Cash Box*, August 31, 1957, 40.

56. "R&B Ramblings," *Cash Box*, September 14, 1957, 38.

57. "Bobbettes Back with a Bigger Hit," *Billboard*, November 18, 1957, 30.

58. "Favorite Small Vocal Group of R&B Jockeys," *Billboard*, November 11, 1957, 126.

CHAPTER NINE: MAYBE (1958)

1. "Singer Julia Lee, Blues Pioneer, Dies in K.C.," *Jet*, December 25, 1958, 23.

2. "Record Reviews," *Cash Box*, March 16, 1958, 12.

3. Birnbaum, *Before Elvis: The Prehistory of Rock 'n' Roll*.

4. "Singer Julia Lee, Blues Pioneer, Dies in K.C."

5. Dik De Heer, "Julia Lee," *Tims This Is My Story*, www.tims.blackcat.nl.

6. "Capitol's Dave Dexter Drops 'News' Chores; Advanced to A&R," *Billboard*, January 13, 1951, 15.

7. Birnbaum, *Before Elvis: The Prehistory of Rock 'n' Roll*.

8. "Rhythm & Blues Record Reviews," *Billboard*, March 24, 1951, 32.

9. "Record Reviews," *Billboard*, October 29, 1951, 78.

10. "Jazz & Blues Reviews," *Cash Box*, February 3, 1951, 18.

11. "Record Reviews," *Cash Box*, September 6, 1952, 8.

12. "Singer Julia Lee, Blues Pioneer, Dies in K.C."

13. "Sleeper of the Week," *Cash Box*, March 19, 1955, 29.

14. "Reviews of New R&B Records," *Cash Box*, August 20, 1955, 50.

15. "Johnny Otis and His Band," *Arizona Sun*, January 6, 1954, 8.

16. "Marie Adams," *Jet*, April 8, 1954, 63.

17. Dik De Heer, "Marie Adams," *Tims This Is My Story*, www.tims.blackcat.nl.

18. "London Lowdown," *Cash Box*, February 15, 1958, 26.

19. De Heer, "Marie Adams."

20. Shaw, *Honkers and Shouters*.

21. Mike Callahan and David Edwards, "The Swan Records Story," https://swanrecords.com/swan-records-history/.

22. Lillie Bryant Howard, interview.

23. Lillie Bryant Howard, interview.

24. Diane Renay, interview.

25. Diane Renay, interview.

26. Lillie Bryant Howard, interview.

27. Major Robinson, "Billy & Lillie," *Jet*, October 23, 1958, 64.

28. Lillie Bryant Howard, interview.

29. "All Star Show to Aid Hepatic Research," *Cash Box*, April 16, 1958, 47.

30. "Sleeper of the Week," *Cash Box*, November 12, 1958, 12.

31. "Record Ramblings," *Cash Box*, November 29, 1958, 16.

32. Lillie Bryant Howard, interview.

33. "Sleeper of the Week," *Cash Box*, August 9, 1958, 11.

34. "Record Ramblings," *Cash Box*, August 23, 1958, 40.

35. "Quin-Tones, America's Finest Musical Quartet," *Billboard*, December 19, 1949, 44.

36. "The Quin-Tones," Girl Groups—A Short History, www.history-of-rock.com/quin.htm.

37. "The Quin-Tones," Brian Lee's Colorradio.com, www.colorradio.com/quintones.html.

38. "District Theaters: Howard," *Evening Star* (Washington, DC), October 9, 1958, B-23.

39. "Award o' the Week," *Cash Box*, August 30, 1958, 38.

40. "A Billboard Pick," *Billboard*, August 25, 1958, 39.

41. Brown and Yule, *Miss Rhythm: The Autobiography of Ruth Brown.*

42. "Atlantic Aims for the Top," *Billboard*, January 13, 1958, 38–39.

43. "Round the Wax Circle," *Cash Box*, June 7, 1958, 18.

44. "R&B Ramblings," *Cash Box*, April 12, 1958, 42.

45. Haskins, *Queen of the Blues.*

46. "On the Beat," *Billboard*, April 14, 1958, 48.

47. "Bobby Shad Leaves Mercury," *Cash Box*, October 11, 1958, 38.

48. "Otis Succeeds Bobby Shad in Mercury Slot," *Billboard*, October 20, 1958, 2.

49. "Reviews of New Pop Records," *Billboard*, Page 35, June 9, 1958.

50. "Sleeper of the Week," *Cash Box*, June 28, 1958, 14.

51. "Mr. Personality—In Person Louis Jordan," *Evening Star* (Washington, DC), April 26, 1958, B-23.

52. Beverly Lee, interview.

53. "R&B Ramblings," "R&B Reviews," *Cash Box*, February 15, 1958, 40, 44.

54. "R&B Reviews," *Cash Box*, November 15, 1958, 56.

55. "R&B Poll Results," *Cash Box*, June 21, 1958, 45.

56. "R&B Sure Shots," *Cash Box*, March 29, 1958, 43.

57. "Blasting Off 1958," *Evening Star* (Washington, DC), October 9, 1958, B-23.

58. Alan Betrock, *Girl Groups: The Story of a Sound*, Delilah Books, 1982.

59. Gaar, *She's a Rebel: The History of Women in Rock & Roll.*

60. Charlotte Greig, *Will You Still Love Me Tomorrow? Girl Groups from the 50s On . . .*, Virago Press, 1989.

61. Ward, Stokes, and Tucker, *Rock of Ages: The Rolling Stone History of Rock & Roll.*

62. Betrock, *Girl Groups: The Story of a Sound.*

63. Greig, *Will You Still Love Me Tomorrow? Girl Groups from the 50s On . . .*

CHAPTER TEN: WHAT A DIFF'RENCE A DAY MAKES (1959 AND BEYOND)

1. "Fred Jay," Discogs, https://www.discogs.com/artist/602864-Fred-Jay/.

2. Marv Goldberg, "Lavern Baker," Marv Goldberg's R&B Notebooks, www.uncamarvy
.com/lavernbaker/lavernbaker.html.

3. "July Best Sales Month in Atlantic Atco History," *Cash Box*, July 29, 1959, 44.

4. "Atlantic Re-Signs LaVern Baker," *Cash Box*, December 19, 1959, 34.

5. "People Are," *Jet*, January 30, 1958, 42.

6. "Riotous Oldsters Halt Youth Rock 'n' Roll Show," *Evening Star* (Washington, DC), October
19, 1959, B-20.

7. "Dick Clark Show," *Evening Star* (Washington, DC), January 10, 1959, A-13.

8. "LaVern Baker," *Evening Star* (Washington, DC), May 1, 1959, C-10.

9. "You Gotta Rock," *Evening Star* (Washington, DC), February 22, 1959, E-2.

10. Brown and Yule, *Miss Rhythm: The Autobiography of Ruth Brown*.

11. "New York Beat," *Jet*, October 15, 1959, 63.

12. "New York Beat," *Jet*, January 23, 1959, 64.

13. "New York Beat," *Jet*, December 8, 1960, 64.

14. "New York Beat," *Jet*, October 18, 1961, 63.

15. Adam Bernstein, "Ruth Brown, 78, R&B Singer Championed Musicians' Rights,"
Washington Post, November 18, 2006.

16. "People," *Jet*, January 22, 1959, 53.

17. "Radio-TV," *Jet*, April 23, 1959, 66.

18. "Radio-TV," *Jet*, May 30, 1961, 66.

19. "New York Beat," *Jet*, December 25, 1958, 64.

20. Chris Morris, "Della Reese, 'Touched by an Angel' Star and R&B Singer, Dies at 86,"
Variety, November 20, 2017.

21. "Reviews of New Pop Records," *Billboard*, July 22, 1957, 71.

22. "When It's a Hit!" *Billboard*, August 9, 1957, 39.

23. Harry MacArthur, "After Dark: Della Has Personality as Well as That Big Voice," *Evening
Star* (Washington, DC), November 15, 1957, C-7.

24. Harry MacArthur, "After Dark: Della Reese Has Style All Her Own," *Evening Star*
(Washington, DC), October 28, 1959, C-15.

25. "Della Reese Signs with Victor," *Cash Box*, August 8, 1959, 44.

26. Harry Bacas, "Top Tunes: Della and La Boheme Produce Current Hit," *Evening Star*
(Washington, DC), October 18, 1959, 2.

27. "Record Ramblings," *Cash Box*, September 5, 1959, 24.

28. Harry MacArthur, "After Dark: Della Returns," *Evening Star* (Washington, DC), February
28, 1962, B-17.

29. "White Fans Favor Billie Holiday," *Jet*, March 6, 1953, 59.

30. "About Sarah Vaughan," *American Masters*, PBS, January 29, 1991. www.youtube.com/
watch?v=cZkFQ3vc-Qc.

31. LeRoi Jones, *Blues People*, William Morrow, 1963.

32. A. B. Spellman, *Black Music: Four Lives*, Schocken Books, 1970.

33. "Entertainment," *Jet*, January 7, 1960, 61.

34. Entertainment," *Jet*, May 18, 1960, 61.

35. "Regional Record Reports," *Cash Box*, October 17, 1959, 49.

36. "Record Review/Pick of the Week," *Cash Box*, July 4, 1959, 10.

37. "Mercury Released 29 LPs for Nov.," *Cash Box*, November 7, 1959, 39.

38. "Talmadge Comments on Mercury's '59 Success," *Cash Box*, December 26, 1959, 56.

39. "Sarah Vaughan Goes to Roulette in 1960," *Cash Box*, August 1, 1959, 41.

40. Nina Simone with Stephen Cleary, *I Put a Spell On You: The Autobiography of Nina Simone*, Da Capo Press, 1991.

41. Birnbaum, *Before Elvis: The Prehistory of Rock 'n' Roll*.

42. Shaw, *Honkers and Shouters*.

43. "Reviews," *Billboard*, April 27, 1959, 41.

44. "Record Review," *Cash Box*, July 11, 1959, 19.

45. "Record Ramblings," *Cash Box*, May 2, 1959, 34.

46. "California Clippings," *Cash Box*, May 23, 1959, 62.

47. "Round Up," *Jet*, August 20, 1959, 60.

48. "New York Beat," *Jet*, July 23, 1959, 63.

49. "L.A. Cops Seize Dinah's Reducing Pills, Up 4 Pounds," *Jet*, January 21, 1960, 61.

50. Haskins, *Queen of the Blues*.

51. "Mercury Hit Wave Belts the Nation," *Cash Box*, November 7, 1959, 15.

52. Anthony Denselow, "A shame about the girl: When she died in 1963, Dinah Washington was the self-appointed 'queen of the blues,'" *Independent*, August 6, 1992, https://www.independent.co.uk/arts-entertainment/rock-a-shame-about-the-girl-when-she-died-in-1963-dinah-washington-was-the-selfappointed-queen-of-the-blues-anthony-denselow-thinks-her-time-has-come-again-1538424.html.

53. Eugene Chadbourne, "Annie Laurie," AllMusic, https://www.allmusic.com/artist/annie-laurie-mn0000490413.

54. Kate Kelley, "Sylvia Robinson: Pioneering Record Producer, Ushered in Era of Rap," obituary, Huffington Post, March 18, 2015, https://www.huffpost.com/entry/sylvia-robinson-pioneer-b-6894924.

55. Birnbaum, *Before Elvis: The Prehistory of Rock 'n' Roll*.

56. Elizabeth Blair, "Rapper's Delight: The One Take Hit," NPR, December 29, 2000, https://www.npr.org/2000/12/29/1116242/rappers-delight.

57. Christopher Weingarten, "Joseph Robinson Jr., Sugar Hill Records Exec, Dead at 53," *Rolling Stone*, July 14, 2015, www.rollingstone.com.

58. James and Ritz, *Rage to Survive: The Etta James Story*.

59. Brian Ray, interview.

60. Brian Ray, interview.

CHAPTER ELEVEN: SALLY GO 'ROUND THE ROSES (1959 AND BEYOND)

1. Jason Ankeny, "The Bobbettes," Allmusic, www.allmusic.com/artist/the-bobbettes-mn0000756518/biography.

2. Dave Edwards and Mike Callahan, "The George Goldner Story," Both Sides Now Publications, https://www.bsnpubs.com/roulette/goldner/goldner.html.

3. Shaw, *Honkers and Shouters*.

4. Clemente, *Girl Groups: Fabulous Females Who Rocked the World.*

5. Gaar, *She's a Rebel: The History of Women in Rock & Roll.*

6. Fanita James, interview.

7. Mark Ribowsky, *He's a Rebel: The Truth About Phil Spector—Rock and Roll's Legendary Madman*, E. F. Dutton, 1989.

8. Beverly Lee, interview.

9. Beverly Lee, interview.

10. Beverly Lee, interview.

11. Dave Marsh, *The Hearts of Rock & Soul: The 1001 Greatest Singles Ever Made*, New American Library, 1989.

12. Louise Murray, interview.

13. Marsh, *The Hearts of Rock & Soul: The 1001 Greatest Singles Ever Made.*

14. Marion, "Zell Sanders and J&S Records."

15. Jimmie Raye, interview.

16. Jimmie Raye, interview.

17. Marsh, *The Hearts of Rock & Soul: The 1001 Greatest Singles Ever Made.*

18. Colin Larkin, *The Virgin Encyclopedia of Sixties Music*, Virgin Books, 1998.

19. Clemente, *Girl Groups: Fabulous Females Who Rocked the World.*

20. "The Jaynetts," Discogs, www.discogs.com/artist/379713-the-jaynetts.

21. Jimmie Raye, interview.

22. Louise Murray, interview.

23. Louise Murray, interview.

24. All Artie Butler quotes from Artie Butler, interview.

25. Jimmie Raye, interview.

26. Artie Butler, interview.

27. Artie Butler, interview.

28. Richard Goldstein, *Richard Goldstein's The Poetry of Rock*, Bantam Books, 1969.

29. Clemente, *Girl Groups: Fabulous Females Who Rocked the World.*

30. "Sheila from Batesville, Ar," comment, "Sally Go 'Round the Roses," Songfacts, https://songfacts.com/lyrics/the-jaynetts/sally-go-round-the-roses.

31. Louise Murray, interview.

32. Betrock, *Girl Groups: The Story of a Sound.*

33. Louise Murray, interview.

34. Spencer Leigh, interview.

35. Clemente, *Girl Groups: Fabulous Females Who Rocked the World.*

36. "Love on a Two-Way Street," Art & Popular Culture, www.artandpopularculture.com/love_on_a_Two-Way_Street.

37. "Lezli Valentine," LaDolceVanessa, www.ladolcevanessa.blogspot.com/2014/03/out-like-a-lion-lioness-heroines-of-soul-music.html.

38. Louise Murray, interview.

SELECTED DISCOGRAPHY

CHARTED SINGLES 1940s, 1950s, 1960s

Based on *Billboard*, Discogs.com, RateYourMusic.com, and https://Archive.org

Faye Adams

Shake a Hand/I've Gotta Leave You (with Joe Morris Orchestra), 1953, Herald 416
I'll Be True/Happiness to My Soul, 1953, Herald 419
It Hurts Me to My Heart/Ain't Gonna Tell, 1954, Herald 434
Keeper of My Heart/So Much, 1957, Imperial 5443

Marie Adams

I'm Gonna Play the Honky Tonks/My Search Is Over (with Bill Harvey's Band), 1952, Peacock 1583
Ma (He's Makin' Eyes at Me)/Romance in the Dark (as Johnny Otis Show with Marie Adams and the Three Tons of Joy), 1957, Capitol 14794
Bye Bye Baby/Good Golly, (as Johnny Otis Show, vocal by Marie Adams), 1957, Capitol 17904

Annisteen Allen

Baby I'm Doin' It/Yes I Know, 1953, King 4608
Fujiyama Mama/Wheels of Love, 1955, Capitol 20558

LaVern Baker

Tweedle Dee/Tomorrow Night (LaVern Baker and the Gliders), 1954, Atlantic 1334
That's All I Need/Bop-Ting-A-Ling (LaVern Baker and the Gliders) 1955, Atlantic 1433
Play It Fair/Lucky Old Sun (LaVern Baker and the Gliders), 1955, Atlantic 1608
Jim Dandy/Tra La La (LaVern Baker and the Gliders), 1956, Atlantic 1784
My Happiness Forever/Get Up Get Up (You Sleepy Head) (LaVern Baker and the Gliders), 1956, Atlantic 1811
Still/I Can't Love You Enough, 1956, Atlantic 2019
Jim Dandy Got Married/The Game of Love (A-One and A-Two), 1957, Atlantic 2365
It's So Fine/Why Baby Why, 1958, Atlantic 2886

I Cried a Tear/Dix-a-Billy, 1958, Atlantic 3122

I Waited Too Long/You're Teasing Me, 1959, Atlantic 3248

So High So Low/If You Love Me, 1959, Atlantic 3586

Tiny Tim/For Love of You, 1959, Atlantic 3587

Shake a Hand/Manana, 1960, Atlantic 3944

Wheel of Fortune/Shadows of Love, 1960, Atlantic 3945

Bumble Bee/My Time Will Come, 1960, Atlantic 4852

You're the Boss/I'll Never Be Free (with Jimmy Ricks), 1961, Atlantic 5171

Saved/Don Juan, 1961, Atlantic 5218

See See Rider/The Story of My Love (I Had a Dream), 1962, Atlantic 6475

Fly Me to the Moon/Ain't Gonna Cry No More, 1965, Atlantic 7720

Think Twice/Please Don't Hurt Me (I've Never Been in Love Before) (with Jackie Wilson),
    1965, Brunswick 55287

Big Mama Thornton (Willie Mae Thornton)

Hound Dog/Night Mare, 1953, Peacock 1612

Big Maybelle (Mabel Smith)

Gabbin' Blues/Rain Down Rain, 1952, OKeh 6931

My Country Man/Maybelle's Blues, 1953, OKeh 7009

Way Back Home/Just Want Your Love, 1953, OKeh 6955

Whole Lotta Shakin' Goin' On/One Monkey Don't Stop No Show (Big Maybelle version didn't
    chart; Jerry Lee Lewis cover did), 1955, OKeh 7060

Candy/That's a Pretty Good Love, 1956, Savoy 1195

The Blossoms (The Dreamers, Bob B. Soxx & the Blue Jeans, and other group names)
(Original line-up: Fanita Barrett, Gloria Jones, Annette Williams, Nanette
Williams. Other lead singers: Darlene (Wright) Love. Fanita (Barrett) James,
Darlene Love, and Bobby Sheen formed Bob B. Soxx & the Blue Jeans. The
Blossoms were backup singers on many hit records.)

He's a Rebel/I Love You Eddie (attributed to Crystals, sung by Blossoms), 1962, Philles 106

Zip-a-Dee-Doo-Dah/Flip and Nitty (Bob B. Soxx & the Blue Jeans), 1962, Philles 107

He's Sure the Boy I Love/Walkin' Along (La La La) (attributed to Crystals, sung by Blossoms),
    1962, Philles 109

Why Do Lovers Break Each Other's Heart?/Dr. Kaplan's Office (Bob B. Soxx & the Blue Jeans),
    1962, Philles 110

(Today I Met) The Boy I'm Gonna Marry/Playing for Keeps (Darlene Love), 1963, Philles 111

Not Too Young to Get Married/Annette (Bob B. Soxx & the Blue Jeans), 1963, Philles 113

Wait 'til My Bobby Gets Home/Take It from Me (Darlene Love), 1963, Philles 114

A Fine, Fine Boy/Nino & Sonny (Big Trouble) (Darlene Love), 1963, Philles 117

Christmas (Baby, Please Come Home)/Winter Wonderland (Darlene Love), 1964, Philles 125

The Bobbettes
(Original line-up: Jannie Pought, Emma Pought, Reather Dixon, Laura Webb, Helen Gathers)

Mr. Lee/Look at the Stars, 1957, Atlantic 2422
I Shot Mr. Lee/Billy, 1960, Triple-X 104
Have Mercy Baby/Dance with Me Georgie, 1960, Triple-X 106
I Don't Like It Like That (Part 1)/I Don't Like It Like That (Part 2), 1961, Gone 5112

Priscilla Bowman (Jay McShann Orchestra)

Hands Off/Another Night, 1955, Vee-Jay 155
A Rockin' Good Way/I Ain't Givin' Up Nothin', 1958, Abner 1018

Hadda Brooks (Hadda Brooks Trio)

Swingin' the Boogie/Just a Little Blusie (with Jimmie Black, Basie Day, Al Wichard), 1945, Modern 102
That's My Desire/Humoresque Boogie, 1946, Modern 147
Out of the Blue/Bully Wully Boogie, 1946, Modern 579

Lillie Bryant (Billy and Lillie)

La Dee Dah/The Monster (with Billy Ford and the Thunderbirds), 1957, Swan 4002
Lucky Ladybug/I Promise You, 1958, 4020
Bells, Bells, Bells (The Bell Song)/Honeymoonin', 1959, Swan 4036

Ruth Brown

So Long/It's Raining, 1949, Atlantic 879
Teardrops from My Eyes/Am I Making the Same Mistake Again, 1950, Atlantic 919
I'll Wait for You/Standing on the Corner (with Budd Johnson Orchestra), 1951, Atlantic 930
I Know/Don't Want Nobody (If I Can't Have You), 1951, Atlantic 941
5–10–15 Hours/Be Anything (But Be Mine), 1952, Atlantic 962
Daddy Daddy/Have a Good Time, 1952, Atlantic 973
(Mama) He Treats Your Daughter Mean/R.B. Blues, 1953, Atlantic 986
Wild, Wild Young Men/Mend Your Ways, 1953, Atlantic 993
Oh What a Dream/Please Don't Freeze, 1954, Atlantic 1936
Mambo Baby/Somebody Touched Me, 1954, Atlantic 1044
Bye Bye Young Men/Ever Since My Baby's Been Gone, 1955, Atlantic 1051
As Long as I'm Moving/I Can See Everybody's Baby, 1955, Atlantic 1059
It's Love Baby (24 Hours a Day)/What'd I Say, 1955, Atlantic 1072
Love Has Joined Us Together/I Gotta Have You, 1955, Atlantic 1077
I Want to Do More/Old Man River, 1956, Atlantic 1082
(Big) Sweet Baby of Mine/I'm Getting Right, 1956, Atlantic 1091
Lucky Lips/My Heart Is Breaking Over You, 1957, Atlantic 1125
This Little Girl's Gone Rockin'/Why Me?, 1958, Atlantic 1197
Jack O'Diamonds/I Can't Hear a Word You Say, 1959, Atlantic 2026

I Don't Know/Papa Daddy, 1959, Atlantic 2035
Don't Deceive Me/I Burned Your Letter, 1959, Atlantic 2052
Shake a Hand/Say It Again, 1962, Philips 40028

Wini Brown

Be Anything—Be Mine/Heaven Knows Why (Wini Brown and Her Boyfriends), 1952, Mercury
8270

The Chantels
(Original line-up: Arlene Smith, Sonia Goring, Renee Minus, Jackie Landry, Lois Harris)

He's Gone/The Plea, 1957, End 1001
Maybe/ Come My Little Baby, 1957, End 1005
Every Night (I Pray)/Whoever You Are, 1958, End 1015
I Love You So/How Could You Call It Off, 1958, End 1020
Summer's Love/All Is Forgiven (Richard Barrett with the Chantels), 1959, Gone 5060
Look in My Eyes/Glad to Be Back, 1961, Carlton 555
Well I Told You/Still, 1961, Carlton 564
Eternally/Swamp Water, 1963, Ludix 101

Savannah Churchill

Daddy Daddy/All Alone, 1945, Manor 1004
I Want to Be Loved (But Only by You)/Foolishly Yours (with the Sentimentalists), 1946, Manor
1046
Time Out for Tears/All My Dreams (If All My Dreams Would Only Come True) (with the
Four Tunes), 1948, Manor 1116
I Want to Cry/Someday (with the Four Tunes), 1948, Manor 1129
(It's No) Sin/I Don't Believe in Tomorrow, 1951, RCA Victor 4280
Shake a Hand/Shed a Tear, 1953, Decca, 28836

Ella Fitzgerald

The Starlit Hour/Is There Somebody Else, 1940, Decca 2988
Sing Song Swing/If It Weren't for You, 1940, Decca 3026
Imagination/Sugar Blues, 1940, Decca 3078
Shake Down the Stars/I Fell in Love with a Dream, 1940, Decca 3199
Five O'Clock Whistle/So Long, 1940, Decca 3420
Louisville, K-Y./Tea Dance, 1940, Decca 3441
Hello Ma! I Done It Again/Wishful Thinking, 1940, Decca 3612
The Muffin Man/I'm the Lonesomest Gal in Town, 1941, Brunswick 3188
My Heart and I Decided/I Must Have That Man (and the Keys), 1942, Decca 18530
Cow-Cow Boogie/When My Sugar Walks Down the Street, 1944, Decca 18587
Once Too Often/Time Alone Will Tell, 1944, Decca 18605
I'm Making Believe/Into Each Life Some Rain Must Fall, 1944, Decca 23356

And Her Tears Flowed Like Wine/Confessin' (That I Love You) (with Johnny Long Orchestra), 1944, Decca 18633

I'm Beginning to See the Light/That's the Way It Is, 1945, Decca 23399

It's Only a Paper Moon/(I'm Gonna Hurry You Out of My Mind And) Cry You Out of My Heart, 1945, Decca 23425

The Frim Fram Sauce/You Won't Be Satisfied (Until You Break My Heart) (with Louis Armstrong), 1946, Decca 23496

Stone Cold Dead in the Market (He Had It Coming)/Petootie Pie (with Louis Jordan and His Tympany Five), 1946, Decca 23546

(I Love You) For Sentimental Reasons/It's a Pity to Say Goodnight (with Delta Rhythm Boys), 1946, Decca 23670

Guilty/Sentimental Journey (with Eddie Heywood Orchestra), 1947, Decca 23844

That's My Desire/A Sunday Kind of Love (with Andy Love Quintet), 1947, Decca 23866

My Happiness/Tea Leaves (with the Song Spinners), 1948, Decca 24446

It's Too Soon to Know/I Can't Go On (Without You), 1948, Decca 24497

Baby, It's Cold Outside/Don't Cry, Cry Baby (with Louis Jordan and His Tympany Five), 1949, Decca 24644

I'll Never Be Free/Ain't Nobody's Business If I Do (with Louis Jordan with The Tympany Five), 1950, Decca 27200

Can Anyone Explain? (No, No, No)/Dream a Little Dream of Me (with Louis Armstrong), 1950, Decca 27209

Smooth Sailing/Love You Madly, 1951, Decca 27693

Trying/My Bonnie Lies Over the Ocean, 1952, Decca 28375

Walkin' by the River/My Favorite Song, 1952, Decca 28433

Crying in the Chapel/When the Hands of the Clock Pray at Midnight, 1954, Brunswick 82789

Melancholy Me/Somebody Bad Stole De Wedding Bell, 1954, Decca 29008

I Need/Baby (with Gordon Jenkins Chorus, Orchestra), 1954, Decca 29108

Beautiful Friendship/Stay There, 1956, Verve 2012

The Swinging Shepherd Blues/Midnight Sun (with Her Shepherds), 1957, Verve 10111

But Not for Me/You Make Me Feel So Young, 1959, Verve 10180

Mack the Knife/Lorelei (with Paul Smith Quartet), 1960, Verve 10209

How High the Moon (Part 1)/How High the Moon (Part 2) (with Paul Smith Quartet), 1960, Verve 10220

Bill Bailey Won't You Please Come Home (with Paul Smith Trio)/Summertime (with Louis Armstrong), 1963, Verve 10288

Can't Buy Me Love/See, See Rider, 1964, Verve 58118

Margie Day

Street Walkin' Daddy/Riffin' with Griffin' (with Griffin Brothers Orchestra), 1950, Dot 1010

Little Red Rooster/Blues All Alone (with Griffin Brothers Orchestra), 1950, Dot 1019

Pretty Baby/Stubborn as a Mule, (Griffin Brothers Featuring Margie Day), 1951, Dot 1070

Varetta Dillard

Easy, Easy Baby/A Letter in Blues, 1952, Savoy 847

Mercy, Mr. Percy/No Kinda Good, No How, 1953, Savoy 897
Johnny Has Gone/So Many Ways, 1955, Savoy 1153

Shirley Goodman (Shirley and Lee; Shirley and Company)

I'm Gone/Sweethearts, 1952, Aladdin 3153
Feel So Good/You'd Be Thinking of Me, 1955, Aladdin 3289
Let the Good Times Roll/Do You Mean to Hurt Me So, 1956, Aladdin 3325
When I Saw You/That's What I Wanna Do, 1956, Aladdin 3362
I've Been Loved Before/Like You Used to Do, 1960, Warwick 535
Well-A, Well-A/Our Kids, 1961, Warwick 664
Shame, Shame, Shame/Shame, Shame, Shame (Instrumental), 1974, Vibration 532

Shirley Gunter (Shirley Gunter and the Queens)

Oop Shoop/It's You, 1954, Flair 1050

Linda Hayes

Yes! I Know (What You're Putting Down) (with Red Callender Sextette)/Sister Anne (with Que
    Martyn), 1953, Hollywood 244
Take Me Back/Yours for the Asking (with Munroe Tucker Band), 1953, Hollywood 512

The Hearts
(Original line-up: Hazel Crutchfield, Forestine Barnes, Louise Harris, Joyce West. Later
    Hearts would include Baby Washington and Lezli Valentine. Many singers from the
    Hearts formed the Jaynetts.)

Lonely Nights/Oo-Wee, 1955, Baton 208

Billie Holiday

God Bless the Child/Solitude, 1941, OKeh 6270
Trav'lin' Light (with Paul Whiteman Orchestra)/All for You/I Can't See for Lookin' (with King
    Cole Trio), 1944, V Disc 286
Lover Man (Oh, Where Can You Be?)/That Ole Devil Called Love, 1945, Decca 23391
Don't Explain/What Is This Thing Called Love?, 1946, Decca 23565

Helen Humes

Be-Baba-Leba/Every Now and Then (with Bill Doggett Octet), 1945, Philo 106
Million Dollar Secret/I'm Gonna Let Him Ride, 1950, Modern 779

Etta James

The Wallflower/Hold Me, Squeeze Me (with the Peaches), 1955, Modern 947
Good Rockin' Daddy/Crazy Feeling, 1955, Modern 962
If I Can't Have You/My Heart Cries (with Harvey Fuqua), 1959, Chess 1760

Spoonful/It's a Crying Shame (with Harvey Fuqua), 1960, Chess 1771

All I Could Do Was Cry/Girl of My Dreams, 1960, Argo 5359

My Dearest Darling/Tough Mary, 1960, Argo 5368

At Last/I Just Want to Make Love to You, 1961, Argo 5380

Trust in Me/Anything to Say You're Mine, 1961, Argo 5385

Fool That I Am/Dream, 1961, Argo 5390

Don't Cry Baby/Sunday Kind of Love, 1961, Argo 5393

Seven Day Fool/It's Too Soon to Know, 1961, Argo 5402

Something's Got a Hold on Me/Waiting for Charlie to Come Home, 1962, Argo 5409

Stop the Wedding/Street of Tears, 1962, Argo 5418

Fool's Rush In/Next Door to the Blues, 1962, Argo 5424

Would It Make Any Difference to You/How Do You Talk to an Angel, 1962, Argo 5430

Pushover/I Can't Hold It in Anymore, 1963, Argo 5437

Pay Back/Be Honest with Me, 1963, Argo 5445

Two Sides (To Every Story)/I Worry Bout You, 1963, Argo 5452

Baby What You Want Me to Do/What I Say, 1964, Argo 5459

Loving You More Every Day/Look Who's Blue, 1964, Argo 5465

Mellow Fellow/Bobby Is His Name, 1964, Argo 5485

I Prefer You/I'm So Glad (I Found Love in You), 1966, Cadet 5552

Tell Mama/I'd Rather Go Blind, 1967, Cadet 5578

Security/I'm Gonna Take What He's Got, 1968, Cadet 5594

I Got You Babe/I Worship the Ground You Walk On, 1967, Chess 8076

Almost Persuaded/Steal Away, 1958, Cadet 5630

Losers, Weepers (Part 1)/Weepers, 1970, Cadet 5676

I Found a Love/Nothing from Nothing Leaves Nothing, 1972, Chess 2125

All the Way Down/Lay Back Daddy, 1973, Chess 2144

You Can Leave Your Hat On/Only a Fool, 1974, Chess 2148

Out on the Streets Again/Feeling Uneasy, 1974, Chess 2153

Jump into Love/I've Been a Fool, 1976, Chess 30001

Piece of My Heart/Lovesick Blues, 1978, Warner Brothers 8545

Ella Johnson (Buddy Johnson and His Band, Buddy Johnson and His Orchestra)

Please Mr. Johnson/Swing Along with Me (vocal by Ella Johnson), 1941, Decca 8507

When My Man Comes Homes/I'll Always Be with You (vocal by Ella Johnson), 1943, Decca 8655

Did You See Jackie Robinson Hit That Ball?/Down Yonder (vocal by Ella Johnson), 1949, Decca 24675

Since I Fell for You/They All Say I'm the Biggest Fool, 1945, Decca 48016

Jewel King

3 × 7 = 21/Don't Marry Too Soon, 1949, Imperial 5055

Eartha Kitt

Uska Dara—A Turkish Tale/Two Lovers (with Henri Rene Orchestra), 1953, RCA Victor 5284

C'Est Si Bon (It's So Good)/African Lullaby (with Henri Rene Orchestra), 1953, RCA Victor 5358

I Want to Be Evil/Annie Doesn't Live Here Anymore (with Henri Rene Orchestra), 1953, RCA
    Victor 5442
Santa Baby/Under the Bridges of Paris (with Henri Rene Orchestra), 1953, RCA Victor 5502
Lovin' Spree/Somebody Bad Stole de Weddin' Bell (with Henri Rene Orchestra), 1954, RCA
    Victor 5610

Christine Kittrell

Every Night in the Week/Evil-Eyed Woman, 1953, Republic 7055–45

Annie Laurie

Since I Fell for You/Love That Man of Mine (with Paul Gayten and His Trio), 1947, De Luxe 1082
Cuttin' Out/My Rough and Ready Man (with Paul Gayten Orchestra), 1949, Regal 3235
I'll Never Be Free/You Ought to Know (with Paul Gayten Orchestra), 1950, Regal 3258
It Hurts to Be in Love/Hand in Hand, 1957, De Luxe 6107
If You're Lonely/It's Gonna Come Out in the Wash Someday, 1960, De Luxe 6189

Julia Lee (Julia Lee and Her Boy Friends)

Gotta Gimme Whatcha Got/Lies, 1946, Capitol 308
(Opportunity Knocks but Once) Snatch and Grab It/I Was Wrong, 1947, Capitol 40028
King Size Papa/When You're Smiling (The Whole World Smiles with You), 1948, Capitol 40082
I Didn't Like It the First Time (The Spinach Song)/Sit Down and Drink It Over, 1949, Capitol 15367
My Man Stands Out/Don't Come Too Soon, 1950, Capitol 4139

Eunice Levy (Gene and Eunice)

Ko Ko Mo/You and Me, 1955, Aladdin 3276
This Is My Story/Move It Over Baby, 1955, Aladdin 3282
Poco Loco/Go-On Kokomo, 1959, Case 1001

Nellie Lutcher

Hurry On Down/The Lady's in Love with You, 1947, Capitol Americana 40002
He's a Real Gone Guy/Let Me Love You Tonight, 1947, Capitol Americana 40017
Fine Brown Frame/The Pig-Latin Song, 1948, Capitol 15032
The Song Is Ended (But the Melody Lingers On)/Do You or Don't You Love Me?, 1947, Capitol
    Americana 40063
Come and Get It, Honey/He Sends Me, 1948 Capitol 15064
Cool Water/Lake Charles Boogie, 1948, Capitol 15148
For You My Love/Can I Come In for a Second (with Nat "King" Cole), 1950, Capitol 5366

Mitzi Mars

I'm Glad/Roll 'Em (with Sax Mallard Orchestra), 1953, Checker 773

Edna McGriff

Heavenly Father/I Love You, 1952, Jubilee 5073

Sarah McLawler

The Blue Room/Let's Get the Party Rockin' (George Auld and Sarah McLawler), 1953, Brunswick 84014

Esther Phillips (Little Esther)

Double Crossing Blues/The Beale Street Gang (with Johnny Otis Quintette and the Robins), 1950, Savoy 731

Mistrustin' Blues/Misery (with Mel Walker and the Johnny Otis Orchestra), 1950, Savoy 735

Cupid's Boogie/Just Can't Get Free (with Mel Walker and the Johnny Otis Orchestra), 1950, Savoy 750

Deceivin' Blues/Lost Dream Blues (with Mel Walker and the Johnny Otis Orchestra), 1950, Savoy 759

Wedding Boogie/Far Away Blues (Xmas Blues) (Johnny Otis Orchestra with Little Esther, Mel Walker, Lee Graves), 1950, Savoy 764

Ring-a-Ding Doo/The Crying Blues (Little Esther and Mel with the J. and O. Orchestra), 1952, Federal 12055

Release Me/Don't Feel Rained On, 1962, Lenox 5555

I Really Don't Want to Know/Am I That Easy to Forget, 1963, Ember 174

You Never Miss Your Water (Till the Well Runs Dry)/If You Want It (I've Got It), 1963, Lenox 5565

Hello Walls/Double Crossing Blues, 1964, Atlantic 7604

And I Love Him/Shangri-La, 1965, Atlantic 8204

When a Woman Loves a Man/Ups and Downs, 1966, Atlantic 10218

Too Late to Worry, Too Blue to Cry/I'm in the Mood for Love, 1969, Roulette 7031

Set Me Free/Brand New Day, 1970, Atlantic 19388

Home Is Where the Hatred Is/'Til My Back Ain't Got No Bone, 1972, Kudu 904

Baby I'm for Real/That's All Right with Me, 1972, Kudu 906

I've Never Found a Man (To Love Me Like You Do)/Cherry Red, 1972, Kudu 910

What a Diff'rence a Day Makes/Turn Around, Look at Me, 1975, Kudu 925

For All We Know/Fever, 1976, Kudu 929

Turn Me Out/Turn Me Out, 1982, Winning 1002

The Quin-Tones
(Original line-up: Roberta Haymon, Carolyn Holmes, Jeannie Crist, Phyliss Carr, Kenny Sexton)

Down the Aisle of Love/Please Dear, 1958, Hunt 321

Lula Reed

I'll Drown in My Tears/Clang, Clang, Clang (Sonny Thompson, vocal by Lula Reed), 1951, King 4527

Let's Call It a Day/Blues Mambo (Sonny Thompson, vocal by Lula Reed), 1952, King 4541

Rock Love/I'm Gone, Yes I'm Gone, 1955, King 4767

Della Reese

And That Reminds Me/I Cried for You, 1957, Jubilee 5292
Sermonette/Dreams End at Dawn, 1958, Jubilee 5343
Don't You Know/Soldier Won't You Marry Me?, 1959, RCA Victor 7591
Not One Minute More/You're My Love, 1959, RCA Victor 7644
Someday (You'll Want Me to Want You)/Faraway Boy, 1960, RCA Victor 7706
Everyday/There's No Two Ways About It, 1960, RCA Victor 7750
And Now/There's Nothin' Like a Boy, 1960, RCA Victor 7784
The Most Beautiful Words/You Mean All the World to Me, 1961, RCA 7833
Won'cha Come Home, Bill Bailey/The Touch of Your Lips, 1961, RCA Victor 7867
After Loving You/How Do You Keep from Cryin', 1965, ABC-Paramount 10691
It Was a Very Good Year/Solitary Woman, 1966, ABC Records 10841

Johnnie Louise Richardson (Johnnie and Joe)

I'll Be Spinning/Feel Alright, 1956, Chess 1641
Over the Mountain, Across the Sea/My Baby's Gone, On, On, 1957, Chess 1654
My Baby's Gone/Darling, 1958, Chess 1706

Sylvia Vanderpool Robinson (Mickey & Sylvia, Little Sylvia, Sylvia, Sylvia Robbins)

Love Is Strange/I'm Going Home, 1956, Groove 0175
There Ought to Be a Law, Dearest, 1957, Vik 0267
Bewildered/Rock and Stroll Room, 1958, Vik 0324
This Is My Story/What Would I Do, 1960, RCA Victor 7811
Baby You're So Fine/Lovedrops, 1961, Willow 23000
Pillow Talk/My Thing, 1973, Vibration 521
Didn't I/Had Any Lately, 1973 Vibration 524
Soul Je T'aime (with Ralfi Pagan)/Sunday, 1973, Vibration 525
Alfredo/If You Get the Notion, 1973, Vibration 527
Private Performance/If You Get the Notion, 1973, 528
Sho Nuff Boogie (Part 1)/Sho Nuff Boogie (Part 2) (with the Moments), 1974, All Platinum 2350
Sweet Stuff/Had Any Lately, 1974, Vibration 529
Easy Evil/Give It Up in Vain, 1974, Vibration 530
LA Sunshine/Taxi, 1976, Vibration 567
Lay It on Me/Stop (Boy), 1977, Vibration 311-GM
Automatic Lover/Stop Boy, 1978, Vibration 326NO
It's Good to Be the Queen/It's Good to Be the Queen (Instrumental), 1982, Sugar Hill

Mabel Scott

Elevator Boogie/Don't Cry Baby, 1948, Exclusive 35x
Boogie Woogie Santa Claus/Every Little Doggie Has Its Day, 1948, Exclusive 75x

The Shirelles (Addie "Micki" Harris, Shirley Owens, Beverly Lee, Doris Coley)

I Met Him on a Sunday (Ronde-Ronde)/I Want You to Be My Boyfriend, 1958, Decca 30588
Dedicated to the One I Love, Look a Here Baby, 1958, Scepter 1203
Tonight's the Night/The Dance Is Over, 1960, Scepter 1208
Will You Love Me Tomorrow/Boys, 1960, Scepter 1211
Mama Said/Blue Holiday, 1961, Scepter 1217
A Thing of the Past/What a Sweet Thing That Was, 1961, Scepter 1220
Big John/Twenty-One, 1961, Scepter1223
Baby It's You/The Things I Want to Hear (Pretty Words), 1961, Scepter 1227
Soldier Boy/Love Is a Swingin' Thing, 1962, Scepter 1228
Welcome Home, Baby/Mama, Here Comes the Bride, 1962, Scepter 1234
Stop the Music/It's Love That Really Counts (In the Long Run), 1962, Scepter 1237
Everybody Loves a Lover/I Don't Think So, 1963, Scepter 1243
Foolish Little Girl/Not for All the Money in the World, 1963, 1248
Don't Say Goodnight and Mean Goodbye/I Didn't Mean to Hurt You, 1963, Scepter 1255
What Does a Girl Do?/Don't Let It Happen to Us, 1963, Scepter 1259
It's a Mad, Mad, Mad, Mad World/31 Flavors, 1963, Scepter 1260
Tonight You're Gonna Fall in Love with Me/20th Century Rock n' Roll, 1963, Scepter 1264
Sha-La-La/His Lips Get in the Way, 1964, Scepter 1267
Thank You Baby/Dooms Day, 1964, Scepter 1278
Maybe Tonight/Lost Love, 1964, Scepter 1284
Are You Still My Baby/I Saw a Tear, 1964, Scepter 1292

Nina Simone

I Loves You, Porgy/Love Me or Leave Me, 1959, Bethlehem 11021
Nobody Knows You When You're Down and Out/Black Is the Color of My True Love's Hair,
    1960, Colpix 158
Trouble in Mind/Cotton Eye Joe, 1960, Colpix 175
I Put a Spell on You/Gimme Some, 1965, Philips 40286
Ain't Got No, I Got Life/Real Real, 1968, RCA Victor 3763
Do What You Gotta Do/Peace of Mind, 1968, RCA Victor 3765
Revolution (Part I)/Revolution (Part II), 1969, RCA Victor 4306
To Be Young, Gifted and Black/Save Me, 1969, RCA Victor 6580

Six Teens (The Sweet Teens)
(Original line-up: Louise Williams, Trudy Williams, Darryl Lewis, Ed Wells, Kenneth Sinclair)

A Casual Look/Teenage Promise, 1956, Flip 315
Send Me Flowers/Afar into the Night (with Ray Johnson Combo), 1956, Flip 317
Arrow of Love/Was It a Dream of Mine (featuring Trudy Williams), 1957, Flip 322

Teen Queens (Betty Collins and Rosie Collins)

Eddie My Love/Just Goofed, 1956, RPM 453

Sister Rosetta Tharpe

Strange Things Happening Every Day/Two Little Fishes and Five Loaves of Bread, 1944, Decca 8669A

Precious Memories/Beams of Heaven (with Marie Knight and the Sam Price Trio), 1948, 48070B

Up above My Head, I Hear Music in the Air/My Journey to the Sky (with Marie Knight and the Sam Price Trio), 1949, Decca 48090 A

Silent Night (Christmas Hymn)/White Christmas (with Rosette Gospel Singers), 1949, Decca 48119

The Tune Weavers
(Original line-up: Margo Lopez, Gilbert Lopez, John Sylvia, Charlotte Davis)

Happy, Happy Birthday Baby/Ol Man River, 1957, Checker 872

Lezli Valentine

I Won't Do Anything/I've Got to Keep on Loving You, 1968, All Platinum 2305

Sarah Vaughan

Tenderly/Don't Blame Me (with George Treadwell Orchestra), 1947, Musicraft 504

It's Magic/It's You or No One (with Richard Maltby Orchestra), 1948, Musicraft 557

Nature Boy/I'm Glad There Is You, 1948, Musicraft 567

Black Coffee/As You Desire Me, 1948, Columbia 38462

That Lucky Old Sun (Just Rolls Around Heaven All Day)/Make Believe (You Are Glad When You're Sorry), 1949, 38559

Our Very Own/Don't Be Afraid, 1950, Columbia 38860

I'm Crazy to Love You/Summertime, 1950, Columbia 38701

(I Love the Girl) I Love the Guy/Thinking of You, 1950, Columbia 38925

These Things I Offer You (For a Lifetime)/Deep Purple, 1951, Columbia 39370

Vanity/My Reverie, 1951, Columbia 39446

I Ran All the Way Home/Just a Moment More (with Percy Faith Orchestra), 1951, Columbia 39576

Sinner or Saint/Mighty Lonesome Feelin' (with Percy Faith Orchestra), 1952, Columbia 39873

I Confess/A Lover's Quarrel, 1953, Columbia 39932

Make Yourself Comfortable/Idle Gossip (with Hugo Peretti Orchestra), 1954, Mercury 70469

How Important Can It Be/Waltzing Down the Aisle, 1955, Mercury 70534

Whatever Lola Wants/Oh Yeah, 1955, Mercury 70595

Experience Unnecessary/Slowly with Feeling (with Hugo Peretti Orchestra), 1955, Mercury 70646

C'est La Vie/Never, 1955, Mercury 70727

Mr. Wonderful/You Ought to Have a Wife (with Hugo Peretti Orchestra), 1955, Mercury 70777

Hot and Cold Runnin' Tears/That's Not the Kind of Love I Want (with Hal Mooney Orchestra), 1956, Mercury 70846

Fabulous Character/The Other Woman (with Hugo Peretti Orchestra), 1956, Mercury 70885

It Happened Again/I Wanna Play House (with Hugo Peretti Orchestra), 1956, Mercury 70947

The Banana Boat Song/I've Got a New Heartache, 1956, Mercury 71020

Leave It to Love/The Bashful Matador with (Hal Mooney Orchestra), 1957, Mercury 71030

Passing Strangers/The Door Is Open (with Billy Eckstine), 1957, Mercury 71122
Separate Ways/Careless, 1959, Mercury 71433
Broken Hearted Melody/Misty, 1959, Mercury 71477
Smooth Operator/Maybe It's Because (I Love You Too Much), 1959, Mercury 71519
Eternally/You're My Baby, 1960, Mercury 71562
Serenata/Let's, 1960, Roulette 4285
A Lover's Concerto/First Thing Every Morning, 1966, Mercury 72543

Baby Washington (Justine Washington, Jeanette Washington, the Hearts)

The Time/You Never Could Be Mine, 1958, Neptune 101
The Bells (On Our Wedding Day)/Why Did My Baby Put Me Down, 1959, Neptune 104
Nobody Cares (About Me)/Money's Funny (Jeanette [Baby] Washington), 1961, Neptune 122
That's How Heartaches Are Made/There He Is, 1963, Sue 783
Leave Me Alone/You and the Night and the Music, 1963, Sue 790
Hey, Lonely One/Doodlin, 1963, Sue 794
I Can't Wait Until I See My Baby/Who's Going to Take Care of Me, 1963, Sue 797
The Clock/Standing Over the Pier, 1964, Sue 104
It'll Never Be Over for Me/Move on Drifter, 1964, Sue 114
Only Those in Love/The Ballad of Bobby Dawn, 1965, Sue 129
I Don't Know/I Can't Afford to Lose Him, 1969, Cotillion 17275
Forever/Baby Let Me Get Close to You (with Don Gardner), 1973, Master Five 9103
Just Can't Get You Out of My Mind/ You (Just a Dream), 1973, Master Five 9104
I've Got to Break Away/Can't Get Over Losing You, 1974, People 107

Dinah Washington

Evil Gal Blues/Homeward Bound (Sextet with Dinah Washington), 1944, Keynote 605
Salty Papa Blues/I Know How to Do It (Sextet with Dinah Washington), 1944, Keynote 606
Blow-Top Blues (with Lionel Hampton and His Octet)/Robbins in Your Hair (Lionel Hampton
    and His Octet only), 1945, Decca 23792
Ain't Misbehavin'/No More Lonely Gal Blues (with the Rudy Martin Trio), 1948, Mercury 8072
West Side Baby/Walkin' and Talkin' and Crying My Blues Away (with the Rudy Martin Trio),
    1948, Mercury 8079
I Want to Cry/Resolution Blues (with Cootie Williams Orchestra), 1948, Mercury 8082
Am I Asking Too Much/I Sold My Heart to the Junk Man, 1948, Mercury 8095
You Satisfy/Laughing Boy, 1948, Mercury 8102
It's Too Soon to Know/I'll Wait, 1948, Mercury 8107
Baby Get Lost/Long John Blues, 1949, Mercury 8148
Good Daddy Blues/Richest Guy in the Graveyard (with Teddy Stewart Orchestra), 1949,
    Mercury 8154
I Only Know/New York, Chicago and Los Angeles, 1950, Mercury 8163
It Isn't Fair/Journey's End, Mercury, 1950, 8169
I Wanna Be Loved/Love with Misery, 1950, Mercury 8181
I'll Never Be Free/Big Deal, 1950, Mercury 8187
Harbor Lights/Cross My Fingers (with Jimmy Carroll Orchestra), 1950, Mercury 5488

Time Out for Tears/Only a Moment Ago (with Jimmy Carroll Orchestra), 1950, Mercury 5503

My Heart Cries for You/I Apologize, 1951, Mercury 8209

I Won't Cry Anymore/Don't Say You're Sorry Again, 1951, Mercury 8211

Cold, Cold Heart/Mixed Emotions, 1951, Mercury 5728

Wheel of Fortune/Tell Me Why, 1952, Mercury 8267

Trouble in Mind/New Blowtop Blues, 1952, 8269

TV Is the Thing (This Year)/Fat Daddy, 1953, Mercury 9750

I Don't Hurt Anymore/Dream, 1954, Mercury 10862

I Diddle/If It's the Last Thing I Do, 1955, Mercury 10865

Teach Me Tonight/Wishing Well, 1954, Mercury 11061

That's All I Want from You/You Stay on My Mind, 1955, Mercury 11107

I Concentrate on You/Not Without You, 1955, Mercury 11553

I'm Lost Without You Tonight/You Might Have Told Me, 1955, Mercury12086

Soft Winds/Tears to Burn, 1956, Mercury 10864

Make Me a Present of You/All of Me, 1958, Mercury 12404

Never Again/Ring-a My Phone, 1958, Mercury 17097

What a Diff'rence a Day Makes/Come on Home, 1959, 18190

It Could Happen to You/The Age of Miracles, 1960, 18411

Unforgettable/Nothing in the World (Could Make Me Love You More Than I Do), 1959,
     Mercury 18818

Baby (You've Got What It Takes)/I Do (with Brook Benton), 1960, Mercury 18863

This Bitter Earth/I Understand, 1960, Mercury 19100

A Rockin' Good Way (To Mess Around and Fall in Love) (with Brook Benton), 1960, Mercury
     19856

Love Walked In/I'm in Heaven Tonight, 1960, Mercury 19774

We Have Love/Looking Back, 1960, Mercury 20525

Early Every Morning (Early Every Evening Too)/Do You Want It That Way, 1961, Mercury 20642

Our Live Is Here to Stay, Congratulations to Someone, 1961, Mercury 21668

September in the Rain/Wake the Town and Tell the People, 1961, Mercury 20643

Tears and Laughter/If I Should Lose You (with Quincy Jones Orchestra), 1962, Mercury 23054

I Want to Be Loved/Am I Blue, 1962, Mercury

Where Are You/You're Nobody Till Somebody Loves You, 1962, Roulette 4424

For All We Know/I Wouldn't Know, 1962, Roulette 4444

You're a Sweetheart/It's a Mean Old World, 1962, Roulette, 4455

Soulville/Let Me Be the First to Know, 1963, Roulette 4490

INDEX

ABOUT THE AUTHOR

Photo courtesy of the author

Steve Bergsman has contributed to a wide range of magazines, newspapers, and wire services for more than thirty years, including the *New York Times*, *Wall Street Journal*, *Barron's*, *Toronto's HomeFront*, *Black Enterprise*, *Oldies*, *The Australian*, *Phoenix Magazine*, *Chief Executive*, and *Reuters*, *Inman*, *Copley*, and *Creators' Syndicate* news services.

His thirteen books fall into four categories, music, travel, memoir, and business. In regard to music, his books include *Chapel of Love: The Story of New Orleans Girl Group the Dixie Cups* (with Rosa Hawkins); *I Put a Spell on You: The Bizarre Life of Screamin' Jay Hawkins*; *The Friends of Billy Preston*; *The Seduction of Mary Wells*; *The Death of Johnny Ace*.

Steve Bergsman's travel books are *Hobnobbing with Ghosts: A Literature and Lyric Junkie Travels the World* and *Hobnobbing with Ghosts II: A Lyric and Literature Junkie Travels the World*.

His sole memoir is *Growing Up Levittown: In a Time of Conformity, Controversy and Cultural Crisis*.

Finally, Steve Bergsman's five business books are *Maverick Real Estate Investing: The Art of Buying and Selling Properties Like Trump, Zell, Simon, and the World's Greatest Land Owners*; *Maverick Real Estate Financing: The Art of Raising Capital and Owning Properties Like Ross, Sanders, and Carey*; *After the Fall: Opportunities and Strategies for Real Estate Investing in the Coming Decade*; *Passport to Exotic Real Estate: Buying U.S. and Foreign Property in Breathtaking, Beautiful, Faraway Lands*; and *Transforming Dirt into Gold, Land Investments: Finding Opportunity Where Others Fail to See It* (with Ronald McRae).

Printed in the USA
CPSIA information can be obtained
at www.ICGtesting.com
LVHW051439240124
769422LV00019B/84

9 781496 848956